# New Testament Essays
## in Honor of
# Homer A. Kent, Jr.

# New Testament Essays

## in Honor of

# Homer A. Kent, Jr.

Edited by

Gary T. Meadors

BMH Books
P.O. Box 544
Winona Lake, Indiana 46590

*Homer A. Kent, Jr.*

ISBN 0-88469-231-0


Copyright 1991
BMH Books
Winona Lake, Indiana

Printed in U.S.A.

# Table of Contents

# Editor's Preface

It is a rare event to honor a professor for forty years of faithful service to one institution. Such is the case with Dr. Homer A. Kent, Jr. With the end of the 1990–1991 academic year, Dr. Kent will retire as a full-time professor at Grace Theological Seminary. His service to Grace will continue with his teaching on a part-time basis, and for this the seminary is grateful.

You may read Ronald Clutter's biographical article to receive an overview of Dr. Kent's life and ministry, so I won't duplicate that material in this preface. Suffice it to say that Dr. Kent's ministry at Grace is virtually immeasurable. He exemplifies the image which we desire to promote at Grace Theological Seminary.

The bibliography which you will find at the end of the festschrift reveals that a major focus of Dr. Kent's ministry has been the education of lay people and pastors. His writings, particularly his commentaries on books of the New Testament, have been widely used in lay Bible study settings, as initial introductions in college courses on the respective books, and by pastors for sermon preparation. In recent years while attending professional meetings with Dr. Kent I have observed on numerous occasions that teachers and pastors from a wide variety of backgrounds have thanked him for his very usable Bible study helps. He often remarked to me afterwards that he himself had no idea that his writings had reached such a variety of people. It was obvious to me that hearing such news was a great encouragement to him.

The articles included in this volume are designed to minister to the diverse audience which Dr. Kent has served. Some articles will provide the new Christian with spiritual food from the Word. Others will challenge the more advanced student to grow in their exegetical and theological horizons. All are a statement of thanks to Homer Kent for his friendship and fidelity over these past forty years.

A few words of an editorial nature are appropriate before I close this preface. A number of decisions arise when working with articles from a variety of sources. The close reader may note some diversity in form and style. As editor, I have endeavored to retain the idiosyncrasies of each author and, therefore, a certain level of diversity has been allowed. All abbreviations for primary sources and periodical literature in the notes may be accessed by reference to the format for the *Grace Theological Journal* found inside the front cover of the journal.

The quality of this production has been enhanced by a number of people in addition to the fine work by the authors. The very existence of this volume is due to the willingness of Mr. Charles Turner of BMH Books to take on a festschrift project. Most publishers refuse such projects because they are usually not profitable from a marketing standpoint. The skill of Ken Herman with the team at BMH Printing and the expert composition typing by Mrs. Barbara Manahan of Eisenbrauns have greatly contributed to this tribute to Dr. Kent. Last but certainly not least, a special word of thanks is due to my secretary, Mrs. Lana Seidel, for caring for a host of details during the process of putting this volume together.

Gary T. Meadors
Easter 1991

# Homer A. Kent, Jr.:
# A Biographical Sketch[1]

## Ronald T. Clutter

While reminiscing during a 1987 visit to his seminary alma mater, Robert A. Clouse, professor at Indiana State University, remarked that Homer A. Kent, Sr., one of his former professors, was the "grace" in Grace Theological Seminary. Two years later, on a return visit, Clouse remarked that Homer A. Kent, Jr., is the "grace" in Grace Theological Seminary. Students and colleagues of this father and son team have voiced agreement with the sentiments of Clouse.

Homer Austin Kent, Jr., was born in Washington, D.C., into a pastor's home on August 13, 1926. He is the eldest of two sons born to Homer and Alice Kent. Wendell was born six years later. Kent, Sr., was serving as pastor of the First Brethren Church of Washington, D.C., at the time of the births of both sons. He had come to the church shortly after graduation from Ashland College in 1925, having graduated from Xenia Theological Seminary prior to completing his college work. Homer Kent[2] and Alice Wogaman were married on August 10, 1925.

The Washington church thrived under the pastorate of Kent, Sr. In his fifteen years of shepherding, he witnessed membership growth from less than one hundred to almost five hundred. There also was spiritual growth in the home as the Kent brothers were exposed to Christian teaching and life in an impressionable way. Homer Kent remembers having stories read to him from *Egermeier's Bible Story Book*. Reading of other good books for young boys was emphasized

Ronald T. Clutter (B.A., Whitworth College; M.R.E., Southwestern Baptist Theological Seminary; Th.M., Th.D., Dallas Theological Seminary) is professor of Church History and Theology at Grace Theological Seminary, Winona Lake, Indiana.

also by parents who were concerned that the raising of two sons in a pastor's home be as normal as possible. Having grown in the atmosphere of Christian commitment, young Homer Kent made a public profession of his faith in Christ on Easter Sunday, 1934.

Growing up in the nation's capital was an exciting experience for Kent. The rich historical heritage of his hometown and its environs produced in him a fascination for American history. This interest was heightened by frequent trips to visit grandparents in Ohio and California. Each excursion followed a different route as much as possible in order to facilitate visiting new sites of historical and geographical interest. These excursions were highlights in the early years of Homer Kent.

Besides having an interest in history and geography, he began stamp collecting. However, the hobby to which he has devoted his interest most is photography. He received his first camera while in the seventh grade. This hobby has proven quite valuable as he often is able to illustrate with slides his different presentations on the expansion of the New Testament church. He has more than ten thousand slides in his collection.

Understandably it was difficult for him to accept his father's decision to leave the pastorate for a teaching ministry at Grace Theological Seminary in Winona Lake, Indiana, in 1940. To leave the allure of Washington, D.C., for a small midwestern town was not what Homer Kent wanted. However, his father had committed himself to join the faculty at Grace due to the strong urgings of Alva J. McClain and Herman A. Hoyt, who had been instrumental in the beginning of the seminary in 1937. They had persuaded Kent, Sr., with the possibility of reproducing his ministry on a wide scale through the training of men and women who would spread the Christian message worldwide. Kent, Sr., accepted the invitation in 1939 but wished to prepare his church for his departure by remaining with it until the summer of 1940.

Though the young Kent did not respond favorably to leaving friends and the excitement of Washington, D.C., he had a change of attitude shortly after moving to the Warsaw-Winona Lake community. It was a new experience for him to have his friends at church also in his school and to find the same families at various community activities. The openness of land provided for biking, hiking, and exploring during his first three years in the community.

Kent attended grades 9–11 in Warsaw and then left home in 1943 to take his senior year at an academy associated with Bob Jones College in Cleveland, Tennessee. Having committed himself to Christian ministry as a vocation while on retreat at Green Mountain Camp in Virginia prior to the move from Washington, Kent was taking courses to prepare him for college. Bob Jones College had been successful in gaining ministerial deferments from the draft for students preparing for ministry. It was decided by the Kent family that his goals and commitment would be served best by his moving to that school. Kent remained at Bob Jones for his college education which he completed in three years by taking a significant number of courses in different summer schools. He distinguished himself in the classroom and was awarded the silver medal for the highest academic average at the college. Upon graduation in 1947, he returned to Winona Lake to begin his seminary education at Grace.

Being the son of one of the professors can prove somewhat difficult for a young man, but Homer Kent excelled in his different classes to such a degree that he did not have to fear being accused of receiving preferential treatment. During his senior year in seminary he was asked to teach English Composition in what was then known as the collegiate division at Grace. This opportunity was beneficial for him in developing more fully oral and written communication skills which he would utilize throughout his ministry. He was awarded the Bachelor of Divinity degree in 1950. The only unmarried man in his graduating class, he did not find churches interested in calling him. Therefore, he decided to remain at Grace another year to enroll in the Master of Theology program. He was called upon by Hoyt, who served as dean, to teach first and second year Greek on the college level. In the fall of 1951, Kent was invited to join the Grace Seminary faculty as a full-time professor in the Department of New Testament.

On a trip to visit family in California, Kent was introduced to Beverly Page. A later renewal of this acquaintance in Winona Lake in the summer of 1952 produced a more serious relationship which led to an engagement announcement the following spring and marriage on August 1, 1953. To this union would be born three children: Rebecca, Katherine, and Daniel. Beverly Kent served Grace College as voice teacher in the music department for twenty-five years. During that time her husband finished his Doctor of Theology program and rose from the ranks of professor to that of seminary dean and then to the post of president of the college and seminary.

It was in 1962 that Kent was appointed dean as Hoyt was elevated to the presidency upon McClain's retirement. The previous year had seen Hoyt make Kent assistant dean of the seminary due to the need that the former had for help, since he held the duty of being both college and seminary dean. Kent maintained a reduced teaching load while carrying out the busy tasks of dean. He enjoyed the involvement in the decision-making processes of a growing institution but also carried the burdens usually associated with deanship.

Teaching and administration were not the only services he rendered to Grace. Through his active writing ministry, he has taken the name of his school into many homes. *The Pastoral Epistles* was published in 1958 as an outgrowth of his doctoral dissertation. He contributed the comments on the Gospel of Matthew in the *Wycliffe Bible Commentary* published in 1962. Other commentaries came forth from his classroom work. *Ephesians: The Glory of the Church* was published in 1971. *Jerusalem to Rome*, a study of the Acts of the apostles, was released in 1972 as was *The Epistle to the Hebrews*. Kent looks back to these as two of his most useful contributions. Others are *Light in the Darkness*, a commentary on John (1974); *The Freedom of God's Sons*, on Galatians (1976); *Treasures of Wisdom*, on Colossians and Philemon (1978); *Studies in the Gospel of Mark* (1981); *A Heart Opened Wide*, on 2 Corinthians (1982), and *Faith that Works*, on James (1986). Kent also contributed comments on Philippians to *The Expositor's Bible Commentary* (1978). *The Pastoral Epistles* has been translated into French, *Ephesians* into Spanish and *Jerusalem to Rome* into Russian.

Homer Kent became the third president of Grace Theological Seminary and College in 1976. His involvement with administrative direction had reached its highest level and Kent can look back upon many achievements. From 1976 to 1986 endowment grew from $300,000 to $1,767,000; the library expanded its holdings from 72,736 volumes to 125,000. The highest enrollment totals for both college and seminary were realized during his presidency. His tenure as president also witnessed the completion of the science building, enlargement of the dining commons, and remodeling of Colonial Hall. However, he had another goal in view, a higher goal. He desired to see a climate created where the pursuit of spiritual growth and a biblical lifestyle was not only possible but would be the normal experience of the students. He did not desire to see lifestyle regimented but, rather, to occur as progress was made in Christian maturity.

On the academic level, the college maintained accreditation from the North Central Association and the seminary achieved accreditation for all of its graduate programs. An extension ministry began at St. Albain in France, making the Grace Seminary presence felt throughout Europe as students came not only from France but from England, Germany, Holland, Italy, Luxembourg, Scotland, Spain, and Switzerland.

Such an expanding program required significant planning in light of the constant financial needs of a Christian institution heavily dependent upon tuition, room and board fees, and financial gifts for the meeting of its annual budget. Kent takes pleasure in having observed nine consecutive years of balanced budgets. His final year in the office of president witnessed some severe cutbacks due to budget restraints. Giving was increasing regularly but costs of education were being driven upwards rapidly. Kent said:

> The reasons that brought these schools into existence are just as important as they ever were. We don't pretend to offer the kind of quality, personal education that we do cheaply. But we think it's worth it. The values that we hold dear are under attack in this country. The education of the next generation is a big and important job for everyone.[3]

On May 11, 1985, Kent surprised the Grace family attending the Faculty and Staff Recognition Banquet by announcing his intention "to relinquish my position as president of Grace Schools at the end of my 1985–86 contract." His announcement, timed as it was, allowed the Board of Trustees sufficient opportunity to select a successor. Kent also expressed his desire to return to full-time teaching in the Department of New Testament in the seminary. September 1986 found him returned to the office in McClain Hall which he had occupied prior to moving into administration responsibilities almost a quarter of a century earlier. From this office he has carried out an open door policy in being available to students and colleagues alike.

Though it might prove difficult for some persons to return to faculty status after a quarter century of administrative leadership, Kent made the transition very smoothly. His humble character facilitated his relating well to his faculty colleagues. He has avoided purposely any situation in which there might be an inappropriate influence due to his having served previously as president over many of the faculty members with whom he is now one. On the other hand, there have been faculty meetings in which after extended discussion, there has not seemed to be a consensus on an action to be taken only to have Kent offer some words out of his wisdom and experience that made clear the best course to be followed. He has been available always to assist his colleagues in discussion on issues of New Testament interpretation and has been willing to come to them for information in areas of their expertise.

A good sense of humor is a quality that probably serves any administrator well. Homer Kent is known among his friends as having a sharp wit and a sense of humor that is often self-effacing. At a banquet, then Senator and now Vice-President Daniel Quayle remarked that he had benefited by Kent's commentary on Acts. Kent responded that he knew that his wife and mother had read the book and that he was pleased to know what had happened to the third copy. On a particular Wednesday morning in the fall semester of 1986, his first after stepping down from the presidency, Kent was met in the parking lot by a member of the administrative team who had served with him for a number of years during which Wednesday afternoons had been given over to administration meetings. The administrator asked Kent why he was smiling, since there was a meeting that afternoon. Kent, no longer required to attend those meetings, quickly responded that that was the reason he was smiling.

He is a man known also for his efficiency. A well-disciplined man, he has been chided by faculty members for posting prospecti for the subsequent semester weeks, or even months, in advance. Upon vacating the president's office he had to move much of his library home. Each day he brought an extra brief case to his office and at the end of the day filled his two cases with his books, allowing for the transfer of this library in three months.[4]

Not wishing to confine his life and witness to Grace Schools, Kent has been active in a wider community. He has regularly taught Sunday School classes at the Winona Lake Grace Brethren Church. In 1983 he served as Moderator of the Fellowship of Grace Brethren Churches. He is a member of the Warsaw Noon Kiwanis Club and a member of the Board of Directors of Lake City Bank. He has been a member of the Greater Warsaw Chamber of Commerce Board of Directors and the Board of Directors of Independent Colleges and Universities of Indiana.

International outreach has also been a part of Kent's ministry. As part of the Institute of Holy Land Studies he has led educational trips to Jerusalem. He also has been involved in teaching Europeans at St. Albain. Already mentioned is the fact that some of his writings have been translated into foreign languages.

Homer A. Kent, Jr., has contributed significantly to his community, his church, his family, and his alma mater. In retirement he continues to minister at Grace Theological Seminary. Realizing that some professors have maintained their positions even after their contributions to their respective institutions have ceased, Kent offered to retire effective at the conclusion of the 1990–91 contract year. In doing so, he allowed the administration at Grace College and Seminary to renew his contract as wished. Colleagues and students are not surprised that he has been encouraged to continue his teaching ministry on a part-time basis, for they realize that he has much grace yet to impart at Grace Theological Seminary.

## NOTES

[1]Much information in this sketch was gained through taped interviews between Kent and the author on December 26, 1986, and September 28, 1990. Tapes are in the possession of the author.

[2]Subsequent references to Homer A. Kent, Sr., will be identified with the appellation, "Sr." All other references are to Homer A. Kent, Jr.

[3]*Warsaw Times-Union*, April 8, 1986, II:4a.

[4]"Out of the Ordinary: Reflections on the Presidency of Homer Kent, Jr.," *Grace Magazine* 2:2 (Summer 1986): 7.

# A Roman Family Tomb at Abila

## John J. Davis

The accurate reconstruction of daily life in Roman Palestine is not only crucial to understanding the New Testament, but gives to it a practical and powerful exegetical force. One of the important processes by which this is done is the careful excavation of rock-cut tombs of the period.

Such tombs provide valuable information about the social organization of the population as well as their religious traditions. During the summers of 1982 and 1984, it was the author's privilege to supervise the tomb excavations at ancient Abila of the Decapolis in Jordan. The site is located just south of Wadi Yarmuk in northern Jordan (see fig. 1).

These two campaigns at Abila were very capably directed by Dr. Harold Mare, Professor

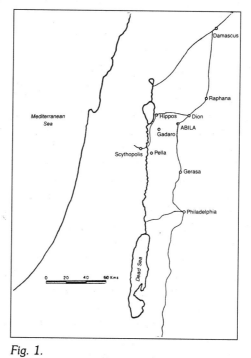

*Fig. 1.*

John J. Davis (B.A., Trinity College; M.Div., Th.M., Th.D., Grace Theological Seminary; D.D., Trinity College) is professor of Old Testament and Hebrew and President at Grace College and Theological Seminary, Winona Lake, Indiana.

17

of New Testament at Covenant Theological Seminary. Since those campaigns, two additional expeditions have been mounted at the site.[1]

Abila was one of the Decapolis cities according to the list of the second century A.D. geographer, Ptolemy (*Geography* 5, 14, 22). Even though the term "decapolis" means "ten cities," it is now known that more than ten were included in some lists. Ptolemy, for example, excludes Raphana which is in some tallies, and adds nine additional cities to the group: Helioplis (Baalbek), Abila (Quailibah), Saana (Sanamyn), Ina, Abila of Lysanias, Capitolias (Beit Ras), Adra (Edre, Derʾa), Gadora and Samoulis.[2]

Pliny (*Natural History*, 5, 7) includes Damascus, Philadelphia, Raphana, Scythopolis, Gadara, Hippos, Dion, Pella, Galasa Trachonitis, Panias, and Abila in his Decapolis list. The Decapolis is mentioned three times in the New Testament (Matt 4:25; Mark 5:20, 7:31), but particular cities are not listed.

Ancient Abila and the adjacent site of Umm el ʾAmad are virtually surrounded by one of the largest cemetery complexes known in northern Jordan. Rock-cut tombs are observable in the southern region along the wadi edge between Abila and Ain Quailibah, at Wadi Abila to the north of the site and Wadi Quailibah on the west.[3]

Prior to the 1982 expedition at Abila, very little scientifically controlled excavation work was done at the cemeteries. In 1888 Gottlieb Schumacher conducted a two-day survey in six of the rock-cut tombs. The architectural character of these tombs is described in some detail by Schumacher, along with accompanying top plans.[4] The majority of tombs described are the standard design of a central chamber with loculi.

The Department of Antiquities conducted excavations in a large painted tomb of the second century A.D. under the direction of Hassan Awad Qutshan in 1959. Three decorated sarcophagi were found in one of the vaults of the chamber.[5] In addition, twenty chamber tombs, twelve shaft graves and one rock-cut tomb were excavated in the same area which lies about 500 meters northeast of the ancient town ruins and on the opposite side of the wadi from them. These tombs are described as containing materials from the Early Bronze, Late Bronze, Hellenistic, Roman and Byzantine periods.[6] Unfortunately, no further published description is given of the work or the finds.

A tomb, located about 500 meters northeast of Abila, was explored in conjunction with the 1980 survey of Abila. A Byzantine lamp was discovered in loculus 13 which is located west of a Greek inscription on the wall.[7]

The above information relates to scientific concerns at the site, but most distressing, to even the most casual observer, has been the widespread clandestine robbery of tombs during the past two millennia. More than 40 tombs were illegally explored between the years 1982 and 1984.

Tomb robbery, of course, is not a new problem. As early as the First Intermediate Period in Egypt, complaints were raised regarding the robbery of the pyramids and the tombs of the nobles.[8] A black basalt sarcophagus of Eshmunazar, king of Sidon in the fifth century B.C., bears this Phoenician inscription, "Whoever you are, ruler and (ordinary) man, (do) not open this resting-place and (do) not search in it for anything, for nothing whatever has been placed in it."[9]

The problem of sepulture violation was apparently common in Palestine as evidenced from an inscription found in Nazareth in 1878. In part, the royal decree reads as follows:

> It is my decision that graves or tombs—whoever has built them for the cult of their ancestors or children or relatives—that these remain forever undisturbed by violence. And if anyone has information that anyone has either demolished them, or has in any other manner exhumed the corpses, or transferred them with malice aforethought to any other place to the prejudice of the corpses, or has displaced the inscriptions or stones, I ordain that against such an offender a trial be instituted. . . .[10]

Roman tombs seemed to be especially susceptible to robbery due to their shallow cut in the rock facing of the hillside. N. P. Toll asserts that at Dura-Europos "most of the tombs were completely plundered in ancient times."[11]

It was the good fortune of the 1982 and 1984 campaigns at Abila to have located four unrobbed tombs and nine undisturbed graves. It is the unrobbed tomb or grave, of course, that yields the best anthropological, artifactual and stratigraphic information.

Some effort has been made by the Department of Antiquities to preserve the more significant of these tombs by sealing off the entrance with iron gates. The 1982 Abila survey team examined, mapped and prepared top plans for many of the opened tombs. In addition to these efforts, a team of French specialists recently copied the tomb paintings and made provision for their preservation.

Assisting the author in the excavation of seven tombs were Neathery Batsell, Bruce Stevens, Ron Jones, Kate McGregor, John McGuire, Shannon McPherron, Nancy Macleod, Laima Ratavicius, Charles Stovall, Michael Fuller, Karen Hutchinson and Russ Adams. The tomb excavation team was also assisted by ten Arab workers provided by the Department of Antiquities.

## EXCAVATION METHODS

All tombs were excavated stratigraphically, with special attention given to the recovery of all materials bearing on the socioeconomic and religious characteristics of the people who used the tombs. Stratigraphic analysis of exterior and interior deposits enabled us to date accurately the origin of the tombs and their sequence of uses. Attention was given to interior geotectural[12] characteristics. All human bone materials were subjected to osteological analysis and soil samples taken from inside the tombs were also examined. Each tomb was carefully studied for characteristics of masonry work. Tool analysis, while not frequently explored in tomb excavation, can provide interesting and important data concerning a tomb's construction and later modification.[13]

The value of analysis of tool marks inside rock-cut tombs was recognized by R. A. S. Macalister:

> The tool marks are always instructive. They show the process followed in excavating the chambers; sometimes also the order in which chambers were cut out; and give much valuable information on the nature of the tools employed. It is just possible that wooden tools were used in some of the caves, but the great majority of the tool marks to be observed can not have been made except by metal chisels.[14]

While the importance of tool analysis has occasionally been recognized, the methods by which this is accomplished are never explained. The writer's special interest in this feature of tomb preparation began in 1976 during the excavation of tombs at Heshbon. We continued the analysis at Abila with fascinating results. Basically three features of tool work were analyzed. The first was to determine the number of actual tools employed in a tomb's preparation. This was accomplished by measuring the blade impressions in the stone with the use of calipers. The end of the blade is most accurately measured and its character is best represented in the soft limestone. Blade tips would often have rounded edges as well as square.

The second feature analyzed focused on the actual stroke patterns in the stone. Each mason developed his own style of working the soft limestone in a tomb setting with some masons using very long strokes, while others employed short powerful strokes. These patterns are clearly discernible in the various parts of a tomb. There are times when the stroke patterns change radically and indicate the presence of another mason.

A third feature analyzed concerned the actual penetration of the tools in the stone. With the varying strengths of working masons, the degree of penetration depended on the type of tool used and the native ability of the worker. When all these data are combined, one is able to determine whether a tomb was cut by one mason or many, and whether it was prepared in phases on demand or at one time.

While tool analysis will not always provide evidence of a final nature, it nonetheless contributes an important complement to soil stratigraphy and pottery analysis. It is an element which must be included in the full interpretation of tomb geotecture.

Tomb exploration in areas H and J during the summer of 1982 produced three basic tomb types: (1) the central type with loculi (Heb. *kokîm*) radiating from its walls, (2) the central chamber type with arcosolia in three of the walls (a cut grave trough was situated in the base of each), and (3) a central chamber type with a stone-cut bench along one wall.

Historically, two tombs were cut in the Early Roman Period (63 B.C.–A.D. 135), while the other five were prepared during the Late Roman Period (A.D. 135–324).

## AN EARLY ROMAN TOMB

Tomb H-2 is located approximately 500 meters northeast of the tell on a gently rolling slope beneath approximately 30 centimeters of soil and its origin is traced to the Early Roman Period (63 B.C.–A.D. 135). The tomb entrance was located by conducting a series of probes with the use of a four-foot steel rod.

Entrance fill above the tomb's sealing stones consisted of three distinguishable strata. The third of these (locus 2003, see fig. 2) was

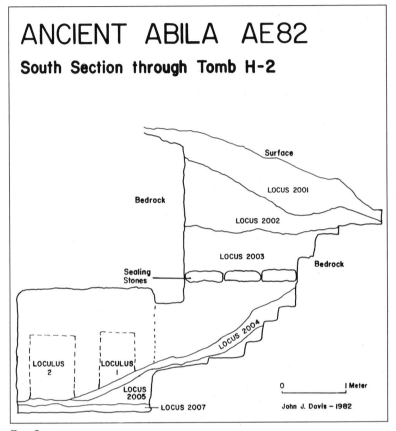

**ANCIENT ABILA AE82**

**South Section through Tomb H-2**

Surface

LOCUS 2001

Bedrock

LOCUS 2002

LOCUS 2003

Bedrock

Sealing
Stones

LOCUS 2004

LOCULUS
2

LOCULUS
1

LOCUS
2005

LOCUS 2007

0          I Meter

John J. Davis – 1982

*Fig. 2.*

situated immediately above the three rectangular blocking stones for the tomb's entrance. The soiled was light brownish gray (Munsell 10 YR-6/2) with heavy rubble interspersed with Late Roman (A.D. 135–324) and Early Byzantine (A.D. ca. 324–491) sherds. The stratigraphic picture would seem to indicate that the blocking stones were exposed for a considerable period of time before a mixed fill covered them over. Inside the tomb there was no ceramic material that dated beyond the Late Roman period when the tomb was last utilized for burial.

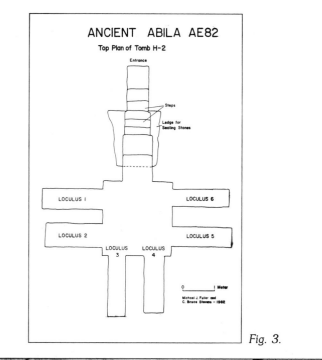

Fig. 3.

Fig. 4. Tomb H-2 before excavation (Photo by Russell Adams).

The tomb entrance was sealed by a series of three rectangular stones positioned on two ledges. A series of steps led to the tomb chamber proper (fig. 2). The position of these stones, coupled with the fact that there was a minimal amount of soil within the tomb and only with Late Roman sherds, indicated that the tomb had not been reopened in modern times. Inside the entrance under the blocking stones and in the tomb chamber there was a limited amount of soil, yet it was still stratigraphically distinguishable (fig. 2). Three distinct layers (loci 2004, 2005, 2007) could be identified, all of which contained sherds and pottery from the Late Roman period.

The tomb had very simple geotecture consisting of a small central chamber with six regularly cut loculi radiating from three of its sides (figs. 3, 4). Unlike many tombs originating in the Early Roman period, this did not have a square-cut depression in the floor (figs. 3, 4). Presumably, the tomb was so small that such a feature was not deemed necessary. Such floor treatments for early Roman tombs are rare but not unknown.[15]

That the tomb had been prepared by masons of considerable skill is evidenced by the fact that the loculi were at proper right angles to the central chamber and the floor was cut level with only a one-centimeter deviance on its north access. Analysis of tool marks in the loculi and central chamber indicated that the tomb was the work of one individual. Stroke pattern peculiarities were observed throughout the tomb, and calibrated measurements of tool impressions indicated that at least two different tools were employed in the preparation of the tomb. It was quite clear from the character of the tomb's geotecture and masonry work that it had been prepared in one operation.

## HUMAN REMAINS

The tomb contained the remains of 17 individuals ranging in age from newborn to adult. Nine of the bodies were children under age 16. The mean height of the adult males was $170 \text{ cm} \pm 4 \text{ cm}$, while that of females was $158 \text{ cm} \pm 4 \text{ cm}$.[16] The measurements accord well with other Mediterranean populations.[17]

Each of the six loculi contained a single inhumation with the body fully extended. In most cases, the head had been placed into the chamber first. Loculus 5, however, gave indication that the head was positioned near the entrance. In the Roman cemetery at Dura-

Europos the "deceased were normally placed in loculi feet first, with the head close to the opening."[18] In Palestine, however, the pattern seems to vary, especially when wooden coffins were utilized. Apparently when the body was not visible due to the use of a coffin, little attention was given to the actual position of the head.[19]

The presence of iron nails in the various loculi of tomb H-2 indicates that wooden coffins had been utilized for burial. While no wood survived from the coffins in this tomb, large fragments of wood were discovered in similar burials in tomb H-1 at Abila. In addition to the 16 burials in the six loculi, one articulated burial was found on the north side of the chamber floor oriented on an east-west axis. Unfortunately, none of the bone materials in this tomb was well preserved.

Osteological analysis of the remains in this tomb, as well as others, indicates that the inhabitants who lived in the Early and Late Roman periods at Abila suffered from a variety of diseases. Pathologies of the bone material included osteoarthritic lipping which affected the joint surfaces and margins of several femurs, tibiae, radii, humeri and ulnas. A number of vertebrae were affected with osteoarthritic lipping as well as abnormal spurs, crushed vertebral bodies and even scoliosis.[20]

Equally fascinating is the fact that of all the burials studied during the 1982 and 1984 seasons, 36 percent died before their 16th birthday.[21] High mortality rates among children were common to this site as well as other biblical cities during New Testament times. Could it be this fact (as well as others) that caused Jesus to give special attention to children?[22]

Tomb H-2 had two lamp niches on the east wall, with two lamps still *in situ* in the niche to the south. Lamps or lamp fragments were also found in loculi 1 and 3. The one lamp in the niche was of early Roman origin, as were the ceramic materials found in loculus 3. These materials, coupled with the geotecture characteristics, point to an origin and first use during the end of the Early Roman period, perhaps about A.D. 100–125. The dominant use of the tomb continued through the next century or century-and-a-half, into the Late Roman period. The majority of the burials in the loculi and the one on the floor are attributable to this period.

The small size of the tomb and the very modest character of the artifactual assemblage point to an ownership of a family with only modest means. This tomb stands in stark contrast to some of the larger, more elaborate loculi tomb complexes at Abila. However, it was its small size that probably caused tomb robbers to miss the entrance. All other tombs in the immediate vicinity had been opened and robbed.

## ARTIFACTUAL ASSEMBLAGE

The various loculi exhibited a very predictable artifactual assemblage. In addition to the iron nails mentioned earlier, there were lamps, glass pieces, juglets, small funerary bowls, bracelets, an alabaster vase, rings, beads, buttons, a bone tool, a fibula, and terra cotta figurines. The pottery materials were of very common quality and indicated manufacture either locally or within the region. Loculi 3 and 6 contained the abundance of materials. Several pottery forms were clearly imitations of earlier Hellenistic and Early Roman I types.

In addition to jugs, juglets, nails, copper coffin braces, and an alabaster vase, loculus 3 contained a complete basalt mortar (figs. 5, 6).

*Fig. 5. Objects in rear of Loculus 3. Note basalt mortar in lower right hand corner. Photo taken before excavation. (Photo by Russell Adams.)*

*Fig. 6. Basalt mortar from Loculus 3 after cleaning. (Photo by John Davis.)*

Such mortars have been found in other tombs of the period.[23] The position of the artifacts in the rear of loculus 3 indicate that they had been pushed to the back in order to make room for a later burial (fig. 4).

Of particular significance were the finds of loculus 6, which included three terra cotta figurines (fig. 7). Figurines of this type were popular among the Romans and were "largely copies or adaptations of famous classical Greek or Hellenistic statues . . . "[24] The smallest of the figurines represented a rider on a horse (fig. 9). This figurine, as well as the others, was made in two sections with considerable finishing work done by the artist or potter. Such riders have a well-known ancestry in ancient Near Eastern art motifs, going all the way back to the Iron Age. They were especially popular in Hellenistic and Parthian periods.[25] One similar figurine found in a cave at Jerash was dated to the last third of the first and the early second century A.D.[26] The second statue was slightly larger and found in badly broken condition. It represented a woman playing a small lyre with another smaller figure standing to her right (fig. 10).

Based upon the foot movement, the playing of the lyre and the facial movement, we posit that this woman is a representation of Terpsichore (the muse responsible for "inspired dance").[27] The third terra cotta figurine, discovered in the back of the loculus near the skull of the skeleton, was in complete form and likely represented Dionysius (fig. 11). Dionysius has a garment covering only the legs, and that garment is held by a young boy standing to his left. In the right hand of Dionysius there appears to be some sort of object being held down toward a panther. This latter feature is very similar to that found on a Dionysius terra cotta discovered at Jerash.[28]

Iron nails, which in a few cases still had wood fragments attached to them, were found in five of the six loculi. Such nails, along with wood, were discovered in tomb H-1 at Abila and in Roman tombs in Nahal Raqafot in Jerusalem.[29] The presence of such iron nails is usually regarded as indicating the use of wooden coffins for burial.[30] The presence of copper braces in the loculi would also argue for this conclusion.

In addition to the significance of the objects which appeared in the tomb, attention also needs to be given to those things which were absent in the assemblage. For example, no coins were found in the tomb in association with the burials. While the custom of placing a

*Fig. 7. Loculus 6 before excavation. Note terracotta figurine of Dionysius in upper left hand corner. (Photo by John Davis.)*

*Fig. 8. Roman cooking pot from Tomb H-2. (Photo by John Davis.)*

(Left)  Fig. 11. Terracotta figurine of Dionysius found in Loculus 6. (Photo by Russell Adams.)

Fig. 9. Terracotta figurine from Loculus 6. (Photo by Russell Adams.)

Fig. 10. Terracotta figurine from Loculus 6. (Photo by Russell Adams.)

coin in the mouth or the hand for the ferryman Charon for the journey over the river Styx was not common, it was nonetheless known in Roman Jordan.[31] These coins appeared with cremations, as well as inhumations.[32]

Also absent in H-2 were the traditional stone slabs used to seal the loculi. Such stones were common in Roman tombs, especially where a cult of the dead was practiced.[33] Also significant was the absence of animal bones and, in particular, the bones of pigs. Traditional Roman funerary practices required that "only when a pig had been sacrificed was a grave legally a grave," and sometimes even pet animals were killed to accompany the soul into afterlife.[34] Only further study of other Early Roman tombs will finally determine whether a cult of the dead was practiced at ancient Abila. The evidence from tomb H-2 would seem to indicate that such a cult was either absent or only practiced to a limited extent.

Tomb H-2 does provide us, however, with significant cultural information as to the burial pattern and assemblage for an average family at Abila. This small tomb was probably utilized over a period that did not exceed two centuries. Its position in a cemetery where other larger, more elaborate tombs were located would indicate that at Abila, socioeconomic standards were not rigidly applied to tomb locations. While it is true that the large tombs of the wealthy tended to be clustered at some locations, it is also important to observe that interspersed with these were common tombs of much less elaborate designs.

## CONCLUSIONS

This Roman family tomb at Abila confirms the fact that the common burial practice during the Early and Late Roman periods in Palestine was by primary extended burials. The bodies, in most cases, were wrapped in a simple shroud and placed in tomb loculi or on the floor of the central chamber. This practice accords well with what we learn from burial patterns followed by the Jews of Jesus' day. Cremation of the corpse was utilized by the Romans, but it does not seem to have been a common practice at Abila.

It appears that there was an absence of a strong and widespread tomb cult at Roman Abila. The general absence of animal bones, and in particular the bones of pigs, supports this conclusion.

Like most Roman cities of Jesus' day, there was a broad socioeconomic distribution of peoples. The elaborately decorated and painted tombs at Abila give indication of careful burials for the wealthy and important individuals. On the other hand, simple graves and cist burials reflect the hasty disposition of the body of individuals of a poorer class.

Infant and youth mortality was high at Abila. While it can be documented that in tomb H-2 these burials constituted 36 percent of the burials, that number might even be low. Regarding the Heshbon bone materials, Professor James Stirling observes:

> Though the infant mortality rate seems high, it is significant that infant bones are the least likely to be preserved in an archaeological site because of their fragility, small size, and incompleteness (lack of fusion); hence the actual rate may have been higher than is represented here.[35]

A 30 percent child mortality rate was noted in the French Hill Cemetery in Jerusalem,[36] while at Merion 40 percent of the individuals at this village died before the age of 18.[37]

Pathologies of the bone materials are those which have been paralleled at many other Roman sites. Among the more common problems were osteoarthritic lipping, enamel wear in the teeth, cavities, periodontal disease and dental attrition. The fusion of vertebrai was also a common condition recognized not only at Abila, but other contemporary sites.

The burial patterns at Abila reflect traditional values originating in Rome but at the same time with strong syncretisms within its Semitic context. The presence of imported materials, along with comparably produced local ware, is an indication of these dynamic processes.

It was not until the Byzantine period that a strong Christian community existed at Abila, at least as reflected in the archaeological tomb data. This fact is amply supported by the discovery of several Byzantine tombs containing carved crosses, Greek inscriptions, and lamps with religious motifs.

The excavations at Abila do give us a good picture of a typical Decapolis city during the days of our Lord on earth. Its material and cultural wealth are impressive and the sophistication of its political systems verified.

# NOTES

[1]For preliminary reports on these campaigns see: W. H. Mare et al., "The 1980 Survey of Abila of the Decapolis: Background Survey Techniques, Ceramic Analysis, Archaeological History and Architectural Features," *Near East Archaeological Society Bulletin*, Part I, 17 (1981) 5–25; Part II, 18 (1981) 5–30;

_____ , "The Decapolis Survey Project: Abila, 1980. Background and Analytical Description of Abila of the Decapolis and the Methodology Used in the 1980 Survey," *Annual of the Department of Antiquities of Jordan* (Amman, 1982) 37–65;

_____ , "1980 Survey of Abila of the Decapolis," *Biblical Archaeologist* 44 (1981) 179–80;

_____ , "1980 Survey of Abila of the Decapolis," *Levant* 31 (1981) 343–45;

_____ , "Tomb Finds at Abila of the Decapolis," *Biblical Archaeologist* 45:1 (1982) 57–58;

_____ , "The 1982 Archaeological Excavation at Abila-Quwailbah," *Levant* 32 (1982) 493–95;

_____ , "Abila Excavation: The Second Campaign at Abila of the Decapolis (1982). A Preliminary Report," *Near East Archaeological Society Bulletin*, Part I, 21 (1983) 5–98; Part II, 22 (1983) 5–55;

_____ , "The Abila Excavation. The Third Campaign at Abila of the Decapolis (1984). A Preliminary Report," *Near East Archaeological Society Bulletin*, Part I, 24 (1985) 5–98; Part II, 25 (1985) 35–90; Part III, 26 (Winter 1986) 5–70;

_____ , "The 1984 Season of Excavation at Abila of the Decapolis, Quwailbah, North Jordan," *Levant* 34 (1984) 440–41;

_____ , "The Abila Excavation. The Fourth Campaign at Abila of the Decapolis (1986). A Preliminary Report," *Near East Archaeological Society Bulletin*, Part I, 27 (1987) 35–78; Part II, 29 (1987) 31–91; Part III (1988) 35–90; Part IV (1988) 35–80;

_____ , "The Abila Excavation. The Fifth Campaign at Abila of the Decapolis (1988). A Preliminary Report," *Near East Archaeological Society Bulletin*, Part I, 31.19–66; Part II, 32–33 (Winter 1989) 2–64.

[2]See W. Harold Mare, "Preface," "The Second Campaign at Abila of the Decapolis (1982)," Near *East Archaeological Society Bulletin* 21 (1983) 6.

[3]See W. Harold Mare, "1980 Survey of Abila of the Decapolis," "News and Notes," *Biblical Archaeologist* 44:3 (Summer 1981) 179, and Gottlieb Schumacher, *Abila of the Decapolis* (London: Palestine Exploration Fund, 1889) 35.

[4]Gottlieb Schumacher, *Abila of the Decapolis* (London: Palestine Exploration Fund, 1889) 35–44.

[5]"Recent Archaeological Discoveries in Jordan," *Annual of the Department of Antiquities* IV, V (1960) 115–16, Plates V–VI and "Chronique Archaeologique," *Revue Biblique* 67 (April, 1960) 229.

[6]"Recent Archaeological Discoveries in Jordan," 116.

[7]W. Harold Mare, "The 1980 Survey of Abila of the Decapolis, Part II," *The Near East Archaeological Society Bulletin* 18 (1981) 17–20, figs. 11, 12, 13.

[8]See John A. Wilson, *The Culture of Ancient Egypt* (Chicago: The University of Chicago Press, 1951) 109.

[9]Leslie Grinsell, *Barrow, Pyramid and Tomb* (Boulder, CO: Westview Press, 1975) 109.

[10]See Frank E. Brown, "Violation of Sepulture in Palestine," *American Journal of Philology*, LII:1.2.

[11]N. P. Toll, "The Necropolis." *The Excavations at Dura-Europos* (New Haven: Yale University Press, 1946) 132.

[12]I am employing the term "geotecture" to describe all subterranean rock-cut tomb features as opposed to "architecture" which more accurately applies to constructed buildings above ground.

[13]See, for example, the importance of geotectural phasing of tomb F.27 at Heshbon resulting from such analysis. John J. Davis, "Heshbon 1976: Areas F and K," *Andrews University Seminary Studies* 16:1 (Spring 1978) 132. On the values of this and other tomb excavation techniques see: John J. Davis, "Excavation of Burials," in *Benchmarks in Time and Culture*, ed. Joel Drinkard, Jr., Gerald Mattingly, and Maxwell Miller (Atlanta: Scholars Press, 1988) 179–208.

[14]R. A. S. Macalister, *Excavations in Palestine, 18981–900* (London: Committee on the Palestine Exploration fund, 1902) 211. See also Warren J. Moulton, "A Painted Christian Tomb at Beit Jibrin," *Annual of the American Schools of Oriental Research* II & III (1921–22) 98.

[15]Tomb 1 at Bethphage is similarly constructed. See Silvester J. Saller, *Excavations at Bethany* (Jerusalem: Franciscan Press, 1957), fig. 20, and a Herodian tomb at Wadi el-Badhan. Awni K. Dajani, "An Herodian Tomb at Wadi el Badhan," *Annual of the Department of Antiquities of Jordan* I (1951) 78–79, fig. 18 (p. 83).

[16]Thomas J. Kick, "Report of the Osteologist, Abila 1982–1984, The Abila Excavation: The Third Campaign at Abila of the Decapolis, Preliminary Report, Part I," *Near East Archaeological Society Bulletin* 24 (1985) 93–98.

[17]See N. Haas, "Anthropological Observations on the Skeletal Remains from Gif'at ha-Mivtar," *Israel Exploration Journal* 20:1–2 (1970) 38–39; and B. Arensburg and Y. Rak, "Skeletal Remains of an Ancient Jewish Population from French Hill, Jerusalem," *Bulletin of the American Schools of Oriental Research* 219 (Oct 1975) 69–71.

[18]Clark Hopkins, *The Discovery of Dura-Europos* (New Haven: Yale University Press, 1979) 230. See also Tomb 1, loculi 20, 21 at Beit Zar'a. Muhammad Murshed A. Khadija, "Beit Zar'a Tombs (1974)," *Annual of the Department of Antiquities of Jordan* 19 (1974) 158.

[19]For additional information on early burial patterns, see John J. Davis, *What About Cremation? A Christian Perspective* (Winona Lake: BMH Books, 1989), and John J. Davis, "Excavation of Burials," 181–94.

[20]Thomas J. Kick, "Report of the Oesteologist: Abila 1982–1984," 93.

[21]Ibid.

[22]See Matt 19:13–14; Mark 10:13–14; Luke 18:16.

[23]D. C. Baramki, "A Byzantine Church at Mahatt El Urdi, Beit Jibrin, 1941–1942," *Studii Biblici Franciscani* 22 (1972) 152.

[24]J. H. Iliffe, "Imperial Art in Trans-Jordan," *The Quarterly of the Department of Antiquities in Palestine* XI (1945) 3.

[25]J. H. Iliffe, "Imperial Art in Trans-Jordan," 5. Moulds for such figurines were recently found in Caesarea. See Varda Sussman, "Moulds for Lamps and Figurines from

a Caesarea Workshop," *Atiqot, English Series* 14 (1980) 70 and Plate XVI.

[26]J. H. Iliffe, "Imperial Art in Trans-Jordan," Plate II, nos. 17–19. This motif is also represented in Nabatean art of the Roman period; see G. and A. Horsfield, "Sela-Petra, the Rock of Edom and Nabatene, IV: The Finds," *Quarterly of the Department of Antiquities of Palestine* 9 (1942), Plates XII:52 and XXX:253.

[27]N. G. L. Hammond and H. H. Scullard, eds., *The Oxford Classical Dictionary*, 2d ed. (Oxford: At the Clarendon Press, 1970), "Muses," H. G. Liddell, R. Scott and H. S. Jones, eds., *A Greek-English Lexicon*, new rev. ed. (Oxford: At the Clarendon Press, 1953) 1778.

[28]J. H. Iliffe, "Imperial Art in Trans-Jordan," Plate IV, no. 44.

[29]L. Y. Rahmani, "Roman Tombs in Nahal Raqafot, Jerusalem," *Atiqot, English Series* 11 (1976) 81.

[30]See D. C. Baramki, "A Byzantine Church at Mahatt El Urdi, Beit Jibrin, 1941–1942," 151.

[31]See Dewey M. Beegle, "Heshbon 1973: Necropolis Area F," *Andrews University Seminary Studies* 13:2 (1975) 204.

[32]Donna C. Kurtz and John Boardman, *Greek Burial Customs* (Ithaca, NY: Cornell University Press, 1971) 211.

[33]J. M. C. Toynbee, *Death and Burial in the Roman World* (New York: Cornell University Press, 1971) 223. See also E. L. Sukenki, "The Earliest Records of Christianity," *American Journal of Archaeology* 51 (1947) 352.

[34]J. M. C. Toynbee, *Death and Burial in the Roman World*, 50.

[35]James H. Stirling, "Human Skeletal Remains from Heshbon," *Andrews University Seminary Studies* 16:1 (1978) 256.

[36]Patricia Smith and Joseph Zias, "Skeletal Remains from the Late Hellenistic French Hill Tomb," *Israel Exploration Journal* 30:1–2 (1980) 114.

[37]P. Smith, E. C. Bornemann, and J. Zias, "Preliminary Report on the Human Skeletal Remains from Tomb 1," *Annual of the American Schools of Oriental Research* 43 (1976) 105–8.

# The Sodom Tradition in Intertestamental and New Testament Literature[1]

## Weston W. Fields

The widespread literary reuse of the Sodom and Gomorrah tradition (Genesis 19) provides an excellent example of how an ancient narrative may be remolded for the purposes of a later writer and the needs of a later audience. This tradition is reused in a variety of ways in the Old Testament itself: direct references,[2] allusions,[3] and recurring literary motifs.[4] The story also captured the imagination of other writers, most notably those responsible for the Apocrypha and Pseudepigrapha and the New Testament, as well as Rabbinic literature.

The present comparative analysis focuses on the reuse of the Sodom tradition by intertestamental and New Testament writers in order to demonstrate the variety of ways in which a single incident, even components of an incident, could be reshaped and differently emphasized to meet changing needs.[5]

A comparative analysis of the references to the Sodom tradition in the Apocrypha and Pseudepigrapha and New Testament enables one both to isolate at least four different lines of emphasis and even to point out a few New Testament allusions to the Sodom tradition which have been frequently overlooked in the past.

Weston W. Fields (B.A., Faith Baptist Bible College; M.Div., Th.M., Th.D., Grace Theological Seminary) is currently completing his dissertation for the Ph.D. degree at the Hebrew University of Jerusalem, and serves on the faculty of the Institute of Holy Land Studies, Jerusalem.

## THE SODOM TRADITION AND SINFUL SEXUAL PRACTICES

We turn first to passages emphasizing the sinful sexual practices of the Sodomites. Jubilees 16:5–10 summarizes the entire Genesis tradition:

> And in this month the Lord executed his judgment on Sodom, and Gomorrah, and Zeboim, and all the region of the Jordan, and He burned them with fire and brimstone, and destroyed them until this day, even as [lo] I have declared unto you all their works, that they are very wicked and sinners, and that they defile themselves and commit fornication with their bodies, and practice uncleanness on the earth. And, in like manner, God will execute judgment, similar to the judgment on Sodom, upon those places where they have imitated the uncleanness of the Sodomites. But Lot we saved; for God remembered Abraham, and sent him out from the midst of the destruction. And he and his daughters committed sin upon the earth, such as had not been on the earth since the days of Adam till his time; for the man lay with his daughters. And so it was commanded and engraved concerning all his seed, on the heavenly tablets, to remove them and root them out, and to execute judgment upon them like the judgment of Sodom, and to leave no seed of the man on earth on the day of condemnation.[6]

The same sin is again recalled in Jubilees 20:5, 6:

> And he told them of the judgment of the giants, and the judgment of the Sodomites, how they had been judged on account of their wickedness, and had died on account of their fornication, and uncleanness, and mutual corruption through fornication.
> "And guard yourselves from all fornication and uncleanness,
> And from all pollution of sin,
> Lest you make our name a curse,
> And your whole life a hissing,
> And all your sons to be destroyed by the sword
> And you become accursed like Sodom,
> And all your remnant as the sons of Gomorrah."[7]

Sexual immorality also figures in four of the references to Sodom in the Testaments of the Twelve Patriarchs. First, the Testament of Levi 14:6:

> And out of greed for gain you teach the commandments of the Lord, wedded women you pollute, and the virgins of Jerusalem you defile;

and with harlots and adultresses you have intercourse, and the gentile women you take as wives, and your sexual relations shall be like those of Sodom and Gomorrah.[8]

The Testament of Naphtali emphasizes this twice. First is 3:4:

But you shall not be so, my children. Recognize in the firmament, in the earth, and in the sea, and in all created things, the Lord who made all things, so that you do not become like Sodom, which departed from the order of nature.[9]

The second reference in this Testament is 4:1:

These things I say unto you, my children, for I have read in the writing of Enoch that you yourselves also shall depart from the Lord, walking according to all the lawlessness of the Gentiles, and you shall commit all the wickedness of Sodom.[10]

Less certainly part of this category is the Testament of Asher 7:1:

My children, do not become like Sodom, which did not recognize the Lord's angels and perished forever.[11]

This passage falls in this category because it seems reasonable to infer that this particular condemnation is not merely for the lack of recognition, since that was understandable and amoral in any event; it was, rather, their sexually abnormal request of the angels, engendered in part by their lack of recognition, that led to their downfall.

Finally, the Testament of Benjamin 9:1 is very explicit on this point:

From the words of Enoch the Righteous I tell you that you will be sexually promiscuous like the promiscuity of the Sodomites and will perish, with few exceptions. You shall resume your actions with loose women, and the kingdom of the Lord will not be among you, for he will take it away forthwith.[12]

The above passages use a variety of expressions to describe the sexual sinfulness of the Sodomites: "wicked and sinners," "define themselves and commit fornication with their bodies," "practice uncleanness on the earth" (*Jub.* 16:5–10); "fornication, uncleanness," "mutual corruption through fornication" (*Jub.* 20:5). The separate category of "sexual relations like those of Sodom and Gomorrah" (*T. Levi* 14:6) may be taken as homosexual relations, as can the phrases "departed from the order of nature" (*T. Naph.* 3:4) and "the wickedness of Sodom" (*T. Naph.* 4:1), but whether the latter refers to hetero- or homosexual relations is ambiguous, as is the phrase "promiscuous like the promiscuity of the Sodomites" (*T. Benj.* 9:1). But the ambiguity is probably only apparent; the Sodomites had long since become proverbial for homosexual relations, and by extension, any sexual relations not sanctioned by Israelite law.[13]

## THE SODOM TRADITION AND ARROGANCE

Another charge against the Sodomites is arrogance. This trait is emphasized by 3 Maccabees 2:3–5:

> For you who created all things, and govern the whole world, are a righteous ruler, and judge those who do aught in violence and arrogance. You destroyed those who previously did iniquity, among whom were giants trusting in their strength and boldness, bringing upon them a boundless flood of water. You burned up with fire and brimstone the men of Sodom, workers of arrogance, who had become known of all for their crimes, and made them an example to those who should come after.[14]

A similar sentiment is found in Sirach 16:8:

> He spared not the place where Lot sojourned,
> Who were arrogant in their pride.[15]

Arrogance as such is not mentioned in Genesis 19. However, the charge appears not only in intertestamental literature, but also in rabbinic literature.[16] It is Ezek 16:46–50 that mediates between the Genesis tradition and this particular emphasis found in later literature, for 16:49 states specifically: "This was the sin of your sister Sodom: arrogance. She and her daughters had plenty of food and tranquility and she did not help the poor or needy."

## THE SODOM TRADITION AND LOT

A third emphasis found in the many early literary references to Sodom is a positive view of Lot, a view which only some, not all, early interpreters found in Genesis 19. Wis 10:6–9 is an example of such a view:

> While the ungodly were perishing, wisdom delivered a righteous man,
> When he fled from the fire that descended out of heaven on Pentapolis

To whose wickedness a smoking waste still witnesses,
And plants bearing fair fruit that ripens not;[17]
(*Yea and* a disbelieving soul has a memorial *there*, a pillar of salt still
 standing.)
For having passed wisdom by,
Not only were they disabled from recognizing the things which are
 good,
But they also left behind them for *human* life a monument of their
 folly;
So that wherein they had offended could not but be known:
But wisdom delivered out of troubles those that waited on her.[18]

Such a view turns up again in Wis 19:17:

And they [Egyptians] too were stricken with loss of sight
(Even as those *others* at the righteous man's doors),
When, being compassed about with yawning darkness,
They sought every one the passage through his own door.[19]

The reference here to "those others at the righteous man's doors"
is certainly to Lot and the blindness of the men of Sodom. This is
corroborated by the reference in Wis 10:6, cited above, which says
that "wisdom delivered a righteous man" from the destruction which
"descended out of heaven on Pentapolis."

2 Pet 2:6–8 also speaks of "righteous Lot," who was distressed by
the immoral conduct of the godless (" . . . for that righteous man, living among them day and night suffered torment as he saw and heard
their immoral lawless deeds.") This tradition is continued by the earliest book of the "Apostolic Fathers," Clement of Rome's first letter to
the Corinthians.[20] Although the book is not strictly intertestamental or
New Testament, like the Qumran material to be discussed later, it
comes out of a very similar literary and cultural milieu. We therefore
include here a reference from 1 Clement 11:1 to the Sodom tradition:

Lot's faith and good deeds saved him from the destruction of Sodom
and Gomorrah; while his own wife perished and remains a monument to all ages of the punishment with which God visits the disobedient and wavering.[21]

It is worth noting that this positive view of Lot found in intertestamental, New Testament, and early Christian literature also surfaces,
but is the minority view, in Rabbinic literature.[22] It is generally supposed that the positive view of Lot may be traced to the fact that he

was the father of Moab, who, through Ruth, was the ancestor of David, and through him, of the Messiah. The negative view of Lot arises from the same fact, but focuses on the incestuous nature of the relationship which produced Moab.

## THE SODOM TRADITION AND DIVINE JUDGMENT

Finally, there is in Intertestamental and New Testament literature an emphasis on the employment of Sodom as an example of divine judgment. This springs from the Old Testament itself, where Israel's sin and/or punishment are compared to that of Sodom. One example of the way in which this biblical emphasis is taken up in later literature is Jubilees 36:10:

> But on the day of turbulence and execration and indignation and anger, with flaming devouring fire as He burnt Sodom, so likewise will he burn his land and his city and all that is recorded in the book of life, but in that which is appointed to destruction, and he shall depart into eternal execration; so that their condemnation may be always renewed in hate and in execration and in wrath and in torment and in indignation and in plagues and in disease for ever.[23]

A reference to Isaiah's comparison of Jerusalem to Sodom (Isa 1:9f.) is found in the Martyrdom of Isa 3:10:

> And Jerusalem also he hath called Sodom, and the princes of Judah and Jerusalem he hath declared to be the people of Gomorrah" (Belchira accusing Isaiah before Manasseh).[24]

Sodom as prototypical of judgment and destruction is also found in Jubilees 22:22:

> And as for all the worshippers of idols and the profane
> (b) There shall be no hope for them in the land of the living;
> (c) And there shall be no remembrance of them on the earth;
> (c) For they shall descend into Sheol,
> (d) And into the place of condemnation shall they go,
> As the children of Sodom were taken away from the earth
> So will all those who worship idols be taken away.[25]

The association of Sodom and judgment recurs as well in the Sibylline Oracles (2d cent. B.C.E.–7th cent. C.E.) 6, 21:

> For you alone, land of Sodom, evil afflictions are in store.[26]

An allusion to Sodom is also found in the Sibylline Oracles, 3, 689–92:

> God will judge all men by war and sword and fire and torrential rain. There will also be brimstone from heaven and stones and much grievous hail.[27]

The allusion here is not only to Sodom ("brimstone from heaven" [Gen 19:24]) but also to the plagues in Egypt ("much grievous hail" [Exod 9:23]).

An interesting connection between judgment and the language of the Sodom story is found in a scroll from Qumran. While Qumran literature is not usually included in "intertestamental literature," it certainly falls within the same time frame and cultural milieu. 1QpHab x, 5 reads: ובתוכם ירשיענו ובאש גופרית ישפטנו ("Then in their midst He will pronounce him guilty and damn him with the fire of brimstone").[28] In this interpretation of Hab 2:9–11, 1QpHab x, 5 applies the passage to "the Priest," evidently the "wicked priest," who is to be judged by God and eventually damned to the fire of brimstone. The combination in 1QpHab of אש, גפרית ("fire," "brimstone," a collocation which usually alludes to Sodom) and the phrase במרום קנו לנצל ("up high he will put his nest," 1QpHab ix, 13) is reminiscent of Jer 49:16–18, where it is predicted that the doom of Edom will be like Sodom and Gomorrah: "though you build your nest high (כי תגביה כנשר קנך, (v 16) . . . Edom will become an object of horror . . . as Sodom and Gomorrah were overthrown (i.e., with fire and brimstone, Gen 19:24) . . . so no one will live there."[29] In the New Testament, fire and brimstone are invariably associated with the place of eternal punishment, a connection also made by 1QS iv, 13f. which describes the miserable lot of those in the "fire of the regions of darkness."[30]

Other possibly important allusions to Sodom based on the words גפרית, הפך, שחת, עמרה, מלח may exist in unpublished non-biblical Qumran fragments, but investigation of the material has not yet been sufficient to enable us to draw any conclusions. It is possible that Beat 15,6, PeshGenB 1 III 2, S1 76 2 II 2, and several other fragments may show allusion upon further investigation.[31]

A whole series of New Testament judgment passages reuses the Sodom story in a similar fashion. The first of these is Matt 10:15 and its parallel in Mark 6:11 (t.r.):[32]

> Indeed, I tell you, it will be better for the land of Sodom and Gomorrah in the day of judgment than for that city.

In the context of sending out the Twelve, Jesus tells his disciples that any city which does not welcome them will have it worse in the judgment than Sodom and Gomorrah. Sodom and Gomorrah, the most wicked cities in antiquity, were harshly judged for their sinfulness. But those who did not welcome the disciples would be considered even more wicked. Consequently, such inhospitable cities would stand in danger of receiving even more punishment. It is *inhospitality* that makes the connection between the ancient tradition and the context in Matthew.

A similar example is found in Matt 11:23–24:

> And you, Capernaum,
> You shall not ascend to heaven,
> But shall be cast down to Hades.
> For if the miracles which have been performed among you had been performed in Sodom, it would have remained until today. Nevertheless, I tell you, it will be better in the day of Judgment for the land of Sodom than for you.

In his condemnation of cities to whom he had preached and who had not repented, Jesus reaches back to the Old Testament for examples of proverbially wicked cities with which to compare and contrast some of the cities rejecting him: Chorazin, Bethsaida, and Capernaum. He contrasts the former two with Tyre and Sidon, which, he says, would have "repented in sackcloth and ashes" had he performed his miracles there.[33] Reusing Isaiah's taunt against the King of Babylon (Isa 14:13, 15), Jesus reserves special contempt for the people of Capernaum who, he says, will have it worse in the day of judgment even than the prototypically wicked Sodom. Had his miracles been performed in Sodom, Jesus says, they at least would have repented. Thus in this reuse of the Sodom tradition, the focus is the unrepentant wickedness of the Sodomites in general and not, as in Matt 10:15 above, their inhospitality.

In the parallel passage, Luke 10:13–16, the reference to Sodom is deleted, probably because Sodom is adduced as an example in the verse immediately preceding, the section about the mission of the seventy-two, which only Luke records.

Also similar to the two previous examples is Luke 10:12:

I say to you that it will be better for Sodom in that day than for that city.

When Jesus commissions the seventy-two[34] in a context similar to the commissioning of the Twelve (Matt 10:15, Mark 6:11) Jesus again emphasizes the *inhospitality* of the Sodomites. Cities which do not welcome his followers will be punished more severely in "that day," i.e., the day of judgment, than will Sodom, notwithstanding that Sodom was the worst ancient example of *inhospitality*.

Luke 17:28–29, 32 also illustrates coming judgment and destruction by reference to the Sodom story.

> It will be just as it was in the time of Lot; they were eating, drinking, buying, selling, planting, and building. But the day Lot left Sodom, fire and brimstone rained down from heaven and destroyed every-one" (ἔβρεξεν πῦρ καὶ θεῖον ἀπ᾽ οὐρανοῦ καὶ ἀπώλεσεν πάντας).

In order to spur his disciples to vigilance for the coming of his kingdom, Jesus adduces two examples of previous destructions over-taking victims who ignored warnings of impending doom. The first of these is the destruction in the time of Noah (Luke 17:26, 27). The second is the destruction of Sodom. Like in days of Noah, when, oblivious to Noah's warnings,[35] everyone went about life as usual (eating, drinking, marrying and giving in marriage, Luke 17:27), the Sodomites carried on with their normal pursuits until the very mo-ment the disaster struck. Jesus lists only a few of many possible activ-ities associated with a normal society. His point is not that any of these occupations was wrong; he wishes only to stress that the Sod-omites' failure consisted of ignoring Lot's warning of the coming de-struction.[36]

Lot's wife is used in v 32 as a negative example. When the Son of Man appears, his disciples are to join him immediately, in contrast to the hesitation and vacillation of Lot's wife: they must not go to the house to get their belongings or come back to the house from the field (17:31).

A slightly different emphasis can be found in Rom 9:29:

> If the Lord Almighty had not left us some descendants, we would have become like Sodom, we would have been like Gomorrah.

In order to emphasize the idea of a remnant saved in Israel, Paul quotes verbatim from the Greek of Isa 1:9. Sodom and Gomorrah were completely destroyed; by way of contrast, Israel was not.

We return once more to 2 Pet 2:6–10, where again the judgment on Sodom and Gomorrah is used as an example.

> If he condemned the cities of Sodom and Gomorrah by burning them with fire (καταστροφῇ), making them an example of what will happen to the godless, and if he rescued righteous Lot, who was distressed by the immoral conduct of the godless (for that righteous man, living among them day and night suffered torment as he saw and heard their immoral lawless deeds), then the Lord knows how to deliver the godly from trials and to hold the unrighteous for the day of judgment while continuing their punishment. This is all the more so for those who follow the perverted lusts of their bodies and despise authority.

The context of 2 Peter includes references to three ancient judgments: (1) the "angels who sinned," and were cast into hell,[37] a reference to a particular interpretation of Gen 6:1–7;[38] (2) the judgment of the Deluge in the time of Noah; and (3) the judgment upon Sodom and Gomorrah during the time of Lot. The passage also contains three of the four emphases which have been demonstrated above from a wide range of intertestamental and New Testament literature. Peter stresses that the destruction of Sodom and Gomorrah provides an example of what the godless can expect. He singles out their immorality. But he also emphasizes that Lot was righteous, and that he was distressed by the godlessness around him in Sodom. Peter uses this fact to demonstrate that if God was able to rescue righteous Lot from the cataclysmic destruction of Sodom, he will also be able to rescue the righteous among his readers from coming judgment. Καταστραφεῖν[39] is noteworthy because it is the only word the LXX uses to translate the Hebrew מהפכה, nearly always a direct reference or an allusion to the Sodom story when it appears in the Old Testament.[40]

Jude 7 is another example which combines more than one emphases in its employment of the Sodom story:

> Similarly, Sodom and Gomorrah and the surrounding cities committed the same kind of sexual immorality and perversion. They serve as an example for those who will be punished with eternal fire (πρόκεινται δεῖγμα πυρὸς αἰωνίου δίκην ὑπέχουσαι).

Jude 7 and 2 Peter 2 are interrelated.[41] As in 2 Peter, the author of Jude emphasizes the rescue of God's people and the punishment of the wicked. He provides only two examples of his points, however, bypassing the example of the Deluge found in 2 Peter. The fate of the "angels who did not stay within the boundaries of their authority" (Jude 6) and the punishment of the people of Sodom and Gomorrah become an illustration of divine retribution upon the wicked. It is sexual sinfulness—ἐκπορνεύσασαι καὶ ἀπελθοῦσαι ὀπίσω σαρκὸς ἑτέρας—for which the Sodomites were punished according to Jude.

Rev 11:8 is also reminiscent of Isa 1:9f.:

> And their bodies will lie in the street of the great city, which is spiritually called Sodom and Egypt, where also their Lord was crucified.

Jerusalem is the city in view. It is "spiritually" Sodom because it is wicked like Sodom. The immediate context alludes to previous punishments and destructions: the plagues in Egypt (Rev 11:6; Exod 7:17–19), the drought during the time of Elijah (Rev 11:6; 1 Kgs 17:1), and, perhaps, the destruction by fire at Sodom (πῦρ ἐκπορεύεται ἐκ τοῦ στόματος αὐτῶν καὶ κατεσθίει τοὺς ἐχθροὺς αὐτῶν, "fire will come out of their mouths and destroy their enemies"). The "two witnesses" who will be killed by "the beast" will lie in the street of Jerusalem as a symbol of its rebellion against God and his prophets. Thus, the application of the symbolism of Isaiah for Jerusalem is apt and to the point. Rev 11:8, however, goes a step beyond Isaiah. Isaiah merely compares Jerusalem to Sodom; Revelation says that Jerusalem may be "spiritually," that is, metaphorically, called "Sodom."

A further development of the Sodom tradition involves the application of certain figures, especially "fire and brimstone," to descriptions of eternal punishment in a symbolic way. That is, from the Sodom story which narrates a *physical* destruction from brimstone and fire, through the reuse of that description as imagery in threats of future punishment, we finally arrive at what can only be a *symbolic* description of the instruments of destruction of the wicked and Satan.

Given the way in which the expressions גפרית ואש invariably refer to the Sodom tradition where they occur in the Old Testament, there is a high degree of probability that the contexts in the New Testament (and other Jewish literature of the period) which employ the Greek translations of these terms (θεῖον [θειώδης, sulphurous, Rev 9:17] and πῦρ) will also be allusive to Sodom.[42] A series of passages from Revelation serve to illustrate this.

This is what the horses and riders I saw in my vision looked like: their breastplates were fiery red, dark blue, and yellow as sulfur (θεῖον). The heads of the horses resembled the heads of lions, and out of their mouths came fire, smoke and sulfur (πῦρ καὶ καπνὸς καὶ θεῖον). A third of mankind was killed by these three plagues of fire, smoke, and brimstone (ἐκ τοῦ πυρὸς καὶ τοῦ καπνοῦ καὶ τοῦ θείου) that came out of their mouths" (Rev 9:17–19).

A third angel followed them and said in a loud voice: "If anyone worships the beast and his image and receives his mark on his forehead or on his hand, then he will drink of the wine of God's wrath, which has been poured full strength into the cup of his anger. He will be tormented with burning brimstone (πῦρ καὶ θείῳ) in the presence of the holy angels and the Lamb" (Rev 14:9, 10).

The two of them [the beast and the false prophet] were cast alive into the fiery lake of burning brimstone (τὴν λίμνην τοῦ πυρὸς τῆς καιομένης ἐν θείῳ)[43] (Rev 19:20).

And the devil, who deceived them, was thrown into the lake of burning sulfur (τὴν λίμνην τοῦ πυρὸς καὶ θείου), where the beast and the false prophet had been thrown (Rev 20:10).

But the cowardly, the unbelieving, the vile, the murderers, the sexually immoral, those who practice magic arts, the idolaters and all liars—their place will be in the fiery lake of burning sulfur (ἐν τῇ λίμνῃ τῇ καιομένῃ πυρὶ καὶ θείῳ). This is the second death (Rev 21:8).

There can be little doubt that the combination of fire, burning sulphur, and judgment is dependent upon the Sodom tradition. One has only to understand that in the Old Testament such a connection is obvious, that passages such as Isaiah 1 and intertestamental literature were mediatory, so that for the audience of the book of Revelation what was obvious need not be stated. Future divine punishment was best described in terms of the most spectacular destruction of all time: the total annihilation of Sodom and Gomorrah by a deluge of fire.

## SUMMARY

The Sodom tradition was "expanded" in different directions by different writers for different purposes, a frequent and familiar biblical pattern. This familiar Old Testament literary technique was continued in other Jewish literature, whether Apocryphal, Pseudepigraphical, New Testament or Rabbinic. It was the literary method of the time. One need apologize neither for these ancient writers, whether these methods were used in what is considered Scripture or what is not considered Scripture. A recognition of the normality of such reuse and reemphasis, illustrated here by examples demonstrating the reworking of the Sodom tradition, can only help, not hinder, in the unending task of understanding the New Testament and applying it to ourselves.

# NOTES

[1]It is a great privilege to dedicate this essay to Dr. Homer A. Kent, Jr., esteemed professor during my student days and President during the years I taught at Grace Schools.

[2]Gen 13:10, 13; Deut 29:22; 32:32; Isa 1:9, 10; 3:9; 13:19; Jer 23:14; 49:18; 50:40; Lam 4:6; Ezek 16:46, 48, 49, 53, 55, 56; Amos 4:11; Zeph 2:9.

[3]E.g., Job 18:15; Ps 11:6; Isa 1:7; 30:33; 34:9; Ezek 38:22.

[4]Most prominently, in Joshua 2 and Judges 19–21.

[5]See J. W. Smart, "The Sodom Tradition and the Hermeneutical Task" (Ann Arbor: UMI, 1988) 1–24.

[6]R. H. Charles, trans., "The Book of Jubilees," *APOT* 2.37. This, and most subsequent translations from *APOT* and *OTP* have been slightly modified by the writer.

[7]Charles, "Jubilees," 2.42.

[8]H. C. Kee, trans., "Testaments of the Twelve Patriarchs," *OTP* 1.793; R. H. Charles, trans., "The Testaments of the Twelve Patriarchs," *APOT* 2.312–13.

[9]Kee, "Testaments," 1.812; Charles, "Testaments," 2.337.

[10]Kee, "Testaments," 1.812; Charles, "Testaments," 2.337.

[11]Kee, "Testaments," 1.818; Charles, "Testaments," 2.345.

[12]Kee, "Testaments," 1.827; cf. Charles, "Testaments," 2.358.

[13]"When a man was evil he was called a Sodomite . . . the men of Sodom were wicked and sinners . . . sinners in adultery . . . " (*Gen. Rab.* 41:7); "The Sodomites made an agreement among themselves that whenever a stranger visited them they should force him to sodomy . . . " (*Gen. Rab.* 50:7).

[14]C. W. Emmet, trans., "3 Maccabees," *APOT* 1.164.

[15]G. H. Box and W. O. E. Oesterley, trans., "The Book of Sirach," *APOT* 1.372.

[16]E.g., *b. Sanh.* 109a.

[17]Cf. Josephus's account of the "Apples of Sodom," in Wars iv.8.4.

[18]S. Holmes, trans., "The Wisdom of Solomon," *APOT* 1.551.

[19]Holmes, "The Wisdom of Solomon," 1.567.

[20]Reputedly written by the first pastor of the church in Rome (ca. 90 C.E.).

[21]J. B. Lightfoot, trans., *Apostolic Fathers* (2 vols.; London: Macmillan and Co., 1890) 1.45. The reference to Sodom in 1 Clement 10:4 is not relevant to our discussion here.

[22]See the expression "wicked Lot" in *Gen. Rab.* 40:7; 51:6–10.

[23]Charles, "Jubilees," 2.37.

[24]R. H. Charles, trans., "The Martyrdom of Isaiah," *APOT* 2.161–62.

[25]Charles, "Jubilees," 2.46.

[26]J. J. Collins, trans., "Sibylline Oracles," *OTP* 1.407. Collins terms this oracle,

addressed to the nation of Israel, "clearly Christian" (1.322).

[27]Collins, "Sibylline Oracles," 1.376. Cf. Ezek 38:22; *Sib. Or.* 3, 543; 5, 274; 5, 377.

[28]W. H. Brownlee, *The Midrash Pesher of Habakkuk* SBLMS 24; Missoula, MT: Scholars Press, 1979) 158.

[29]1QpHab x, 13 should also be noted: למשפטי אש אשר גדפו ויחרפו את בחירי אל, "the judgments of fire, since they have reviled and insulted the elect of God" (Brownlee, *The Midrash Pesher of Habakkuk*, 167).

[30]A. Dupont-Sommer, *The Essene Writings from Qumran* (trans. G. Vermes; Gloucester, MA: Peter Smith, 1973) 81. Brownlee points out that Hippolytus, *Adv. haer.* (as pointed out by K. Shubert, *ZKTh* [1952] 36) ascribes to the Essenes the doctrine that the world will be destroyed by fire and that the wicked will be punished forever (Brownlee, *The Midrash Pesher of Habakkuk*, 165–66). This is unremarkable, however, given similar widespread beliefs in various sects of Judaism, including Christianity, in the period. Cf. further Josephus, *War* 2.155–58.

[31]These are preliminary designations for the fragments found in the catalog of nonbiblical fragments in the scrollery of the Rockefeller Museum, Jerusalem. I would like to thank Profs. E. Tov and S. Talmon for arranging for me to have access to these fragments.

[32]Found in the *textus receptus* of Mark 6:11, but not in the tradition of the Alexandrian text type, and the editors of the eclectic UBS text did not include it.

[33]Cf. the condemnations of Tyre and Sidon in Isa 23:1–8; Ezekiel 26:28; Joel 3:4–8; Amos 1:9–10; Zech 9:2–4).

[34]Or, seventy, as many manuscripts read, including א A C and a number of other uncials and minuscules, in contrast to the seventy-two of $p^{75}$ B and D.

[35]The conception of Noah as a preacher is evidently based on Gen 6:9 and is derived from tradition current at the time. Cf. Josephus, *Ant.* 1.3.1; *Jub.* 7:20–39.

[36]In the Genesis account only Lot's sons-in-law are warned.

[37]ταρταρώσας, i.e., cast into Tartarus.

[38]Found in the LXX (e.g., the translation γίγαντες for נפלים [Gen 6:4]); *Jub.* 5:1–16; *1 Enoch* 9:8–11; Josephus, *Ant.* 1.3.1.

[39]Καταστροφῇ (v 6) is read by א A C² other uncials, many minuscules, as well as the Byz text type. It is omitted in $p^{72txt}$ B C* and a few other witnesses.

[40]See E. C. Dos Santos, *An Expanded Hebrew Index for the Hatch-Redpath Concordance to the Septuagint* (Jerusalem: Dugith Publishers, n.d.) 106; E. Hatch and H. A. Redpath, *A Concordance to the Septuagint* (3 vols. reprinted in 2; Grand Rapids: Baker Book House, 1983) 2.745–46. Ετέφρωσα, from τεφρόω is used only here in the NT, but is found in *Sib. Or.* 5, 124 (see reference below in *Sib. Or.* 6, 21ff.) and Philo, *Ebr.* 223, where it is used with reference to Sodom and Gomorrah.

[41]The most common view is that 2 Peter depends upon Jude, but the reverse is also possible. In any event they both appear to rely on Jubilees and 1 Enoch or traditions similar to those represented by them.

[42]Most of the Revelation references are probably based to some extent on the LXX of Isa 30:33, in which the valley of Tophet (Gehenna) is mentioned, but the last half of the verse may base its imagery ultimately on the Sodom story (ὁ θυμὸς κυρίου ὡς φάραγξ ὑπὸ θείου καιομένη).

[43]Following NIV version.

# Form and Function in the Letters
# of the New Testament

## D. Brent Sandy

The simple act of writing a letter is ubiquitous across time and culture. And letter writing is likely to outlast even the megatrends of modern society, despite the advancing technology of the information revolution.

Yet the "simple" act of writing a letter is neither simple nor something to be taken for granted, for the significance and complexity of a letter are more than meet the eye. A letter bonds the author and reader together as the author concentrates on the reader while he writes, and as the reader concentrates on the author while he reads. Thus, a letter is a form of conversation but with a more lasting value: it can be read again and again and even passed on to another reader. Writing a letter, therefore, requires very careful choice of wording, much more so than conversation, since the sender will not be able to explain the meaning of his words. Letters are also portraits of an author's personal values and feelings at any given time. Thus, letters preserve moments in time, they are chapters in a relationship. And letters serve many purposes: there are keep-in-touch letters, letters of praise and commendation, letters of petition and demand, letters of complaint, letters to initiate or to end a relationship, and letters to give a report. Letters, then, can tug at emotions, console, uplift, stir to action, and even transform.[1]

The complexity of letter writing is confirmed by the importance of the elements of letters, and how the elements establish the desirable

D. Brent Sandy (B.A., Grace College; M.Div., Grace Theological Seminary; Ph.D., Duke University) is Professor of New Testament at Liberty University, Lynchburg, Virginia.

relationship or tone for the letter. The form of greeting and closing are especially important, but so are the sentiments expressed in the body of the letter, the type of paper, the placement of the letter on the page, and the presence of the date and an address. A handwritten letter denotes ever more increasingly—given the availability of mechanical means of composing letters—a special relationship between author and recipient. If not handwritten, a letter requires at least a handwritten signature to guarantee to the reader the personal touch of its author.[2]

## EARLY CHRISTIAN LETTER WRITING

The earliest preserved documents from the Christian movement are letters written by the Apostle Paul; and letters became the most widely used form of written expression in the first one hundred years of Christianity. Thirty letters are preserved in the NT: twenty-one of the twenty-seven books of the NT are "letters," though some of these lack the salutations and conclusions typical of ancient letters; two letters are preserved in Acts;[3] and Revelation 2–3 includes seven "letters," though these also lack some features typical of letters. Similar to the predominance of letters in the NT, the collection of writings composed by the Apostolic Fathers during the first half of the second century includes twelve compositions in letter form out of a total of fifteen compositions. Christians continued writing letters throughout succeeding centuries so that more than nine thousand ancient Christian letters are extant today.[4]

The Christian attraction to letter writing is not surprising. (1) Important to the success of Christianity was the ability to keep in touch, to maintain close relationships, to build community. Letters bonded Christians together beyond city or territorial boundaries, helping preserve a oneness of experience and purpose. (2) For the earliest Christians, the lack of written expressions of their faith could most readily be filled by letters. The unusual popularity of the genre of letter writing in the Roman world in the century before and after Christ provided the needed medium for Christians to articulate their beliefs. (3) A letter could function as a written sermon, to encourage and admonish individuals or a group of believers, or if passed from place to place, it could reach many groups of believers spread over a wide area. In this sense a letter was a surrogate for the author's personal presence with his readers. (4) The typology of ancient letters was sufficiently varied to allow Christians to express a diversity of ideas without creating a new genre. Letters could include praise, rebuke, consolation, advice, exhortation, vice and virtue lists, dues for members of the community, doxologies, benedictions, prayers, autobiographical information, and travel plans. (5) Letters served the early Christian community well because they were not pretentious. While letters were a form of literary art, they could express goodwill, friendship, and encouragement in simple terms without an elegant or elaborate style. Christians would later be attracted to the neoclassicism of their culture and attempt to write lofty essays patterned after the heroes of the classical Greek past. But the early Christians were completely satisfied simply to write letters.

## UNDERSTANDING THE LETTERS IN THE NT

At the heart of all accurate interpretation of any literary document is culture, for meaning is a function of culture.[5] While truth transcends culture, every expression of truth is culturally conditioned. Thus, the particular words chosen to reveal timeless truths are in themselves limited by time, and those ephemeral words are empty symbols without recourse to the culture that gives them meaning. The symbolic universe of a language, then, is the sum total of all that the symbols of that language can designate. Culture is much more, however, than archaeological artifacts—pottery, buildings, armor, jewelry, etc.—however valuable they are. Culture is a world of ideas, values, and ways of thinking. This is the heart of culture, and it is those ideas which hold the promise of opening up the pages of any text.

The necessity of culture is especially pressing when reading the letters canonized in the NT. Letters universally presume a common base of information, more so than any other genre, for they are usually prompted by an experience or relationship common to two or more people. A recounting in the letter of what is held in common is therefore usually not needed. The principle is that the closer the bond and shared knowledge between the sender and recipient, the more will be presumed in the exchange of letters. Furthermore, letters have certain codes embedded in the specific forms used to write the letter. The greeting, certain kinds of phrases, the ending, all can contribute to the meaning of the contents of the letter.

The interpreter of letters in the NT faces serious challenges, therefore, in doing exegesis. The larger issues of culture, i.e., the symbolic universe, are important as they are for any portion of the NT. But the very nature of letter writing adds another dimension: the life situation of the author and the readers must be reconstructed as completely as possible. All that might have been presumed between sender and recipient is important to understanding what is explicitly stated in the letter. In a sense, reading the letters in the NT, especially those responding to specific situations in the lives of the recipients, is like listening to one side of a telephone conversation.[6] To piece together the full significance of what is being said when hearing just half of a conversation demands careful attention to everything that can be discovered about both parties involved in the conversation including their ways of speaking and the issues involved.

Fortunate for the study of NT letters is the treasure of information from antiquity about the forms and functions of letters and their components. In addition to thousands of letters preserved in collections by various ancient authors[7] and in the papyri,[8] valuable handbooks have survived that prescribe the typology of ancient letter writing.[9] With the classification of letters into various types, with the clarification of the functions of letter components provided by these handbooks, and with the ability to analyze many examples of ancient letter forms, the study of NT letters can be placed on much surer footing. For NT letters represent a variety of forms: some are personal, some are impersonal, some are anonymous, some are letter essays, some are strings of moral exhortations, and some are prophetic proclamations. The following presentation, then, of letter forms and functions will provide the basis for specific insight into the interpretation of the letters in the NT.

## ANCIENT LETTER WRITING

The act of writing a letter was the result of the desire to communicate when face to face communication was impossible or undesirable. Hence, a letter was an exchange between two or more people and consisted of an opening (usually personalized), the contents, and a closing (generally dated). Most common in NT times, a letter was written with a reed pen and black ink on a sheet of papyrus. The document was then folded (sometimes rolled) and the name of the addressee written on the outside, which served as the envelope. For business correspondence, the outside of the letter might also be docketed for filing purposes.[10] Since the postal service of the Roman Empire was largely for official business only, personal letters were sent with couriers or with someone known to be traveling to the vicinity of the addressee.[11] Letter carriers could often convey a personal greeting and bring additional information to the recipient of the letter. Sometimes professional letter writers were hired to compose a letter, if the author was illiterate or unskilled in writing a particular type of letter. In this case, the real author wrote something in his own hand at the end of the letter, often in larger letters, to guarantee his personal touch.[12]

More important than the pen and paper with which a letter was composed were the deeply embedded cultural values that shaped the contours of ancient letters.[13] (1) Social status determined the nature of the letter that could be sent from one person to another. (2) The forms of expression in letters regularly followed the taxonomy of rhetoric, since ancient society was primarily an oral culture. (3) When admonition was included in letters, the patterns of dialectical methodology set by philosophers affected how authors expressed themselves. A closer inspection of these basic concepts is essential for a proper perspective on the letters of antiquity.

First, social interactions at the time of the NT were ordered along horizontal lines—relationships between equals—and along vertical lines—patron-client relationships. In horizontal relationships, friendship was thoroughly integrated into all spheres of life, including labor, politics, learning and recreation.[14] This close bonding between friends meant the sharing of two selves, the absence of individualism, and most importantly an ethic of reciprocity in the exchange of goods and services.

This friendship was so important in antiquity that it was considered the primary basis for the act of writing a letter.[15] In letters, the expression of the affections of friendship became commonplace, for letters permitted absent friends to share with each other and to maintain their friendship. It was in the opening and closing elements of letters where these sentiments of friendly relations were especially expressed. Some letters, with the maintenance of contact their sole purpose, consisted only of opening and closing elements.

The patron-client relationships, on the other hand, reveal a basic hierarchical pattern of life in the Roman world.[16] Everyone depended on close ties with those at a higher social status than themselves to gain influence and security. Patrons were liberal with benefactions and assistance for their clients, in exchange for which the clients gave praise and honor to the patrons. In civil affairs, for example, wealthy aristocrats funded major public works, and in turn the townspeople honored the patrons with the erection of statues and inscriptions in their honor.

Essential to the success of the patron-client relationships was the rhetoric of praise and blame, or the giving and taking away of honor.[17] Honor was the basis of status in society, and a person's status above others was determined by the honor shown. Honor was shown to a superior, but it was received from an inferior. In letter writing, the rhetoric of praise and blame is clearly evident, for a client would not write to a patron without praising the goodness of that patron. For some letters the sole purpose is to give honor to a patron as part of the preservation and enhancement of the patron-client relationship. On the other hand, a patron may use blame in writing to a client, not to end the relationship, but to maintain the status of it.

Implicit to every social situation, therefore, is either a relationship of friends or of patron-clients. This is especially clear in the guidelines for a farewell speech (Menander Rhetor 395.4–30): if the traveler is socially inferior, the speech should give advice; if the traveler is a superior, the speech should give praise; if the traveler is a friend, i.e., equal in social status, the speech should display affection. Determining the status of the relationship, then, is the basis of a proper understanding of most examples of ancient correspondence.

Second, the orality of ancient culture is evident throughout the NT. Ancient literature was more often heard than read, and it was composed with rhetorical qualities intended to have an impact on the people to whom it was read. Even for private readers, literature retained its orality and linearity, for they read aloud to themselves.[18] All this is confirmed by the transfer of rhetorical techniques from speech to letter. Since rhetoric was the primary subject of secondary education in the Greco-Roman world, handbooks of rhetoric were in common circulation and affected almost all forms of oral and written communication. Thus, letters were considered "written conversation"

(Libanius/Proclus 14.1), or as Cicero said in a letter, "I am speaking to you in your presence" (*Letters to Atticus*, 1.16.8). Thus, the highly developed stratigraphy of oratory, with specific rules for certain types of speeches, was adapted for letter writing, and resulted in the ancient treatises on epistolary theory defining at least twenty-one epistolary types.[19] The rhetorical techniques common to speaking, therefore, became common in letter writing.

Though ancient letters fictionalized personal presence, the acts of speaking and writing were not equated. While ancient theorists prescribed writing letters as if the author was speaking face to face with the reader, they realized that letters needed to be more articulate than actual conversation, for letters could not convey the inflection and gestures that speech could. Furthermore, writing was permanent and potentially non-private. Thus, this second best means of communicating personal presence, in many ways similar to the speech-act, was yet unique in its own ways.

Third, philosophy in antiquity had the practical goal of discovering the way to meaning and happiness in life.[20] Finding normal society inadequate, most philosophies attempted to convert people to an improved approach to life. To this end, philosophers developed distinctive styles of teaching in their schools that usually involved dialogue and a conversational style. In addition to teaching, philosophers communicated their ideas through letters, with the primary purpose of persuading readers to adhere to the values of the philosophy. The extensive letter writing of the philosophical schools, originating with the disciples of Socrates, but continuing through Epicurus, Diogenes, and others, created a well established tradition of what the contents of the conversion literature should be. Philosophical correspondence could include positive and negative exhortation, encouragement, rebuke, and advice, but most importantly, the letters were to be dialogical.

A sub-category of this philosophical style is the diatribe,[21] a mix of philosophical dialogue with rhetorical declamation. Common to diatribe are rhetorical figures, elliptical expressions, irony, sarcasm, vice and virtue lists, and censorious rebuke. This wide-ranging philosophical style of teaching and writing, in the course of communicating with widely scattered disciples, left a legacy of rhetorical technique that often appears to be very polemical, but which is no more than a pedagogical style.

## FORMS OF ANCIENT LETTERS

Accurate analysis of letters can be facilitated by studying together the letters with the same features. Unfortunately, the classification of letters is complicated by the complexity of the letter writing process, and no one system is adequate to account for all the features of ancient letters. The various criteria that can be used to classify letters include:

(a) writing materials: papyri, wood tablets with a waxed surface (etched with a stylus), ostraca (for very brief letters), and inscriptions on stone;

(b) means of preservation: letters collected, published, and passed on; letters discarded but preserved in ideal climatic conditions; and letters embedded in historical or biographical literature;

(c) languages: in relation to the NT, primarily Greek, Latin, Hebrew, Aramaic, Demotic, and Coptic;

(d) authorship: letters written by specific individuals or groups, such as philosophers, Jews,[22] or Christians;

(e) formal epistolary features: letters written according to different formulas appearing in the opening, body, and closing of the letters;

(f) nature of the correspondence: official letters from government representatives that were often inscribed on stone for public display,[23] documentary letters generally of private, family, or business matters, preserved primarily on papyri;[24] literary letters that were valued for their artistry or special contents;[25]

(g) forms of rhetoric: judicial, deliberative, and epideictic;[26]

(h) themes (*topoi*): friendship, joy upon receiving a letter, longing to be together, consolation for separation, and anticipated reunion;[27]

(i) function: letters of recommendation, petition, friendship, family, praise and blame, exhortation and advice, mediation, and accusation.[28]

These nine classifications of letters, though overlapping and not exhaustive, form the basis of an ongoing analysis of ancient epistolography. And they form the basis of proper interpretation of the NT. For the dynamics of the NT text, in a dialogue of give-and-take with the culture of the Greco-Roman and Jewish societies—while the various forms of religious life and literary expression of Christian beliefs were being shaped—demonstrate that rather than creating new literary forms, Christians adopted the current mediums of communication and adjusted their message accordingly. Consequently, any informed excursion into the meaning of NT letters or portions thereof will need to appreciate the larger setting of epistolary conventions.

## INSIGHTS INTO NT LETTERS

From the letters in the NT it becomes clear that the authors were eclectic in their approach to ancient letter conventions, for they creatively drew from numerous letter techniques rather than using a single letter type. Thus their letters tend to be multifunctional and multi-formal, in response to complex life situations that called for a mixture of rhetorical styles. Nevertheless, NT letters clearly fall within the diverse framework of ancient letter writing forms and functions, meaning that an almost endless list of parallels can be compiled between NT and Greco-Roman-Jewish letters, a list that would include almost every feature of the letter writing process. All of these parallels have the potential of impacting a proper interpretation of the epistolary portions of the NT, though some parallels will be of more significance than others. The following discussions focus on certain aspects of NT letters that seem to benefit from a comparison with non-biblical letters. These discussions, albeit selective and exploratory, are indicative of the benefits of studying NT letters in their cultural milieu.

### Circumstantial letters, general letters, letter essays

The letters in the NT can be categorized in various ways, but the most basic is the distinction between circumstantial letters, general letters and letter essays. In circumstantial letters, the author knows his readers and their situation and is writing to stay in touch or to respond to particular circumstances. In general letters, the relationship between author and readers is more distant, and the contents of the letter transcend a specific historical situation. In letter essays, the author may have no relationship with his readers, for he simply used epistolary prescripts and postscripts to bracket his composition. Which of these categories a letter belongs to is based partly on: (a) whether the letter is monological or dialogical, i.e., does the author interact with the ideas and particular situations of the readers or does he speak generally to Christians; (b) whether the formulaic letter conventions of opening and closing are prominent and complete—suggesting close ties between sender and recipient—or whether the conventions are suppressed and in some cases absent; and (c) whether the letter has the characteristics of a friendly letter, e.g., does the author refer to specific individuals, mention travel plans, or express a wish for the well-being of the readers.

The letters in the NT are arranged in essentially two groups: Paul's letters, thought of as circumstantial; and the other epistles, thought of as general (or catholic). But these groupings are misleading: 2 and 3 John are clearly circumstantial not general, while Hebrews and Romans fall somewhere between circumstantial and general. And 1 and 2 Peter, James, and Jude may be treatises or homilies that the author bracketed with the popular letter opening and/or closing formulas,[29] while 1 John has no formal epistolary features.

Paul's letter to a community of believers in Rome that he had not founded or visited is a useful example of the necessity of distinguishing between circumstantial letters and general letters. The textual history of Romans shows that in antiquity it was considered a general letter, for two shortened versions were in circulation, one without chapter 16 and one without chapters 15 and 16.[30] Furthermore, the extended list of greetings in chapter 16, usually indicating close ties between author and readers, may be Paul's attempt to establish those close ties even before his arrival in Rome. Determining, therefore, whether Paul's arguments in Romans are in response to the particular situation in Rome, even though he had not visited there, or whether he is simply presenting his view of the gospel, is important to the interpretation of the book. For if Paul is responding to a particular theological crisis at Rome, the interpreter of Romans is dealing with a circumstantial letter and must examine two questions: What were the problems in Rome? and, Has Paul presented his views in certain ways to convince his readers that their view was wrong and his right?—a situation that tended to affect an author's rhetoric.[31]

The circumstantial, general, or letter essay categories of NT letters are important, then, to proper interpretation, but recognizing whether a letter is general or circumstantial will also be important to the application of the NT, i.e., determining what in the NT applied to specific situations, and what had a more universal application. Relating the regulations of the NT to the specific situations of twentieth century life calls into question whether some of the biblical directives were for circumstances unique to the people to whom the NT was addressed.[32] While determining which of the NT letters were circumstantial and which were general will not resolve these problems, that determination may contribute to the solution.

*Opening and closing formulas*

The general organizational pattern of ancient letters fell into three parts: the author began with an attempt to secure the good will of the readers; he ended with the hope that the good relationship that had been established would continue; and in the body of the letter he expanded on the subject which he usually had introduced in the opening comments. Paul consistently followed this pattern and drew his epistolary prescripts and postscripts largely from the conventions of friendly and family letters, resulting in an unmistakably friendly tone of an equal writing to equals. As with ancient letters in general, the more Paul gave attention to opening and closing remarks the more he was placing special emphasis on friendship with his readers, hoping thereby to enhance that relationship.[33]

NT letters begin with the author's name, followed by epithets stating the author's position, e.g., apostle, servant, and in the letter to Philemon, prisoner. These epithets, which can be expanded into a whole paragraph as in the letter to the Romans, reflect the conventions of the official correspondence of Roman politicians, where titles established the authority of the author. The inclusion of epithets in letters that are characteristically friendly in tone exemplifies the borrowing from different letter forms that is typical of the eclecticism of NT letters. More importantly, epithets in a friendly letter reveal the author's relationship to his readers: Paul is mostly an equal writing on the basis of friendship, but with some appeal to his position of authority. Letters with more extensive epithets, as in Romans and Galatians, indicate that Paul is giving more emphasis to his authority.

After the author identifies himself in the opening formula, he states who the addressees are. Accompanying the designation of the addressees are usually words of commendation or affection, e.g., "saints who are faithful," words that are part of the author's attempt to secure the good will of his readers. The glaring exception to this practice in Paul's letters is Galatians, where he simply writes, "To the churches in Galatia."

In the next portion of the opening formula, the NT letters use a Christianized equivalent of the common word for greeting in Greco-Roman letters. With a simple play on words, the universal "greetings" (*chairein*) becomes "grace" to you (*charis*). And appended to "grace," is "and peace," certainly reflecting the Hebrew *shalom*.

Perhaps the most important part of the opening remarks, and almost always the longest, is the thanksgiving. Here Paul went to great lengths to praise his congregations, heaping compliments on them for their achievements. And like the common wish for good health in family letters, Paul prayed that the believers would continue to prosper in their Christian lives. The function of the rhetoric in these thanksgiving *topoi* in NT letters was threefold: it endeared the author to his readers, it put the readers in a position of obligation to the author,[34] and it functioned as encouragement for the readers to live up to what the author was already praising them for.[35]

Two of Paul's epistles are noteworthy in light of the function of the thanksgiving. Paul's generous words of praise to the Corinthians (1 Cor 1:4–9), which seem incredulous in view of his later accusations, take on new meaning in light of the rhetoric of the thanksgiving *topoi*, for Paul's words may have been prompted by their function more than by a sincere expression of his feelings about the Corinthians.[36] In contrast, Paul's letter to the Galatians replaces the thanksgiving with harsh words of blame and rebuke;[37] here Paul puts the minimum of customary material in the prescript. In the case of the Corinthians, Paul is friendly in his approach, hoping to have influence on them out of their respect for his friendship. But his letter to the Galatians lacks almost all of the typical signs of friendly correspondence. Apparently, friendship is an insufficient basis for Paul's attempt to correct the problems confronting the Galatians.[38]

The closing formulas in NT letters continue the author's appeal to friendship with his readers, adding to the obligation that the readers feel to comply with what the letter has requested. By naming specific individuals in the congregations and giving them his greetings, and by naming friends common to both Paul and his readers—when he sends greetings from his associates to the congregations—Paul underscores his close ties with the recipients of his letters. In the letter to the Romans, in particular, Paul goes to great lengths to list the names that will help establish his friendship with the believers there: he greets twenty-six people by name and refers to others associated with the ones he specifically names; in addition he sends greetings from seven of his fellow workers and commends to them Phoebe, who apparently was the courier of the letter.

Other elements of the closings of NT letters also function to endear Paul to his readers. He requests that they pray for him and that they greet each other with a holy kiss,[39] he expresses his intention to visit them, he sends a fellow worker to them, usually the courier, who will represent him, and he includes an autographed greeting. These latter three elements of the closing have a particularly important function. For by mentioning his travel plans, by sending an envoy, and by greeting them in his own hand,[40] Paul creates a special closeness between himself and his readers and brings to climax a letter's primary role, that of making the author seem present to the reader.

A function common to both the opening and closing formulas is the intended use of letters in early Christian worship. NT authors wrote their letters to be read aloud before the congregations that they addressed,[41] and they naturally included liturgical forms that would be appropriate in a worship setting. The presence, therefore, of prayers, thanksgivings, confessions, hymns, doxologies, and benedictions—especially in the opening and closing portions of NT letters—attest to the role of letters in early Christian liturgies.

## Paul's relationship with his readers

The cordial tone that Paul establishes in the opening and closing elements of a letter tends to permeate the entire communication. In support of his commendatory prescripts and the close ties highlighted in his postscripts, Paul commonly refers throughout the letters to his longing to be present with his readers and to his being "present in spirit though absent in body."[42] The use of these phrases from typical friendly correspondence enhances the intimacy of Paul's relationship with his hearers. Paul also borrows from the conventions of friendly letters by using the terminology of family relationships to refer to his congregations. These conventions are most commonly seen in letters in the papyri, where it is impossible in many cases to distinguish between friends and family members, for friends will call each other "brothers," an older man will call a younger man "son," a husband will call his wife "sister," etc.[43] The NT letters continue this practice with the very common "brothers," as well as "sister" and "children," to refer to fellow believers, thereby promoting the close ties of friendship among believers.

The letters of the NT are shaped, therefore, by the social ethic of friendship, a traditional value rooted in Greco-Roman-Jewish society. If two people were bonded together in a close relationship, they were to give up their individualism and exist for each other. Paul's appeals to Christians to continue in the process of conversion from paganism to Christianity are rooted, therefore, in his friendship with his hearers, a friendship that carried an obligation of reciprocity. The accountability needed to insure the progress of the believers in the gospel was uniquely provided by the bond of friendship between Paul and his congregations.

Another dimension to Paul's relationship with his readers is the terminology of familial bonding. Paul looked at the converts from all his journeys as united together in one large family unit. Given the size of ancient households, encompassing a patriarch's entire family—married sons with their wives and children—along with slaves, the family metaphor seemed especially appropriate. More importantly, the family was a cohesive unit in which individuals functioned for the benefit of the whole. Even as the family was a microcosm of the larger Roman society with its combination of vertical and horizontal relationships, so in the NT the family unit represented the sum of converts to Christianity.[44]

Paul's philosophy of the early church is evident then from the contents and form of his letters: the church is a society of friends, existing for the mutual benefit of the members, and it is a household, where the individual finds his place in the context of the community. Paul writes his letters to build up communities of believers who will mutually build each other up.

## CONCLUSIONS

Correct interpretations of the letters of the NT depend on understanding them in their cultural setting, and it is the form and function of each element of a letter that determines the meaning of the letter. For circumstantial letters in particular, a reconstruction of the historical settings that occasioned the letters is essential. Using internal clues alone to make the reconstruction catches exegetes in circular reasoning. Only when interpreters understand how the different types of letters functioned and what the conventions they followed meant can they gain control over the circular reasoning of interpretations based on internal data alone.

The following recapitulation of the most important conclusions from this study will sum up the research on the letters of the NT:

(1) NT letters were substitutes for the personal presence of the author. The author made himself present to his readers by writing a letter and by using conventions in the letter that heightened the sense of his presence.

(2) NT letters were written to increase the bond of friendship between the author and reader as well as to communicate the concerns of the author to the reader.

(3) NT letters addressed issues and expressed Christian truths in the context of friendship. It was not out of a position of authority that converts were urged to follow the Christian lifestyle, but rather out of the obligation of friendship.

(4) Each element of NT letters had a significant role in enhancing the quality of the relationship between author and reader.

(5) Some NT letters were written in response to specific circumstances. These situations need to be ascertained as precisely as possible in order to determine how the letters should be interpreted and applied.

(6) NT authors used widely accepted rhetorical techniques to communicate the urging of their hearts. Correct interpretations of what NT authors meant by what they said must carefully take into account the rhetorical conventions of the first century.

(7) The NT authors' theology of the church is underscored by their choice of letter forms and conventions. To them the church was a community of believers joined together in a mutual process of encouragement and growth.

This brief survey of the forms and functions of NT letters has introduced the basic concepts of ancient letter writing, though only a few of the insights from those concepts on the letters in the NT have been explored. That is partially due to limitations of length in this study, but more importantly it indicates the amount of work yet to be done on understanding NT letters in their cultural setting.

# NOTES

[1]Various collections of letters by single authors underscore the value and enduring significance of good letters. See, e.g., the letters of Elizabeth Barrett Browning, Benjamin Franklin, Emily Dickinson, Robert Frost, E. B. White, Ernest Hemingway, John Donne, Edith Wharton, and C. S. Lewis.

[2]A sociology of letter writing, using modern social scientific analysis, has apparently not been written. For a popular treatment, see Alexandra Stoddard, *Gift of a Letter* (New York: Doubleday, 1990).

[3]Acts 15:23–29, from the believers at Jerusalem to those at Antioch; and 23:25–30, from Claudius Lysias, the Roman commander in Jerusalem, to Felix, the Roman governor of Judea.

[4]Stanley K. Stowers, *Letter Writing in Greco-Roman Antiquity*, Library of Early Christianity, ed. W. A. Meeks (Philadelphia: Westminster, 1986) 15; Stowers includes more than 70 examples of ancient letters. Another collection of ancient letters, complete with helpful indices and appendices, is John L. White, *Light from Ancient Letters* (Philadelphia: Westminster, 1986). In addition to these recent and important studies of ancient letters from the perspective of NT studies, see the two chapters on letters in David E. Aune, *The New Testament in Its Literary Environment*, Library of Early Christianity, ed. W. A. Meeks (Philadelphia: Westminster, 1987); also John L. White, "Ancient Greek Letters," *Greco-Roman Literature and the New Testament*, ed. D. E. Aune, SBL Sources for Biblical Study 21 (Atlanta: Scholars Press, 1988); and the older but still useful William G. Doty, *Letters in Primitive Christianity*, Guides to Biblical Scholarship (Philadelphia: Fortress, 1973).

[5]On hermeneutics, see E. D. Hirsch, Jr., *Validity in Interpretation* (New Haven: Yale University Press, 1967); idem, *The Aims of Interpretation* (Chicago: University of Chicago Press, 1976); and Jerome H. Neyrey, *Paul in Other Words: A Cultural Reading of His Letters* (Louisville: Westminster/John Knox, 1990).

[6]Artemon, editor of Aristotle's letters, characterized a letter as "one side of a literary dialogue" (Demetrius, *On Style*, 223). Cicero conceived of his letters (*Letters to Atticus* 9.10.1) as talking in written form. Someone who tries to understand the correspondence between two people is a "third party" or outsider to the letter event; John H. Hayes and Carl R. Holiday, *Biblical Exegesis: A Beginner's Handbook* (Atlanta: John Knox, 1987) 8–9.

[7]E.g., the letters of Isocrates, Demosthenes, Epicurus, Cicero, Horace, Pliny, Fronto, Seneca, Jerome, John Chrysostom, Augustine, Gregory, and Basil. See Klaus Thraede, *Grundzüge griechisch-römischer Brieftopik*, Monographien zur klassischen Altertumswissenschaft 48 (Munich: Beck, 1970); Robert G. Ussher, "Letter Writing," in *Civilization of the Ancient Mediterranean: Greece and Rome*, 3 vols., ed. Michael Grant and Rachel Kitzinger (New York: Charles Scribners, 1988) III, 1573–1582; and Aune, *The New Testament in Its Literary Environment*, 170–72.

[8]For selections and analysis of letters preserved in papyri, see: Adolf Deissmann, *Bible Studies*, trans. A. Grieve (Edinburgh: T. & T. Clark, 1901); idem, *Light from the Ancient East*, trans. L. R. M. Strachan (London: Hodder & Stoughton, 1927); A. S. Hunt and C. C. Edgar, trans., *Select Papyri*, 2 vols., Loeb Classical Library (Cambridge: Harvard University Press, 1932); and Heiki Koskenniemi, *Studien zur Idee*

*und Phraseologie des griechischen Briefes bis 400 n. Chr.*, Annales Academiae scientiarum fennicae, series B, vol. 102.2 (Helsinki: Suomalainen Tiedeakatemian, 1956). See also above n. 4. Students practicing writing letters according to different letter types is attested in the papyri: *P. Bon.* 5; *UPZ* I 110, 111, 144, 145. For these and other references to papyri, see John F. Oates, Roger S. Bagnall, William H. Willis, and K. A. Worp, *Checklist of Greek Papyri and Ostraca*, 3rd ed., *BASP* Supplements 4 (Atlanta: Scholars Press, 1985).

[9]*Forms of the Letter (Typoi Epistolikoi)*, attributed to Demetrius of Phalerum, classifies twenty-one types of letters; *Styles for Letters (Epistolimaioi Charakteres)*, transmitted under the name of Libanius or Proclus, classifies forty-one types of letters; see also *On Style (De Elocutione)*, also attributed to Demetrius. For translation and introduction of these handbooks—among other primary sources on ancient letters—see Abraham Malherbe, *Ancient Epistolary Theorists*, SBL Sources for Biblical Studies 19 (Atlanta: Scholars Press, 1988) [originally published in *Ohio Journal of Religious Studies* 5 (1977) 3–77].

[10]See, e.g., John L. White, "A Note on Zenon's Letter-Filing," *BASP* 13 (1976) 129–31.

[11]W. L. Westermann, "On Inland Transportation and Communication," *Political Science Quarterly* 43 (1928) 364–87; and John L. White, "New Testament Epistolary Literature in the Framework of Ancient Epistolography," *Aufstieg und Niedergang der römische Welt*, ed. Wolfgang Haase and Hildegard Temporini (Berlin: De Gruyter, 1984) II.25.2, 1732.

[12]This commonplace in the papyri can be illustrated by *BGU* I 37, 287; *P.Cair.Zen.* II 59154; *P.Eleph.* 13; *P.Flor.* II 127, 142; *P.Giss.Univ.* III 20, 21; *P.Oxy.* II 275; XIV 1664, 1676; *P.Ryl.* II 183, 238, 262. For this practice in literary letters, see Cicero, *Letters to Atticus* 12.32; 13.28; 14.21. See also below, n. 40.

[13]The best discussion of these values in relation to letter writing is in Stowers, *Letter Writing*, 27–60.

[14]Horst Hutter, *Politics as Friendship* (Waterloo, Ontario: Wilfrid Laurier University Press, 1978; and Erich Gruen, *The Hellenistic World and Coming of Rome* (Berkeley: University of California Press, 1984) 54–95.

[15]Demetrius, *On Style* 229 (cf. 225, 231–32); Demetrius, *Forms of Letters* [1]; Seneca, *Moral Epistles* 40.1. Cicero's admissions in his letters that he wrote even though he had nothing to write about suggests that the function of the letters was simply to maintain and enhance the friendship; Cicero, *Letters to Atticus* 8.14.1; 9.4.1; 9.10.1; 12.53.

[16]On patronage in ancient Rome, see: Richard P. Saller, "Roman Class Structures and Relations," *Civilization of the Ancient Mediterranean: Greece and Rome*, in 3 vols., ed. Michael Grant and Rachel Kitzinger (New York: Charles Scribners, 1988); *idem, Personal Patronage under the Early Empire* (Cambridge: Cambridge University Press, 1982); in relation to the NT, see John E. Stambaugh and David L. Balch, *The New Testament in Its Social Environment*, Library of Early Christianity, ed. W. A. Meeks (Philadelphia: Westminster, 1986) 63–64; on the relation of social status to letter writing, see Stanley K. Stowers, "Social Typification and the Classification of Ancient Letters," *The Social World of Formative Christianity and Judaism: Essays in Tribute to Howard Clark Kee*, ed. Jacob Neusner et al. (Philadelphia: Fortress, 1988) 78–90.

[17]Demetrius, *Forms of Letters* [3], [10]; Libanius/Proclus, *Styles for Letters* [30], [53], [77]; Stowers, *Letter Writing* 77–90.

[18]Walter Ong, *Orality and Literacy: Technologizing of the Word* (New York: Methuen, 1982); and Paul J. Achtemeier, "Omne *verbum sonat*: The New Testament and the Oral Environment of Late Western Antiquity," *JBL* 109.1 (Spring 1990) 3–27. The best studies of ancient rhetoric are by George A. Kennedy: see especially *New Testament Interpretation through Rhetorical Criticism* (Chapel Hill: University of North Carolina Press, 1984); but also: *The Art of Persuasion in Greece* (Princeton: Princeton University Press, 1963); *The Art of Rhetoric in the Roman World: 300 B.C. to A.D. 300* (Princeton University Press, 1972); *Classical Rhetoric and Its Christian and Secular Tradition from Ancient to Modern Times* (Chapel Hill: University of North Carolina Press, 1980); and *Greek Rhetoric under Christian Emperors* (Princeton: Princeton University Press, 1983).

[19]Demetrius describes twenty-one types; Libanius/Proclus forty-one types. See above, n. 9. Julius Victor emphasized the similarity of oral discourse and letter writing; *The Art of Rhetoric* 27.

[20]The best study of Greek philosophy is William K. C. Guthrie, *A History of Greek Philosophy* in 6 vols. (Cambridge: Cambridge University Press, 1962–1981). Also see A. A. Long, *Hellenistic Philosophy: Stoics, Epicureans, Sceptics*, 2nd ed. (Berkeley: University of California Press, 1986); and M. L. Clarke, *The Roman Mind: Studies in the History of Thought from Cicero to Marcus Aurelius* (Cambridge: Harvard University Press, 1956). On philosophical letters, see Stowers, *Letter Writing*, 36–40.

[21]Abraham J. Malherbe, "Hellenistic Moralists and the New Testament," *Aufstieg und Niedergang der römischen Welt*, ed. Wolfgang Haase and Hildegard Temporini (Berlin: De Gruyter, forthcoming in II.27); Stanley K. Stowers, "The Diatribe," *Greco-Roman Literature and the New Testament: Selected Forms and Genres*, ed. David E. Aune, SBL Sources for Biblical Study 21 (Atlanta: Scholars Press, 1988) 71–83; and *idem*, *The Diatribe and Paul's Letter to the Romans*, SBL Dissertation Series 57 (Chico: Scholars Press, 1981).

[22]For letters by Hellenistic Jews, see the numerous embedded letters in Josephus, twelve in 1 Maccabees, seven in 2 Maccabees, four in 1 Esdras, two in the Additions to Esther, and one in *Paraleipomena Jeremiou*. The Letter of Jeremiah and the *Letter of Aristeas* have some letter features. For documentary Jewish letters, see Victor A. Tcherikover, A. Fuks, and M. Stern, *Corpus Papyrorum Judaicarum* in 3 vols. (Cambridge: Harvard University Press, 1957–64).

[23]See C. Bradford Welles, *Royal Correspondence in the Hellenistic World* (New Haven: Yale University Press, 1934); and Robert K. Sherk, *Roman Documents from the Greek East: Senatus Consulta and Epistulae to the Age of Augustus* (Baltimore: Johns Hopkins, 1969).

[24]These documentary letters are an especially valuable resource on the forms and functions of private letter writing, an endeavor that shows little change from the third century B.C. to the third century A.D. See above n. 8 for collections of these letters.

[25]Here can be included treatises written in epistolary form, fictional letters written to pass on anecdotes, as well as personal letters written without realizing that they would be preserved for their literary value. Epistolary forms, especially opening and closing conventions, could be used to frame almost any composition. This tendency underscores the dominant and widely accepted role of letters in antiquity.

[26]On the forms of rhetoric, see Carolyn DeWald, "Greek Education and Rhetoric," *Civilization of the Ancient Mediterranean: Greece and Rome*, in 3 vols., ed. Michael Grant and Rachel Kitzinger (New York: Charles Scribners, 1988) II, 1093–95.

[27]Aune, *The NT in Its Literary Environment*, 172–73.

[28]This functional typology of letters is based in the main on Stowers's simplification of Demetrius's and Libanius/Proclus's numerous letter types; *Letter Writing*, 51–173.

[29]Martin Luther Stirewalt, Jr., "The Form and Function of the Greek Letter-Essay," *The Romans Debate*, ed. K. P. Donfried (Minneapolis: Augsburg, 1977) 175–206.

[30]Karl P. Donfried, "A Short Note on Romans 16," *The Romans Debate*, ed. K. P. Donfried (Minneapolis: Augsburg, 1977) 50–60; and Harry Gamble, Jr., *The Textual History of the Letter to the Romans*, Studies and Documents 42, ed. I. A. Sparks (Grand Rapids: Eerdmans, 1977).

[31]On rhetoric in Romans and the occasion of the letter see: Willhelm Wuellner, "Paul's Rhetoric of Argumentation in Romans: An Alternative to the Donfried—Karris Debate over Romans," *The Romans Debate*, ed. K. P. Donfried (Minneapolis: Augsburg, 1977) 152–74; John W. Drane, "Why Did Paul Write Romans?" *Pauline Studies: Essays Presented to Professor F. F. Bruce on His 70th Birthday*, ed. D. A. Hagner and M. J. Harris (Grand Rapids: Eerdmans, 1980) 208–27; J. N. Aletti, "Incoherence ou coherence de l'argumentation paulinienne?" *Bib* 69.1 (1988) 47–62. For the most important recent bibliography on Paul, see Hans Dieter Betz *et al.*, "The Editor's Bookshelf: New Literature on the Authentic Letters of the Apostle Paul," *JR* 68.1 (January 1988) 186–203. For comparative analysis of Paul's letters, see Fred O. Francis and J. Paul Sampley, *Pauline Parallels*, SBL Sources for Biblical Study 9 (Philadelphia: Fortress, 1975).

[32]Cf. D. A. Carson, *Biblical Interpretation and the Church: The Problem of Contextualization* (Nashville: Thomas Nelson, 1985).

[33]For general information on the formulas in NT letters see Franz Schnider and Werner Stenger, *Studien zum Neutestamentlichen Briefformular*, NTTS 11 (Leiden: Brill, 1987). On thanksgiving formulas, see Paul Schubert, *The Form and Function of the Pauline Thanksgiving* (Berlin: Topelmann, 1939); and P. T. O'Brien, *Introductory Thanksgiving in the Letters of Paul*, NovTSup 49 (Leiden: Brill, 1977).

[34]On the obligation of reciprocity, see Stowers, *Letter Writing*, 59.

[35]Demetrius, *Epistolary Types* [10], says that the function of praise was encouragement/exhortation.

[36]Benjamin Fiore, "'Covert Allusion' in 1 Corinthians 1–4," *CBQ* 47 (1985) 85–102; Hans Dieter Betz, "The Problem of Rhetoric and Theology according to the Apostle Paul," *L'apotre Paul: Personnalité, style et conception du ministère*, Bibliotheca Ephemeridum Theologicarum Louvaniensium, vol. 73, ed. A. Vanhoye (Leuven: University Press; Peeters, 1986) 16–48; L. L. Welborn, "On the Discord in Corinth: 1 Corinthians 1–4 and Ancient Politics," *JBL* 106.1 (1987) 85–111; and Linda L. Belleville, "Continuity and Discontinuity: A Fresh Look at 1 Corinthians in the Light of First Century Epistolary Forms and Conventions," *EvQ* 59.1 (January 1987) 15–37

[37]Paul says that he is "astonished" that they have "deserted" and turned to a gospel that is "no gospel at all" and have been thrown into "confusion" by those who are "perverting" the gospel and who deserve "eternal condemnation." These are severe words for Paul, especially in the part of the letter where thanksgiving is expected.

[38]See Hans Dieter Betz, "The Literary Composition and Function of Paul's Letter

to the Galatians," NTS 21 (1975) 353–79; *idem*, *A Commentary on Paul's Letter to the Churches in Galatia*, Hermeneia: A Critical and Historical Commentary on the Bible (Philadelphia: Fortress, 1979); and G. Walter Hansen, *Abraham in Galatians: Epistolary and Rhetorical Contexts*, JSNTSup 29 (Sheffield, 1990).

[39]Aune suggests that the kiss greeting is possibly an enactment of Paul's greetings; *The New Testament in Its Literary Environment*, 187.

[40]See above n. 12 for examples of this practice. In 2 Thess 3:17, Paul notes that he closes all of his letters in his own hand. The common practice of the author signing off, even though he does not necessarily state that he is doing so, is confirmed in the papyri; Deissmann, *Light from the Ancient East*, 172.

[41]Col 4:16; 1 Thess 5:27; cf. Rev 1:3; 22:18. On liturgical forms, see Aune, *The New Testament in Its Literary Environment*, 192–94.

[42]1 Cor 5:3; 2 Cor 10:1–2; Phil 1:7–8; Col 2:5; 1 Thess 2:17; 3:6; Phlm 22; cf. 2 John 12; 3 John 14.

[43]Deissmann, *Light from the Ancient East*, 168; and W. Hersey Davis, *Greek Papyri of the First Century* (New York: Harper, 1933; reprinted Chicago: Ares, 1980) 2.

[44]On the relationship of the literary genre of household codes to the NT, see David L. Balch, "Household Codes," *Greco-Roman Literature and the New Testament*, ed. D. E. Aune, SBL Sources for Biblical Study 21 (Atlanta: Scholars Press, 1988) 25–50.

# Inspiration, Preservation, and New Testament Textual Criticism

## Daniel B. Wallace

### INTRODUCTION

The Bible has always been of central importance to evangelicals. It not only defines what we are to believe; it also tells us how we are to behave. A clear and faithful exposition of the scriptures has, historically, been at the heart of any relevant pastoral ministry. Now in order for a particular passage to be applied legitimately, it must first be understood accurately. Before we ask "How does this text apply to me?" we must ask "What does this text mean?" And even before we ask "What does this text mean?" we must first ask, "What does this text say?" Determining what a text says is what textual criticism is all about. In other words, textual criticism, as its prime objective, seeks to ascertain the very wording of the original. This is necessary to do with the books of the Bible—as with all literary documents of the ancient world—because the originals are no longer extant. Not only this, but of the more than five thousand manuscript copies of the Greek New Testament no two of them agree completely. It is essential, therefore, that anyone who expounds the Word of God be acquainted to some degree with the science of textual criticism, if he or she is to expound that Word faithfully.

The relevance of textual criticism, however, is not shut up only to those who have acquaintance with Greek, nor only to those in explicitly expository ministries. Textual criticism is relevant to every

Daniel B. Wallace (B.A., Biola University; Th.M., Th.D. candidate, Dallas Theological Seminary) is Assistant Professor of New Testament Studies at Dallas Theological Seminary, Dallas, Texas.

Christian, precisely because many of the textual differences in Greek can be translated into another language. Thus the differences between the New Testament of the King James Version, for example, and that of the New American Standard Version are not just differences in the English; there are also differences in the Greek text behind the English—in fact, over 5,000 differences! And with the publication of the New King James New Testament in 1979[1] (in which the KJV was rendered in modern English), the translational differences are diminished while the textual differences are heightened. The average modern American Christian who lacks the requisite educational background to read Elizabethan English now has no excuse for not reading the (new) King James Version. In light of the heavy promotion by Thomas Nelson Publishers,[2] that oft-asked question, "What is the most accurate New Testament?," is increasingly a question about a version's textual basis as much as it is of the translational philosophy behind it.

What is the textual difference, then, between the (new) KJV NT and other modern translations? In a nutshell, most modern translations are based on a few ancient manuscripts, while the (new) KJV NT is based on a printed edition of the Greek New Testament (called the Textus Receptus or TR) which, in turn, was derived from the majority of medieval manuscripts (known collectively as the majority text [MT] or Byzantine text). In one respect, then, the answer to the question "What is the most accurate New Testament?" turns on the question, "Which manuscripts are closest to the original—the few early ones or the many late ones?"

In this paper it is not my objective to answer that question.[3] Rather, I wish to address an argument that has been used by TR/MT advocates—an argument which is especially persuasive among laymen. The argument is unashamedly theological in nature: inspiration and preservation are intrinsically linked to one another and both are intrinsically linked to the TR/MT. That is to say, the doctrine of verbal-plenary inspiration necessitates the doctrine of providential preservation of the text, and the doctrine of providential preservation necessarily implies that the majority text (or the TR)[4] is *the* faithful replica of the autographs. Inspiration (and inerrancy) is also used for the Byzantine text's correctness in two other ways: (1) only in the Byzantine text do we have an inerrant New Testament; (2) if any portion of the New Testament is lost (no matter how small, even if only one word), then verbal-plenary inspiration is thereby falsified.

If inspiration and preservation can legitimately be linked to the text of the New Testament in this way, then the (new) KJV NT is the most accurate translation and those who engage in an expository ministry should use this text alone and encourage their audiences to do the same. But if this theological argument is not legitimate, then New Testament textual criticism needs to be approached on other than a theological *a priori* basis. And if so, then perhaps most modern translations do indeed have a more accurate textual basis after all.

Our approach will be to deal first with the arguments from preservation, then to deal with the arguments related more directly to inspiration and inerrancy.[5]

## I. PRESERVATION

### A. *The Statement*

On a popular level, the TR-advocating and "King James only" fundamentalist pamphleteers have waged a holy war on all who would use any modern version of the New Testament, or any Greek text based on the few ancient manuscripts rather than on the many late ones.[6] Jasper James Ray is a highly influential representative of this approach.[7] In his book, *God Wrote Only One Bible*,[8] Ray says that no modern version may properly be called the Bible,[9] that salvation and spiritual growth can only come through versions based on the TR,[10] and that Satan is the prime mover behind all versions based on the more ancient manuscripts.[11] If Ray's view is correct, then those who use modern translations or a Greek New Testament based on the few ancient manuscripts are, at best, dupes of the devil and, at worst, in danger of forfeiting their immortal souls.

Ray's chief argument on behalf of the TR is based on preservation. In the following statements, notice how closely inspiration and preservation are linked—and how both are linked to the Textus Receptus. Ray says, for example, that "the Textus Receptus . . . was given by the inspiration of God, and has been providentially preserved for us today."[12] He further adds that "the writing of the Word of God by inspiration is no greater miracle than the miracle of its preservation in the Textus Receptus."[13] Preservation, then, for

Jasper James Ray, takes place on the same level as inspiration—i.e., extending to the very words.[14]

Even in works which are dressed in more scholarly garb, this theological presupposition (along with the witch-hunting invectives[15]) is still present. David Otis Fuller, for example, has edited several volumes in which professors and Bible scholars have contributed—all for the purpose of proving that the TR or MT is the best Greek New Testament. In *Which Bible?* he declares:

> Naturalistic New Testament critics seem at last to have reached the end of the trail. Westcott and Hort's broad highway, which appeared to lead so quickly and smoothly to the original New Testament text, has dwindled down to a narrow foot path and terminated finally in a thicket of trees. For those who have followed it, there is only one thing to do, and that is to go back and begin the journey all over again from the consistently Christian starting point; namely, the divine inspiration and providential preservation of Scripture.[16]

The sequel to *Which Bible?*, entitled *True or False?*, is "DEDICATED TO All lovers of the Book; who believe in the Verbal, Plenary Inspiration of the Scriptures; and who, of necessity [,] *must believe* in the Providential Preservation of the Scriptures through the centuries; and who hold that the Textus Receptus (Traditional Text) is nearest to the Original Manuscripts."[17]

This theological refrain—the linking of inspiration to preservation, and both to the majority text—got its major impetus from John William Burgon. Burgon, a high Church Anglican, Dean of Chichester, toward the end of the nineteenth century was both prolific and vituperative in his attacks against Westcott and Hort (the Cambridge scholars who produced the Greek text which stands, more or less, behind all modern translations). There is no question that Burgon is the most influential writer on behalf of the TR—indeed, that he is the father of the majority text movement—for he is quoted with extreme approbation by virtually every TR/MT advocate.[18] He argued that "there exists no reason for supposing that the Divine Agent, who in the first instance thus gave to mankind the Scriptures of Truth, straightway abdicated His office; took no further care of His work; abandoned those precious writings to their fate."[19]

Wilbur Pickering, president of the Majority Text Society, has continued this type of argument into the present debate. In his 1968 master's thesis done at Dallas Seminary ("An Evaluation of the Contribution of John William Burgon to New Testament Textual Criticism") he argued that this doctrine is "most important" and "what one believes does make a difference."[20] Further, he linked the two together in such a way that a denial of one necessarily entails a denial of the other: "the doctrine of Divine Preservation of the New Testament Text depends upon the interpretation of the evidence which recognizes the Traditional Text to be the continuation of the autographa."[21] In other words, Pickering seems to be saying: "if we reject the majority text view, we reject the doctrine of preservation."[22]

E. F. Hills, who wrote his doctoral dissertation on NT textual criticism at Harvard Divinity School, argued:

> If the doctrine of the Divine inspiration of the Old and New Testament scriptures is a true doctrine, the doctrine of providential preservation of the scriptures must also be a true doctrine. It must be that down through the centuries God has exercised a special providential control over the copying of the scriptures and the preservation and use of the copies, so that trustworthy representatives of the original text have been available to God's people in every age.[23]

Hills adds that "all orthodox Christians, all Christians who show due regard for the Divine inspiration and providential preservation of Scripture, must agree with Burgon on this matter."[24]

These writers are just the tip of the iceberg. Indeed, so universal is the doctrinal underpinning of preservation found among MT/TR advocates that Bart Ehrman could say:

> One cannot read the literature produced by the various advocates of the Majority text without being impressed by a remarkable theological concurrence. To one degree or another, they all (to my knowledge, without exception) affirm that God's inspiration of an inerrant Bible required His preservation of its text.[25]

And even Theo Letis, a TR advocate himself, flatly states, "The only reason that the Majority Text proponents even argue for the Byzantine text is because theologically they have both a verbal view of inspiration—and as a hidden agenda an unexpressed (at least as part of their present method) belief in providential preservation."[26]

To sum up: on a lay level, as well as on a pseudo-scholarly level, and even on a scholarly level, inspiration, preservation and the TR/MT are linked intrinsically. According to Byzantine text advocates, you cannot have one without the other.

## B. The Critique

There are a number of serious problems with the theological premise of Byzantine text advocates. Generally speaking, however, they all fall into one of three groups: (1) a question-begging approach, (2) faulty assumptions, and (3) a non-biblical doctrinal basis. As will be readily seen, there is a great deal of overlap between these three areas.

### 1. Question-Begging Approach

Majority text proponents beg the question for their view on at least three fronts.

*a. What do you count?* First, they only count Greek manuscripts. Yet, there are almost twice as many Latin NT manuscripts as there are Greek (over 10,000 to approximately 5,500). If the Latin manuscripts were to be counted, then modern translations would be vindicated rather than the King James, because the early Greek manuscripts which stand behind the vast bulk of Latin manuscripts and behind modern translations are quite similar.[27] At one point, E. F. Hills argued that "God must preserve this text, not secretly, not hidden away in a box for hundreds of years or mouldering unnoticed on some library shelf, but openly before the eyes of all men through the continuous usage of His Church."[28] Preservation is therefore linked to public accessibility. It is precisely at this point that the argument for counting only Greek manuscripts begs the question. As Ehrman points out:

> [According to Hills,] the subsequent preservation of the New Testament text did not extend to guaranteeing the accuracy of its translation into other languages, but only to protecting the relative purity of the Greek text itself. Here, of course, his prior argument that God preserved the text for the sake of His church becomes irrelevant—since only a select minority in the church has ever known Greek.[29]

*b. When do you count?* Majority text advocates tacitly assume that since most Greek manuscripts extant today belong to the Byzantine text, most Greek manuscripts throughout church history have belonged to the Byzantine text. But this assumption begs the question in the extreme, since there is not one solid shred of evidence that the Byzantine text even existed in the first three centuries of the Christian era.[30] Not only this, but as far as our extant witnesses reveal, the Byzantine text did not become the majority text until the ninth century. Furthermore, for the letters of Paul, there is no majority text manuscript before the ninth century. To embrace the MT/TR text for the *corpus Paulinum*, then, requires an 800-year leap of faith. Not only is this a severe instance of *petitio principii*, but it also is a cavalier treatment of historical evidence unbecoming of those who boast a faith which cannot be divorced from history. No majority text advocate would tolerate such a fideistic leap regarding the person and work of Christ;[31] how then can they employ it when it comes to the text?

c. *Where do you count?* Suppose we were to assume that only Greek manuscripts should be counted. And suppose further that public accessibility is a legitimate divine motive for preservation. Given these two assumptions, one would expect the Byzantine text-type to be readily accessible in all pockets of the ancient Greek-speaking world. But that is demonstrably not true. For example, it was not readily available to Christians in Egypt in the first four centuries. After carefully investigating the Gospel quotations of Didymus, a fourth-century Egyptian writer, Ehrman concludes, "These findings indicate that no 'proto-Byzantine' text existed in Alexandria in Didymus' day or, at least if it did, it made no impact on the *mainstream* of the textual tradition there."[32] What confirms this further is that in several places Origen, the great Christian textual scholar, speaks of textual variants that were in a majority of manuscripts in his day, yet today are in a minority, and vice versa.[33] Granting every gratuitous concession to majority text advocates, in the least this shows that no majority text was readily available to Christians in Egypt. And if that is the case, then how can they argue for a majority on the basis of public accessibility?

## 2. Faulty Assumptions

More serious than a question-begging approach are several decidedly faulty assumptions made by MT/TR advocates. These assumptions are shown to be faulty either by the force of logic or empirical evidence.

*a. Preservation is a necessary corollary of inspiration.*   E. F.
Hills argued:

> If the doctrine of the divine inspiration of the Old and New Testament
> Scriptures is a true doctrine the doctrine of the providential preserva-
> tion of these Scriptures must also be a true doctrine. It must be that
> down through the centuries God has exercised a special providential
> control. . . . God must have done this . . . [34]

In other words, preservation proceeds from and is a necessary conse-
quence of inspiration. Or, in the words of Jasper James Ray, "the
writing of the Word of God by inspiration is no greater miracle than
the miracle of its preservation . . . "[35] Ehrman has ably pointed out
the logical consequences of such linkage:

> Any claim that God preserved the New Testament text intact, giving
> His church actual, not theoretical, possession of it, must mean one of
> three things—either 1) God preserved it in all the extant manuscripts
> so that none of them contain any textual corruptions, or 2) He pre-
> served it in a group of manuscripts, none of which contain any cor-
> ruptions, or 3) He preserved it in a solitary manuscript which alone
> contains no corruptions.[36]

The problem with these first and second possibilities is that neither
one of them is true: no two NT manuscripts agree completely—in
fact, there are between six and ten variations per chapter for the
closest two manuscripts.

Is it possible that the NT text was preserved intact in a single manuscript? No one argues this particular point, because it is easily demonstrable that every manuscript has scribal errors in it. However, one
group does argue that a particular printed edition of the NT has been
providentially preserved. Proponents of the Textus Receptus (as opposed to those who argue for the majority text[37]) believe that the TR
satisfies this third requirement. There are numerous problems with
such a view,[38] but it should be noted that TR advocates are at least
consistent in putting preservation on the same level with inspiration.

Nevertheless, there seems to be one major flaw in their approach,
from a biblical standpoint: If the TR equals the original text, then the
editor must have been just as inspired as the original writers, for he
not only selected what readings were to go in this first published edition, but he also created some of the readings. To be specific, the
last leaf of Erasmus' copy of Revelation was missing, so he "back-

translated" from Latin into Greek and thereby created numerous readings which have never been found in any Greek manuscript. This should cause some pause to those conservative Protestants who hail Erasmus' text as identical with the original, for such a view implies that revelation continued into at least the sixteenth century. Not only this, but Erasmus was a Roman Catholic who battled papists and Protestants alike—the very man against whom Martin Luther wrote his famous *Bondage of the Will*. Are conservative Protestants willing to say that this man was just as inspired as the apostle Paul or John? What is especially ironic about this is that most TR advocates reject the text of Westcott and Hort because (in part), as high church Anglicans, they had Roman Catholic leanings![39]

*b. Preservation must be through "majority rule."* To be sure, most scholars who employ the doctrine of preservation as a text-critical argument do not embrace the TR as equal to the original text. In this, they are not as consistent about the corollary between inspiration and preservation, but they are certainly more rational in other ways. Nevertheless, there are four serious objections to the argument that preservation must be through "majority rule." First, no where does the Bible state how God would preserve the NT text. Thus their argument is based squarely on silence.

Second, as Sturz points out,

> . . . the Bible itself reveals that there have been occasions when there has been a famine or dearth of the Word of God. One thinks, for example, of the days of Josiah (II Kings 22:8ff.) when apparently the Scriptures were reduced to one copy. Nevertheless, it still could be said that God's Word was preserved.[40]

Third, in light of this biblical precedent of how God preserved a portion of the Old Testament, can we not see the hand of God guiding a man such as Constantin von Tischendorf to St. Catherine's monastery at the base of Mount Sinai, only to discover codex Sinaiticus—the oldest complete NT known to exist—shortly before it would have met an untimely demise as kindling for the furnace?[41] There are, in fact, countless stories of manuscript discoveries which seem to speak quite eloquently for God's providential preservation of the text.[42] A more biblically based view of God's providential ways would not argue that God's hand is only seen or always seen in "majority rule."

Fourth, theologically one may wish to argue against the majority: usually it is the remnant, not the majority, that is right. If the history of Christianity teaches us anything, it teaches us that the majority is rarely right. Taylor points out a particularly cogent analogy:

> ... Hills' understanding of God's providential dealings in history fails to account for greater problems than the comparatively minor differences between the Textus Receptus and its modern rival. For example, God in His providence allowed in the medieval ages the doctrine of justification by faith to be almost eclipsed from public understanding until the Reformation leaders again called attention to that doctrine. Would Hills have God concerned that an exact form of the New Testament text be available but unconcerned about serious and widespread soteriological misunderstandings?[43]

The weight of this argument is especially felt when one considers that the variations between the majority text and modern critical texts are qualitatively very minor; most would say that no doctrine is affected by such differences.[44] If God did not protect a major doctrine like justification, on what basis can we argue that he would protect one form of the text over another when no doctrinal issues are at stake?[45]

   c. *Public accessibility of a pure text is a theological necessity.* We have touched on this to some degree already—at least by way of analogy. But the argument is also contradicted by direct evidence. Pickering believes that "God *has* preserved the text of the New Testament in a very pure form and it has been readily available to His followers in every age throughout 1900 years."[46] There are two fundamental problems with this view.

   First, assuming that the majority text (as opposed to the TR) is the original, then this pure form of text has become available only since 1982.[47] The Textus Receptus differs from it in almost 2,000 places —and in fact has several readings which have "never been found in any known Greek manuscript," and scores, perhaps hundreds, of readings which depend on only a handful of very late manuscripts.[48] Many of these passages are theologically significant texts.[49] Yet virtually no one had access to any other text from 1516 to 1881, a period of over 350 years. In light of this, it is difficult to understand what Pickering means when he says that this pure text "has been readily available to [God's] followers in every age throughout 1900 years."[50] Purity, it seems, has to be a relative term—and, if so, it certainly cannot be marshaled as a theological argument.

Second, again, assuming that the majority text is the original, and that it has been readily available to Christians for 1900 years, then it must have been readily available to Christians in Egypt in the first four centuries. But this is demonstrably not true, as we have already shown.[51] Pickering speaks of our early Alexandrian witnesses as "polluted" and as coming from a "sewer pipe."[52] Now if these manuscripts are really that defective, and if this is all Egypt had in the first three or four centuries, then this peculiar doctrine of preservation is in serious jeopardy, for those ancient Egyptian Christians had no access to the pure stream of the majority text. Therefore, if one were to define preservation in terms of the majority text, he would end up with a view which speaks very poorly of God's sovereign care of the text in ancient Egypt.[53]

*d. Certainty is identical with truth.* It seems that the underlying motive behind MT/TR advocacy is the equation of certainty with truth. For TR advocates, certainty is to be found in a printed edition of the New Testament. Hills' despair of finding absolute textual certainty through the standard means of textual criticism ultimately led him to abandon textual criticism altogether and replace it with a settled text, the Textus Receptus. Theo Letis, the self-proclaimed heir of Hills' mantle, argues that "without a methodology that has for its agenda the determination of a continuous, obviously providentially preserved text . . . we are, in principle, left with maximum uncertainty, as Edward Hills characterizes it, versus the maximum certainty afforded by the methodology that seeks a providentially preserved text."[54]

For MT advocates, certainty is found in the majority of manuscripts. Pickering argues, for example, that "If the Scriptures have *not* been preserved then the doctrine of Inspiration is a purely academic matter with no relevance for us today. If we do not have the inspired Words or do not *know* precisely which they be, then the doctrine of Inspiration is inapplicable."[55] At one point Pickering even states that uncertainty over the text also makes inspiration untrue.[56]

In response, several things can be mentioned. First, it should be noted that in one respect TR advocates are much more consistent than MT advocates: not only do they put preservation on exactly the same level as inspiration, but they also can be more certain about the text, since they advocate a printed edition. But their argumentation is so palpably weak on other fronts that we will only make two

observations here: (a) since the TR itself went through several different editions by Erasmus and others, TR advocates need to clarify
which edition is the inspired one; (b) one simply cannot argue for
the theological necessity of public accessibility throughout church
history and for the TR in the same breath—for the TR did not exist
during the first 1500 years of the Christian era. (Rather inconsistent,
for example, is the logic of Theo Letis when he, on the one hand,
argues that God must have preserved the pure text in an open, public, and accessible manner for Christians in every generation[57] and,
on the other hand, he argues that "the Latin and non-majority readings [of the TR] were indeed restorations of ancient readings that fell
out of the medieval Greek tradition"![58])

Second, regarding MT proponents, several criticisms can be lev-
eled, two of which are as follows. (a) Pragmatically, there is in reality
less certainty in their approach than there is among reasoned eclec-
tics. In the Byzantine text, there are hundreds of splits where no
clear majority emerges. One scholar recently found 52 variants
within the majority text in the spaces of two verses.[59] In such places
how are majority text advocates to decide what is original? Since
their method is in essence purely external (i.e., counting manuscripts), in those places the majority text view has no solution, and
no certainty. At one point, Pickering recognized this lack of certainty: "Not only are we presently unable to specify the precise
wording of the original text, but it will require considerable time and
effort before we can be in a position to do so."[60] Ironically, therefore, according to Pickering's own theological construct, inspiration
for him must be neither relevant nor true. (b) Logically/theologically,
the equation of inspiration with man's recognition of what is inspired (in all its particulars) virtually puts God at the mercy of man
and requires omniscience of man. The burden is so great that a text
critical method of merely counting noses seems to be the only way
in which human beings can be "relatively omniscient." In what other
area of Christian teaching is man's recognition required for a doctrine to be true?

Finally, a general criticism against both the MT and TR positions:
the quest for certainty is not the same as a quest for truth. There is
a subtle but important distinction between the two. Truth is objective reality; certainty is the level of subjective apprehension of something perceived to be true. But in the recognition that truth is

objective reality, it is easy to confuse the fact of this reality with how one knows what it is. Frequently the most black-and-white, dogmatic method of arriving at truth is perceived to be truth itself. Indeed, people with deep religious convictions are very often quite certain about an untruth. For example, cultists often hold to their positions quite dogmatically and with a fideistic fervor that shames evangelicals; first-year Greek students want to speak of the aorist tense as meaning "once-and-for-all" action; and almost everyone wants simple answers to the complex questions of life. At bottom this quest for certainty, though often masquerading as a legitimate epistemological inquiry, is really a presuppositional stance, rooted in a psychological insecurity.[61]

To sum up so far: The TR/MT advocates get entangled in numerous question-begging approaches and faulty—even contradictory—assumptions in their arguments concerning the providential preservation of the text. That is not the worst of it, however. Their view also is non-biblical.

### 3. Non-Biblical Doctrinal Basis

We are often told that the consistently Christian view, or the only orthodox view of the text is one which embraces the Byzantine text-type, and that to embrace a different form of the text is to imbibe in heresy. Although this charge is vigorously denied by non-MT/TR evangelicals, the tables are rarely turned. It is our contention, however, that to use the doctrine of preservation in support of the MT/TR is to have a non-biblical view which cannot consistently be applied to both testaments. The majority text-preservation connection is biblically unfounded in four ways, two of which have already been touched on.

*a. Biblical silence.* As we have argued concerning the faulty assumption that preservation must be through "majority rule," the scriptures nowhere tell us how God would preserve the NT text. What is ironic is that as much ink as MT/TR advocates spill on pressing the point that theirs is the only biblical view, when it comes to the preserved text being found in the majority of witnesses, they never quote one verse. Although they accuse other textual critics of rationalism, their argument for preservation via the majority has only a rational basis, not a biblical one. "God must have done this"[62]—not because the Bible says so, but because logic dictates that this must be the case.

*b. Old Testament examples of preservation.* Again, as we have already pointed out, the few OT examples of preservation of scripture do not herald the majority, but only the mere existence of a written witness. This fact leads to our third point—that the argument from preservation actually involves bibliological contradictions.

*c. A Marcionite view of the text.* Marcion was a second century heretic whose literary remains are found only in essays written against him. Metzger points out that

> The main points of Marcion's teaching were the rejection of the Old Testament and a distinction between the Supreme God of goodness and an inferior God of justice, who was the Creator and the God of the Jews. He regarded Christ as the messenger of the Supreme God. The Old and New Testaments, Marcion argued, cannot be reconciled to each other.[63]

It is our contention that majority text advocates follow in Marcion's train when it comes to their doctrine of preservation because their theological argument does not work for the Old Testament. If our contention is true, then the dogmatic basis for the majority text is bibliologically schizophrenic. The evidence is of two kinds.

First, the argument that the divine motive for preservation is public availability—as poor an argument as it is for the Greek text—is even worse for the Hebrew. Not only is it alleged that "God must do more than merely preserve the inspired original New Testament text. He must preserve it in a public way . . . through the continuous usage of His Church,"[64] but that "down through the ages God's providential preservation of the New Testament has operated only through believers . . . "[65] But the Hebrew scriptures were neither preserved publicly—on display through the church as it were, nor only through Christians. In light of this, how can majority text advocates escape the charge of Marcionism? In what way can they argue that a bibliological doctrine is true for the NT but is not true for the OT?

Second, it is demonstrable that the OT text does not meet the criteria of preservation by majority rule. Although the Masoretic textual tradition (which represents almost the entirety of the extant Hebrew manuscripts) is highly regarded among most OT textual critics, none (to my knowledge) claim that it is errorless.[66] Most OT scholars today would agree with Klein that "Samuel MT is a poor text, marked by extensive haplography and corruption—only the MT of Hosea and

Ezekiel is in worse condition."[67] In fact, a number of readings which only occur in versions (i.e., not in the extant Hebrew manuscripts at all), or are found only in one or two early Qumran manuscripts, have indisputable claim to authenticity in the face of the errant majority.[68] Furthermore, in many places, all the extant Hebrew manuscripts (as well as versions) are so corrupt that scholars have been forced to emend the text on the basis of mere conjecture.[69] Significantly, many such conjectures (but not all) have been vindicated by the discovery of the Dead Sea scrolls.[70] Majority text advocates simply do not grapple with these OT textual phenomena. And if they were to do so and were even to prove many minority text readings or conjectures false, our point would still stand. Only if they could demonstrate that all minority text readings and all conjectures were inferior (or at least probably so), could their argument hold water. The indisputable fact is that OT textual criticism simply cannot be conducted on the basis of counting noses. Since this is the case, either majority text advocates must abandon their theological premise altogether, or else be subject to the charge of a bibliological double standard.

   *d. The biblical doctrine of preservation.*   In light of the occasional necessity of conjectural emendation for the OT text, it is our contention that not only is the majority text argument for preservation entirely wrong-headed, but so is any doctrine of preservation which requires that the exact wording of the text be preserved at all. In spite of the fact that even opponents of the MT/TR view embrace such a doctrine,[71] it simply does not square with the evidence. Only three brief points will be made here, in hopes of stimulating a dialogue on this issue.

   First, the doctrine of preservation was not a doctrine of the ancient church. In fact, it was not stated in any creed until the seventeenth century (in the Westminster Confession of 1646). The recent arrival of such a doctrine, of course, does not necessarily argue against it—but neither does its youthfulness argue for it. Perhaps what needs to be explored more fully is precisely what the framers of the Westminster Confession and the Helvetic Consensus Formula (in 1675) really meant by providential preservation.

   Second, the major scriptural texts alleged to support the doctrine of preservation need to be reexamined in a new light. I am aware of only one substantial articulation of the biblical basis for this doctrine by a majority text advocate. In Donald Brake's essay, "The

Preservation of the Scriptures," five major passages are adduced as proof that preservation refers to the written Word of God: Ps 119:89, Isa 40:8, Matt 5:17–18, John 10:35, and 1 Pet 1:23–25.[72] One of the fundamental problems with the use of these passages is that merely because "God's Word" is mentioned in them it is assumed that the written, canonical, revelation of God is meant.[73] But 1 Pet 1:23–25, for example, in quoting Isa 40:8, uses ῥῆμα (not λόγος)—a term which typically refers to the spoken word.[74] Brake's interpretation of Ps 119:89 ("For ever, O Lord, your word is settled in heaven") is, to put it mildly, improbable: "The Word which is settled in heaven was placed there by a deliberate and purposeful act of God Himself."[75] It seems that a better interpretation of all these texts is that they are statements concerning either divine ethical principles (i.e., moral laws which cannot be violated without some kind of consequences) or the promise of fulfilled prophecy.[76] The assumptions that most evangelicals make about the doctrine of preservation need to be scrutinized in light of this exegetical construct.

Third, if the doctrine of the preservation of scripture has neither ancient historical roots, nor any direct biblical basis, what can we legitimately say about the text of the New Testament? My own preference is to speak of God's providential care of the text as can be seen throughout church history, without elevating such to the level of doctrine. If this makes us theologically uncomfortable, it should at the same time make us at ease historically, for the NT is the most remarkably preserved text of the ancient world—both in terms of the quantity of manuscripts and in their temporal proximity to the originals. Not only this, but the fact that no major doctrine is affected by any viable textual variant surely speaks of God's providential care of the text. Just because there is no verse to prove this does not make it any less true.[77]

## C. Conclusion on the Arguments concerning Preservation

In conclusion, MT/TR advocates argue from a theological vantage point which begs the question historically and logically. More serious than *petitio principii*, they make several faulty assumptions which not only run aground on rational and empirical rocks, but ultimately backfire. The most telling assumption is that certainty equals truth. This is an evangelical disease: for most of us, at some point, the quest for certainty has replaced the quest for truth. But even for majority text advocates, this quest must, in the last analysis, remain unfulfilled. The worst feature of their agenda, however, is not the faulty assumptions. It is that their view of preservation not only is non-biblical, it is also bibliologically schizophrenic in that it cannot work for both testaments. And that, to a majority text or Textus Receptus advocate—as it would be to any conservative Christian—is the most damaging aspect of their theological agenda.

## II. INSPIRATION

Under the general topic of inspiration are two arguments: (1) if any portion of the NT is lost, then verbal-plenary inspiration is thereby falsified; and (2) only in the Byzantine text-type do we have an inerrant NT. This first argument is really the converse of the argument from preservation, while the second argument is a corollary of a corollary.

### A. Does Loss of Text Falsify Inspiration?

In his paper, "Mark 16:9–20 and the Doctrine of Inspiration,"[78] Wilbur Pickering argues that if any portion of the NT is lost, then inspiration is not only irrelevant—it also is not true:

> Among those who wish to believe or claim that Mark's Gospel was inspired by the Holy Spirit, that it is God's Word, I am not aware of any who are prepared to believe that it could have been God's intention to terminate the book with εφοβουντο γαρ.[79]
>
> Are we to say that God was unable to protect the text of Mark or that He just couldn't be bothered? I see no other alternative—either He didn't care or He was helpless. And either option is fatal to the claim that Mark's Gospel is "God-breathed."[80] . . . if God was powerless to protect His Word then He wouldn't really be God and it wouldn't make all that much difference what He said.[81] . . . If God permitted the original ending of Mark to be lost then in fact we do not have an inspired text.[82]
>
> Anyone who denies the authenticity of Mark 16:9–20 cannot consistently affirm the Divine Inspiration of Mark 1:1–16:8. I now submit the question to the reader: have I not demonstrated that to reject

Mark 16:9–20 is to relinquish the doctrine of Divine Inspiration—for Mark, certainly, but by extension for the rest of the Bible?[83]

Majority text advocates, as we have seen, argue that if there is uncertainty over the wording of the text, inspiration becomes irrelevant. Pickering's argument goes one step beyond: if part of the text is lost, then "we do not have an inspired text."

This argument seems flawed on five fronts. First, it is special pleading. One has to accept Pickering's (incomplete) syllogism for this to be true: if God was not able or did not care to protect the text, then inspiration is not true. Why is it not possible for the text to be originally inspired but now lost? Apparently, once again, inspiration necessitates preservation. Further, why is it necessary to impugn either God's power or his goodness if part of the NT is lost? Analogously, would anyone argue that if Christians—who are born of God—sin, then God is either powerless or not good enough to prevent them from sinning?

Second, as we have already mentioned in the first section of this paper, Pickering assumes that inspiration necessitates preservation. Yet, if our arguments against this supposition are correct, then this new argument (viz., lack of preservation implies non-inspiration) carries no weight.

Third, this approach is also Marcionite if there is ever a need for conjectural emendation for the Old Testament. Since that is the case, the loss of text (whether it be one word or a whole chapter) in principle cannot be used as a theological argument for a text critical viewpoint—otherwise proponents of such a view have to say that the OT is not inspired.

Fourth, there is a tacit assumption on the part of Pickering that everything a biblical author writes is inspired. But this is almost certainly not true, as can be seen by the lost epistles of Paul and the agrapha of Jesus. The argument is this: there seem to be a few, fairly well-attested (in patristic literature), authentic sayings of Jesus which are not found in the Gospels or the rest of the New Testament. Of course, evangelicals would claim that they are inerrant. But they would not be inspired because inspiration refers strictly to what is inscripturated within the canon. Further, Paul seems to have written three or four letters to the Corinthians, perhaps a now-lost letter to the Laodiceans,[84] and apparently more than a few letters before 2 Thessalonians.[85] If some NT epistles could be lost, and even some authentic sayings of Jesus could show up outside the NT, then either they were not inspired or else they were inspired but not preserved. Assuming the former to be true, then the question facing us in Mark's Gospel is whether an inspired writer can author non-inspired material within the same document—material which is now lost. Such a possibility admittedly opens up a Pandora's box for evangelicals, and certainly deserves critical thought and dialogue. Nevertheless, the analogies with the lost epistles of Paul and the authentic, non-canonical agrapha of Jesus seem to damage Pickering's contention that if the last portion of Mark's Gospel is lost, then inspiration is defeated.

Finally, although Pickering is unaware of any evangelical who thinks Mark ended his Gospel at verse 8, there does indeed seem to be an increasing number of scholars who believe this, evangelicals included among them.[86] Ernest Best states, for example, that "It is in keeping with other parts of his Gospel that Mark should not give an explicit account of a conclusion where this is already well known to his readers."[87] Further, he argues that "it is not a story which has been rounded off but an open story intended to draw us on further."[88] At one point he makes a rather intriguing suggestion:

> Finally it is from the point of view of drama that we can appreciate most easily the conclusion to the Gospel. By its very nature the conclusion forces us to think out for ourselves the Gospel's challenge. It would have been easy to finish with Jesus' victorious appearances to comfort the disciples: they all lived happily ever after. Instead the end is difficult . . . The readers or hearers of Mark know the disciples did see Jesus . . . Listen to the story as a believer and work it out for yourself. It is like one of Jesus' own parables: the hearer is forced to go on thinking.[89]

Although one would not say that Ernest Best is an arch-conservative, his overall interpretation of the reason for the shorter ending should cause no offense to evangelicals, as is evident by the fact that a number of evangelicals do believe that the Gospel was intended to end at verse 8.[90]

The argument that loss of text invalidates inspiration is, therefore, seen to be logically fallacious, bibliologically inconsistent, and irrelevant for those evangelicals who believe that Mark intended to end his Gospel at the eighth verse of chapter sixteen.

## B. Does the Byzantine Text-type Have Sole Claim to Inerrancy?

Occasionally, MT/TR advocates appeal to inerrancy in support of the Byzantine text-type's superiority. The argument is not new,[91] but it has received a clear articulation recently by James A. Borland. In his article, "Re-examining New Testament Textual-Critical Principles and Practices Used to Negate Inerrancy,"[92] Borland argues that the Alexandrian readings of Ἀσάφ in Matt 1:7, Ἀμῶς in 1:10, and τοῦ ἡλίου ἐκλιπόντος in Luke 23:45 are errors and must, for this reason, be rejected (for otherwise they impugn the character of the biblical authors and thereby falsify inerrancy). The reason such are errors, according to Borland, is that, with regard to the Matthean passage, Asaph and Amos were not kings (thus, spelling errors on the part of early Alexandrian scribes); and with regard to the Lukan passage, since "a solar eclipse is impossible astronomically during the full moon of the Passover when sun and moon are 180 degrees apart in relation to the earth"[93] and since the verb ἐκλείπω, when used with ἥλιος, normally indicated an eclipse,[94] Luke would err if he had written this. In both the Matthean texts and the Lukan passage, the Byzantine text-type has readings which do not involve such errors (respectively, Ἀσά, Ἀμών, καὶ ἐσκοτίσθη ὁ ἥλιος ["and the sun was darkened"]). Borland's conclusion is that (1) only in the Byzantine text-type do we have an inerrant Bible and (2) we must pour our text-critical methodology through the doctrinal grid of inerrancy.[95]

Our critique of Borland's linking of inerrancy to the Byzantine text-type is fourfold. First, his argument seems to question either the intelligence or the doctrinal conviction of virtually all members of the Evangelical Theological Society as well as any other non-MT/TR inerrantists—stretching from B. B. Warfield to D. A. Carson. Carson goes so far as to say: "I cannot think of a single great theological writer who has given his energies to defend a high view of Scripture and who has adopted the TR, since the discovery of the great uncials and, later, the papyri and other finds."[96]

Second, Borland's view suffers from historical myopia. That is to say, he is superimposing his modern-day, twentieth-century definition of inerrancy on the text. But should not our definition of inerrancy be shaped by both the biblical statements which imply this doctrine as well as the phenomena which indicate how the biblical authors understood it? One is reminded of a typical layman's understanding of inerrancy: the events of the Gospels must be in strict chronological sequence, the red letters in the Bible refer to the *ipsissima verba* (exact words) of Jesus, etc. Faced with the contrary evidence, would it be appropriate to change the text to suit one's doctrine? More analogous still is the Purist controversy in the seventh century.

> The beginning of the seventeenth century was marked by the rise of the Purist controversy. The Purists maintained that to deny that God gave the New Testament in anything but pure classical Greek was to imperil the doctrine of inspiration. The Wittemberg Faculty, in 1638, decreed that to speak of barbarisms or solecisms in the New Testament was blasphemy against the Holy Ghost. Hence, a correct conception of the peculiar idiom of the Apostles was impossible, and the estimate of different readings was seriously affected by this cause. Readings of existing editions were arbitrarily mingled, the manuscripts employed and the sources of variants adopted were not properly specified, and a full survey of the apparatus was impossible.[97]

In other words, in the seventeenth century many evangelicals argued that the Textus Receptus was not inspired and that many of its readings were even "blasphemy against the Holy Ghost." They too had a myopic view of inerrancy, and they too poured their text-critical method through a dogmatic grid—but their conclusions were exactly the opposite of Borland's!

Third, in letting his doctrinal position dictate the outcome of his textual criticism, Borland proves his own position wrong. There are plenty of passages far more troublesome to inerrancy than Matt 1:7 or Luke 23:45. In fact, these passages hardly constitute a serious difficulty.[98] To be consistent, Borland ought to advocate conjectural emendation wherever inerrancy seems to be in jeopardy. Who would not like a clean harmony between the two records of Judas' demise, uniform parallel accounts of Peter's threefold denial of Jesus, or an outright excision of the census by Quirinius? If Borland is unwilling to perform such radical surgery to the text under the guise of inerrancy, then why does he wave this doctrinal stick at significantly lesser problems? One can only suspect that inerrancy is not driving his decisions; rather, a preservation-majority connection is.[99]

Finally, we question whether it is an epistemologically sound principle to allow one's presuppositions to dictate his text-critical methodology. It is our conviction that this is neither honest to a historical investigation nor fair to one's evangelical heritage. If our faith cannot stand up to the scrutiny of rigorous investigation, then our beliefs need to be adjusted. But if we always jerk back the fideistic reins when the empirical horse goes too fast for us, then the charges of obscurantism, scholasticism, even pietistic dribble are well deserved. Borland believes that "unhappily our widely accepted textual-critical principles and practices may help to accommodate them in their jesting against the inerrancy of Scripture."[100] But surely the jesting will be louder and stronger if we change the rules of the game because the other team is winning!

## CONCLUSION

In many respects, the theological premise of the TR/MT proponents is commendable. Too many evangelicals have abandoned an aspect of the faith when the going gets tough. That certain students of the NT have held tenaciously to a theological argument concerning the text of the NT speaks highly of their piety and conviction. If their view were biblically founded, it would also speak highly of their orthodoxy. But, as we have seen, their theological *a priori* is neither biblically, nor logically, nor historically sound.

Concerning preservation, their underlying motive that the quest for certainty is identical with the quest for truth speaks volumes about their method. Their most self-defeating argument is that truth must be found in the majority—for not only does this contradict God's normal *modus operandi*, but it does not at all work for the Old Testament. Thus those who practice textual criticism by "majority rule" end up with a doctrine which promotes a bibliological double standard. At precisely this point they are out of step with orthodoxy, resembling more the ancient heretic Marcion in their view of the text.

Byzantine text advocates' arguments which are related more directly to inspiration and inerrancy also falter. Pickering's argument that loss of text falsifies inspiration is, once again, Marcionite (for there is loss of text in the OT), and his lone example—the longer ending of Mark—is irrelevant to anyone who thinks that the evangelist intentionally ended his Gospel at 16:8. Borland's argument is that the presuppositions of inerrancy must drive our text-critical methodology and that, consequently, only in the Byzantine text-type do we have an inerrant text. This view was found to be not only isolationist (in which inerrancy is defined only in twentieth century terms which are, moreover, not shared by the vast bulk of twentieth century iner-rantists), not only inconsistent (otherwise he would have to appeal to conjectures wherever he felt the text erred), but also epistemologi-cally, historically, and evangelically unsound.

In sum, there is no valid doctrinal argument for either the Textus Receptus or the majority text. A theological *a priori* has no place in textual criticism. That is not to say that the majority text is to be re-jected outright. There may, in fact, be good arguments for the major-ity text which are not theologically motivated. But until TR/MT advocates make converts of those who do not share with them their peculiar views of preservation and inspiration, their theory must re-main highly suspect.

# NOTES

[1]*The New King James Bible, New Testament* (Nashville: Thomas Nelson Publish-ers, 1979).

[2]One of the promotional means of the publisher is the sponsoring of concerts. On July 18, 1988, I attended one of these concerts at Reunion Arena in Dallas, Texas, where approximately 18,000 people were in attendance. At the end of the concert, Dr. Arthur L. Farstad, editor of the NKJV, promoted this Bible. His chief "sales pitch" was text-critical in which he argued that Mark 16:9–20 was authentic and that modern translations, by deleting it (or at least by casting doubts on its authenticity), delete Christ's resurrection from Mark's gospel. His statement, however, was not altogether accurate, for although there is no resurrection appearance by Christ if the gospel ends at v 8, there is still a resurrection! Whether intentional or not, the impression left on the audience was that the NKJV is a more orthodox translation than other modern versions.

[3]For a discussion of this, see my article, "The Majority Text and the Original Text: Are They Identical?," *Bibliotheca Sacra* 148:590 (April–June 1991) 151–69.

[4]This statement is not meant to imply that MT = TR, but that within this school of thought are two divisions—those who hold that the printed edition of Erasmus (TR) is the original and those who hold that the reading of the majority of extant Greek wit-nesses is the original.

[5]This breakdown is somewhat artificial, since the arguments from inspiration and inerrancy are closely tied to preservation as well. However, our organization is due chiefly to the fact that the arguments from preservation are more traditional and uni-versal among TR/MT advocates, while the arguments from inspiration/inerrancy are of more recent vintage and are more idiosyncratic.

[6]In passing, Peter Ruckman could be mentioned as the most extreme "King James only" advocate, going so far as to argue that even the Greek and Hebrew text need to be corrected by the KJV! Cf. his *The Christian's Handbook of Manuscript Evidence*

(Pensacola: Pensacola Bible Institute, 1970) 115–38; *Problem Texts* (Pensacola: Pensacola Bible Institute, 1980) 46–48.

[7]Not only has he influenced many laymen, but David Otis Fuller dedicated the book, *Counterfeit or Genuine[:] Mark 16? John 8?*, of which he was the editor (2d ed.; Grand Rapids: Grand Rapids International Publications, 1978), to "Jasper James Ray, Missionary Scholar of Junction City, Oregon, whose book, *God Wrote Only One Bible*, moved me to begin this fascinating faith-inspiring study" (p. v). Further, even Zane C. Hodges, formerly professor of NT at Dallas Theological Seminary, and arguably the prime mover in the modern revival of the "Traditional Text," "admits that it was the reading of Ray which began his investigation of textual criticism" (David D. Shields, "Recent Attempts to Defend the Byzantine Text of the Greek New Testament" [Ph.D. dissertation, Southwestern Baptist Theological Seminary, Fort Worth, Texas; December, 1985] 26. This is based on an interview Shields had with Hodges on January 15, 1985).

[8]Junction City, OR: Eye Opener Publishers, 1955.

[9]"A multiplicity of differing Bible versions are in circulation today, resulting in a state of bewildering confusion. Some versions omit words, verses, phrases, and even chapter portions . . . Among these [versions] you'll not find the Bible God gave when holy men spake as they were moved by the Holy Spirit . . . " (ibid., 1).

[10]The following are representative statements: " . . . the TEXTUS RECEPTUS . . . is God's sure foundation on which to rest our eternal salvation" (32). "It is impossible to be saved without 'FAITH,' and perfect-saving-faith can only be produced by the 'ONE' Bible God wrote, and that we find only in translations which agree with the Greek Textus Receptus refused by Westcott and Hort" (122). "Put poison anywhere in the blood stream and the whole becomes poisoned. Just so with the Word of God. When words are added or subtracted, Bible inspiration is destroyed, and the spiritual blood stream is poisoned. In this respect the revised Bibles in our day seem to have become spiritual guineapigs, with multiple hypodermic shots-in-the-arm by so called Doctors of Divinity, who have used the serum of scholasticism well mixed with modern free-thinking textual criticism. When the Bible words are tampered with, and substitution is made, the Bible becomes a dead thing with neither power to give or sustain life. Of course, even under these conditions, it is possible to build up church membership, and report many professions. But what about regeneration? Are they born again? No person can be born again without the Holy Spirit, and it is evident the Holy Spirit is not going to use a poisoned blood stream to produce healthy christians. Therefore, beware, beware, lest your faith become marred through the reading of corrupted Revised Versions of the Bible" (9).

[11]In his introduction, Ray states that he "knows that the teaching of this book, regarding Textual Criticism, goes contrary to what is being taught in almost every college, seminary, and Bible school. . . . The reader may say, 'How can so many good, sincere educated people be wrong?' Herein lies the 'mystery of iniquity' (2 Thess. 2:7)" (ii). Later he argues: "*Many of these men* [who use modern versions] *are true servants of the Lord, and we should, with patience and love, try to reveal the truth to them.* They have been 'brain-washed' by their teachers; who were 'brain-washed' by other teachers in a 'chain-reaction' on back to *Westcott and Hort who, in 1881, 'switched' most of our seminaries and Bible schools from the dependable TEXTUS RECEPTUS to inferior manuscripts*, such as codex Sinaiticus and Codex Vaticanus. Of

course this 'chain-reaction' could be traced on back to its beginning in Genesis 3:1, where (Satan) the serpent said unto the woman, 'Yea, hath God said?' In the humanistic theology of today we would hear something like this: 'These words are not in the best manuscripts'" (101).

[12]Ibid., 102.

[13]Ibid., 104.

[14]Further, inspiration and preservation are linked to tradition—especially the tradition of the English Bible, for Ray argues: "The Bible God wrote has been providentially preserved for us in the Greek Textus Receptus, from which the King James Bible was translated in 1611. Any version of the Bible that does not agree with this text, is certainly founded upon corrupted manuscripts" (ibid., 106).

[15]David Otis Fuller, for example, in *Counterfeit or Genuine*, speaks of "bastard Bibles" (10) and echoes J. J. Ray in condemning virtually all evangelical institutes of higher learning for using other than the *Textus Receptus* or the King James Version: "This is a David and Goliath battle with practically all of the evangelical seminaries and colleges, Bible institutes, and Bible schools slavishly following essentially the Westcott and Hort Greek Text and the Westcott and Hort theory, both of which are fallacious in every particular" (12). He adds further, as did Ray, that Satan is the mastermind behind this defection from the King James and TR: "born-again Christians in this twentieth century are facing the most malicious and vicious attack upon God's inspired Holy Word since the Garden of Eden. And this attack began in its modern form in the publication of the Revised Version of the Scriptures in 1881 in England" (9).

Donald A. Waite, a Dallas Seminary graduate, argues in his *The Theological Heresies of Westcott and Hort* (Collingswood, NJ: Bible for Today, 1979), that the two Cambridge dons were unregenerate, unsaved, apostate, and heretical (39–42). David D. Shields in his dissertation on "Recent Attempts to Defend the Byzantine Text of the Greek New Testament," points out that "the evidence on which [Waite] bases these conclusions often would indict most evangelical Christians. Even in the author's perspective, Westcott and Hort have theological problems, but the extreme severity of Waite's approach would declare anyone apostate and heretical who does not hold to his line" (55).

Wilbur Pickering, another alumnus of Dallas Seminary, and the president of the Majority Text Society, although normally not as prone as many others to such language, does sometimes imbibe in vitriolic speech. For example, in his master's thesis, "An Evaluation of the Contribution of John William Burgon to New Testament Textual Criticism" (Dallas Theological Seminary, 1968), he declares that the most ancient manuscripts came from a "sewer pipe" (93). In his book, *The Identity of the New Testament Text* (Nashville: Thomas Nelson, 1977)—a book which has become the standard text in support of the majority text—Pickering states, for example, that "Aleph and B have lied" and that "Aleph is clearly a bigger liar than B" (126), and that all the ancient manuscripts on which modern critical text are based are "convicted liars all" (135). Pickering has toned down his language in his second edition (1980), perhaps due to book reviews such as R. A. Taylor's in *JETS* 20 (1977) 377–81, in which such "emotionally-loaded language" is seen as clouding the issue (379). (In this second edition he says that "Aleph and B have . . . mistakes, . . . Aleph is clearly worse than B" [135], and the ancient manuscripts are "blind guides all" [145].)

Theodore P. Letis, editor of *The Majority Text: Essays and Reviews in the Continuing Debate* (Fort Wayne, IN: Institute for Biblical Textual Studies, 1987), seems to use fulminatory language against everybody, for he is in something of a theological no man's land: his volleys are directed not only at modern textual criticism, but also at *majority text* advocates (since he advocates the TR)—and even against inerrantists! He speaks, for example, of "the idolatrous affair that evangelicals are having with the red herring of inerrancy" (22); those who advocate using modern-language Bibles (including the translators of the New King James Version) are "in pragmatic league with the goddess of modernity—Her Majesty, Vicissitude" (81); virtually all modern translations imbibe in Arianism (203); *ad hominem* arguments are everywhere to be found in his book.

[16]*Which Bible?*, 5th ed. (Grand Rapids: Grand Rapids International Publications, 1975) 8–9.

[17]*True or False? The Westcott-Hort Textual Theory Examined*, ed. D. O. Fuller (Grand Rapids: Grand Rapids International Publications, 1973) 5. This linking of inspiration and preservation is also seen most clearly in Fuller's statement that "The Scriptures make it quite clear that He [God] is also well able to insure the providential preservation of His own Word through the ages, and that He is the Author and Preserver of the Divine Revelation. The Bible cannot be accounted for in any other way. It claims to be 'Theopneustos,' 'God-breathed' (II Timothy 3:16)" (*Which Bible?*, 5). It is significant that Fuller gives no proof-text for preservation here, for to him if the Bible is inspired it must be providentially preserved.

[18]In Shields' dissertation ("Recent Attempts"), the first three chapters are entitled "The Popular Defenders of the Textus Receptus," "The Scholarly Defenders of the Textus Receptus," and "The Defenders of the Majority Text." In each chapter there is a section (or two) on Burgon and the impetus he provided for the various groups (there is even a Dean Burgon Society which quite explicitly promotes his views). One may, with some justification, feel that very little new has been said by MT/TR advocates after Burgon.

[19]J. W. Burgon, *The Traditional Text of the Holy Gospels Vindicated and Established* (arranged, completed, and edited by E. Miller; London: George Bell and Sons, 1896) 12.

[20]Wilbur N. Pickering, "An Evaluation of the Contribution of John William Burgon to New Testament Textual Criticism" (Th.M. thesis, Dallas Theological Seminary, 1968) 86.

[21]Ibid., 91.

[22]More recently, Pickering has linked inspiration and preservation so closely that he argued that a denial of one was a denial of the other: "Are we to say that God was unable to protect the text of Mark or that He just couldn't be bothered? I see no other alternative—either He didn't care or He was helpless. And either option is fatal to the claim that Mark's Gospel is 'God-breathed'" ("Mark 16:9–20 and the Doctrine of Inspiration" [a paper circulated to members of the Majority Text Society, September, 1988] 1).

[23]E. F. Hills, *The King James Version Defended* (4th ed.; Des Moines: Christian Research, 1984) 2.

[24]"The Magnificent Burgon," in *Which Bible?*, 90.

[25]Bart D. Ehrman, "New Testament Textual Criticism: Quest for Methodology"

(M.Div. thesis, Princeton Theological Seminary, 1981) 40. Shields echoes the same viewpoint in his dissertation ("Recent Attempts") where in each of his first three chapters in which he interacts with various proponents of MT/TR, there is extensive material on "theological perspective," including inspiration and providential preservation. He summarizes that "the strong theological basis from which all advocates for primacy [of the Byzantine text-type] argue is a poor starting-point for determining the text of the New Testament and creates a history of the text which contradicts known facts" (p. 3 of abstract). Since Ehrman wrote his thesis and Shields his dissertation, Theo Letis has altered this picture to some degree: he is the first member of the MT/TR school (as far as I am aware) who, though affirming providential preservation, denies inerrancy (see n. 15).

[26]Letis, *Continuing Debate*, 9. One might argue that Zane Hodges does not have such an agenda and that therefore he is an exception to the rule. At one point, in fact, Hodges himself seems to say this. In his interaction with Gordon Fee over this issue, Hodges states: "To speak of 'all modern advocates of the TR' as having a 'hidden agenda' is an impermissible *argumentum ad hominem*. It also is not true. I, for one, would be quite happy to accept the Westcott-Hort text as it stands if I thought that the grounds on which it rested were adequate. . . . My agenda at least—and I speak here only for myself—is precisely what I have expressed it to be—namely, a call to re-examine the claims of the majority text in the light of increasingly perceived deficiencies of the theory that underlies today's editions. I happen to think that a man's theology *can* affect his textual theories, but I am perfectly willing to entertain sensible arguments from any quarter no matter what theology they may be associated with" ("Modern Textual Criticism and the Majority Text: A Response," *JETS* 21 [1978] 145–46).

As Ehrman points out, however, there are two objections to Hodges' alleged neutral stance: (1) "While Hodges is right that some theological presuppositions may have no effect on one's approach toward textual criticism, it is equally clear that others certainly will. If one affirms as a theological 'given' that God would not allow a corrupted form of the New Testament text to be widely accepted, then, despite disclaimers, any argument to the contrary must be rejected out of hand. For the sake of personal integrity an individual such as Hodges may adduce strictly historical arguments for his position; but if one assumes this doctrine to be true and refuses to reconsider, then any textual method that does violence to it will be automatically rejected. For this reason, Hodges cannot 'entertain sensible arguments from any quarter no matter what theology they may be associated with'" (49–50). (2) "The other problem with Hodges's position is that he himself does not hold to it consistently. In another work ["A Defense of the Majority Text," Dallas Seminary, n.d., p. 18], Hodges openly states that his historical (note, historical, not theological) arguments for the superiority of the Majority text will appeal only to those of similar theological conviction. . . . " (50). Not only this, but elsewhere Hodges rejects Hort's views because of their rationalistic presuppositions, arguing that the "New Testament text is not like any other ancient text" and that "the logic of faith demands that documents so unique cannot have had a history wholly like that of secular writings" (Hodges, "Rationalism and Contemporary New Testament Textual Criticism," *BSac* 128 [1971] 29–30). Ehrman concludes from this that "apart from the fact this amounts to little more than rhetoric, a paradigmatic *argumentum ad hominem*, it is clear that Hodges chooses to reject the principles of Wes[t]cott and Hort simply because they do not accept his doctrine of revelation and preservation.

Under such circumstances, to turn around and say that all arguments for the contrary position will be given rational consideration is nothing short of misleading" (51).

[27]B. M. Metzger, *The Early Versions of the New Testament: Their Origin, Transmission and Limitations* (Oxford: Clarendon, 1977) 359.

[28]E. F. Hills, *The King James Version Defended!*, 31.

[29]Ehrman, "Quest for Methodology," 43.

[30]See Wallace, "The Majority Text and the Original Text," 159–66.

[31]Ironically, in this instance majority text advocates—all of whom are theologically conservative—share by analogy some similarities with Bultmann's separation of the Christ of history and the Christ preached by the early church (i.e., the Christ of faith or Kerygmatic Christ).

[32]B. Ehrman, *Didymus the Blind and the Text of the Gospels* (Atlanta: Scholars Press, 1986) 260 (italics added).

[33]See Wallace, "The Majority Text and the Original Text," 166.

[34]Hills, *King James Version Defended!*, 8.

[35]Ray, *God Wrote Only One Bible*, 104.

[36]Ehrman, "Quest for Methodology," 44.

[37]These two text deposits are not identical: there are almost 2,000 differences between them.

[38]E.g., which TR? One of the editions of Erasmus, or Beza, or the Elzevir brothers? The TR has gone through numerous changes, not the least because Erasmus did a rather poor job of editing the text. Further, once one argues for the infallibility of the TR, any arguments drawn from public accessibility must be limited to the time of the Reformation and beyond, since the TR has scores of readings which not only were not in the majority beforehand, but were also nonexistent.

[39]Not infrequently MT/TR advocates quote from the *Life and Letters of Fenton John Anthony Hort*, 2 vols. (London: Macmillan, 1896). A favorite passage is where Hort writes to Westcott on October 17, 1865: "I have been persuaded for many years that Mary-worship and 'Jesus'-worship have very much in common in their causes and their results" (2:50). Cf. B. C. Wilkinson, "Our Authorized Bible Vindicated," in *Which Bible?*, 279; D. A. Waite, *The Theological Heresies of Westcott and Hort*, 39–42.

In passing, it could, with equal justification, be mentioned that not only was Erasmus more Catholic than either Westcott or Hort, but even Burgon had a hidden agenda in his vigorous defense of the longer ending of Mark: he held to baptismal regeneration and Mark 16:16 seemed to him to be the strongest proof-text of this doctrine. E. F. Hills writes that he was "strenuously upholding the doctrine of baptismal regeneration" ("The Magnificent Burgon," in *Which Bible?*, 87). That this is not an *argumentum ad hominem* is evident by the fact that his personal beliefs directly affected his text-critical approach. (It is perhaps not insignificant that when Hills' essay was reproduced in *True or False?* [in Fuller's introduction], this line about Burgon's beliefs was dropped.)

[40]H. A. Sturz, *The Byzantine Text-Type and New Testament Textual Criticism* (Nashville: Thomas Nelson, 1984) 41–42.

[41]Contrary to popular belief, although the monks were indeed burning old biblical manuscripts to keep warm, codex Sinaiticus was not the next in line. (Cf. B. M. Metzger, *The Text of the New Testament: Its Transmission, Corruption, and Restoration*, 2d ed. [Oxford: University Press, 1968] 42–45.) Nevertheless, one could not

argue that this manuscript was out of harm's way, in light of the midwinter practice at the monastery.

[42]One thinks, for example, of C. H. Roberts rummaging through the basement of the John Rylands Library of Manchester University in 1935, only to chance upon a small scrap of papyrus which included portions of five verses from John's gospel (18:31–33, 37–38), and was dated in the first half of the second century. In light of the radical German view of the date of John as c. A.D. 170 (harking back to F. C. Baur a century earlier), this small fragmentary copy of John's gospel, as one scholar put it, "sent two tons of German scholarship to the flames."

[43]R. A. Taylor, "The Modern Debate Concerning the Greek Textus Receptus: A Critical Examination of the Textual Views of Edward F. Hills" (Ph.D. dissertation, Bob Jones University, 1973) 156.

[44]Cf., e.g., D. A. Carson, *The King James Version Debate: A Plea for Realism* (Grand Rapids: Baker, 1979) 56.

[45]Sturz gives some further helpful analogies (*Byzantine Text-Type*, 38): "Preservation of the Word of God is promised in Scripture, and inspiration and preservation are related doctrines, but they are distinct from each other, and there is a danger in making one the necessary corollary of the other. The Scriptures do not do this. God, having given the perfect revelation by verbal inspiration, was under no special or logical obligation to see that man did not corrupt it. He created the first man perfect, but He was under no obligation to keep him perfect. Or to use another illustration, having created all things perfect, God was not obligated to see that the pristine perfection of the world was maintained. In His providence the world was allowed to suffer the Fall and to endure a defacement of its original condition."

[46]Pickering, "Burgon," 90.

[47]Pickering states, "In terms of closeness to the original, the King James Version and the *Textus Receptus* have been the best available up to now. In 1982 Thomas Nelson Publishers brought out a critical edition of the Traditional Text (Majority, "Byzantine") under the editorship of Zane C. Hodges, Arthur L. Farstad, and others which while not definitive will prove to be very close to the final product, I believe. In it we have an excellent interim Greek Text to use until the full and final story can be told" (*Identity*, 150).

[48]Metzger, *The Text of the New Testament*, 100.

[49]Cf., in particular, 1 John 5:7–8 and Rev 22:19.

[50]To be sure, Pickering was unaware that there would be that many differences between the TR and *Majority Text* when he wrote this note. Originally, his estimate was between 500 and 1,000 differences ("Burgon," 120). But in light of the 2,000 differences, "purity" becomes such an elastic term that, in the least, it is removed from being a doctrinal consideration.

[51]Literally scores of studies have been done to prove this, none of which Pickering seems to be aware. Gordon Fee speaks of Pickering's "neglect of literally scores of scholarly studies that contravene his assertions" and "The overlooked bibliography here is so large that it can hardly be given in a footnote. For example, I know eleven different studies on Origen alone that contradict all of Pickering's discussion, and not one of them is even recognized to have existed" ("A Critique of W. N. Pickering's *The Identity of the New Testament Text*: A Review Article," *WTJ* 41 [1978–79] 415).

[52]"Burgon," 93.

[53]We could add here an argument concerning the early versions. None of the versions produced in the first three centuries A.D. was based on the Byzantine text. But if the majority text view is right, then each one of these versions was based on polluted Greek manuscripts—a suggestion that does not augur well for God's providential care of the NT text, as that care is understood by the majority text view. But if these versions were based on polluted manuscripts, one would expect them to have come from (and be used in) only one isolated region (for if only *some* Christians did not have access to the pure text, God's sovereignty might be supposed still to be left intact). This, however, is not the case: the Coptic, Ethiopic, Latin, and Syriac versions came from all over the Mediterranean region. In none of these locales was the Byzantine text apparently used. (For further discussion and documentation, see Wallace, "The Majority Text and the Original Text," 161–62.)

[54]Letis, *Continuing Debate*, 200.

[55]Pickering, "Burgon," 88.

[56]W. N. Pickering, "Mark 16:9–20 and the Doctrine of Inspiration" (unpublished paper distributed to members of the Majority Text Society, September, 1988) 1.

[57]Letis, *Continuing Debate*, 192–94.

[58]Ibid., 17.

[59]K. Aland, "The Text of the Church?" (*TrinJ* 8 [1987] 136–37), commenting on 2 Cor 1:6–7a. To be fair, Aland does not state whether there is no clear majority 52 times or whether the Byzantine manuscripts have a few defectors 52 times. Nevertheless, his point is that an assumption as to what really constitutes a majority is based on faulty and partial evidence (e.g., von Soden's apparatus), not on an actual examination of the majority of manuscripts. Until that is done, it is impossible to speak definitively about what the majority of manuscripts actually read.

[60]*Identity of the New Testament Text*, 150. In Pickering's theological construct, then, the doctrine of inspiration has no significance, for elsewhere he argued "If we do not have the inspired Words or do not *know* precisely which they be, then the doctrine of Inspiration is inapplicable" ("Burgon," 88).

[61]Along this line is a significant corollary: those Christians who must have certainty in nonessential theological areas have a linear, or "domino," view of doctrine: if one falls, all fall. A more mature Christian, in our view, has a concentric view of doctrine: the more essential a doctrine is for salvation (e.g., the person of Christ), the closer it is to the center of his theological grid; the less essential a doctrine is (e.g., what he believes about eschatology), the more peripheral it is.

[62]Hills, *King James Version Defended!*, 8.

[63]B. M. Metzger, *The Canon of the New Testament: Its Origin, Development, and Significance* (Oxford: Clarendon, 1987) 91–92.

[64]Hills, *King James Version Defended!*, 29.

[65]Ibid., 26.

[66]E. Würthwein, *The Text of the Old Testament* (Grand Rapids: Eerdmans, 1979), for example, argues that "an arbitrary procedure which hastily and unnecessarily dismisses the traditional text . . . can lead only to a subjective form of the text which is uncertain historically and without any claim to theological relevance" (111). He further argues that the Masoretic text "has repeatedly been demonstrated to be the best witness to the text. Any deviation from it therefore requires justification" (113). Yet, as conservative as he is, he hastens to add, "But this does not mean that we should

cling to [the Masoretic text] under all circumstances, because it also has its undeniable faults . . . " (ibid.). For similar statements regarding the value, but not inerrancy, of the Masoretic textual tradition, see F. E. Deist, *Toward the Text of the Old Testament* (Pretoria: Kerkboekhandel Transvaal, 1978) 247–49; R. W. Klein, *Textual Criticism of the Old Testament: The Septuagint after Qumran* (Philadelphia: Fortress, 1974) 62–63; F. F. Bruce, *Second Thoughts on the Dead Sea Scrolls* (Grand Rapids: Eerdmans, 1964) 61–69.

[67]Klein, *Textual Criticism of the Old Testament*, 70. Cf. also F. M. Cross, *The Ancient Library of Qumran and Modern Biblical Studies* (Garden City: Doubleday, 1958) 179–81; E. Tov, "The State of the Question: Problems and Proposed Solutions," in *1972 Proceedings: IOSCS and Pseudepigrapha*, ed. R. A. Kraft (Missoula, MT: Scholars Press, 1972) 3; and especially E. C. Ulrich, *The Qumran Text of Samuel and Josephus* (Missoula, MT: Scholars Press, 1978) 193–221.

[68]Cf. the discussions (and demonstrations) to this effect in D. Barthélemy, *Critique Textuelle de l'Ancien Testament: 2. Isaïe, Jérémie, Lamentations* (Göttingen: Vandenhoeck & Ruprecht, 1986) 361–62 (Isa 49:12), 403–7 (Isa 53:11); Würthwein, *Text of the Old Testament*, 106–10 (on 108 he argues that Qumran MS 1QIsa$^a$ at Isa 2:20 is superior to MT); J. A. Sanders, *The Dead Sea Psalms Scroll* (Ithaca: Cornell University, 1967) 17; E. Tov, *The Text-Critical Use of the Septuagint in Biblical Research* (Jerusalem: Simor, 1981) 70–72, 288–306; W. H. Brownlee, *The Meaning of the Qumran Scrolls for the Bible* (New York: Oxford University Press, 1964) 216–35; G. Vermes, *The Dead Sea Scrolls: Qumran in Perspective*, rev. ed. (Philadelphia: Fortress, 1977) 203–9; Cross, *Ancient Library*, 169, 189, 191; Bruce, *Second Thoughts*, 61–62, 66–69; Klein, *Textual Criticism of the Old Testament*, 62, 71, 74–76; C. E. Pfeiffer, *The Dead Sea Scrolls and the Bible* (Grand Rapids: Baker, 1969) 101–9.

[69]Cf. especially J. Kennedy, *An Aid to the Textual Amendment of the Old Testament* (Edinburgh: T. & T. Clark, 1928). In the editorial note N. Levison comments that "Dr. Kennedy was very conservative theologically. . . . [yet] he was possessed with an intense passion for the correction of the Massoretic Text, and, as will be seen from the contents of this book, it was no mere speculation but considered and conscientious study that led him to his conclusions" (p. vii). But note also Brownlee, *Meaning of the Qumran Scrolls*, 231 (where he accepts an emendation by C. C. Torrey for Isa 53:11, since "if the verse is to be scanned as poetry at all, some such alteration is necessary"); Klein, *Textual Criticism of the Old Testament*, 76 (on 1 Sam 14:47); Würthwein, *Text of the Old Testament*, 108 (on Jer 2:21); Bruce, *Second Thoughts*, 69 (on Isa 21:8; 53:11; and Deut 32:8); Deist, *Towards the Text of the Old Testament*, 247–49, 260; D. M. Fouts, "A Suggestion for Isaiah XXVI 16," forthcoming in *Vetus Testamentum* (prepublication draft courtesy of the author).

[70]Ulrich notes that Josephus preserved "at least four genuine Samuel readings which were preserved by no other witness until 4QSam$^a$ was recovered" (*Samuel and Josephus*, 2). Cf. also Cross, *Ancient Library*, 189 ("4QSam$^a$ and I Chron. 21:16 preserve a verse [2 Sam. 24:16b] which has dropped out of *MT* by haplography . . . "); Würthwein, *Text of the Old Testament*, 142 (1QIsa$^a$ confirms conjectures at Isa 40:6 and 40:17); Barthélemy, *Critique Textuelle*, 361–62 (1QIsa$^a$ at Isa 49:12) 403–7 (Isa 53:11); Brownlee, *Meaning of the Qumran Scrolls*, 218–19 (Isa 11:6; 21:8) 225–26 (Isa 49:12) 226–33 (Isa 53:11).

[71]Taylor's comments in "Modern Debate" are representative: "It is essential, then, that this distinction be maintained between the concepts of inspiration, which insures the reliability of the divine revelation, and preservation, which insures the availability of the divine revelation" (148); "It is certain that if God took such pains to insure by inspiration the accuracy of the original manuscripts, He would not leave to an undetermined fate the future of those writings" (154); "Nothing of the inspired writings has been lost as a result of the transmission of the text. This, too, is in keeping with God's preservation of the Scripture" (163). Cf. also Sturz, *Byzantine Text-Type*, 37–49, *et al.*

[72]Donald L. Brake, "The Preservation of the Scriptures," in *Counterfeit or Genuine?*, 175–218. This essay is a modification of Brake's Th.M. thesis (Dallas Seminary, 1970), "The Doctrine of the Preservation of the Scriptures."

[73]In passing, it should be noted that all these proof-texts, if they refer to the written word at all, refer to the OT. The bibliological inconsistency is thus heightened, for MT/TR advocates apply this doctrine only to the NT.

[74]BAGD, 735 (1).

[75]Brake, "Preservation," 181–82. Apparently Brake means by this that an exact written copy of the originals was brought to heaven. Not only is this difficult to believe, but it renders the "public accessibility" idea absolutely worthless.

[76]"The scripture cannot be broken" (John 10:35), in its context, means "all will be fulfilled" or "all of it is true" rather than "we must have every word preserved." "Not one jot or tittle from the law will pass away until all is fulfilled" (Matt 5:18) plainly refers either to the ethical principles of the law or the fulfillment of prophecy, or both. (The validity of each of these options turns, to some degree, on how πληρόω is used elsewhere in Matthew and the weight given to those texts—e.g., are Matthew's OT quotation introductory formulae [ἵνα πληρωθῇ in 1:23; 2:15; 4:14, etc., connecting the term to eschatological fulfillment] more significant or is Jesus' own use of πληρόω [in 3:15, connecting it to ethical fulfillment] more significant?) Either way, the idea of preservation of the written text is quite foreign to the context.

Occasionally Matt 24:35 ("Heaven and earth will pass away, but my words will not pass away") is used in support of preservation. But once again, even though this text has the advantage of now referring to Jesus' words (as opposed to the OT), the context is clearly eschatological; thus the words of Jesus have certainty of fulfillment. That the text does not here mean that his words will all be preserved in written form is absolutely certain because (1) this is not only foreign to the context, but implies that the written gospels were conceived at this stage in *Heilsgeschichte*—decades before a need for them was apparently felt; (2) we certainly do not have all of Jesus' words recorded—either in scripture or elsewhere (cf. John 20:30 and 21:25).

[77]A possible objection to this statement might be that, on the one hand, we criticize MT advocates for their rational leap of linking preservation to the majority, while on the other hand, here we argue for providential care without having a biblical basis. Is this not the same thing? No. That preservation is to be seen in the majority is an *a priori* assumption turned into a doctrine; that the doctrinal content of the Bible is not affected by the variants is an *a posteriori* demonstration which stops short of dogma. Thus if a viable variant were to turn up that affected a major doctrine, our view of God's providential care would not be in jeopardy, though it would be reworded. An analogy might be seen in two twentieth century wars: One could say that God's hand was seen in the Allies' defeat of the Axis in World War II, as well as the

Coalition's defeat of Iraq in the Persian Gulf War. But on occasion, a given battle in which the weather conditions had previously been reported as quite favorable to the Allies'/Coalition's cause turned out to be unfavorable, this would not alter our overall picture of God's sovereignty. Rather, we simply could not appeal to that battle in support of our view. Similarly, our view of God's providential care of the text does not depend on the nonexistence of viable variants which teach heresy precisely because we are not affirming such on a doctrinal level. Our statement is made solely on the basis of the evidence. And just as historical investigation might uncover certain environmental conditions, or mechanical failures, etc., which were unfavorable to the Coalition forces for a given battle, still the outcome of the Persian Gulf War is not at all altered by such evidence—even so any new discoveries of manuscripts may cause us to reshape how we speak of God's providential care of the text, but the overall fact derived from empirical evidence is still the same.

[78]A paper circulated to members of the Majority Text Society, September, 1988.

[79]Pickering, "Mark 16:9–20 and the Doctrine of Inspiration," 1.

[80]Ibid.

[81]Ibid.

[82]Ibid.

[83]Ibid., 4.

[84]Col 4:15–16 speaks of a letter coming to the Colossians from the Laodiceans. This is either now lost (the known "Letter to the Laodiceans" is forged) or is the letter to the Ephesians which circulated counterclockwise through Asia Minor, going from Ephesus, to Laodicea, to Colossae.

[85]The statement in 3:17 ("this greeting is in my own hand, Paul's, which is a sign in every letter [of mine]") seems to imply a well-known practice. Yet, most NT scholars would date only Galatians and 1 Thessalonians as coming prior to this letter—i.e., among the known letters of Paul.

[86]So much so that W. R. Telford could argue, "While a number of scholars would still adhere to the view that the Gospel originally extended beyond 16:8, more and more are coming to the opinion that it was intended to end at 16:8, and that it does so indeed, in literary terms, with dramatic appositeness" ("Introduction: The Gospel of Mark," in *The Interpretation of Mark*, ed. W. R. Telford [Philadelphia: Fortress, 1985] 26). Cf. also C. S. Mann, *Mark: A New Translation with Introduction and Commentary*, Vol. 27 in the Anchor Bible (Garden City: Doubleday, 1986) 659 ("Mark did indeed finish his gospel at v. 8, and . . . he had a specific and well-defined purpose in doing so"); R. P. Meye, "Mark 16:8—The Ending of Mark's Gospel," *BibRes* 14 (1969) 33–43; H. Anderson, *The Gospel of Mark*, in the New Century Bible Commentary (Grand Rapids: Eerdmans, 1976) 351–54; H. Paulsen, "Mark xvi. 1–8," *NovT* 22 (1980) 138–70; N. R. Petersen, "When Is the End Not the End? Literary Reflections on the Ending of Mark's Narrative," *Interp* 34 (1980) 151–66; T. E. Boomershine and G. L. Bartholomew, "The Narrative Technique of Mark 16:8," *JBL* 100 (1981) 213–23. Among those who are evangelicals (in the strictest sense of the word—i.e., inerrantists), a number of authors antedating Pickering's essay held to this view: cf., e.g., N. B. Stonehouse, *The Witness of Matthew and Mark to Christ* (Philadelphia: Westminster, 1944) 86–118; W. L. Lane, *The Gospel of Mark* in the New International Commentary on the New Testament (Grand Rapids: Eerdmans, 1974) 582–92; J. D. Grassmick also seems to lean toward this view (*Mark* in the Bible

Knowledge Commentary [Wheaton: Victor Books, 1983] 193–94).

[87]E. Best, *Mark: The Gospel as Story* (Edinburgh: T. & T. Clark, 1983) 73.

[88]Ibid., 74.

[89]Ibid., 132.

[90]See n. 86. Besides literary criticism, another argument could be used to support the view that the gospel ended here: only if Mark's Gospel were originally published in codex form (in which case the last leaf could have possibly fallen off) could one argue that the ending of Mark was lost. But if, as extrabiblical parallels are increasingly showing to be more likely, the Gospel was originally written on a scroll, then the last portion of the book, being at the center of the scroll, would be the least likely portion of the book to be lost.

[91]Cf., e.g., G. Salmon, *Some Thoughts on the Textual Criticism of the New Testament* (London: John Murray, 1897) 26; H. C. Hoskier, "Codex Vaticanus and Its Allies," in *Which Bible?*, 143.

[92]J. A. Borland, "Re-examining New Testament Textual-Critical Principles and Practices Used to Negate Inerrancy," *JETS* 25 (1982) 499–506; reprinted in Letis, *Continuing Debate*, 46–57. All references in this paper are to the original article in *JETS*.

[93]Borland, "Negate Inerrancy," 504.

[94]Ibid., 505, n. 22.

[95]Ibid., 506.

[96]D. A. Carson, *The King James Version Debate: A Plea for Realism* (Grand Rapids: Baker, 1979) 71.

[97]M. R. Vincent, *A History of the Textual Criticism of the New Testament* (New York: Macmillan, 1899) 94. Timothy J. Ralston of Dallas Seminary is to be credited with pointing out this quotation to me.

[98]All that needs to be noted is that variant spellings of proper names were in existence in the first century, as well as in the LXX (thus, "Asaph" and "Amos," though unusual spellings, are hardly to be classified as errors); and, as Borland himself admits, ἐκλείπω with ἥλιος, though usually meaning "to eclipse," does not always have this technical nuance. Nevertheless, Borland is quite right that both passages strike one as a bit peculiar. But if they strike us a little odd, then surely they did the same for the ancient scribes—who would have changed the text out of their own pietistic motives. What Borland simply cannot explain is how the Alexandrian readings arose in the first place, rendering them more probably original.

[99]Throughout his article Borland speaks of "the vast numerical superiority" of his preferred reading ("Negate Inerrancy," 504). He concludes the article by saying, "In our quest for the true reading we must not confine ourselves to a few early MSS while forgetting the thousands of MSS that each bear an independent testimony to the text" (ibid., 506).

[100]Ibid., 506.

# Rhetorical Allegories Among the Parables of Jesus?

## Robert Duncan Culver

If this investigation is to achieve any success there must be first some agreed definition of the principal words of the topic.

### DEFINITIONS

First, about rhetoric and rhetorical: This we must rescue from "the media," where anybody's speech, persuasive or not, conversational or formal, correct or incorrect (the distinction is denied) is often labeled "rhetoric" in an uncomplimentary way. By definition, rhetoric is "the *art* or *science* of using words effectively in speaking or writing, so as to influence or persuade [from Gr. *rhetor* orator] . . . especially now, the art or science of literary composition . . . including the use of figures of speech" (Webster's *New World Dictionary*). Hence, what the newscaster calls rhetoric may be really the absence of rhetoric.

Allegory is a figure of speech, especially public speech or writing, being by derivation from Gr. *allos*, other, plus *agora*, the public place of assembly. So whatever allegory may be, being a device for persuasion of listeners (or readers) in public assembly by an effective rhetorician (orator) it seems *a priori* perfectly proper, even to be expected, that Jesus should have employed allegories.[1]

Robert Duncan Culver (A.B., Heidelberg College; B.D., Th.M., Th.D., Grace Theological Seminary) is a retired Professor of Theology, most recently at Trinity Evangelical Divinity School, and is a free-lance author residing in Houston, Minnesota.

## HISTORICAL CONSIDERATIONS

Shortly we must define allegory more precisely, as well as parable, but meanwhile it is important to observe what careless use of the word allegory has done even among some great names of Gospel criticism. John W. Sider has written: "from Jülicher[2] onward for the past century, the *literary* practice of parable criticism rests on principles which have either been described perfunctorily or simply assumed by writers glancing *at* the parables before looking through them. (For example Jeremias gives no definition of allegory.)"[3]

Jülicher happens to be the putative father of present-day critical parable study and Jeremias the author of *The Parables of Jesus*, which in our time, has shaped most liberal parable scholarship. Sider's thoroughly researched article shows that logic has been neglected to erect the now self-generating flood of books and articles related to the critical study of Jesus' parables.[4] The main concern of the literature has not been to discover and expound the text of the parables as they stand in the Gospels. That text is regarded as largely unauthentic by the liberal critical community

> . . . the parables do go back to Jesus, but not the parables as we know them. Why do Jeremias and others believe this to be the case? There is more than one reason. A significant factor is that Jeremias accepted the now discredited view of Adolf Jülicher that Jesus' parables were simple single-point parables . . . this led inevitably to the conclusion that, for example, the four-point interpretation of the parable of the sower . . . is not original. Jeremias believed that this was shown by a variety of other considerations.[5]

Unless one has spent a long time examining in detail some of the thousands of pages of literature, liberal and conservative, existential and Freudian, etc., the full significance of David Wenham's summary statement can only be guessed.

Since Jeremias himself had a gift for clear expository statement, I cite a single page from his famous work on this subject.

> As they have come down to us the parables of Jesus have a double historical setting. (1) The original historical setting of the parables, as of all his utterances, is some specific situation in the pattern of the activity of Jesus. Many of the parables are so vividly told that it is natural to assume that they arise out of some actual occurrence. (2) But subsequently, before they assumed a written form, they "lived" in the

primitive Church, of whose proclamations, preaching, and teaching, the words of Jesus were the content, in its missionary activities, in its assemblies, or in its catechetical instruction. It collected and arranged the sayings of Jesus according to their subject matter, created a setting for them, sometimes modifying their form, expanding here, allegorizing there, always according to its own situation between the Cross and the *Parousia*. In our study of the parables of Jesus it is important to bear in mind the difference between the situation of Jesus and that of the primitive Church. In many cases it will be necessary to remove sayings and parables of Jesus from their setting in the life and thought of the primitive Church, in the attempt to recover their original setting in the life of Jesus, if we are to hear once more the original tones of the utterances of Jesus, and to experience anew the vital qualities of force, conflict, and authority in the historical events. As soon as we attempt to ascertain the original historical setting of the parables, we meet with certain principles of transformation.[6]

Jeremias then devotes the next 92 pages of his book to a statement and explanation of how his famous ten principles of transformation changed what Jesus really said to the expanded, allegorized form they presently take in the text of the Gospels.

Allegory is the word which the above-mentioned Gospel critics use most frequently to designate the character of the additions to the parables and modifications of them made by the early church, which they designate the early "creative community."

These changes took place after Jesus' death but before the supposed final redactor-theologians composed the Gospels. The changes, dictated by the unexpected delay in the *parousia* (second advent of Christ) and the presence of a new Gentile constituency are said to be "hortatory" expressions of "pastoral concerns." In the case of the parables these non-dominical portions are labeled allegory, hence the sting of Sider's criticism that Jeremias, a father of the enterprise, never defined "allegory" in his pivotal book, *The Parables of Jesus*, though he assigned central importance to allegory.

"The mode of speech which says other things (than the mere letter) and hints at different things from what it expresses, is called appropriately *allegory.*" This definition was first phrased by Heraclitus (1st century A.D.) about 1900 years ago, as noted by J. Massie's article on "Allegory" in *A Dictionary of the Bible* (vol. 1, pp. 64–66), edited by James Hastings. After defining many rhetorical figures such as type, fable, parable, Massie goes on to say: "All these tropes may indeed be classed under the allegorical or figurative," i.e., allegorical in a non-specific sense simply means figurative. The specific, however, not the general sense, is in view in this essay. *Metaphor* likewise has a specific and a general sense.

A survey textbook of "The Literature of England" usually includes many lengthy specimens of allegory as well as short ones: Spenser's *The Faerie Queen*, Swift's *The Tale of a Tub*; Addison's *The Vision of Mirza* and, above all, Bunyan's *The Pilgrim's Progress*, as well as others. They can run from a paragraph in length to a book, but never as short as a simple metaphor. The reader recognizes quickly the meaning of an allegory as something *other* than (not necessarily entirely *different* from) the story. There may be many, not usually complicated, aspects of the meaning of an allegory and for the most part the meaning is self-explanatory. The successful allegory is its own exegete and exhorter. Bunyan preaches still to the reader about progress toward holiness and heaven; Swift to the wrangling sectaries of all Christendom and Addison about the perilous brevity of life and need for caution, discipline and perseverance.

Allegory, then, when used as a tool of liberal criticism in the interpretation of parables, is *not employed in explicating the meaning*, but of stripping away excrescences which obscure the supposed obvious, plain meaning of the simple illustrative story spoken by Jesus in the first place. In Jülicher's time the reconstructed lessons read like 19th century enlightenment moral maxims. Recent critics make them read like existentialist theology. How allegory came to be a tool of interpretation among pagan commentators before the opening of the Christian era and by Christian theologians near the beginning of our era I defer to a note at the end of this article. Allegorical interpretations of Genesis or Kings and Chronicles is remote from the focus of this essay, but the issues are easily confused.

The medieval predilection for treating all the parables as allegories prevailed until the Reformation. It was interrupted most severely and successfully by Calvin. As one reads his *Commentary on a Harmony of the Evangelists*[7] one quickly becomes aware that Calvin, the trained linguist and humanist, knew he was breaking new ground. For example, the Parable of the Good Samaritan receives this comment which focuses on the single main point: " . . . the chief aim is to show neighborliness which obliges us to do our duty by each other is not restricted to friends and relations, but open to the whole human race."[8] He then proceeds to demolish three then extant "allegorical interprelations" [his term], ending with this caustic remark: "Anyone may see that these speculations have been cooked up by meddlers, quite divorced from the mind of Christ."[9]

Modern study has agreed that most of Jesus' parables have one main point to make. "The kingdom of heaven is like"—not the several details, each standing for something, as in allegory—but "like" indicates some important single truth brought out by the whole parable.

## DEFINING PARABLE

We have given attention to "rhetorical" and "allegory" in relation to our essay on "Rhetorical Allegories among the Parables of Jesus," and now we address "parable." Here we encounter a genuine biblical-linguistic nuisance, namely, important English words, biblical and otherwise, come across without much modification from Greek into common speech, thence into the English Bible. But in common speech the words frequently are modified to mean something different from the original Greek word (or Hebrew) found in the biblical text. So en route from the original source in Greek into English and thence into our English Bible the word's meaning gets skewed enough to affect our exegesis if we do not check the Greek original. For example our word "method" is a direct transfer of the Greek *methodeia*, meaning *scheming*, and rendered "wiles of the devil" in Eph 6:11, thus giving the term a morally defective tone. The English word, *method*, however, is morally neutral. One could rightly refer to the methods of a holy God, but not His *methodeia*. Thus etymology of a word does not necessarily relate to its meaning in current usage. *Parabolē* comes across into English almost unmodified in form as "parable." The Greek word receives its simplest sense of "comparison" (like its OT Hebrew equivalent, *mashal*) by derivation from a verb meaning to compare. In the Greek OT, *parabolē* with only one exception translates *mashal*—of which only a few usages are equivalent in meaning to our word parable. Each of Balaam's oracles is a *parabolē* (Num 23:7, 18; 24:3, 15, 23) as also the pithy comparisons and contrasts of Proverbs (1:6) and the strange taunting song of Isa 14:3–11, put by Isaiah in the mouth of dead kings and potentates. Enigmas, fables, wise sayings, catchy sing-songs, bywords, wisdom, laments, riddles, aphorisms are all designated by *mashal* and regularly rendered *parabolē* by the Greek OT.

By analogy, the English proverb: "A man is known by the company he keeps" applies to the word *parabolē* in the Greek OT. In this case it is bad company. Jer 24:9 (KJV) reads, "And I will deliver them to be removed into all kingdoms of the earth for their hurt, to be a *reproach* and a *proverb* [*parabolē*], a *taunt* and a *curse.*" The Hebrew is even worse, where *mashal* (= *parabolē*) is fourth among six terms meaning terror (*zewaᶜah*), misfortune (*raᶜah*), reproach (*ḥerpah*), byword or proverb (*mashal*= *parabolē*), mockery (*sheninah*) and a curse (*gelalah*). It is even in parallel with the Septuagint's *ainigma* (astonishment) and *diegema* (an idle tale) in Deut 28:37. So there is clear OT precedent for using a parable as a "curse" (Mark 4:1, 13).

These citations clearly show (1) that the biblical word *parabolē* does not necessarily, not even usually, designate something helpful to understanding, though it may do so. (2) It designates a great variety of rhetorical-literary devices, including several figures of speech. (3) Among these rhetorical devices is what we might legitimately call allegory (see Ezek 17:2), though Gr. *allegoria* does not appear in the Septuagint. (4) In the biblical sense of *parabolē*, *all* allegories are parables; *some* parables are allegories; but *not all* proverbs are allegories. Our concern here is to determine if some of Jesus' parables are allegories.

Perhaps this sheds some light on why all the Synoptic Gospel writers chose *parabolē* as a name for "the parables." They were not in each case the very same rhetorical device. Furthermore, what was a similitude (transparent comparison) to an enlightened disciple might be a taunt to a hardened pharisee or mere entertainment to a careless bystander and certainly a judgment on all incorrigible unbelievers (Mark 4:10, 11). Readers of the Greek Bible would have known already that some parables were designed more to puzzle the hearer than initially to enlighten him.

Among the numerous figures of speech in the OT there are several acknowledged allegories. F. F. Bruce has written: "Ezekiel's picture of Israel as the foundling baby girl . . . (Ezek 16), is more allegory than parable . . . the same is true of the account of Oholah and Oholibah (Ezek 23)."[10] There is also the allegory of a "Great Eagle" (Ezek 17:1–10). Of these three only the "Great Eagle" is called a *mashal* (*parabolē*), also *hidah* (LXX *diegma*). The others receive no name at all. They are nonetheless allegories. Isa 5:1–7 is another undesignated but clear example of allegory, probably the key to our Lord's *parabolē* of the Wicked Husbandmen (Matt 22:1–12 and parallels). Another is Ps 8:8–16 representing Israel as a "Vine out of Egypt" and still another is the extraordinary representation of the advance of old age as the progressive decay and decrepitude of a magnificent house and garden in Eccl 12:1–6.

In the NT the Vine and Branches of John 15 and the Good Shepherd of John 10 are neither parable nor allegory in the usual sense of these words [see extended end note].

## ALLEGORIES AMONG PARABLES?

Now to the question: Are other extended rhetorical figures of Jesus, designated each as a *parabolē*, really allegories, rather than the simple single-idea which "modern" scholarship has until very lately said to be the *only* kind of *parabolē* spoken by Jesus?

There are three "parables" which Jesus set forth to his followers during the last seven or eight days of his life which, in my judgment, ought to be regarded as outright allegories and a possible fourth. True, according to the standards of the Jülicher-Jeremias model, allegory was missing from the stories as Jesus ordinarily propounded them. Jeremias set forth ten "canons"[11] by which the original non-allegorical *Parabole* could be recovered. Those canons have not been accepted *en toto* by every critic and one recent article,[12] I think, demolishes all of them as ill conceived.

Even some liberal-critical writers on parables who accept the usual conclusions of form and redaction criticism express less respect for the Jülicher-Jeremias orthodoxy than might be expected. J. D. Crossan, for example, readily acknowledges that several parables, especially the parable of the Wicked Husbandmen, are allegories. He goes to great length, however, to explain that all the allegorical elements were absent from the parable as originally expounded by Jesus. The seven "elements" of Mark's account are reduced to the four which the story contains in "The Gospel of Thomas," a document included in the Nag Hammadi materials. So the allegory which Crossan introduces with his right hand he removes with his left and is not so very different from Jülicher and Jeremias after all.[13] The same is true, it seems to me, of the treatments by Hans Weber[14] and D. O. Via.[15] Since these authors find such authority as they believe, in the veritable but uncertain words of Jesus, rather than in the canonical Gospels as such, they offer the orthodox interpreter little guidance and less comfort in accepting allegory as having a rightful place among rhetorical devices employed by Jesus.

It is not wrong for expositors to begin and end their work on the assumption that the Gospel parables are authentic, granted the fruit of modern *textual* criticism. Textual criticism at least tries to work objectively with the evidence of factual data.

Fifty years ago my professors at Grace Theological Seminary, including A. J. McClain and H. A. Hoyt, pointed out (without reference to the question of allegory) that at a certain time, just before his Last Week, Jesus began to drop hints and warnings which gave a sort of time structure to the disciples' future — beyond Calvary. There were some details which no single-idea *parabolē* could convey and which he was not ready yet plainly to state. True, my professors spoke from a Dispensational perspective, but that perspective is hardly necessary for the point made.

To carry the disciples patiently and hopefully through the coming decade or two, they needed some information about the long age to follow the Lord's death, resurrection, ascension and onward to the Second Advent.

If the Spirit was to "bring all things to your remembrance" about "whatsoever I have said unto you," explain the meaning and "show you things to come" as John plainly reports Jesus' promise (John 14–16), such hints and warnings were exceedingly appropriate at this time.

## The parable of the pounds

Jesus spoke the first of the four parables (Luke 19:11–27) at the very brink of his sea of troubles called "holy week." He had just passed through Jericho along the ascent to Bethany where he was to overnight and enjoy the last sabbath of his natural life: "And as they heard these things, he added and spake a parable, because he was nigh to Jerusalem and because they supposed the kingdom of God was immediately to appear" (Luke 19:11). [That they kept on expecting the kingdom to appear immediately is evidenced by their robust enthusiasm on Palm Sunday.]

It is to be expected that any instruction from the Lord in such circumstances would predict some details of the close of his earthly career and the long, long wait for his return as well as of some causes and effects. "After he was risen from the dead" they would be assisted by the Spirit to remember ("bring all things to your remembrance whatsoever I have said to you," John 14:26). They would be informed thereby (as we are today) and "believe" (John 2:22).

> Christ's meaning was that the disciples were very deceived in thinking that his kingdom was already established and that he was going to Jerusalem to set up a prosperous state. He takes from them the hope of a present kingdom and exhorts them to hope and patience . . . they must undergo troubles for a long time before they enjoy that glory which they do not greatly desire.[16]

Though the parable is called the Parable of the *Pounds*, Luke has informed us that the message was not primarily about stewardship of money or any special moral duty. It is about time, a long time—about ordering life in light of the long absence of the Lord during the inter-advental period. The "long" time is symbolized by "the far country" (= heaven) where the nobleman goes and sets up residence.

With minor variations, liberals and conservatives agree that the meaning is about like this: the crowd of followers was excited about the prospects of immediate assumption of kingly powers by Jesus to inaugurate an external kingdom, the promised restoration of Israel. It looked to them as though this might occur as soon as he reached Jerusalem, only a long day's march from the environs of Jericho where the parable was propounded. In the parable the "nobleman" is Jesus; the "far country" is heaven; the "kingdom" is his reign inaugurated at the session at the Father's right hand; "to return" is His Second Advent; the ten servants and the ten pounds represent the believers of the time of Jesus' absence and their Christian duties; the hate of "his citizens" is the rejection of Jesus by his people, the Jews; "when he was come back again" refers to the Second Advent after an unspecified but long period of time; the servants of the nobleman (vv 15–26) are the Christians who will be rewarded at His return and the slaying of "these mine enemies" the judgments on evil men, vaguely indicated, at the Second Advent.

J. A. Fitzmyer identifies the authorial (Luke) allegorical additions as vv 12, 14, 24a and 27. He interprets these verses as follows: v 12 (far country = delayed coming of Christ in His kingdom); v 14 (citizens hate him = rejection of Christ by Jews); v 15 (come back = Second Advent); v 27 ("slay them before me" = judgment of enemies, though Fitzmyer does not think it is eschatological). [17]

I note that among the recent commentators I consulted on this parable, the liberals have no trouble finding abundant allegory in the "present form" of what amounts to Luke's rather than Jesus' parable, so far is it from the simple original spoken by Jesus. Some very recent evangelical, conservative writers seem gun-shy of observing very many of the details characteristic of allegory. It may be they are fearful of being accused of lapsing into pre-modern assumptions or ignorance of assured findings of accredited critics or even worse, obscurantism, said to be characteristic of writers out of step with progressive interpretation.

David Wenham pointedly avoids finding any reference to the delayed appearance of the kingdom of God, discovering only spiritual lessons. Like the parable of the Talents the meaning appears "to refer to the resources that the Lord entrusts to his people." [18]

Even though Fitzmyer, obedient to the Jülicher-Jeremias orthodoxy, thinks allegory was absent from the original parable, being added by tradition-makers and redactors, he is not mistaken about the parable's pronounced allegorical features. Nor is he mistaken in seeing the specific allegorical features as too obvious to require proof, speaking of the material cited above as "the obvious allegorizing which these verses give to the parable." [19]

## The parable of the wicked husbandmen

Jesus propounded the second of the series early in that long Tuesday of Holy Week. It is reported at Matt 21:33–46 with parallels at Mark 12:1–12 and Luke 20:9–19. It is the Parable of the Wicked Husbandmen [or tenants].

Among recent writers, allegory is enthusiastically acknowledged by liberals. C. S. Mann says: "The element of allegory in Matthew and Mark was recognized early. The influence of Isa 5:1–9 (and in the text of the Septuagint) is unmistakable. The scenario (to use a modern expression) was as follows: vineyard = Israel; owner = God; the tenant

winegrowers = Israel's leaders and rulers; the various messengers = the prophets, former and latter; the son = Jesus; the inevitable
punishment = the ruin of Israel; the other [new] tenants = the Gentile
Church."[20] Though I did not find the word allegory in Wenham's
work, his exposition gives some place to it. He sees prophecy of judgment on the old tenants (Israel) but I noted no reference in his comments to the obvious, mainly Gentile character of the new tenants.[21]

That the parable, as is usual with allegory, was self-interpreting is
supported by the fact that even the least discerning then present so
understood it, namely, "and when the chief priests and the Pharisees
heard his parables [i.e., of the Two Sons, vv 28–32 and Wicked Hus-
bandmen] they perceived that he spake of them" (Matt 21:45).

## *The parable of the marriage feast*

Let us give brief attention to the allegorical character of the third
of these parables. It is the Parable of the Marriage Feast (Matt
22:1–14), coming immediately after the Parable of the Wicked
Husbandmen.

Identifiable correspondences which are characteristic of allegory
are present, although not as numerous as in the previous two. Some,
however, are exceedingly striking. I will limit my treatment to citing
the comments of David Wenham on a portion of the passage. We
have already observed that Professor Wenham has no special predi-
lections for discovering allegory in the Parables, though he acknowledges its presence there.

> The parable refers, like that of the tenants [husbandmen] to the
> Jewish leaders' rejection of Jesus and the gospel of the kingdom, in
> this case the "son" is not one of the messengers, but he is the one
> whose wedding is being celebrated. The implied reference is to Jesus
> again, and it is most significant that the kingdom of God is all to do
> with Jesus as God's son. We are reminded of Revelation 19, with its
> vision of God's reign and of the "wedding of the Lamb." The lamb in
> Revelation is Jesus, and the comment is made "Blessed are those who
> are invited to the wedding supper of the Lamb!" (Rev 19:9).
>
> Jesus' parable portrays the Jewish leaders' rejection of this invita-
> tion. Their refusal of the most important invitation of all time is por-
> trayed as an inexcusable insult to the author of the invitation (i.e., God
> himself). The parable is a warning of judgment on those leaders (they

will be killed) and on "their city" (it will be burnt with fire). The reference is evidently to the events of A.D. 66–70, when in the aftermath of a Jewish rebellion against their rule the Roman imperialists invaded Palestine and after a prolonged and horrible war captured and destroyed Jerusalem.

As for the command to the servants to go on and to invite . . . "whoever you find," the reference must be both to the tax collectors, prostitutes and sinners who responded to the message of the kingdom in Jesus' lifetime (Mt 21:31), but also, by implication to the biggest group of outsiders of all (i.e., the Gentiles).[22]

If Wenham is correct—and he is in the mainstream of interpretations of the Parable of the Wedding Feast of all schools—then this parable is not quite pure allegory (there are some non-analogies too), although it certainly has pronounced allegorical features.

### The parable of the talents

This does not exhaust the number of allegories or allegory-like parables of Jesus. Some recent interpreters include the Parable of the Sower and the Parable of the Wheat and the Tares. As indicated earlier, I had intended to include the Parable of the Talents (Matt 25:14–30) in this essay, but on further examination it seems to me the specific correspondences to persons, events, etc., characteristic of allegory are minimal—chiefly "another country" (v 14) referring to our Lord's ascension to heaven and "after a long time the lord of those servants cometh" (v 19), referring to the now lengthening present age and Second Advent.

## CONCLUSIONS

I think it is clear that Jesus did not lock himself into employment or non-employment of any sort of rhetorical figure or figures in propounding his message. The notion that he could not use the multiple metaphor of allegory but only simple similitudes demanding "radical repentance" and "immediate decision" with no foresight of a church and the long age to follow is the invention of modern liberal and existential criticism. The real Jesus was more complicated than that. The parables have to be trimmed drastically to make the apocalyptic, existential or liberal models of Jesus fit the scheme; hence the variegated maze of book-learning among the critical writers on the parables. Take this sort of alleged scholarship out of the two large volumes of Fitzmyer on Luke and there is precious little left. They would deprive the Lord Jesus of his prophetic foresight and turn him into a partially deluded, if admirable, fanatic. They would also deprive the Church, truly in God's eternal plan, of her natural birthright, depriving believers of important specific guidance in their agelong missionary task. This would especially include the "kingdom of heaven" parables, as I tried to set forth in *A Greater Commission: A Theology for World Missions.*[23]

Jesus was not bound to employ any pure form of a figure of speech. If he wished to mix a metaphor or simile with irony, sarcasm, parable, paradox, or to fill out a similitude with allegory or some other rhetorical flourish, that was his prerogative. Jesus' rhetorical methods resist modern critical stereotyping.

Yet, in view of flagrant misuse of allegory in interpretation, that is, treating *every* parable as an allegory, the warnings I have cited from Calvin and others are well taken. The single-lesson parable type is the most numerous, so much so that it should be assumed unless compelling evidence to the contrary is present. My limited observation indicates that with possible exception of the Parables of the Four Soils and of the Wheat and Tares, the allegories were all spoken very late in Jesus' ministry, for reasons I have already addressed. The Cursing of the Fig Tree, prominently featured in the story of the Lord's last week, should be included as an acted parable. Many of his miracles were acted parables. Like the Parables of the Wicked Husbandmen and of the Wedding Feast the Cursing of the Unproductive Fig Tree denounces a curse on Israel for rejection of God's Messiah.

I endorse the following guidance of Robert H. Stein:

> One cannot therefore say *a priori* that a parable cannot contain any allegorical elements or that Jesus could not have included allegorical details in his parables. Whether the parables of Jesus at times contain allegorical details and whether the details are authentic must be demonstrated on exegetical grounds, not on philosophical or *a priori* grounds. It would appear, nevertheless, to be a wise rule not to interpret the parables of Jesus allegorically unless such an interpretation is absolutely necessary. We should find allegory in the parables of Jesus only when we must, not simply when we can.[24]

## PROPOSED CRITERIA FOR DETECTION OF ALLEGORY

I continue with some proposed criteria for determining when a *parabolē* is an *allegoria* or *has* what have been called allegorical elements in a parable.

It has been shown early in this essay that in the Hebrew OT many kinds of figures of speech and other rhetorical devices are designated *mashal*, uniformly translated *parabolē* in the Greek OT (LXX) current in NT times and employed by the Gospel writers. This is the word rendered *parable* in English versions of the OT. This being true we should expect variation in the types of figures or devices (all called parables) in the Synoptic Gospels. It would be strange to find it otherwise.

1. Perhaps most uncontroversial are indications (stronger than hints) in the very text, especially the way the parable is introduced. According to Luke, Jesus spoke the Parable of the Pounds (Luke 19:11–27) "because he was nigh to Jerusalem and because they [his followers] supposed that the kingdom of god was immediately to appear" 19:11). A simple moral lesson or single idea would hardly have solved the problems latent in these two circumstances. I have already dealt with this verse as key to this essentially allegorical narrative called by Luke a *parabolē*. This is the most striking of such textual pointers to allegory among the parables. A search for such indicators in all of Jesus' parables could not be undertaken within the limits of the present project.

2. Somewhat less decisive, but important, is information in the context suggesting allegory, i.e., detailed symbolical information, in the parable. A simple reading of Matthew 21–25 finds Jesus toe to toe in fierce controversy with bloodthirsty Jewish leaders. They understood some of his parables in detail as directed against themselves. They saw themselves as the wicked husbandmen who mistreated the king's (God's) servants (prophets). This is of greatest importance and leads to the next point.

3. Usually there is nothing in the text of a parable or its context to suggest allegory in one of Jesus' stories. In such a case allegory must be an inference from the text of the story itself. I go so far as to say it must be an *obvious* inference. This is to be expected. Poets do not say, Now I'm going to employ such and such a literary device, before saying "Our hearts like muffled drums are beating" (simile). Nor did

orator Churchill notify the Missouri audience that he was about to use a metaphor when he referred to the Soviet enclosure of eastern Europe as an "iron curtain." Nor did Swift anywhere call *The Vision of Mirza* an allegory. Yet no one who reads it fails to catch what the piece is, even if he has not the word *allegory* in his vocabulary. As stated previously in this article, "an allegory . . . is self-explanatory. The allegory is its own *exegete* and *exhorter.*"

This is the main contention of this essay and I will proceed to show by quotation of several writers of many schools of theology and criticism that this may be the chief criterion of allegory in the Gospel parables. I will quote several relevant articles, monographs and commentaries to show that whether acknowledged or not, consciously or not, this is *the* criterion for recognizing allegory in the parables. [Emphases in the following quotations is mine, not the authors'.]

William Barclay treats Matt 21:33–46 as two parables rather than as entirely the Parable of the Wicked Tenants. Yet he gives an allegorical twist to each and introduces the discussion in an unusual way:

> In interpreting a parable it is normally a first principle that *every* parable has *only one point* and that details are not to be stressed. Normally to try to find a meaning for every detail is to make the mistake of treating the parable as an allegory. But in this case it is different. In this parable the details do have a meaning and the chief priests and the Pharisees well knew what Jesus was meaning his parable to say to them.[25]

The only clue as to *why* Barclay thinks this is so is a reference to Isa 5:7, a prophetic allegory in which "the vineyard" is the nation of Israel. He adds: "the vineyard is the nation of Israel, and its owner is God. The cultivators are the religious leaders of Israel . . . The messengers . . . are the prophets sent by God and so often rejected and killed. The son . . . is none other than Jesus himself." Evidently Barclay *just knows*, i.e., *obviously* there are allegorical meanings. The multiple metaphors are so numerous and impressive one cannot avoid interpreting the *parabolē* as an *allegoria*.

A. Carr nearly a century ago said about the same:

> No parable *interprets itself* more clearly than this. [All allegories are self-interpreting in ordinary literature, i.e., they are obvious.] Israel is represented by an image which the prophets had made familiar and unmistakable—the Vineyard of the Lord. The householder who

planted the Vineyard and fenced it signifies God the Father, Who created the nation for Himself—a peculiar and separate people. The husbandmen are the Jews, and especially the Pharisees, the spiritual
leaders of the Jews. The servants are the prophets of God, the Son is
the Lord Jesus Christ.[26]

D. A. Carson remarks in his treatment of the Parable of the
Wicked Husbandmen that "the metaphorical equivalences are *obvious* [that is, the allegory is obvious, for allegory consists of multiple
"metaphorical equivalences"]: the landowner is God, the vineyard Israel, the tenants the leaders of the nation, the servants the prophets,
and the son is Jesus Messiah."[27] Carson seems reluctant to apply the
word "allegory" to any of Jesus' parables, perhaps in want of a clear
definition common to the scholarly literature of parables and a certain stigma attached to it among critical authors.

Regarding the Wicked Husbandmen, J. D. Crossan writes in the
same tenor: " . . . this parable is, *apparently*, the most perfect example of an allegory from his teaching. . . . Other authors who insist
that it is not an allegory but a parable have had little success in explaining it as such and, in effect, have usually interpreted it allegori-
cally while hailing it as a parable."[28] The governing word here is
"apparently." Crossan means the parable as Mark and Luke present
it. He later says they have overlaid it with additions to the original,
which was a simple parable. So it is an allegory of the first generations of Christians, not of Jesus. He thinks the original simple parable
of Jesus is found in "The Gospel of Thomas," as we have reported
earlier.

*Ellicott's Commentary* declares, "The interpretation of the parable (Mt 22:1, 2) is *on the surface."* He goes on to interpret the entire parable pretty much as though there was a *surface* or *near
surface allegorical meaning.*[29]

Fitzmyer, whom I have cited earlier in this essay, frequently uses
words like "obvious allegorizing," "allegorizing verses," "the allegorized parable" (twice) in his treatment of the Parable of the Pounds.
He does not, of course, assign much of the allegory part to the original story spoken by Jesus, but to later additions to "the tradition."

William Hendrickson, commenting on the Parable of the Pounds
remarks, "What Jesus was really telling his audience in symbolical
phraseology, was *probably* this, that he himself at the conclusion of
his suffering would ascend to the Father in heaven; that the Father,

as a reward upon his son's accomplished work would . . . [bestow] on him rulership . . . and . . . he would return to earth after a *long* (but indefinite time) symbolized by the 'far country,' etc."[30]

Harry Ironside, a respected dispensational interpreter of recent memory, makes no apologetic for treating the parable of the Wicked Husbandmen as an allegory of the beginning and ending of the present Church age.[31] Without saying this is an allegory, he treats it as such.

Heinrich Meyer treats the same parable (Wicked Husbandmen) largely as an allegory without any apologetic for it, even though, of all truly great commentators, he was perhaps least sparing in citing reasons for critical decisions.[32]

T. W. Manson subscribes to the Jülicher-Jeremias orthodoxy in explaining how the simple, non-allegorical Parable of the Pounds reached its final form as found in Luke 19:11–27. He does not need to say why he thinks so, but he then says, "The effect of the additions is to make the parable, as it now stands, an allegory of the Christian life in the interim between the Ascension and the Parousia. The nobleman (Christ) has departed to a distant country (heaven) to receive a kingdom. Meanwhile he entrusts the management of his affairs to his servants (Christians)."[33]

The quotations might go on indefinitely. Some of Jesus' parables must be interpreted as allegories—rhetorical allegories—by an "orator" employed as convincing argument to persuade certain people simply because common sense dictates that no other interpretation quite fits. We will not deal with the important questions of how and why only certain people get the meaning of metaphors and allegorical language. It has been discussed by some of the literary giants— Goethe, Eliot, Yeats, Lewis, Coleridge, Ricoeur, even Marcuse and Frost.

It is fitting to conclude this part of the essay with a quotation from Matthew Black, one of the first "modern" scholars to break from the iron frame of Jülicher-Jeremias orthodoxy:

> On purely *a priori* grounds there does not seem to be any reason why there should not be allegory in the teaching of Jesus. . . . The Old Testament does not know of any distinction between allegory and parable, for the one can easily pass into the other as more than one detail comes to assume a symbolic significance. The Oxford Dictionary also fails to make the distinction, and, in fact, gives "allegory" as one of the

meanings of "parable." Differences are of degree not of kind, and while we must beware of attaching absurd allegorical meanings to details which form no more than the scenic background of a story, we may well be impoverishing our understanding of the parables of Jesus by excluding allegory simply on the basis of the Jülicher canon that the parables are not allegorical. As Dr. Vincent Taylor has written, "The shade of Jülicher must not affright us from admitting allegory when we see it."[34]

## A NOTE ON ORIGIN OF ALLEGORICAL INTERPRETATION OF ALL SCRIPTURE

Authorities (mine are the *Oxford Classical Dictionary* and *Smith's Dictionary of Greek and Roman Antiquities, Biography and Mythology*) point out that allegorical interpretation of important, ancient, national literature was first devised and employed by Greek authors. Certain learned writers among the Greeks had been reading their classics this way for several centuries when the Latins, now catching up on their humane letters, found the method useful at about the turn of the Christian epoch. In each case allegorical interpretation was a hermeneutical device (not a writer's or speaker's device) employed to make the coarse national myths and epics acceptable to educated people. These "enlightened" folk conceived themselves too scientific and morally sensitive to accept a straightforward, literal understanding of the Cosmogony of Hesiod and the immoral carryings on of their gods and heroes in the mythical epics—Iliad and Odyssey of Homer. At first "hidden meanings" (Gr. *huponoiai*) were sought by the exegetes to neutralize the defective morality of offensive passages. As the procedure developed it was later called *allegoriae*.[35] The leading allegorists were philosophers who applied their treatment to offensive and inoffensive passages alike. The allegorists, as near as I can determine, did not concern themselves very much with questions about the historical reality of affairs reported in their classical literature. Its significance, they had come to think, lay in something *other* than what the classics said. To discover and set forth that meaning is to allegorize, a term found only once in the NT in Gal 4:24. When one reads the racy, mythical accounts of the begetting of the members of the Greek pantheon and of their scandalous behavior, by any civilized standard, one can understand why sensitive ancient people might have hoped the truth of the stories lay not in any literal sense, but rather in some *other* sort of sense—perhaps metaphysics, epistemology, ethics, etc.

This method was applied to interpretation of the OT by learned hellenized Jews of the diaspora at Alexandria. Later when Christian theologians brought their Platonism along as they interpreted scripture, they had this respectable precedent to follow, which they proceeded to do. They proceeded to allegorize not only the indiscretions of biblical saints and patriarchs but also biblical history and Gospels, including, of course, the parables of Jesus.

Allegorization came to be the usual way of interpreting Jesus' parables until the Protestant Reformation. Robert H. Stein provides a helpful, brief survey of the sad story of parable interpretation in the early Fathers and up to the Middle Ages, at the time of the Protestant Reformation.[36] The most thorough discussion of allegorizing as a hermeneutical technique for interpreting scripture, tracing antecedents and the course of the sad story through Jewish and Christian history known to me, is *History of Interpretation* by F. W. Farrar, a 19th-century work of 600 pages recently reprinted by Baker Book House.

## A NOTE ON PARABLE SCHOLARSHIP

That there should be something called "parable scholarship" is apt to be news to those uninitiated to NT scholarship. There is indeed a very large literature of the subject, but the trend of it is not to enlarge understanding of what stands before the reader in Matthew, Mark and Luke. It has, however, been a fecund field for monographs, articles and doctoral theses—mostly within the 20th century. An accessible brief introduction to this literature is found in D. A. Carson's "Matthew," in *The Expositor's Bible Commentary* 8 (Grand Rapids: Baker, 1984) 301–2. For a thorough survey of the literature, read *The Parables of Jesus: a History of Interpretations and Bibliography* by W. S. Kissinger (Metuchen, N.J.: Scarecrow, 1979). It will not be settling. When I had finished the book I was sure that scholarship has turned up many needless doubts and questions as to whether scripture conveys any "sure word of prophecy" at all. The situation reminds one of a quip by G. K. Chesterton on Hamlet's indecision: "Hamlet failed to act because he had been taught in a German University." Interesting that the supposed father of 20th-century parable "research" was a professor in a German university. To this day parable literature of this sort is in response to German authors, in the main. This is confirmed by the unintentionally revealing comment in Robert Funk's introduction to Kissinger's bibliography: "The appearance of this volume will do much to stimulate the round of advances and will contribute to its own obsolescence. Such is the reward of productive scholarship" (Kissinger, *The Parables of Jesus*, vi). I quote myself in a previous comment on Kissinger's book: "The writer was correct in judging the lasting power of the work he was evaluating. It would not endure. But he did pinpoint the cause of the lack of vitality. It is not the crowding of new theories that will condemn their work to early obsolescence, but their work's lack of a truly Christian sense of religious authority [i.e., Christ as he speaks to us through inspired scripture]" (*A Greater Commission*, 159).

## A NOTE ON THE FIGURES OF JOHN 10 AND 15

There are in each case sentences which say "I am the door of the sheep" or "I am the vine," etc., but there is no story about sheep and sheepfolds, etc. The "story," so to speak, was already in people's minds, for they were familiar with sheep-raising and vine-culture. It is as though Jesus was indicating something like this: "You are familiar with sheep, shepherds, sheepfolds and gates. Well, in the sphere of salvation I am the shepherd and the door, etc. You are familiar with vine culture. Well, in the sphere of salvation I am the vine, you are the branches, the Father is the farmer," etc. It seems to me each figure of speech is exactly what John calls the first (John 10:6), a similitude" (Gr. *paroimian*), or "illustration" (NKJV). NIV "figure of speech" dodges the problem. Since the Bible does not designate this figure either parable or allegory, why should we? It is neither, in the precise sense those words are currently used. The KJV is in error in rendering *paroimia* "parable," as though it were *parabolē*.

# NOTES

[1]Let us agree with J. D. Crossan: " . . . there is no presumption that the term 'allegory' has a pejorative connotation or that allegory is a bad or inferior literary form, for Jesus or for anyone else. The only question is whether Jesus' stories *are* allegories in

whole or in part, and if not what are they?" (*In Parables* [New York: Harper & Row, 1973] 10).

[2]Adolph Jülicher's massive work is *Die Gleichnisreden Jesu*, 2 vols. (Tübingen: J. C. B. Mohr, 1899, 1910) and Joachim Jeremias's primary work is *Die Gleichnisse Jesu*, available in English as *The Parables of Jesus* (New York: Scribners, 1972).

[3]"Rediscovering the Parables: The Logic of the Jeremias Tradition," *Journal of Biblical Literature* 102:1 (1983): 83.

[4]*The Parables of Jesus: A History of Interpretations and Bibliography*, by W. S. Kissinger (Metuchen, N.J.: Scarecrow Press, 1960), a large book, and the list continues to grow.

[5]David Wenham, *The Parables of Jesus* (Downers Grove, IL: InterVarsity Press, 1989) 219.

[6]*The Parables of Jesus*, 23.

[7]*A Commentary on A Harmony of the Gospels Matthew, Mark and Luke*, trans. T. H. L. Parker, 2 vols. (reprinted; Grand Rapids: Eerdmans, 1972).

[8]Calvin, vol. II, 8.

[9]Calvin, vol. II, 39.

[10]*Zondervan Pictorial Encyclopedia of the Bible*, s.v. "Parable," by F. F. Bruce, 4.592a.

[11]Jeremias, *The Parables of Jesus*, 24, 91ff.

[12]See n 3.

[13]*In Parables*, 86–96.

[14]*Die Gleichnisse Jesu als Metaphoren* (Göttingen: Vandenhoeck & Ruprecht, 1978).

[15]*The Parables of Jesus* (New York: Harper & Row, 1973).

[16]Calvin, vol. II, 286.

[17]*The Anchor Bible: The Gospel According to Luke I-IX* (Garden City: Doubleday, 1981) loc. cit.

[18]*The Parables of Jesus*, 84, 85.

[19]Fitzmyer, *Luke*, 1231.

[20]*The Anchor Bible: The Gospel according to Mark* (Garden City: Doubleday, 1986) 460.

[21]Wenham, *The Parables of Jesus*, 125–33.

[22]Wenham, *The Parables of Jesus*, 134, 135.

[23]Cf. Part 2, Principles for the "Mission of World Evangelism" in Matt 13:1–53 and Mark 4:21–29. Robert D. Culver, *A Greater Commission: A Theology for World Mission* (Chicago: Moody Press, 1985).

[24]*The Method and Message of Jesus' Teachings* (Philadelphia: The Westminster Press, 1978) 52.

[25]*The Gospel of Matthew*, 2 vols. (Philadelphia: The Westminster Press, 1958) 2:261–71.

[26]*The Cambridge New Testament* (Cambridge: Cambridge University Press, 1894) 247.

[27]D. A. Carson, "Matthew," in *The Expositor's Bible Commentary* 8 (Grand Rapids: Zondervan, 1984) 451.

[28]Crossan, *In Parables*, 86.

[29]*Ellicott's Commentary*, in. loc.

[30]*Luke*, in *New Testament Commentary* (Grand Rapids: Baker Book House, 1978) 859.

[31]*Notes on Matthew* (New York: Loizeaux Bros., 1948) 276–79. Dr. Ironside presented me an autographed copy of his then new book when I gave him a free ride from Warsaw town square to his retirement cottage at Winona Lake.

[32]H. A. W. Meyer, *Critical & Exegetical Handbook to the Gospel of Matthew* (London: T. & T. Clark, 1884).

[33]*The Sayings of Jesus* (Grand Rapids: Eerdmans, 1949) 313.

[34]"The Parables as Allegories," *Bulletin of the John Rylands Library* 42 (1959–60): 275, 276. Very shortly after Black's article was published an article of similar point of view by R. A. Brown appeared, "Parable and Allegory Reconsidered," *Novum Testamentum* 5 (1962) 36–45. In this article Brown "argued against much of the oversimplification that is characteristic of parable-interpretation . . . (since A. Jülicher), rightly stressing that the lines between allegory and parables have been too tightly drawn . . . maintaining that some parables do contain allegorical elements and that there is no reason why Jesus in his ministry could not have used allegory as well as parable" (from Fitzmyer, *Luke I–IX*, 711).

[35]*Oxford Classical Dictionary*, 46.

[36]*The Method and Message of Jesus' Teachings* (Philadelphia: Westminster, 1978) 45–49.

# ΓΕΝΕΑ in Matthew 24:34

## Duane A. Dunham

Among the teachings of our Lord Jesus, none has elicited more curiosity and interest than the Olivet Discourse with its descriptions of future events. It has been called, "The most difficult of all His deliverances to understand."[1] This is no overstatement, for, in spite of a sometimes passionate interest in prophecy, not a few have despaired of anything like a consistent literal exegesis.[2] His declaration that "this generation shall not pass until all these things shall come to be" (Matt 24:34; Mark 13:30; Luke 21:32), certainly demands some investigation. The primary questions of interest to those who accept the integrity of the text, and by that the writer means its divine inspiration and all that this entails, is: Was Jesus prophesying the soon coming of the end of the age and, if so, was he therefore mistaken (cf. the disciples' questions, Matt 24:3)?[3] Corollary questions include: does this eschatological discourse refer in any way to the historical events of A.D. 70 when Jerusalem fell to the Roman armies under Titus? Is this a prediction of the coming fall of Jerusalem by the Lord Jesus, or a history of it, constructed by redactors out of various threads of authentic utterances?[4] Since it is with the discussion focused upon Matt 24:34 and its parallels that some critics have launched attacks on Scripture, if not on the Saviour himself. Questions which reflect not only on eschatology, but on apologetics as well.[5] Fitzmyer says that this particular text proposes "a difficult question to answer, and in the long run the most difficult phrase to interpret in this complicated eschatological discourse."[6] However, unlike the treatment of other very difficult passages, the commentaries are

Duane A. Dunham (B. A., Biola College; B.D.,3 Talbot Seminary; Th.M., Western Conservative Baptist Seminary; Th.D., Grace Theological Seminary) is Professor of New Testament Language and Exegesis at Western Conservative Baptist Seminary in Portland, Oregon.

often not reticent to take dogmatic positions. The majority position is expressed by Beasley-Murray: "On the lips of Jesus, 'this generation' *always* signifies the contemporaries of Jesus."[7]

This view leaves us with several choices, none of which are acceptable: either Jesus made a mistake, or his words are incorrectly reported, or he did not utter these words, or the fulfillment is to be found in the fall of Jerusalem in A.D. 70, which demands undesirable compromises in our hermeneutic. This article will propose a different position by addressing two topics: (1) the setting of the discourse and (2) the meaning of "generation" in Matt 24:34 (Mark 13:30; Luke 21:32).

## THE SETTING OF THE DISCOURSE

There are a number of complicated issues which are far beyond the limits of this discussion. They would take one into the theories of the sources of the discourse in particular and the synoptics in general.[8] We offer only a brief analysis of some opinions on the general setting of this passage which in turn have impact on how one explains the phrase "this generation."

### The Historical View

This position maintains that the discourse is not prophecy but history, composed, either completely or in large part, after the events described. The more radical opinions include a total rejection of the authenticity of this text as a discourse of Jesus, "It is quite clear that this whole proclamation has nothing to do with the historical Jesus. It is a creation of the first generation of the Christian community."[9] Goppelt has expressed essentially the same opinion except he sees a distant connection to Jesus as having some validity.

> The apocalyptic discourse (Mk. 13 par.) is a composition of the evangelist. It was extensively reworked in Mt. 24:1–37 and Lk. 21:5–36. The traditions drawn upon here by Mark extend back—somewhat unusually—only in very modest proportions to Jesus.[10]

Very few evangelicals could hold either of these positions.

### The Historical-Eschatological View

This is probably the most widely held view. It views the contents as describing both the fall of Jerusalem in A.D. 70 and that of the return of Christ. For instance, Carr divides Matthew 24 into (1) the fall of Jerusalem vv 5–22; and (2) the Second Advent vv 23–31.[11] In his discussion of Luke 21, Fitzmyer says: "The discourse proper falls in two main parts: a) vv 8–24 *What will precede the end of Jerusalem. . . .* b) vv 25–36 *What will precede the end of the world.*"[12] George Fuller has divided the discourse into more detail, but maintains the same basic twofold aspect: (a) the fall of Jerusalem, Matt 24:3–38; (b) the return of Christ, Matt 24:29–31; (c) the relation of these two events to each other, Matt 24:32–36; and (d) the proper Christian attitude in light of the certain coming of Christ, Matt 24:37–25:46.[13] It is obvious that there is little unanimity regarding the precise point where the change is made from the destruction of Jerusalem, to the end of the age. Kidder argues for a chiastic structure of Matthew 23–25, contending that these chapters constitute "one broad literary unit."[14] He proposes the following chiastic parallels:

Scribes and Pharisees sit on Moses' seat, 23:1–22 and Son of man sits on throne of glory, 25:31–46.

Characteristics of Scribes and Pharisees, 23:23–35 and characteristics of two classes, 24:45–25:30.

"This generation," 23:36 and "this generation," 24:34. Prediction of destruction of Jerusalem 23:37–24:3 and the end of the world, Christ's second coming 24:30–33.

False messiahs 24:5 and false messiahs 24:23–28.

Signs on earth 24:6–8 and signs in heaven 24:29.

Preliminary tribulation 24:9–13 and great tribulation 24:16–22.

The Gospel to the world 24:14 and the abomination of tribulation 24:15.[15]

To him, the crucial point, indicating the division between prophecies of the fall of Jerusalem and those of the parousia of Christ, is found in vv 14 and 15. The preaching of the gospel to the whole world is said to serve "the function of a pivot, so as to look back" (to the historical section), but also "has relationship to both of the culminating events—the destruction of Jerusalem in the first Christian century, and the end of the age when Christ returns."[16] His conclusion indicates that, "the proclamation of the gospel relates to *both* of them."[17] He also holds that "the abomination of desolation" (Matt 24:15; Mark 13:14) has a kind of double fulfillment, since it "suggests not only the *culmination of the series* at the left . . . but also a *typological prefiguring* for the final judgment at the end time."[18]

There are some who see certain segments referring to either one or the other period, but not both, while making other portions refer to both. A major problem with this position, in addition to the remarkable lack of unanimity, is the tendency most of its adherents have to espouse a double fulfillment of portions of the discourse. There is also the presence of a confusing inconsistency which appears to be endemic to the position. Hendriksen explains his hermeneutical theory:

> By the process of prophetic foreshortening, by means of which before one's eyes the widely separated mountain peaks of historic events merge and are seen as one . . . two momentous events are here intertwined, namely, a. the judgment upon Jerusalem (its fall in the year A.D. 70), and b. the final judgment at the close of the world's history. Our Lord predicts the city's approaching catastrophe *as a type* of the tribulation at the end of the dispensation.[19]

While generally refusing to espouse a double reference in specific passages, he finds an alternation of topics throughout the discourse: "The prophetic material found in this sixth discourse has reference not only to events near at hand . . . but also to those stretching far into the future."[20] This is a great improvement from suggesting that the *same* texts refer to two different events. However, when we come to 24:15 he believes:

> The first part of the question . . . "When shall this—destruction of the Temple—be?" Jesus answers it now, but in such a way that the answer suits more than one event in history. To begin with it was without doubt appropriate for the days immediately referred to by Daniel.[21]

This leads him to the position that this reference to Daniel's prophecy fulfilled "long ago," is "showing that . . . a divine oracle may apply to more than one historical situation: the sacrilege that results in the desolation of city and temple takes place more than once in history."[22] He explains: "Just as the pagan altar and the swine offered upon it in the very temple of Jehovah in the second century B.C. pointed forward to the idolatrous legions of Rome, so these in turn foreshadowed the great and final violation by the antichrist of all that is sacred."[23] Hence we have three historical events referred to by one prophecy!

To cite another brief example, consider the line of argument taken by Tasker. After deciding that vv 15–28 must refer to the fall of Jerusalem in A.D. 70, he admits the difficulty of v 29: "It would seem that the words "Immediately *after the tribulation of those days*" in v 29 make it necessary . . . to assume that the events . . . would take place directly after the downfall of Jerusalem."[24] The result of such a determination leaves "the unsatisfactory conclusion that Jesus was mistaken."[25] His method of avoiding such is to ask: "Is it not also possible to regard these verses as a cryptic description in the symbolism of poetry?"[26] This is most unsatisfactory and amounts to special pleading. Where is the justification for the sudden change from the plain literal meaning of the preceding verses to a poetic symbolism? Only if one is placed in the untenable position occasioned by understanding *genea* as Jesus' contemporaries is this an attractive explanation.

Therefore, it appears that at the center of these opinions, giving both help and difficulty to expositors is the interpretation of *genea* in Matt 24:34.

*The Eschatological View*

This position holds all of the discourse in Matthew 24–25 and the parallels as unfulfilled; it refers entirely to the future return of Christ.[27] It is a more recent view, essentially limited to some dispensational expositors.[28] Its newness is its primary weakness, but its strengths outweigh the charges of its limited influence and recent advocacy.[29]

Among its strengths are: (1) freedom from defending and explaining how any portion has been fulfilled, either in the fall of Jerusalem, or in the years since. For instance, to see a fulfillment during the intervening years between the time of the prophecy and the fall of Jerusalem will fail even in the first section, without even examining the rest of the discourse. The early edition of the Scofield Bible in an attempt to overcome this subtitled Matt 24:4–14, "The course of this age."[30] This, too, fails. Attempting to find some fulfillment by counting either wars or earthquakes (Matt 24:6–7) in the past century or centuries, suggesting they are signs of the imminent parousia is an exercise in futility. The New Scofield Bible has wisely eliminated this problematic heading. (2) Freedom from the hermeneutical problem of double reference.[31] (3) Freedom from any need to spiritualize any portion of the discourse. These strengths, if valid, certainly outweigh those of other views.

## THE MEANING OF *GENEA*

Many problem passages which a student of Scripture encounters often have only two positions with which to contend. This is not the case before us. Fitzmyer lists four viable meanings for the key term, *genea*. Each is held by one or more competent scholars:

(a) Jesus' own contemporary generation: So A. Plummer, W. G. Kummel, et al; (b) the Jewish people: so W. Grundman, W. Marxen, et al; (c) human beings in general or all humanity: So A. R. C. Leaney, J. Zmijewski, et al; (d) the generation of end signs: So H. Conzelmann, G. Schneider, et al.[32]

Marshall adds a few more options: (a) "Wicked men (cf. 9:41; Acts 2:40; W. Michaelis. . .)" and (b) "The contemporaries of the evangelist (cf. Klosterman. . .)."[33] We would immediately reject both the evil men and humanity in general options since it would be unnecessary to state such obvious facts. The other views are more substantial and demand some analysis.

The proliferation of possible solutions makes an acceptable resolution seem impossible. Any explanation that ignores or skews the context must be rejected, hence "generation" cannot be understood apart from "all these things" which must come to pass before that particular generation passes which heard the words. The primary weaknesses of many positions are focused here. The decision for *genea* is taken prior to its immediate context, then "all these things" is brought into conformity, thus disregarding the serious difficulties which attend their interpretation.

### All These Things Shall Come to Be

What did Jesus mean by his statement: "All these things shall come to be?" The meaning of *genea* cannot be considered without an understanding of its relationship to this clause. G. B. Caird's comment on Luke 21:32 shows the difficulty:

As in Mark's Gospel, this parable is followed by a declaration that all things will be accomplished within a generation. Mark undoubtedly understood this prediction to include the parousia, and he was writing near enough to the time of Jesus to feel no embarrassment about such a prophecy. But Luke, writing . . . later, was in a different case; we should expect him to interpret the saying otherwise, and there is every indication that he did so.[34]

In an effort to resolve it, he then refers to the phrase "all these things" in Luke 21:36. His assumptions are, (a) "things" must mean the same events, (b) Jesus told his followers to pray for deliverance from them in v 36, (c) there can be no deliverance from the parousia, (d) "nor can we imagine the disciples of Jesus being taught to pray for any" deliverance.[35] Fault may be found with each of these, but he then concludes that "all these things" must be "the preliminary crises of persecution and the siege of Jerusalem; and these . . . were the events which Jesus declared would happen before a generation has passed away."[36] While this explanation makes an earnest attempt to deal with the context, it leaves us without an explanation of Mark's (and presumably Matthew's) "embarrassment," and hence is unsatisfactory.[37] One cannot in effect "rob Peter to pay Paul" and deal convincingly with the problem. Further, it completely ignores the statement which immediately precedes our text, "When you see all these things, you know that he is near, at the very gates" (Matt 24:33, RSV). Luke is even more strongly eschatological: "You know that the Kingdom of God is near" (Luke 21:29, RSV). Beasley-Murray is correct to suggest that we must consider the questions asked by the disciples (Mark 13:4) as the primary context. He then adds, "however, it is difficult to exclude from "*all* these things" the description of the parousia in [Mark 13:24–27]."[38] Whatever else they may have thought, it is virtually impossible to deny that the disciples thought that the destruction of the Temple was associated with the end of the age, and nothing in the discourse clearly takes away from them that idea.

Many scholars have agreed that Jesus (or the evangelist) is speaking of the details of the parousia, and the fact that the parousia has not yet taken place leaves them in an untenable position, after deciding much of the prophecy is referring to A.D. 70. Guthrie follows one line when he suggests:

> The Messiah was looking ahead to the destruction of Jerusalem. In Matthew's and Mark's account, he spoke of the "desolating sacrilege," a term from the book of Daniel. . . . In Luke's account, the reference is more specifically to "Jerusalem surrounded by armies."

Undoubtedly, both records refer to the siege of Jerusalem in A.D. 70, during which both city and Temple were laid waste.[39]

The difficulty we are left with is how to account for those passages which obviously did not come to pass in the fall of Jerusalem? To avoid a mistake by Jesus, the answer seems to be either to spiritualize them in some way, or to yield to a double fulfillment. Tasker comments:

> The sack of "the holy city" in which over a million people were slain would inevitably appear to those who witnessed it a world-catastrophe of the greatest magnitude; and only language symbolic of cosmic disturbance, such as the darkening of the sun, the failure of the moon to give light, and stars falling from the sky, was adequate to describe it.[40]

While one is sympathetic to the enormous effect the fall of Jerusalem had upon the followers of both Christ and Judaism, it is doubtful whether or not any would have associated this description of heavenly phenomena with the catastrophe. Further, this fails to explain the immediately following statement in Matt 24:30, "Then will appear the sign of the Son of Man . . . and all the tribes of the earth will mourn and they will see the Son of Man coming. . . . " This approach simply exchanges one difficult question for another which is more difficult. There is no escaping the material which describes the parousia, and no satisfactory way to divide between it and the supposed references to the fall of Jerusalem.

A further weakness by many commentators is their silence about the meaning of "not one stone upon another" (Matt 24:2) to describe the destruction of the Temple. Taken literally, it must mean that not even a single stone (probably those used for building the Temple) could be left in its position.[41] In light of the absence of any records of such a complete destruction, how can it be maintained that this was fulfilled in A.D. 70? This is too unreliable a foundation upon which to build an argument. It could have been so totally destroyed and not recorded, but the enormous religious and political significance of the temple makes this unlikely.[42]

> The history of Israel and all their prospects were intertwined with their religion; so that it may be said that without their religion they had no history, and without their history, they had no religion. Thus, history, patriotism, religion, and hope alike pointed to Jerusalem and the Temple as the centre of Israel's unity.[43]

It is hardly likely that such complete destruction would have passed without comment by those Jews who recorded the fall of the city and reflected upon its significance.[44] If there is any reason not to take this emphatic prophecy literally, apart from a determination to see A.D. 70 as a fulfillment, it is not apparent.

Gundry supports a double fulfillment since, "Jesus makes 'these things . . . all these things' signal the near coming of the Son of man; yet that event did not occur soon after A.D. 70, . . . ."[45] He concludes: "So either Jesus made a mistake. . . . Or we are to expect a second fulfillment of 'these things' . . . shortly before the coming of the Son of Man, . . . ."[46] He then argues for this double fulfillment, defending the principle on the grounds that Christ is "predicting a further 'abomination of desolation' after the one . . . perpetrated in 168 B.C. to say nothing about messianic prophecies that received initial fulfillments in the near future of OT history and further fulfillments in Jesus."[47] Beyond the legitimate hermeneutical question of double fulfillment, there are two considerations which should caution us: first, any possible double fulfillment to which he refers can be understood in the light of later revelation, which is lacking in this case. Second, the formulaic statement: "All these things will come to be" is far more definite than the OT passages to which he could appeal.[48] Another factor is the intent of the disciples' questions in v 3 which dealt with the end of the age. Would Jesus now speak of a fulfillment that was not the end in such an indefinite way?

It seems fair, seeing the evidence offered, often scanty at best, that we understand the words, "all these things will come to be" to be best accepted as intended to refer to the literal events of the parousia, not the fall of Jerusalem. One gets the distinct impression that underlying most of the debate about the meaning of these important words is a commitment to an interpretation of *genea* that demands the conclusions reached.

### The Meaning of Genea

As we noted above, there are at least six theories of the meaning Jesus had in mind when he used this term. The majority views are associated in one way or another with time. (a) Jesus' own contemporary generation; (b) the generation of end signs; and, (c) the contemporaries of the evangelist. The other primary position is slanted towards the character: (a) human beings in general or all humanity, and (b) wicked men (cf. 9:41; Acts 2:40). A distinctly minority position is that it refers to the Jews as a people; however, this is the one we find most convincing.

The meaning of any term that travels from one language to another is more difficult to ascertain than is often admitted. The baggage that terms carry from the native language into the target language is too easily read back into the source, and seldom acknowledged.[49] The English term "generation" might well be an example of this inclination. It is most often used in modern speech nontechnically of a period of time. One dictionary gives eleven possible meanings, with the fourth being: "The period between successive steps in natural descent, usually taken at 30 years in humans."[50] While the Greek term of NT times is not so versatile, it can mean:

> 1. lit., those descended fr. a common ancestor, a *clan* . . . then *race, kind* . . . 2. basically, the sum total of those born at the same time, expanded to include all those living at a given time, *generation, contemporaries* . . . 3. *age*, the time of a generation. . . .[51]

In the classical idiom, it is not markedly different:

> I. of the persons in a family, 1. race, a family . . . of horses, breed . . . hence tribe, nation; 2. race, generation; 3. offspring . . . 4. metaph. class, kind . . . II. of time or place, 1. birthplace . . . 2. age, time of life. . . .[52]

The cognate term *genos* (21 times in the NT) as used in classical literature also shows a marked preference for the meaning of "kind" rather than "contemporary."[53] It would not be out of line to say that "the primary meaning" of this word group is race or kind, and not contemporaries.

Appealing to the lexicons can in some measure benefit any of the views we have listed, but the final test must be the context. Several factors in discovering the meaning of terms must be observed. First, arguments from so-called primary meanings are only helpful, "where there is little or nothing to help the receptor in determining meaning."[54] Second, what is "most natural" is an individual matter, depending upon "their individual background and experience."[55] Third, "To always award one meaning to one word is incorrect since it denies the basic fact of polysemy."[56] Fourth, it is the context that must decide precise meanings of terms.[57] Another aspect of proper evidence must also be recognized: a majority does not necessarily confirm or disconfirm a solution.

Beasley-Murray has concluded:

> The meaning of "this generation" is now generally acknowledged. While in earlier Greek, *genea* meant "birth," "progeny," and so "race," in the sense of those descended from a common ancestor, in the LXX it commonly translates the term *dor*, meaning "age," "age of man," or "generation" in the sense of contemporaries.[58]

The decision is fallacious in that it depends entirely upon the allegedly most usual use of the Hebrew term as rendered in the LXX. It remains to be proved that Jesus was using or relying upon the Hebrew *dor*, and if he were, that the "commonly" translated meaning of *genea* is what he meant here. That *dor* may mean "race" or "kind" is implied in one lexicon,[59] and stated in another.[60] We must rest on the immediate context to determine the meaning in Matthew.

The view that *genea* in this passage has any sense of time, such as the contemporaries of Jesus, the generation of the Evangelist, or of the parousia must be rejected on the basis of the context. In the cases of either those who heard Jesus or those who heard the evangelist,[61] similar objections from context can be raised: (1) there is no legitimate way to escape the obvious force of "all these things" referring to the parousia, which has not happened yet. (2) The phenomena in the heavens cannot be understood of the fall of Jerusalem. (3) The fall of Jerusalem did not fulfill the promise that Jesus made: "Not one stone shall be left upon another." (4) The meaning of "generation" to indicate the people of a given time period is too vague and subject to too many variables to be meaningful. The term "contemporary" is likewise only helpful on any given day, but cannot be accurate of either the past or future, having no certain *termini* apart from a context. How does one determine the precise beginning or ending of a generation? If Jesus were 33 years old when he gave the prophecy, is he saying his generation is now beginning? To know in even a general way when a generation passes to the next is virtually impossible. Do we begin a new generation every two, five, ten, or thirty years, and who decides?

The view that the "generation" is the people of the time of the parousia must also be rejected. Several indicators of time are given in Rev 11:2, 3; 12:6; 13:5, etc., but they are too brief for a time period of a generation to be of any substantive help. Many are the mistakes made in deciding the precise, or even the general, time of the parousia, built upon the supposed length of a generation. Some have calculated the beginning of the establishment of the modern state of Israel to be the beginning of the "terminal generation." When Jesus said, "no one knows of that day and the hour" (Matt 24:36), was he not indicating the futility of this very endeavor?

The ultimate reason to reject *genea* as a time word comes from logic. What would be the purpose of such a prediction? How would they know which generation they were in? Does "my generation" include only people whose age is within five years of mine? Of what possible comfort would it be for those caught in the maelstrom of the great tribulation to know it would be finished in around thirty years?[62]

The view which best fits the context is to take *genea* as meaning the Jews as a nation, a race. We have a great reason for the oracle: he is assuring them that in spite of all the deadly events of the great tribulation, God has not and will not forsake his people, Israel. This fits everything in the context: (1) an acceptable meaning of the noun; (2) the literal meaning of "all these things"; (3) Israel as the focus of the entire discourse; and, (4) a simple statement of a great truth which avoids all the difficulties about a time schedule. Hence, we need not speculate about why our Saviour could have made such a mistake or what the Evangelist might have done in revising an oral tradition, or how to calculate the time of the return of Christ for his Church by deciding when Israel was or shall be reestablished in the land.

The purpose of the text is not to provide a time frame, but to give a plain and simple promise that reinforces God's promises to Abraham, Isaac and Jacob as stated in Isa 62:1–4:

> For Zion's sake I will not keep silent
>   and for Jerusalem's sake I will not rest,
>     until her vindication goes forth as brightness, and
>     her salvation as a burning torch.
> The nations shall see your vindication,
>   and all the kings your glory;
>     and you shall be called by a new name which the mouth of the
>     Lord shall give.
> You shall be a crown of beauty in the hand of the Lord,
>   and a royal diadem in the hand of your God.

You shall no more be termed Forsaken,
    and your land shall no more be termed Desolate;
    But you shall be called My Delight in Her,
    and your land Married;
For the Lord delights in you,
    and your land shall be married.

## NOTES

[1]J. W. Shepard, *The Christ of the Gospels* (Grand Rapids: Eerdmans, 1939) 512. It is interesting that Robert Stein does not deal with any part of the discourse in his *Difficult Passages in the Gospels* (Grand Rapids: Baker, 1984).

[2]See H. A. W. Meyer, *Critical and Exegetical Hand-Book to the Gospel of Matthew* (New York: Funk and Wagnalls, 1884) *in loc* for various references to the at times outlandish efforts to exegete the discourse in the last century and earlier. This century has not brought a resolution that is widely accepted. For a confusing alternation between double fulfillment, spiritualizing and literal exegesis see: R. V. G. Tasker, *The Gospel According to Matthew*, Tyndale New Testament Commentaries (Grand Rapids: Eerdmans, 1961) 223–40. Leavell asserts: "Possibly some of the predictions in chapter 24 refer both to the destruction of Jerusalem and the return of Christ to the earth. No verse in the chapter can be a dividing point between the two topics." Rolland Q. Leavell, *Studies in Matthew: The King and the Kingdom* (Nashville: The Convention Press, 1962) 122. Guthrie describes the discourse as "a curious mixture of allusions to the more immediate event of the fall of Jerusalem and the more remote parousia. . . . " Donald Guthrie, *New Testament Theology* (Downers Grove, IL: InterVarsity, 1981) 794. Morris agrees with C. E. B. Cranfield: "In one sense the interval between the Ascension and the Parousia might be long or short . . . this whole period is the 'last days'—the epilogue . . . of history. . . . " *The Gospel According to St. Mark* (Cambridge: University Press, 1959) 238. Cited by Leon Morris, *New Testament Theology* (Grand Rapids: Zondervan, 1986) 108. Desmond Ford concludes: "The period of the church age is characterized as 'the last time,' 'the end of the world,' 'the last hour.' The church itself is that generation which will not pass till all be fulfilled. It lives in 'lover's time' which is not reckoned by the clock." *The Abomination of Desolation in Biblical Eschatology* (Washington, D.C.: University Press of America, 1979) 31. One sympathizes with Blackman who, in speaking of the gospels in general, concludes: "Sometimes the sense is baffling, even forbidding . . . especially Mark xiii." E. C. Blackman, *Biblical Interpretation* (London: Independent Press Ltd., 1957) 19.

[3]The form, source, tradition, and redaction critics have plowed this turf considerably in their search for solutions to the various Synoptic problems. Beasley-Murray has asserted: "The title 'Q Apocalypse' (for his title of Luke 17:22–37) is time-honored. . . . It is acknowledged by all that the heart of the discourse is from Q. . . . " G. R. Beasley-Murray, *Jesus and the Kingdom of God* (Grand Rapids: Eerdmans, 1986) 313. Whether or not an actual Q document existed, of which there is no record or even any compelling tradition, is not a question which needs to be addressed here. However, I remain skeptical of the existence of any specific Q document, any solutions

it may offer to several of the problems faced in the Synoptics notwithstanding. See Hans-Herbert Stoldt, *History and Criticism of the Marcan Hypothesis* (Macon, GA: Mercer Univ. Press, 1980) 123.

[4]A. B. Bruce asked: "Were the words here collected, all of them, or even the greater number of them, ever spoken by Jesus at any time; have the evangelists not worked up into the discourse a Jewish, or Jewish-Christian, apocalypse, or given us a composition of their own, consisting of certain *logia* of the Master as the nucleus, with additions, modifications, and comments in the light of subsequent events?" *The Expositor's Greek Testament*, W. Robertson Nicoll, ed. (Grand Rapids: Eerdmans, reprint, 1961) I:287.

[5]Henry Alford has noted: "This is one of the points on which the rationalizing interpreters . . . lay the most stress to shew that the prophecy has *failed, . . .* " *The Greek Testament*, revised by Everett Harrison (Chicago: Moody, 1958) I:244.

[6]Joseph A. Fitzmyer, *The Gospel According to Luke (X–XXIV)*, in The Anchor Bible (New York: Doubleday & Co., 1985) 1353.

[7]G. R. Beasley-Murray, *Jesus and the Kingdom of God* (Grand Rapids: Eerdmans, 1986) 334. My emphasis.

[8]See, for example, David Wenham, *The Rediscovery of Jesus' Eschatological Discourse* (Sheffield, England: JSOT Press, 1984); Werner Kummel, *Introduction to the New Testament* (Nashville, TN: Abingdon Press, 1966) 94–95.

[9]E. Meyer, *Ursprung und Anfange des Christentums* (Berlin: Cotta, 1921) I:129. Cited by Fitzmyer, *The Gospel According to Luke*, 1325.

[10]Leonard Goppelt, *The Theology of the New Testament*, translated by John Alsup (Grand Rapids: Eerdmans, 1981) I:59.

[11]A. Carr, *The Gospel According to St. Matthew* in The Cambridge Greek Testament for Schools and Colleges (Cambridge: University Press, 1906) 265.

[12]Fitzmyer, *The Gospel According to Luke*, 1334.

[13]"The Olivet Discourse: An Apocalyptic Timetable," *WTJ* 28 (May 1966) 157.

[14]S. Joseph Kidder, "'This Generation' in Matthew 24:34," *Andrews Seminary Studies*, vol. 21, no. 3, 1983, 203. Hendriksen rejects a combination of chapter 23 with 24 and 25 on the basis of several facts: (1) they were spoken in different places. This assumes that Matthew and Mark are accurate and that Luke's omission of the leaving of the Temple does not require that he views them as still there. We concur with this assumption. Contra I. H. Marshall, *Commentary on Luke* [Grand Rapids: Eerdmans, 1978], p. 752; Fitzmyer, p. 1323; et al. (2) they are addressed to a different audience; (3) the themes are different. William Hendriksen, *Exposition of the Gospel According to Matthew* [Grand Rapids: Baker, 1973] 846.

[15]Kidder, 208.

[16]Ibid., 206–7.

[17]Ibid.

[18]Ibid., 207.

[19]William Hendriksen, *Exposition of the Gospel According to Matthew* (Grand Rapids: Baker, 1973) 846–47. This is not to imply that interpreting prophecy is a simple task. See, for example, David Aune, *Prophecy in Early Christianity* (Grand Rapids: Eerdmans, 1983) 1–22; Berkeley Mickelsen, *Interpreting the Bible* (Grand Rapids: Eerdmans, 1963) 280–305; Paul Tan, *The Interpretation of Prophecy* (Winona Lake, IN: BMH Books, 1974); Henry Virkler, *Hermeneutics: Principles and*

*Processes of Biblical Interpretation* (Grand Rapids: Baker, 1981) 190–209.

[20]Hendricksen, *Matthew*, 846.

[21]Ibid., 857.

[22]Ibid. This is not so different from Robert Gundry's position: "This history stretches from the final phase of Jesus' conflict with the Jewish religious leaders, who represent antinomian leaders in the church, to the last judgment." *Matthew: A Commentary on His Literary and Theological Art* (Grand Rapids: Eerdmans, 1982) 474.

[23]Ibid.

[24]*The Gospel According to Matthew*, 225. Alan McNeile comments: "It is impossible to escape the conclusion that Jesus, as Man, expected the End within the lifetime of His contemporaries." *The Gospel According to St. Matthew* (London: Macmillan, 1957) 355. See also George Beasley-Murray, "Despite all attempts to establish the contrary, there seems to be no escape from the admission that ἡ γενεὰ αὕτη here is to be taken in its natural sense of the generation contemporary with Jesus." *A Commentary on Mark Thirteen* (London: Macmillan, 1957) *in loc.*

[25]Ibid.

[26]Ibid.

[27]Pretribulationists have generally denied the doctrine of a rapture in the discourse. See Gerald Stanton, *Kept From the Hour* (Grand Rapids: Zondervan, 1956) 51–69; John Walvoord, *The Rapture Question* (Findlay, Ohio: Dunham, 1957); Everett Harrison, "The Time of the Rapture in the Light of Matthew 24," *Bibliotheca Sacra* 115 (1956): 109–15. Posttribulationists have found the rapture in the references to the coming of the Son of Man, as in Matt 24:27–31. See George Ladd, *The Blessed Hope* (Grand Rapids: Eerdmans, 1956) 130–61; Robert Gundry, *The Church and the Tribulation* (Grand Rapids: Zondervan, 1973) 129–39.

[28]For one of the most recent expositions from this perspective, see John MacArthur, Jr., *The MacArthur New Testament Commentary: Matthew 24–28* (Chicago: Moody, 1989). The earliest expositor I could find holding this opinion is Robert Govett, *The Prophecy on Olivet* (Norwich, England: Fletcher and Son, 1881).

[29]In any attempt to discover truth, it is not a matter of how many scholars might hold a given view, or how recent any alternative position might be. Even going against a prevailing unanimous opinion is not to be disregarded simply on that basis. Our primary criterion should be accuracy of exegesis. With such problematic passages as this one, with nothing like unanimity at many points, and with serious unexplained difficulties, a new position is often to be preferred, not because of its novelty, but because of the failure of the older views to resolve such difficulties.

[30]*The Scofield Reference Bible*, C. I. Scofield, ed. (New York: Oxford, 1909) 1032.

[31]While Terry's well-known observation may be overstated, it nevertheless should be carefully weighed: "The moment we admit the principle that portions of Scripture contain an occult or double sense we introduce an element of uncertainty in the sacred volume, and unsettle all scientific interpretation." Milton Terry, *Biblical Hermeneutics* (New York: The Methodist Book Concern, 1883) 383.

[32]*The Gospel According to Luke*, 1353.

[33]I. H. Marshall, *Luke*, 780.

[34]G. B. Caird, *The Gospel of St. Luke* (New York: The Seabury Press, 1963) 233.

[35]Ibid.

[36]Ibid., 234.

[37]See the pretribulationist explanation of this text in John Walvoord, *The Rapture Question* (Findlay, OH: Dunham, 1957) 112–13.

[38]*Jesus and the Kingdom of God*, 334.

[39]Donald Guthrie, *Jesus the Messiah* (Grand Rapids: Zondervan, 1972) 297.

[40]Tasker, *Matthew*, 226.

[41]The language of Jesus in 24:2 is very strong: οὐ μὴ ἀφεθῇ ὧδε λίθος ἐπὶ λίθον ὃς οὐ καταλυθήσεται. The double negative is unmistakably emphatic. We could render it: "There shall absolutely not be left here a stone upon a stone which shall not be utterly thrown down." See the descriptions in Josephus, *Wars of the Jews*, book VI; H. Graetz, *A History of the Jews* (Philadelphia: The Jewish Publication Society of America, 1893) II:305–8. It is inferred, for instance, that the Temple was not completely destroyed, although it burned. The huge stones of Herod's Temple were hard, white limestone with some blocks thirty feet long, eighteen feet wide, and twelve feet thick. The Babylonian Talmud says: "He who never saw the temple of Herod never saw a fine building." It was overlaid with beautiful artifacts. Including all the courtyards it covered some twenty acres. "For strength it was like a fortress and it crowned an eminence, making it visible from afar like a snow-capped hill." See the descriptions in Bo Reicke, *The New Testament Era*, David Green, trans. (Philadelphia: Fortress, 1968) 97–100; Josephus, *Wars of the Jews*, book V, chapter V; Tacitus, *Histories*, book V, chapter 8, 1.

[42]"A great building continues to evoke such emotions long after the first time it has been seen, and the writings of Josephus indicate the national pride that Jews had in their temple." I. Howard Marshall, *Commentary on Luke* (Grand Rapids: Eerdmans, 1978) 760.

[43]Alfred Edersheim, *The Life and Times of Jesus the Messiah*, vol. 1 (New York: E. R. Herrick, n.d.) 4.

[44]E. G. Josephus indicates that Titus was disposed to deal more gently with the Jews than would otherwise be the case, due to his affair with Bernece, a Jewess (Josephus, *Wars of the Jews*, book VI; Graetz, *History*, II:305–8). Others have doubted much of what he reports regarding any kindnesses he may attribute to the Roman general. See Lea Roth, "Titus," in *Encyclopaedia Judaica* (Jerusalem: Keter, 1971), vol. 15, 1167–70.

[45]Robert Gundry, *Matthew: A Commentary on His Literary and Theological Art* (Grand Rapids: Eerdmans, 1982) 491.

[46]Ibid.

[47]Ibid.

[48]A problem is in the meaning of "fulfilled." If it were in any way possible to interpret the Greek ἕως ἂν πάντα ταῦτα γένηται differently than as referring to a definite event, it escapes me.

[49]This is often humorously displayed. A recent publication spoke of the great University of Notre Dame football coach, Knute Rockne, indicating his name was pronounced Can-ute. One letter to the editor responded: "Even I k'now that this k'not be right." A Sunday School teacher and seminary professor was once stymied by an adult student who explained that the name Adam in Genesis must mean "an obstruction," since that is what "a dam" is.

[50]*Funk & Wagnalls* Standard Dictionary (New York: Funk & Wagnalls, 1958) I:526.

[51]Walter Bauer, William Arndt and F. Wilbur Gingrich, revised by Wilbur Gingrich and Frederick Danker, *A Greek-English Lexicon of the New Testament* (Chicago: University of Chicago, 2nd ed., 1979) 153–54.

[52]Henry Liddell and Robert Scott, revised by Robert Scott, *A Greek-English Lexicon* (Oxford: Clarendon, 1968) 342.

[53]"Race, stock, kin . . . II. Offspring . . . III. Race . . . b. clan, house . . . c. tribe . . . d. caste . . . e. breed . . . " Ibid., 344.

[54]J. P. Louw, *Semantics of New Testament Greek* (Philadelphia: Fortress, 1982) 34. See also Peter Cotterell and Max Turner, *Linguistics and Biblical Interpretation* (Downers Grove, IL: InterVarsity, 1989) 129–39.

[55]Ibid.

[56]Ibid., 40.

[57]Moises Silva, *Biblical Words and Their Meaning* (Grand Rapids: Zondervan, 1983) 138–59.

[58]*Jesus and the Kingdom of God* (Grand Rapids: Eerdmans, 1986) 333–34.

[59]Francis Brown, S. R. Driver, and Charles Briggs, *A Hebrew and English Lexicon of the Old Testament* (Oxford: Clarendon, 1953) 190.

[60]*Gesenius' Hebrew and Chaldee Lexicon*, Samuel Tregelles, trans. (Grand Rapids: Eerdmans, 1949) 194.

[61]The position that the text is the creation of the evangelist without continuity with the words of the historical Jesus demands a view of the source of the Synoptics which we reject.

[62]This time span is more modern. Older authorities suggested it meant one hundred years to the patriarchs. Robert D. Culver cites as evidence for this *Gesenius' Lexicon*, 26th ed., and C. F. Keil's *Commentary On Genesis.* "dor" in *Theological Wordbook of the Old Testament*, R. Laird Harris et al., eds. (Chicago: Moody, 1980) I:186.

# The Background to the Good Shepherd Discourse in John 10

## Donald L. Fowler

There are few more beloved images from the Bible than that of Christ as our "Good Shepherd." God as our shepherd is a well-known biblical idea common to both testaments. After the NT period, this image of Christ remained popular with the church as it spread west through the gentile world. As it left its original Semitic setting, however, it is clear that the context of the image was quickly lost. While the Shepherd image for Christ would be the most popular pictorial representation in the first four centuries, by the middle of the fifth century A.D., it had all but disappeared from the Church's art.[1] A modest exception to this observation might be made for certain branches of the church whose language was Syriac.[2] As this study is begun, it is important to search for possible explanations for this startling change in imagery. The best place to begin the search is to analyze the biblical "context" where the Shepherd imagery occurs.

### THE HISTORICAL CONTEXT

Students of the Bible who have been introduced to the study of hermeneutics know that the first rule of interpretation is to determine the context.[3] To be more specific, what is the contextual relationship of the term Shepherd to the Old Testament? As is so often the case in biblical studies, the answer is neither simple nor conclusive.

Donald L. Fowler (B.A., Pillsbury Baptist College; M.Div., Th.M., Th.D., Grace Theological Seminary) is Professor of Old Testament and Hebrew at Grace Theological Seminary, Winona Lake, Indiana.

The first point that must be made with vigor is to demonstrate the span of time shepherd appears in various cultures related to the entire biblical period. Scores of ancient Sumerian kings called themselves "shepherd" as early as the third millennium.[4] Often the title was graced with an adjective such as "righteous," "humble," "obedient," "loving," etc.[5] This practice continued until Sumerian fell into disuse. Concurrent with Sumerian were the Akkadian and Babylonian languages where the same usage prevailed. There are slight changes in that the title is now somewhat more common and often becomes descriptive. An example of this may be seen in the title of Adad-nirari I (ca. 1307–1275), "The Shepherd who himself is the door of his heart," or "The Shepherd who provides for the needs of this sanctuaries/temples of the great gods."[6] This same kind of literary imagery was continued in Mesopotamia from its earliest literary period down through the fall of Babylon to Cyrus the Great. It is much more difficult to trace the origins of its usage in Syro-Palestine since so few inscriptions have survived. There are some occurrences in royal literature from Ugarit and, of course, the Old Testament.[7] Also, the title did continue to be used in the intertestamental literature and was attested in the Qumran literature.[8]

The use of the shepherd as a royal title was even more popular in Egypt than elsewhere. So ancient is the image that the Egyptian hieroglyph for the verb "to rule" is that of a shepherd's crook.[9] The basic difference, of course, between kingship in Egypt compared with those around her was that all of Egypt's kings were regarded as a deity.[10] Nonetheless the highly favored title had the same imagery as elsewhere—kingship.

In the Mediterranean world, the oldest references appear to be Homeric.[11] In the Odyssey, "Shepherd of the people" is a standard title for Menelaus, Nestor, Agammemnon, Laertes and Odysseus.[12] The use of shepherd continued as a title throughout the Greek world but perhaps the most famous of its writers was Philo, for whom it was a common literary device.[13]

> . . . for the chase of wild animals is a drilling-ground for the general in fighting the enemy, and the care and supervision of tame animals is a schooling for the king in dealing with his subjects, and therefore kings are called "shepherds for their people," not as a term of reproach but as the highest honor. And, my opinion, based not on the opinions of the multitude but on my own inquiry into the truth of the

matter is that the only perfect king is one who is skilled in the knowledge of shepherding, one who has been trained by management of the inferior creatures to manage the superior.[14]

The use of Philo for comparison requires caution due to his allegorical style, but the fact is that he understood the connection between the image of the shepherd and kingship. The same general connection continued into the Roman era when Tiberius, emperor at the time of Christ's birth chided: "To the governors who recommended burdensome taxes for his provinces, he wrote in answer that it was the part of a good shepherd to shear his flock, not skin it."[15]

One other point needs to be made in concluding this discussion of historical context. The title shepherd was especially revered among the gods, especially those who ranked highest in the pantheon.[16] Just as with the geographical and chronological distribution among earthly kings as described above, so there is also attested the usage of the title among the deities. This leads to the conclusion about the title that it equated automatically with leadership in general and kingship, whether mortal or divine, in particular. Its particular nuance was that it identified that leadership which was benign or meek and reverent, particularly in light of religious faithfulness and the cultus.

While there is not sufficient space to exegete the various Old Testament passages, several can be seen which illustrate that this same literary idiom can be found in the Old Testament as it was in Mesopotamia. It is clearly a title for God as in Ps 80:1: "Oh, give ear, Shepherd of Israel, thou who dost lead Joseph like a flock; Thou who are enthroned above the cherubim, shine forth!"[17] In Isa 40:10–11 the Lord God rules (מֹשְׁלָה). "Like a shepherd He will tend His flock, in His arm He will gather the lambs, and carry them in His bosom; He will gently lead the nursing ewes."[18] Scores of these kinds of passages could be cited but for the present study these will suffice. We should note that the title shepherd is never used of an ancient Israelite king. Rather, Israel's kings were said to have "shepherded." Moses said near his death, "May the Lord, the God of the spirits of all flesh, appoint a man over the congregation, who will go out and come in before them, and who will lead them out and bring them in, that the congregation may not be like sheep which have no shepherd" (Num 27:16–17). The idea of the earthly king "shepherding" was a more common metaphor in the Old Testament than using shepherd as a divine title.[19]

The shepherd metaphor was also used of the leaders of the country in such passages as Jer 2:8, 23; 25:34–36; 50:8, and most importantly Ezekiel 34 which is likely to be the chapter Christ had in mind for his discourse in John 10.

Last, the shepherd metaphor is applied to the coming Messiah in the Old Testament in such passages as Mic 5:1–4 where the ruler (מוֹשֵׁל) was to "go forth for Me to be a ruler in Israel" from "Bethlehem Ephratah . . . of Judah." Ezek 34:22–24 refers to this coming one: "I will set over them one shepherd, My servant David, and he will feed them; he will feed them himself and be their shepherd" (see also 37:24ff.). This juxtapositioning of the coming Shepherd King with Yahweh Himself occurred in Psalm 45 (although the word Shepherd is missing) where at 45:6 God is exalted, "Thy throne O God, is forever and ever; a scepter of uprightness is the scepter of Thy kingdom."[20] Ps 45:6–7 is quoted by the writer of Hebrews in 1:8–9 as proof that Jesus was the Messiah.[21]

In conclusion a number of points can be made from the discussion above. One, the Shepherd title and image is one of the common images of ancient Near Eastern royal designations. Two, the image is also used in the same way in the Old Testament. Three, it is used for the Messiah who, at times, is clearly identical to God.

## JOHANNINE CONTEXT

The explanation for John's usage of the Old Testament often hinges on the presuppositions of the interpreter. Generally, scholars trained in semitics are more likely to see the source of John's appeal to be the Old Testament. Scholars trained in the classics are more likely to explain the book in light of hellenistic motifs and ideas which penetrated the semitic world.[22] There can be no doubt that hellenism had made inroads into the ancient semitic world.[23] It is quite another matter, however, to argue that the various books of the NT were written with that world view in mind in either its content or audience.[24] In his *New Testament Introduction* Guthrie wrote, "So much emphasis has been placed on Hellenistic influences on John's Gospel that the part played by Old Testament ideas has not always been fully realized."[25] Happily, the tide has today moved overwhelmingly in the direction of the Old Testament.[26] Du Plessis has said that "It is without a doubt the most Jewish Gospel among the four."[27]

If it may be agreed that John's citations[28] and ideas are drawn from the Old Testament, the point also needs to be made that John's gospel, for all its uniqueness, fits well with the other Synoptics. "The attitude of the Johannine Jesus toward the Old Testament is very close to that reported in the synoptic tradition."[29] This is, in my opinion, specifically true in the shepherd imagery. Concerning Matthew it has been written, "more than any other Gospel, Matthew emphasizes Jesus' messiahship."[30] One of the images that all the gospels share in identifying Christ is that He is Israel's shepherd.[31] In a seminal work, Francis Martin has shown that Matthew used shepherd as a primary means of identification of Christ as Messiah. He comments that " . . . Mt builds upon the following combinations to construct an inclusive figure: Shepherd-king; Shepherd-Son of David; Shepherd-servant; Shepherd-Vicar of Yahweh."[32] In every instance in his gospel the Shepherd is the long-predicted messiah who heals. The image of the Shepherd who heals is, nonetheless, discarded in Matthew's book beginning with His final entry into Jerusalem. Now the Messiah would lay down His life and suffer for the sheep as does the messianic shepherd in Zechariah 9–14.[33]

If the term shepherd was so common in the ancient Near East and that same idiom is repeated in the Old Testament and, with only slight modifications, taken up in the gospels, it is most surprising to see how many commentators do not see the Good Shepherd as either royal or messianic. Bultmann admits the chapter in John 10 "corresponds to the Old Testament tradition." But then he says, "There is, however, a decisive difference in John 10, namely that the shepherd is not thought of as the Messianic ruler; there are no traces whatsoever of the kingly figure."[34] While few would agree with that stark evaluation, very few commentators are willing to interpret the series of discourses in 9–10 as messianic, and especially as royal.

Perhaps the chief reason for this is that they treat John 10 as if it was an allegory.[35] John does not introduce the story with the word allegory but *paroimia* which is certainly an equivalent of the Hebrew *māšāl*. In the rest of the New Testament it only appears in 2 Peter 2:22 and John 16:25 (twice) and 16:29. In John's usage it appears to mean "hidden, obscure speech."[36] Concerning a definition of allegory Stein has written:

> In an allegory the subject is described by circumstances and details
> that indicate that the subject as well as the circumstances and details

refer to something else. An allegory is therefore a guise under which the intention of the story is different from what it first appears. In an allegory the details of the story are not simply local coloring to fill out the story, as in the story and example parables, but are of great importance and must be "interpreted."[37]

Since it is quite impossible to identify key elements in this *paroimia*, it does not fit well with Stein's definition of an allegory. Perhaps it would be best to avoid nomenclature like parable and allegory since there is little consensus on definition. Even if John's *paroimia* was classified as an extended metaphor or parable,[38] too often there is the failure to "perceive the distinction between the metaphor and its significance."[39] It is now clear that the parables of Jesus were not meant to be clear.[40] When it was imperative that his disciples understand the parable, Jesus would then explain it to them. More often than not, then, the parable was an important means for the self-presentation of Christ to the public but usually understood only by His inner circle. The message of this parable is the same in all three discourses: it is christological which results in salvation for those who "know" His voice.

Another objection to John using the Good Shepherd as a messianic symbol is that he doesn't quote specifically from the Old Testament. C. K. Barrett wrote that it's not

> . . . that John had no use for the Old Testament; what they suggest is that he used it in a way of his own. It is his method to deal not so much with Old Testament texts as with Old Testament themes. One of the clearest examples is provided by his description of Jesus as the Good Shepherd (10:1–16). In this passage no part of the Old Testament is quoted, but no one familiar with the Old Testament can read it would recalling a number of places where similar imagery is used— for example, Psalms 23; 80; Ezekiel 34; and not the least the fact that David, the ancestor and prototype of the Messiah was a shepherd. Without pinning himself to a particular prophecy, John takes up a central Old Testament theme and familiar Old Testament language and concentrates them upon the figure of Jesus.[41]

Furthermore, "symbolism in John is not an element in the Gospel but a dimension of the Gospel as a whole, namely, its characteristic revelatory mode."[42] The symbol in John 10 is the Shepherd (and that may be taken to mean he is proclaiming Himself as a political leader, king, Messiah or God) and the response to the symbol is found in v 24, "If you are the Christ, tell us plainly."[43]

The structure of this chapter has often led commentators to deny a direct connection with the Old Testament.[44] The literary integrity of the chapter has, however, been proven to be of the highest quality in a massively important work by Menken.[45] He has shown that chapters 9–10 are a literary triumph of the first order.[46] "Careful attention to the literary character of the Fourth Gospel will quickly reveal how pervasive has been the influence of the OT in its composition."[47] This is also evidenced in his use of numbers.

> The writer of the fourth gospel makes much use of number pattern, in a manner similar to that which pervades Revelation. There is repeated use of sets of three. The narrator, for example, records three Passovers and three other feasts that Jesus attended. Early in the book John the Baptist three times states his witness to Christ's messiahship. Late in the narrative Jesus is three times condemned. He also speaks three times from the cross and makes three appearances after His resurrection. There are three denials by Peter and three stages in Christ's restoration of Peter. There is a similar use of the number seven. The writer structures the central part of his narrative around seven great miracles or "signs" that Jesus performed. Equally important is the pattern of seven statements by Jesus beginning with the important formula "I am" and followed by a metaphoric description of Jesus' person and work. . . .[48]

The effect of these observations is to take special note that one must not approach John's text as if its meaning was obvious.[49]

The last point of introduction is to understand the ἐγώ εἰμι (*egō eimi*) phrases. "The christological ἐγώ in John's Gospel is the catchword for a christocentric view of the world."[50] The emphasis is truly striking as McArthur has shown: "Passages where the word order is reversed or words intervene between the *egō* and the *eimi* are not included in the following figures":

| | | | |
|---|---|---|---|
| Total NT | 47 | Mark | 3 |
| John | 24 | Luke | 4 |
| Apocalypse | 4 | Acts | 7 |
| Joh. Ep. | 0 | Rest of NT[51] | 0 |
| Matthew | 5 | | |

There are two current explanations for the meaning of the phrase. Schnackenburg wrote that " . . . the formal structure of the revealer's utterance was probably influenced by the soteriological type of discourse current in Eastern Hellenism."[52] The overwhelming majority of scholars, however, seek its origins in the Old Testament where two primary locations have been proposed. Stevens has pointed out that

> The phrase *egō eimi* appears in the LXX, however, as the translation for many direct proclamatory statements by YHWH. The most important in the light of Bultmann's objection is the rendering of *ănî* YHWH ("I am Yahweh") by the simple *egō eimi* in Isa 45:18. Frequently the statement by God, *ănî hû* (literally "I he," meaning "I am he") receives the translation *egō eimi* (cf. Isa 41:4, 43:10, 46:4). *Anî hû* is an alternate for *ănî YHWH* and it is an appropriate way of expressing that he is the only God.[53]

There can be little doubt that John's *egō eimi* is his way of telling us that the Christ was the *anî hû* which was Isaiah's way of saying YHWH.

An alternative view has been put forth by Odeberg who sought to relate *egō eimi* to the revelation of the tetragrammaton in Exod 3:14[54] "'Εγὼ εἰμί = *ehyeh*, again, as implying the appropriation of the Divine Name, would equal 'I and the Father are one', the central, reiterated thesis of Jesus in John."[55] Harner has objected to this because the full etymological phrase *ehyeh ʾser ʾehyeh* "I am who I am" in the LXX because "In the clause *egō eimi ho ōn*, the *egō eimi* is used not absolutely but merely to introduce the predicate *ho ōn*. Only this predicate can be regarded as a proper name." Since approximately half of John's *egō eimi* sayings are absolute rather than predicate, he feels that the *anî hû* formula from Isaiah is the source.[56] Stauffer, however, is correct in writing, "This emphatic formula (egō eimi) [addition mine] rests ultimately on the 'I am that I am' of Exodus 3:14."[57] The great revelation of the etymology of the divine name in Exodus 3 is the vehicle John uses for the revelation of the divine Person in his gospel. It would seem, therefore, that John was actually uniting the title *anî hû* in Isaiah with the idea of "I will be with you," an idea which is at the core of the revelation of the divine name in Exodus 3.

The opening "parable" in John 10 is divided into either a five or six verse unit. It should, however, be understood as a continuation of the events in chapter 9. Beasley-Murray has suggested that 10:1–21 is set in close association with the narrative of the healing of the blind man[58] in the period following the Festival of Tabernacles, while 10:22–39 falls within the Festival of Dedication, shortly after the preceding events.[59] This would mean that there were several months between the festivals, but John has not made clear in his text where the chronological disposition should be made.[60] There are, however, a number of things which connect 10:1–21 with chapter 9. There is the common element of unbelief that the two chapters share. Furthermore, as Brown suggested, " . . . the example of the blind man who refused to follow the guidance of the Pharisees and turned to Jesus is not unlike the example of the sheep in x 4–5 who will not follow a stranger but recognize the voice of their true master."[61] Last, both chapters open with the predicate *egō eimi* (I am the light of the world in 9:5 and I am the door of the sheep in 10:7).

Concerning the structure of 10:1–6 Menken has some pertinent suggestions:

> In 10,1b–2, Jesus speaks first about the "thief and robber," who enters the sheepfold in an illegal way, and secondly about the "shepherd of the sheep," who enters in a legal way; in 10,4b–5 he speaks first about the shepherd whom the sheep follow, and secondly about the "stranger" who they will not follow. So, the two parallelisms together constitute in 10,1–5 an inclusion in chiastic order: thief and robber—shepherd (10,1b.2)—shepherd—stranger (10,4b–c.5).[62]

The purpose of v 3 is to be a hinge in which the door is opened only to the shepherd and he leads them out and thus anticipates vv 4–5.

It is difficult to know how to interpret the various persons in the *paroimia*. They are a shepherd, a doorkeeper, thieves, hirelings, and the question whether the door is to be personalized. It is perhaps no surprise that his audience is confused! I doubt that there is any character identification that is possible beyond the idea that there is one legitimate leader of the flock, Christ, and, perhaps, the illegitimate leaders might be the Pharisees. For John to have mixed his metaphors here is not at all unusual in his book:

> But such statements are not uncommon in this Gospel. Jesus is the Bread of Life (6:35), and He gives it (6:51). He speaks the truth (8:45f.) and He is the truth (14:6). Throughout the Gospel He is depicted as showing men the way, and He is the way (14:6).[63]

Since "shepherd" in v 2 is anarthrous, it might be argued that such a christological interpretation of the term is premature but

Colwell has argued that "The absence of the article does not make the predicate indefinite or qualitative when it precedes the verb; it is indefinite in this position only when the context demands it. The context makes no such demand in the Gospel of John."[64] Or as Schnackenburg put it,

> The contrasting of "thief and robber" with "shepherd of the sheep" is a general and typical procedure when, as here, normal conditions are described. And herein lies the explanation of why there is no article and of the fact that "thief and robber" is singular. In verse 2, "shepherd of the sheep" can thus stand for one shepherd among others and equally for the one shepherd looking after all the sheep. Not till verse 3f do we gather that a particular shepherd is meant. . . .[65]

At any rate, this *paroimia* sets the stage for the clearer christological revelation that follows. The ambiguity of the *paroimia* is clarified for those who know his voice by his skillful employment of the word "voice" which in John's gospel is only used in a supernatural sense.[66] The message of the *paroimia* is subtle and able to be heard with varying capacities.

It is impossible to know for certain if the new discourse begun in v 7 was made at the same occasion as the *paroimia*. There are, however, a number of observations that would lead the interpreter to think it was. John's use of "therefore" (οὖν) would seem to suggest this new discourse is a commentary on the first and seeks to answer their confusion—"they did not understand what those things were which he had been saying to them." The repeated use of "truly, truly" suggests a continuity with the same words starting the *paroimia*. He interprets the meaning of the *paroimia* with the revelation "I am the door of the sheep." Because of the way John uses the formula, we no longer have a *paroimia*; He is now making His claim clear.

It is not possible to identify the Old Testament source for this title although Ps 118:20 is perhaps the best guess: "This is the gate of the Lord; the righteous will enter through it." Indeed, vv 22–27 are clearly messianic. At any rate, it is most natural to interpret the Door here in relation to the sheep who enter by the Redeemer into the salvation of the kingdom of God.[67] Schnackenburg captured the importance of vv 7–10 with his comment.

> Jesus' double self-predication unfolds less from the image (door) than from the subject matter. Through the first I-word, false claims and

seizures are parried (verse 8), and, through the second, Jesus' salvational importance for those who are his own is illustrated (verse 9).[68]

The "double self-predication" is the fact that the *egō eimi* formula starts the discourse (v 7b) and repeats it (v 9a). Menken sees the structure:

| 10:7b | a | Amen-formula |
|---|---|---|
| 7b | | 'I am the door . . .' |
| 8 | b | thieves and robbers |
| 9 | a | 'I am the door . . .' |
| 10a | b | the thief |
| 10b | a | 'I came . . .'[69] |

Moreover, the passage displays a bipartition: 10,7–8.9–10. Both parts begin with and ἐγώ εἰμι saying and contain a sentence about the "thieves and robbers" or the "thief." In the first part, the sentences end in προβάτων and πρόβατα respectively; the second begins and ends with a sentence starting with ἐγώ. 10,10 contains a clear antithetic parallelism.[70]

This pericope, then, has made clearer to the audience that Christ is making divine claims but they are still confused.

This third discourse (vv 11–18) is not only longer but more complex with characters and activity. At first blush, it looks like genuine allegory. Even a quick glance at Ezekiel 34 shows that this is the source for Christ's self-revelation in John 10:11–18. In John 10:3, Jesus said ἐξάγει αὐτὰ while in Ezek 34:13 (LXX) God said ἐξάξω αὐτοῦ. Again, in the Good Shepherd story, great emphasis is laid on the fact that there is a knowing relationship between the sheep and the Shepherd. In 10:4 it is said that "the sheep follow him because they know his voice," and the idea is preceded in Ezek 34:27, 31 where in that day "they will know that I am the Lord."

Still another example of this interdependence may be seen in the reference to pasture in John 10:9 and ἐν νομῇ ἀγαθῇ in Ezek 34:14. The predations of the beasts in Ezek 34:5, 8 compare favorably with the attacks mentioned in John 10:12 as well as the Synoptics. There is conceptual similarity in that there is severe judgment on the bad shepherds whose flocks are scattered. The general theme of scattered sheep and regathering by YHWH compare favorably. Finally, the reference to one flock in 10:16 (μία ποίμην) may well have been prompted by the messianic prediction in Ezek 34:27–31. So similar are the two accounts that Gerhardsson has suggested that " . . . we should think of John 10:1–16 as a *messianic midrash* [his emphasis] on Ezekiel 34."[71]

The similarities are so numerous and striking that they actually highlight the few differences. In John 10, the Good Shepherd gives ζωὴν αἰώνιον, a gift unique to the New Testament picture of the Shepherd. In addition, the basis for this "eternal life" is taken from Zech 13:7ff. rather than Ezekiel. In a striking reversal, it is the Shepherd who searches out the wolf so that he may die, thereby granting life for His flock. Ezekiel 34 is much more allegorical than the Good Shepherd story which has scarcely any pastoral imagery beyond the Shepherd, a wolf and a hireling. Concerning the various characters in this discourse it has been observed:

> But in the Johannine perspective, wolf (singular) is simply the symbol of threatening danger and brings the hirelings conduct to light. As for "hireling," it is not an image for those sub-shepherds appointed by the chief shepherd; rather, it stands in contrast to the owner who loves his sheep and devotes himself entirely to them.[72]

Indeed, it is senseless in a genuinely pastoral setting for a hireling to run from a single wolf which would then kill a larger number of sheep.[73] Then too, any sturdy and properly armed shepherd was more than a match for the wolf.[74] The most glaring inconsistency with pastoral imagery is the repeated declaration "I lay down my life for my sheep." The good shepherd would do better to take the life of the wolf because with the shepherd's death the sheep now have no shepherd! It would seem, in retrospect, that all three discourses use pastoral imagery only as a foil as each sought to make its main point.

It will always be impossible to know exactly how His audience understood His statements, but this last discourse has led some of them to say he has a demon (v 20). Still, His message was just ambiguous enough to be understood in several ways. He may have been simply picturing Himself as the Messiah, or He may have been claiming something new and scandalous. "How long will You keep us in suspense? If you are the Christ, tell us plainly." This led to the point of the parable itself, "I and the Father are one." It is especially important to note that in vv 25–29 Christ returned to the sheep/shepherd imagery to answer their question. No better image from the Old Testament could be found to communicate that YHWH and His Messiah were identical.

## CONCLUSION

In conclusion, a number of statements need to be brought together. It was noted initially that the title/epithet of shepherd was used throughout the ancient world by both kings and deities. Invariably, it evoked the idea of a beneficent leader who piously exercised his rule. The Old Testament continued that practice except that the title is reserved for God. It was not uncommon, however, for the image or its nomenclature to be used for leaders. There are evidences that it was used in the intertestamental literature, occasionally in messianic texts. Most importantly, both the Synoptic gospels and John use it in a messianic way.

John alone combined most dramatically the person of the Messiah with YHWH Himself. His unique use of the formula ἐγώ εἰμι with the predicate was the means by which he made that self-revelation clearer. This finds its climax at the end of the discourses in John 9–10 with the unprecedented statement, "I and the Father are One." Up to this point, in John's gospel, Jesus had not yet made it public that He was the Messiah. "By his subtle and careful use of the phrase ἐγώ εἰμι he taught the truth concerning his own divinity and at the same time his submission to the Father."[75] The result is such that the theme of the story, indeed of his book, is christological. Because of the new understanding that Messiah and God are one, the Messiah is uniquely able to offer those who believe eternal life.[76] "But these have been written that you may believe that Jesus is the Christ, the Son of God; and that believing you may have life in His name" (John 20:31).

# NOTES

[1]See Boniface Ramsay, "A Note on the Disappearance of the Good Shepherd from Early Christian Art," *HTR* 76:3 (July 1983): 375. Henry Leclerq is able to cite more than 300 examples from the first four centuries in *Dictionnaire d'archéologie chrétienne et de liturgie* (Paris: Letouzey et Ané, 1924); see the long quotation that forms the conclusion to the article by William R. Cook and Samuel D. Accorso, "The Image of the Good Shepherd in pre-Reformation Christianity," *Proceedings of the PMR Conference* 1 (1976): 102, where they wrote: "In the first fifteen hundred years of Christianity, therefore, the image of the Good Shepherd underwent a significant series of metamorphoses. At first a pagan motif was borrowed and associated with John 10 and Luke 15 as well as a series of the Old Testament texts and had strong

eschatological overtones. Gregory the Great applied the pastoral imagery to the bishops and especially the pope, relying on John 21. Advocates of the papal hierocratic theory used especially the John 21 text to strengthen their claims. Finally, in the late Middle Ages, poets and theologians employed the image to criticize the ecclesiastical hierarchy and even the local parsons. Thus, a study of Good Shepherd imagery is not only interesting in its own right but reflects the great changes that took place from the time when Christians were a small and persecuted minority to the corruption and neglect which was in large part responsible for the Protestant Reformation."

[2]Robert Murray, *Symbols of Church and Tradition: a Study in Early Syriac Tradition* (Cambridge: University Press, 1975). As the church moved west, the iconography for the Shepherd was clearly adapted from pagan art forms, particularly for the Greek god Hermes. See Paula Savage, "The Good Shepherd Theme in Ancient Art," *Biblical Illustrator* (Winter 1985): 59–64. It seems quite clear that whatever it meant in the ancient oriental setting has been lost over these many years.

[3]There is a great deal being written in this area but several fine works are to be commended: D. A. Caron and John D. Woodbridge, eds., *Hermeneutics, Authority, and Canon* (Grand Rapids: Zondervan, 1986), and Earl D. Radmacher and Robert D. Preus, eds., *Hermeneutics, Inerrancy, and the Bible* (Grand Rapids: Zondervan, 1984).

[4]The standard work listing such examples is M.-J. Seux, *Épithèts Royales: Akkadiennes et Sumériennes* (Paris: Letouzey et Ané, 1967) especially 441–46. Also helpful is William W. Hallo, *Early Mesopotamian Royal Titles: A Philogic and Historical Analysis*, AOS 43 (New Haven: American Oriental Society, 1957). The classic for the titles of deities is Knut Leonard Tallqvist, *Akkadische Götterepitheta*, Studia Orientalia Edidit Societas Orientalis Fennica, 7 (Helsingforsia: Societas Orientalis Fennica, 1938) reprinted in 1984 by Georg Olms.

[5]Seux, *Épithèt Royales*, 441–46.

[6]Seux, *Épithèt Royales*, 248.

[7]For the most complete work on the subject, see Donald Fowler, "The Context of the Good Shepherd Discourses," unpublished Th.D. dissertation, Grace Theological Seminary, 1981.

[8]See Theodor H. Gaster, *The Dead Sea Scriptures* (Garden City: Doubleday, 1964) 332–39.

[9]"The shepherd's crook denoted especially the kingship of Osiris, and the sign for it, *ḥek*, was also used as the ideogram of the small letters word *ḥek*, 'to rule.'" Maurice A. Canney, "Ancient Concepts of Kingship," Oriental Studies in Honour of Cursetji Pavry (London: Oxford, 1953) 64.

[10]There was no "gradual" development of this phenomena because the first king was already regarded as god incarnate. See the opening chapters in John A. Wilson, *The Culture of Ancient Egypt* (Chicago: University of Chicago, 1971). The classic volume for studying kingship in the semitic world is Henri Frankfort, *Kingship and the Gods: A Study of Ancient Near Eastern Religion as the Integration of Society and Nature* (Chicago: University of Chicago, 1948). He also deals with Egyptian views.

[11]Homer, *The Odyssey*, translated by A. T. Murray, LCL, ed. E. Capps et al. (Cambridge: Harvard, 1927), in vol. 1, see 79, 103, 109; in vol. 2, see 71, 85, 159, 201, 281, 429, and 437.

[12]Fowler, "Good Shepherd," 64–66.

[13]See especially J. Quasten, "Der Gut Hirt in hellenistischer und früchristlicher Logostheologie," in *Heilige Ueberlieferung: Auschnitte für der Geschichte des Monchtums und des heiligen Kultes*, ed. O. Casel (Munster: Herwegen, 1938) 51–58.

[14]"Moses," translated by F. H. Colson, in *Philo*, Vol. 6, Loebs Classical Library, 309. The point might be added that Philo's use of this as a term for royalty is all the more striking because he was so deeply influenced by Greek thought and literary techniques.

[15]Suetonius, "The Lives of the Caesars, Book III: Tiberius," in *Loebs Classical Library*, 341.

[16]Indeed, the very idea of kingship among mortals is only possible because the great gods have given it. See the translation by Thorkild Jacobsen, *The Sumerian King List, Assyriological Studies* 11 (Chicago: University of Chicago, 1939), where the text emphasizes that kingship was given to the first kings following the flood and three are called "shepherd." Note also the pious statements of king Urninurta:

> The wise god, the lord, who determines the destinies,
> has spoken faithfully to him, An to Urninurta,
> in the land of Sumer he has made him the highest . . .
> a royal throne on an eternally fixed foundation,
> the highest shepherd's crook which gathers all the *mes* in the land of Sumer,
> a righteous sceptre which keeps watch over the numerous men he has given
> Urninurta

Quoted from Helmer Ringgren, *Religions of the Ancient Near East* (Philadelphia: Westminster, 1973) 37.

[17]"Thou who are enthroned above the cherubim" is a royal title also found in Ps 99:1 and goes back to 1 Sam 4:4 and 2 Sam 6:2 where it was an ancient title descriptive of Yahweh's presence above the ark. Mitchel Dahood, *Psalms II (51–100)*, AB 17 (Garden City: Doubleday, 1968) 255.

[18]One cannot help but notice the same kind of metaphorical language in Hammurabi's epilogue to his law code: "The great gods have called me, and I am indeed a shepherd who brings peace, whose sceptre is just; my pleasant shade is spread over my city, in my bosom I have carried the people of the land of Shumer and Accad. . . . " G. R. Driver and John C. Miles, *The Babylonian Laws*, Vol. 2 (Oxford: Clarendon Press, 1955) 97.

[19]This is likely due to the nature of the OT literature which contains very little of the kind of official documents found in the Mesopotamian royal archives. Probably the most important example of royal shepherding would be 2 Samuel 7, especially v 7, although much of the chapter is characterized by royal language and metaphors identical to those in the ancient Near East. Notice also 2 Sam 5:2 where David speaks to the tribes at Hebron, "Previously, when Saul was king over us, you were the one who led Israel out and in. And the Lord said to you, 'You will shepherd My people Israel, and you will be a ruler over Israel.'"

[20]The scepter and the shepherd are virtually inseparable in the ancient literature as it speaks about kingship. See E. Douglas Van Buren, *Symbols of the Gods in Mesopotamian Art*, Analecta Biblica 23 (Rome: Biblical Institute, 1945) 142ff. Perhaps the best known pairing of the two is Psalm 23. Note the quotation from Hammurabi in fn 18 above.

[21]Besides the commentaries see Simon Kistemaker, *The Psalm Citations in the*

*Epistle to the Hebrews* (Amsterdam: Wed. G. van Soest N.V., 1961) and Sidney G. Sowers, *The Hermeneutic of Philo and Hebrews*, Basel Studies of Theology 1 (Zurich: Evz-verlag, 1965). Reim has said, "Psalm 45.7 f. is the only OT passage where, as it seems, God speaks to God, God speaks to the Messiah, the Messiah is God." Gunter Reim, "Jesus as God in the Fourth Gospel: The Old Testament Background," *NTS* 30:1 (Jan. 1984): 158–60. On the problem of the citation itself, see the articles by Roger Nicole, Ronald F. Youngblood and S. Lewis Johnson in *Hermeneutics*, ed. by Earl D. Radmacher and Robert D. Preus, 765–99.

[22]Since 1982, the following articles analyzing scholarly literature on John have been published. John F. O'Grady, "Recent Developments in Johannine Studies," *BTB* 12:2 (April 1982): 54–58; Adela Yarbro Collins, "New Testament Perspectives: The Gospel of John," *JSOT* 22 (Feb. 1982): 47–53; D. A. Carson, "Recent Literature on the Fourth Gospel: Some Reflections," *Them* 9:1 (Sept. 1983): 8–18; R. Kysar, "The Fourth Gospel: A Report on Recent Research," *Principat* 25:3, *Aufstieg und Niedergang der Römischen Welt*, ed. Wolfgang Haase (New York: Walter de Gruyter, 1985): 2389–480; Donald Foster, "John Come Lately: the Belated Evangelist," *The Bible and Narrative Tradition*, ed. Frank McConnell (New York: Oxford University Press, 1986) 113–31; John A. Burns, "Commenting on Commentaries on the Book of John," *CurTM* 3:1 (Fall 1988): 185–98; Moises Silva, "Approaching the Fourth Gospel," *CurTM* 3:1 (Fall 1988): 17–29; D. A. Carson, "Selected Recent Studies of the Fourth Gospel," *Them* 14:2 (Jan./Feb. 1989): 57–64.

[23]Probably the best single treatment showing those inroads is Martin Hengel, *Judaism and Hellenism*, 2 vols. (Philadelphia: Fortress, 1974). It is one thing, however, to demonstrate the concrete evidences of hellenism and quite another to show that the uniqueness of hellenism was embraced by the populace. My own view is that hellenistic thought and practices were accepted by the aristocratic class rather than the masses. In fact, the terrible events of the Maccabean war, in all likelihood had alienated all but the nobility. See the interesting, but occasionally contradictory, discussion in Donald E. Gowan, *Bridge Between the Testaments: a Reappraisal of Judaism from the Exile to the Birth of Christianity*, Pittsburgh Theological Monograph Series, 14 (Pittsburgh: The Pickwick Press, 1976), especially 89–109.

[24]The classic example of a hellenistic approach to this gospel is C. H. Dodd, *Historical Tradition in the Fourth Gospel* (Cambridge: University Press, 1963) and his earlier work, *The Interpretation of the Fourth Gospel* (Cambridge: University Press, 1953). This approach has been continued in the highly influential work of Rudolf Schnackenburg, *The Gospel According to John*, 3 vols. (New York: Seabury Press, 1980).

[25]Donald Guthrie, *New Testament Introduction* (Downers Grove: InterVarsity Press, 1973) 237. Other sources for John's material have been suggested. Rudolf Bultmann, *The Gospel of John: A Commentary*, translated by G. R. Beasley-Murray (Philadelphia: Westminster, 1971), in 1925 originally published the view that the origin for John's imagery was Mandaean and for decades influenced the majority of scholars working on John's gospel. This view has now been completely rejected. Some have argued for a gnostic influence such as J. Becker, "Beobachtungen zum Dualismus in Johannesevangelium," *ZNW* 65 (1–2, 1974): 71–87 and G. Stemberger, "'Er kam in sein Eigentum.' Das Johannesevangelium im Dialog mit der Gnosis," *Wort und Warheit* 28 (6, 1973): 435–52. This view also has faded. Note the highly influential book by Edwin Yamauchi, *Pre-Christian Gnosticism: A Survey of the Proposed Evidences*

(Grand Rapids: Eerdmans, 1973).

[26]Kysar, "The Fourth Gospel," 2417, wrote, "If anything, the shift of scholarship in recent decades has been toward the elucidation of OT and rabbinic thought in the gospel. It is instructive that when W. F. Howard wrote his survey of then recent criticism of the FG [fourth gospel] in 1931 the chapter devoted to the background of the thought of the gospel was devoid of any discussion of OT and rabbinic thought. Today our attention must in contrast give extensive attention to this alternative."

[27]I. J. Du Plessis, "The Lamb of God in the Fourth Gospel," *A South African Perspective on the New Testament*, ed. J. H. Petzer and P. J. Martin (Leiden: Brill, 1986) 146. This dramatic shift is also evidenced in the view that John may now be understood to be the earliest of the gospels. See John A. T. Robinson, *The Priority of John* (Oak Park, IL: Meyer-Stone, 1987), where he argues for the view although the final redaction according to him, was much later. The discussion may be followed in Ralph P. Martin, *New Testament Foundations: A Guide for Christian Students*, vol. 1 (Grand Rapids: Eerdmans, 1975) 271–87, and especially 281. Note also the book review of Robinson in *JBL* 108:1 (Spring 1989): 156–58 by D. Moody Smith.

[28]See especially Edwin D. Freed, *Old Testament Quotations in the Gospel of John*, NovTSup 11 (Leiden: Brill, 1965).

[29]Robert M. Grant, "Jesus and the Old Testament," *The Authoritative Word: Essays on the Nature of Scripture*, ed. Donald McKim (Grand Rapids: Eerdmans, 1983) 23.

[30]Lloyd Gaston, "The Messiah of Israel as Teacher of the Gentiles: The Setting of Matthew's Christology," *Interpreting the Gospels*, ed. James Luther Mays (Philadelphia: Fortress, 1981) 87.

[31]Note, for example, the article by Kenneth E. Bailey, "Psalm 23 and Luke 15: A Vision Expanded," *IBS* 15 (1990): 54–71, where he makes an interesting attempt to connect the shepherd imagery of Psalm 23 with Luke's story of the Prodigal.

[32]Francis Martin, "The Image of Shepherd in the Gospel of Saint Matthew," *ScEs* 27:3 (1975): 297. This is an excellent article which should be studied further.

[33]Ibid. See also the excellent work by R. T. France, *Jesus and the Old Testament: His Application of Old Testament Passages to Himself and His Mission* (London: Tyndale, 1971), especially 103–10. Speaking of Zechariah 9–14 he said, "This section introduces four figures which may be taken as messianic: the king riding on an ass (9:9–10), the good shepherd (11:4–14), the one 'whom they have pierced' (12:10), and the smitten shepherd (13:7). Thus the four passages are seen as four aspects of a single Messianic conception, 'the Shepherd-King', presenting successive phases of his coming and the reaction of the people. It is a conception built up through reflection on the figure of the Servant of Yahweh in Isaiah, and therefore concentrating on the problem of rejection, suffering and death of the Messiah" (104). These are precisely the themes and issues of John 9–10.

[34]Bultmann, *John*, 387. Consider also the statement by Vincent Taylor, *The Names of Jesus* (London: Macmillan, 1954) 90, "While, then, we can hardly call the title (shepherd) a technical name for the Messiah, it has distinct Messianic associations." As Martin, "The Image of Shepherd," 272–73, showed in Matt 2:6, it is the theme that introduces Christ's kingship. There Matthew has conflated Mic 5:1 and 2 Sam 5:2 to answer the Magi's question in 2:2: "Where is He who has been born *King* of the Jews?" By quoting Micah he is answering the Magi's question "where" (Bethlehem) and

by quoting 2 Sam 5:2 he is answering "who," that is, the shepherd/king.

[35]Thus William Hendriksen, *The Gospel of John* (London: Banner of Truth Trust, 1959) 97, wrote: "In the interpretation of this sublime allegory commentators differ widely." The overwhelming number agree: "The allegory of the sheep and shepherd makes an immediate appeal to the imagination. It provides the most endearing aspect of the Johannine portrait of Jesus, which otherwise tends to be remote and forbidding." Barnabas Lindars, *The Gospel of John*, NCB (Greenwood, SC: Attic, 1977) 352.

[36]*TDNT*, s.v. "παροιμία," by Friedrich Hauck, 5:856.

[37]Robert H. Stein, *The Method and Message of Jesus' Teachings* (Philadelphia: Westminster, 1978) 38.

[38]Ibid., 15–16, where he observes that "A metaphor like a simile, is a comparison between two essentially unlike things. In contrast to a simile, however, where an explicit comparison is made ('The eye is like a lamp for the body'), the metaphor makes an implicit comparison ('The eye is the lamp of the body'). The Gospels contain numerous examples of such figures of speech, for Jesus was fond of using analogies. As in the case of the simile, so here also it is evident that some metaphors can also be defined as parables, so that any absolute distinction between the two is impossible." In fact, the "Parable of the Good Shepherd" is rarely treated in books specifically on parables. It is not mentioned in David Wenham, *The Parables of Jesus* (Downers Grove: InterVarsity, 1989); Bernard Brandon Scott, *Hear then the Parable: A Commentary on the Parables of Jesus* (Minneapolis: Fortress, 1989); Warren S. Kissinger, *The Parables of Jesus: A History of Interpretation and Bibliography*, The American Theological Library Association Series, 4 (Metuchen, NJ: Scarecrow, 1979).

[39]Francis Lyall, "Of Metaphors and Analogies: Legal Language and Covenant Theology," *SJT* 32:1 (1979): 3. This excellent article clarifies that "appearance" and "intent" are often confused in parabolic and metaphorical language. This has been the precise problem in John 10. See also the intriguing article by Birger Gerhardsson, "The Narrative Meshalim in the Old Testament Books and in the Synoptic Gospels," *To Touch the Text: Biblical and Related Studies in Honor of Joseph A. Fitzmyer*, ed. by Maurya P. Horgan and Paul J. Kobelski (New York: Crossroad, 1989) 289–304 who calls for the terms aphoristic meshalim (Proverbs) and narrative meshalim (a broad term similar to "story"). Interestingly, the narrative meshalim in the synoptics all concentrated on one theme, that is, "the one necessary thing" (p. 303).

[40]See discussion in Wenham, *Parable*, 239–45.

[41]C. K. Barrett, "The Interpretation of the Old Testament in the New," *The Authoritative Word: Essays on the Nature of Scripture*, ed. Donald McKim (Grand Rapids: Eerdmans, 1983) 53.

[42]Sandra Schneiders, "History and Symbolism in the Fourth Gospel," *L'evangile de Jean: Sources, Redaction, Theologie*, ed. M. de Jonge, Bibliotheca Ephemeridum Theologicarum Lovaniensium, 44 (Louvain: Louvain University, 1977) 376. Two excellent works need to be mentioned about the categories of language in John: John Beekman and John Callow, *Translating the Word of God* (Grand Rapids: Zondervan, 1974) and G. B. Caird, *The Language and Imagery of the Bible* (Philadelphia: Westminster, 1980), especially 144–71.

[43]C. H. Dodd, *The Interpretation of the Fourth Gospel* (Cambridge: University Press, 1970) 362, pointed out that "The only place in the Synoptic Gospels where a similar demand is made is in Mark 14:61 (and parallels), where the High Priest asks,

'Are you the Messiah, the Son of the Blessed?'" Our Lord's response was ἐγώ εἰμι.

[44]See Kysar, "The Fourth Gospel," 2391–2411, for a listing of the various approaches.

[45]M. J. J. Menken, *Numerical Literary Techniques in John: The Fourth Evangelist's Use of Numbers of Words and Syllables*. NovTSup 60 (Leiden: Brill, 1985) 189–228. His work is too detailed to be incorporated in this brief study.

[46]Edwin C. Webster, "Pattern in the Fourth Gospel," *Art and Meaning: Rhetoric in Biblical Literature*, ed. David J. A. Clines et al. JSOTSup 19 (Sheffield: JSOT, 1982) has provided a very important article on the structure of the book. His "thesis is that the Gospel, as a literary whole, is meticulously constructed on the basis of symmetrical design and unbalanced units" (230). On page 231 he identifies the literary devices as:

1. a balancing of incident against incident and theme against theme in paired complementary units;
2. triadic (with some quadratic arrangements of paired units in consecutive (a,a'–b,b'–c,c'), sequential (a,b,c–a',b',c'), or chiastic order (a–b–c–b'–a'): a pattern consisting of two overlapping triads—a,a' and b,b' being the paired units);
3. parallel sequences within complementary units;
4. word or formula repetitions to mark units;
5. a close balance as to length between complementary units.

He then divides the book into 5 sections based on the christological revelation that dominates each section. The redactional approaches to John's gospel will certainly have to be revised.

[47]Moises Silva, "Approaching the Fourth Gospel," *CTR* 3:1 (1988): 27.

[48]Leland Ryken, *The Literature of the Bible* (Grand Rapids: Zondervan, 1974): 279–80.

[49]E. Richard, "Expressions of Double Meaning and their Function in the Gospel of John," *NTS* 31 (1985): 96–112. Although he does not deal with the double meaning possibility of shepherd, it is an enlightening introduction to this subject.

[50]*TDNT*, s.v. "ἐγώ," by Ethelbert Stauffer, 2:351.

[51]Harvey K. McArthur, "Christological Perspectives in the Predicates of the Johannine Egó Eimi Sayings," *Christological Perspectives*, ed. Robert F. Berkey and Sarah A. Edwards (New York: Pilgrim, 1982) 79.

[52]Schnackenburg, *John*, 2.86. Calvin Stevens, "The 'I AM' Formula in the Gospel of John," *Studia Biblica et Theologica* 7:2 (Oct. 1977): 24 wrote, "It appears unlikely that Jesus was introducing a foreign, Hellenistic idea with its source in the Mystery religions. His Palestinian audience would probably have been baffled by such a concept. In addition the absolute use of ego eimi does not appear in any Hellenistic literature." See also Raymond Brown, *The Gospel According to John I–XII*, AB 29 (Garden City: Doubleday, 1966) 535–38. The obvious explanation for the formula lacking in Greek sources is because the verb has its own subject, thus the ego would be superfluous.

[53]Stevens, "The 'I AM' Formula," 25.

[54]Hugo Odeberg, *The Fourth Gospel Interpreted in its Relation to Contemporaneous Religious Currents in Palestine and the Hellenistic-Oriental World* (Amsterdam: B. R. Gruner, 1968) 308–9.

[55]Ibid., 310.

[56]Philip B. Harner, *The 'I Am' of the Fourth Gospel*, Facet Books Biblical Series 26 (Philadelphia: Fortress, 1970) 16–17. He does say, "At most it is indirectly related to the Fourth Gospel in the sense that it may have influenced the Septuagint translators in their rendering of ani hu in Second Isaiah as ego eimi" (60). He also makes the very important observation that "In Second Isaiah, for example, the phrase 'I am He' is spoken only by Yahweh, and in the Fourth Gospel the absolute ego eimi is used only by Jesus." See his most recent monograph, *Grace and Law in Second Isaiah: 'I am the Lord'*, Ancient Near Eastern Texts and Studies, vol. 2 (Lewiston, NY: Edwin Mellen, 1988).

[57]Stauffer, "ἐγώ," 352.

[58]It should be remembered that in every mention of shepherd in Matthew, Christ was healing. See again Martin, "The Shepherd Image."

[59]George R. Beasley-Murray, *John*, WBC 36 (Waco: Word, 1987) 167.

[60]This is probably because John's desire is to make us see that it is the same crowd with the same questions and doubts. This kind of approach to chronology is a well-documented phenomena in Hebrew historiography.

[61]Brown, *John I–XII*, 389. Note that the blind man's response to their repeated questioning in 9:27 εἶπον ὑμῖν is identical to Jesus' response in 10:25.

[62]Menken, *John*, 214.

[63]Leon Morris, *The Gospel According to John* (Grand Rapids: Eerdmans, 1971) 599 n. 5.

[64]E. C. Colwell, "A Definite Rule for the Use of the Article in the Greek New Testament," *JBL* 52 (1932): 21.

[65]Schnackenburg, *John*, 2.282.

[66]See M. Vellanickel, *The Divine Sonship of Christians in the Johannine Writings*, AnBib 72 (Rome: Biblical Institute, 1977) 201.

[67]Beasley-Murray, *John*, 169. Others have argued for contemporary ancient Jewish examples. See Odeberg, *John*, 320ff. for examples. John Bowman, *The Fourth Gospel and the Jews: A Study of R. Akiba, Esther and the Gospel of John*, Pittsburgh Theological Monograph Series 8 (Pittsburgh: Pickwick, 1975) 200–201, argues that the imagery comes from Lev 16:7 where the Hebrew reads "lipne YHWH petaḥ ʾōhel môʿēd" (normally translated "before the Lord at the doorway of the tent of meeting) should actually be translated "before the Lord, the door of the tent of meeting." The problem is that his suggestion hangs on a legitimate grammatical possibility but it can never be proven or disproven. Further, one wonders whether Jesus' audience would have caught such a minute point.

[68]Schnackenburg, *John*, 2:289.

[69]Menken, *John*, 217.

[70]Ibid.

[71]B. Gerhardsson, *The Good Samaritan—the Good Shepherd*, Coniectanea Neotestamentica (Lund: C. W. K. Gleerup, 1958) 13.

[72]Schnackenburg, *John*, 2.296.

[73]The Greek word for wolf only appears 6 times and only John uses it in the singular. The Hebrew counterpart only appears 10 times. It may be that Ezek 22:27 was in the Lord's mind as he spoke of this creature in John 10. The wolf is, in this part of the world, a solitary creature who hunts at night. If allowed, it will kill numerous sheep while making off with only one. See *Encyclopedia Judaica*, s.v. "Wolf," Jehuda Feliks,

16:602, and *Fauna and Flora of the Bible*, Help for Translators, 11 (London: United Bible Societies, 1972) 85–86.

[74]If Exod 22:12–13 can be used here, it makes the hireling's behavior all the more unbelievable. Verse 13 reads "If it (the animal) is torn to pieces (by a wild beast), let him bring it as evidence; he shall not make restitution to its owner." This ancient practice for showing the shepherd's innocence was likened to God and Israel in Amos 3:12 where God threatened Israel, "Just as the shepherd snatches from the lion's mouth a couple of legs or a piece of ear, so will the sons of Israel dwelling in Samaria be snatched away . . . " Presumably, anyone who knew the shepherd's calling would have found this picture in John 10 to be strange.

[75]Stevens, "The 'I AM' Formula," 28.

[76]MacArthur, "Christological Perspectives," 88, pointed out that the word "life" occurs 36 times in John. "So it is no exaggeration to affirm that all occurrences of egō eimi with predicates are affirmations that Jesus is the life-bearer and life-giver." This, however, is not just because of His act of love but because of His person, namely Israel's Messiah.

# The Relationship of the Law to Christ in Matt 5:17-20 and Its Implications for Moral Theology

## James Murray Grier, Jr.

### INTRODUCTION

A philosophical shift in the controlling motifs of western philosophy has made a significant contribution to the growth of ethical relativism in our culture. The Post-Renaissance notions of the twin ultimacy of process and autonomy has finally moved from epistemological issues and penetrated the discipline of ethics. With no fixed values and no transcendent base for obligation, consequential ethics has become the approved societal practice. No doubt the emergence of pressing ethical issues in medicine has contributed to the revival of the serious discussion of ethics in the community.

Since moral theology is logically built on exegetical theology, biblical theology, historical theology, systematic theology, and ministry theology, tension has developed between the method of doing ethics in exegesis and the method of doing ethics in moral theology. When exegetes set the agenda for doing ethics the focus usually turns to critical problems. They normally reject all ethical categories and distinctions in order to do exegesis without an informing moral theology. This usually leads to a set of exegetical observations that

James M. Grier (Th.B., Baptist Bible Seminary; M.Div., Grace Theological Seminary; Th.M., Westminster Theological Seminary; Th.D., Grace Theological Seminary) is Academic Dean and Professor of Theology and Apologetics at Grand Rapids Baptist Seminary, Grand Rapids, Michigan.

comprise the total of what can be known on the subject. On the other hand, when the moral theologian sets the agenda the process usually ends up using the text to support a philosophical schema. On this model an extra canonical structure is superimposed on the data of exegesis. Neither of these extremes is adequate for doing ethics in theological curricula. The order and relationship of the disciplines of theology necessitate a contextual overlap between the disciplines. There is not only a logical order to the disciplines, but there is also an interdependent relationship between them.

This essay attempts to offer limited exegetical data as an answer to some questions posed by moral theology. The answer will be limited to the exegetical data of Matt 5:17–20 and their implications for moral theology. The questions include the following: (1) Does the Bible teach one ethic? (2) Is the Biblical ethic of such a nature that it is comprised of antithetical elements? (3) Is there any moral continuity in biblical theology that runs from creation to the final judgment? Exegetical theology needs moral and ministry theology to raise appropriate questions to guide exegesis toward the production of authentic Christian witness in the church and in the world. Moral and ministry theology depend on exegetical theology to provide the exegetical content to be used by the church in her enactment of ministry in the world.

The specific research question for the essay is: What is the relationship of the law to Christ in Matt 5:12–20? The relevance of the Mosaic law to church ethics has been debated for generations in the church. Although the issue is complex and much broader than the context of Matt 5:17–20, it is generally agreed that this passage is one of the crucial pericopes in the continuing discussion of the relation of the authority of the law to Jesus. Given the breadth of the task it will be necessary to deal with this pericope as it exists in the canon without reference to the problems of its history of interpretation.

Douglas Moo gives six positions which adequately summarize the main tendencies in the relation of the law to Christ:[1]

1. Jesus abrogated the law.
2. Jesus' teaching is a new law which replaces the Mosaic law.[2]
3. Jesus is the last and greatest expositor of the law of God. He upholds the moral law, showing obedience to its demands, and demonstrating its original intent by his teaching.[3]

4. Jesus radicalized the law, intensifying the demands of the law beyond what they originally intended. Some commands are abrogated by this radicalization.[4]

5. Jesus intensified the requirements of the law and brought new demands of his own, without clearly abrogating any moral commands.

6. Jesus' teaching fulfills the law, in the sense that the law pointed forward to his teaching. His demands move in a different sphere, above and apart from the law, whose continuing validity exists only in and through Him.[5]

There are many other ways to organize the positions on this subject. Moo's structure has the value of being more comprehensive than the other structures.[6]

## ANNULLING AND FULFILLING

Matthew begins this pericope by indicating that some false assumptions were about to be made concerning the relation of the law and the prophets to Jesus. It appears that some were about to suppose that Jesus' teaching and actions were devoid of respect for the Torah. In Jesus' day the primary works of piety included Torah study, Sabbath observance, Temple reverence, almsgiving, prayer and fasting.[7] So far Jesus has asserted that acceptance before God includes poverty of spirit, mourning, meekness, hunger and thirst for righteousness, mercy, purity of heart, peacemaking, and persecution. In order to correct this untenable supposition, Jesus asserts in both negative and positive terms the relation of the law and the prophets to himself.

καταλύω is used twice to state negatively what Christ has not come to do. The use of καταλῦσαι (an aorist infinitive of purpose) with νόμος in both the LXX and classical literature indicates it has the basic meaning to annul or abolish rather than to tear down a building piece by piece.[8] The stress falls on invalidating something that has been in force and could be translated, "do away with."[9] This negative statement of what the relationship of the law is to Christ is intensified by the repetition of καταλῦσαι in the second clause of the sentence.

Matthew combines the law and the prophets as the entities which Jesus has not come to abolish. There is almost universal agreement that the denotation of this combination title is the Old Covenant

Scriptures. The question arises as to whether the connotation in this context is general or if it is specific? Subsequent verses indicate the permanent validity for the law as well as the importance of relaxing and keeping the commands. It appears that the stress in vv 18–20 falls on the Old Testament's imperative statements. Although it would be inappropriate to suggest that the law or the prophets equals the will of God, it does seem appropriate to suggest the Old Testament deposit in this context is primarily focused on its moral content.[10] The scriptures definitely contained a normative ethical moment for Matthew.[11]

The crux of v 17 is the contrasting positive statement that Jesus came to fulfill the law and the prophets. Πληρῶσαι is the key to understanding the relation of the law to Christ. Matthew uses the idea of fulfillment as a central theme of continuity in his theology.[12] Douglas Moo asserts that the most appropriate way to interpret πληρόω in 5:17, is to do so in light of examples provided in 5:21–48.[13] Although it is clear that there can be no tension between the supposed antitheses of vv 21–48 and 5:17, it is not apparent why the purported antitheses should not be interpreted in light of 5:17–20. It is admitted by all that "fulfill" is a notorious crux in the sense that it is difficult to give it meaning and significance when its antecedent is commandments and not prophecy.

πληρόω is used about 70 times in the LXX for various forms of מָלֵא. Its significance includes the range of: (1) to fill up the measure, (2) to fill up to the top, (3) to fulfill a word of Yahweh, (4) to fill completely, (5) to complete, and (6) to fill.[14] The LXX does not render forms of *qûm* with πληρόω which we would expect if the sense was to establish, to bring into effect.[15] Contrary to Bahnsen's thesis, the contrast between abolish and fulfill is not characterized by thesis-antithesis.[16] The opposite of abolish is not fulfill. If Matthew's intent was to assert this, he had at his disposal the word ἵστημι to state the idea of establishing the law and the prophets. One thing seems clear in this text and that is that Jesus' fulfillment of the law and the prophets does not have reference to Jesus' acts, but does have reference to Jesus' teaching.

Matthew uses the verb πληρόω 16 times as compared to three uses by Mark and nine uses by Luke.[17] Of the 16 uses in Matthew, 12 fit the formula-citation pattern (1:22; 2:15, 17, 23; 4:14; 8:17; 12:17; 13:35; 21:4; 26:54, 56; 27:9). Two uses of the verb clearly mean to fill up (13:48) with fish and (23:32) to fill up the measure of the fathers who killed the prophets. The 12 formula-citation occurrences are aorist subjunctive passive verbs. The reference in 23:32 is an aorist imperative. Neither the 13:48 or the 23:32 references use the verb in a theological sense. Two references remain, i.e., 3:15 (aorist infinitive) and 5:17 (aorist infinitive). Since 12 of the 16 references in Matthew are formula-citations, Banks argues that this is the appropriate meaning of πληρόω in 5:17.

> What I would argue then, and it is this possibility that seems to have been consistently overlooked, is that precisely the same meaning should be given to the term when it is used of the Law as that which it has when it is used of the Prophets. The prophetic teachings point forward (principally) to the actions of Christ and have been realized in them in an incomparably greater way. The Mosaic laws point forward (principally) to the teachings of Christ and have also been realized in them in a more profound manner. The word "fulfill" in 5:17, then, includes not only an element of discontinuity (that which has now been realized *transcends* the Law) but an element of continuity as well (that which *transcends* the law is nevertheless something to which the Law itself *pointed forward*).[18]

Banks affirms that Jesus fulfills the law by conserving it through perfecting and surpassing the whole didactic content of the Old Testament and not just its moral content.[19]

Banks' interpretation is based primarily on the 12 uses of πληρόω by Matthew as formula-citations with reference to the fulfillment of prophecy. Because the law and prophets are placed in conjunction in this passage, he assumes that fulfill for law must be identical to fulfill for prophecy as in the formula-citations. Should such an identity exist, one would expect the formula-citation in 5:17. It is interesting to note that the formula-citation structure is not used in 5:17. The verb in 5:17 is an aorist active infinitive. In the formula-citations the verbs are aorist passive subjunctives. The closest parallel to 5:17 is 3:15 where the aorist active infinitive occurs. In that passage Jesus tells John that what is to be fulfilled is "all righteousness." Whatever righteousness means in the passage, it is certainly hard to read it as a conjunction of prophetic fulfillment. In point of fact, righteousness suggests a moral focus that relates to the maintenance and development of normative relationships. Fulfillment in 3:15 has the action of baptism as its primary referent rather than an Old Testament passage that is being fulfilled.

In this regard Ulrich Luz suggests that Matthew may be thinking primarily of the demands (precepts) of the law and the prophets because both the law and the prophets demand as well as predict.[20] Matthew uses the phrase "law and prophets" with this emphasis on precept in 7:12 and in 22:40. The reference in 7:12 is of particular importance because of its inclusion in Matthew's ordered memorandum of Jesus' moral teaching. Dale Brunner may go too far with this emphasis when he concludes that to fulfill means Jesus' personal obedience to the precepts of the old covenant. He does seek to temper his view by suggesting that Jesus' teaching is an aspect of his doing and thus can be correlated with his obedience.[21]

The 12 formula-citations use the aorist passive subjunctive in the sense of to cause to happen, to make happen, to fulfill.[22] Matthew's use of the aorist active infinitive suggests that Christ did something in relation to the moral content of the Old Testament. This does not fit the formula-citation pattern of predict/fulfill whether taken in the shallow sense of Moule or in the theological sense of France.[23] To make the contrast equal fulfill in the sense of point forward/predict does not coincide with Jesus' assertion that no one should suppose that he has come to annul or abolish the law or the prophets. Καταλύω cannot carry the weight of "not point forward to" or "not fulfill." It clearly carries the connotation to set aside or abolish the law or prophets as they embody the perceptive will of God.

Donald Carson suggests that Jesus fulfills the law and the prophets in many ways. Because they point to him he has come to fulfill them in "a rich diversity of ways, a richness barely hinted at in these paragraphs."[24] Perhaps this suggestion will keep us from arguing for a single focus and cause us to appreciate the value in the predict/fulfill and the demand/fulfill viewpoints. Even with a commitment to appreciate the richness of the idea of fulfillment, it remains to be suggested that the disparity between "annul" and "fulfill" is best explained by reference to Jesus' moral action and teaching.[25]

## UNTIL ALL THINGS ARE ACCOMPLISHED

Jesus affirms that until heaven and earth pass away, not the smallest part of the law will drop out of the law until it all happens. This reference builds on the contrast of the supposition that Jesus was annulling the law. The problem in the passage is the two temporal clauses. The first clause, "until heaven and earth pass away," clearly points to the eschatological consummation of the age. No doubt the intent of the clause is not to teach the temporal limitation of the law, but rather to show that it is inconceivable that the smallest part of the law should fail.

The second temporal clause, "until all takes place," is much more difficult to interpret. Banks asserts that the second temporal clause conditions the first and should be taken as a reference to Jesus' accomplishment of the law in his passion and resurrection.[26] There is thus a movement from the teaching of Jesus fulfilling the law (5:17) to an action of Jesus fulfilling the law, i.e., his death and resurrection. The validity of the law continues until Jesus makes all things happen by his redemptive mediacy. This signals the end of the law's function and the inception of the messianic age.

There is need to admit that to give the "accomplishment of all things" a specific referent in the redemptive actions of Jesus does not seem to fit the argument of 5:17 or the time reference in the first temporal clause. At best these clauses make this verse difficult no matter what interpretation is accepted. "Until all takes place" does not state a clear terminal point for the validity of the law. Should it be assumed that the reference for "all takes place" is the same as the demands (precepts) of the law fulfilled in 5:17, then it would imply that the law's validity is sustained until all of the commands are done.[27] From this perspective both temporal references would be to a future apocalyptic consummation.

It does not appear obvious that an interpretive decision can be made solely on this verse. Reflection on 5:19 may help to focus the issue as well as evaluate the interpretive options.

## THESE COMMANDMENTS

There is a distinct change in subject from 5:17, 18 to 5:19, 20. In 5:17–18 the content has to do with Jesus while in 5:19–20 the content has to do with his followers. The key issue in this verse is to identify the appropriate antecedent of ἐντολῶν. There seems to be little doubt that the purpose of vv 18 and 19 is to preclude any kind of antinomian interpretation of 5:17.[28]

Matthew uses οὖν as an inferential particle that logically connects 5:19 to 5:18. Banks argues that the connection supports his thesis that the commandments do not refer to the law, but rather they refer to the commandments given by Jesus as the one who brings the law to its completion. Since Jesus in his passion has brought the accomplishment of all things in the law, Matthew must now be using commandments to identify the moral teaching of Jesus. Since the law has been accomplished (5:18) there must be a new referent for commandment in Jesus' instruction.[29]

As France points out, ἐντολὴ in Matthew's other five uses refers to the Old Testament law.[30] Jesus asserts that relaxing in 5:19 (λύσῃ) defines the abolishing that is not a part of Jesus' purpose in relation to the law. To relax the least of these commandments identifies the commandments with the *yod* and *serif* of 5:18.[31] Davies argues that the flow of the passage plus the inferential particle shows that commandments revert back to 5:18 and thus to the Torah. In light of the connection of λύω 5:19 to καταλύω in 5:17, where the law is the subject, it seems almost impossible to take commandments as a reference to Christ's past accomplishment and his present moral instruction.[32]

These observations form the strongest lines of diverging evidence from the interpretive hypothesis that "until all things are accomplished" (5:18) refers to Christ's death and resurrection. It makes no sense to argue that *yods* and *serifs* have fallen away since Jesus' accomplishment of all things and then demand no relaxing of the least commandments for life in the kingdom of heaven. In fact, greatness in the kingdom is predicated on doing and teaching others to do these commandments. Jesus' teaching in 5:19 precludes the possibility that the time of the law's validity has ended. The second temporal clause of 5:18 (until all things are accomplished) has not yet come to pass in light of 5:19. Even though the time reference is ambiguous in the second temporal clause of 5:18, it appears that it must refer to a future time when the law will be accomplished.[33]

## SURPASSING RIGHTEOUSNESS

Entrance into the kingdom demands a righteousness that surpasses that achieved by the scribes and the Pharisees. "Righteous" should be understood in terms of conduct and the comparative construction in which it occurs can be best described as quantitative.[34] Jesus' teaching incorporates the moral demands of the law which are related to entrance into the kingdom of heaven. This verse is a transitional hinge to Jesus' teaching about the commandments in 5:21–48. Righteousness is conduct in accord with the demands of Jesus. Jesus' demand for surpassing righteousness is essential for entrance into the kingdom. Gundry summarizes: "The reason is that even to enter the kingdom requires more righteousness than the Scribes and the Pharisees have . . . The following part of the sermon tells how to surpass the righteousness of the Scribes and the Pharisees."[35]

## EXEGETICAL CONCLUSIONS

Matt 5:17–20 was intended to correct the supposition that Jesus annulled the Torah. This suspicion does not appear in the antecedent material of Matthew's Gospel. So it would appear that this supposition is found in the material that is yet to be presented. This pericope functions as an introduction to the demands of Jesus in 5:21–48 and gives the reader appropriate parameters for the understanding of the anticipated discussion. It is suggested that rather than interpreting 5:17–20 by 5:21–48, it is more appropriate to Matthew's intent to understand Jesus' teaching in 5:21–48 in light of 5:17–20, that is, as not annulling the law or the prophets but fulfilling them.[36]

The contrast of καταλύω and πληρόω in 5:17 suggests that Jesus' purpose in relation to the moral content of the law, or for that matter the prophets, was not annulment but fulfillment. Jesus is the one to whom all the moral content of the Old Testament points. In his life he embodied this content and gave flawless, spontaneous obedience to every precept of the Father. The law is filled full in Him and He advances it by reinterpretation for conduct in the kingdom.

It is inconceivable that even the smallest components of the Old Testament revelation will fall away until the consummation of all things. In fact, rather than relaxing the commandments, keeping them and teaching others to keep them is the basis for being graded great in the kingdom.

Matthew's focus through this pericope is on the imperative content of the Old Testament. The connotation of fulfillment does not match the formula-citations of Matthew as noted by the active aorist infinitive. What is fulfilled by Jesus are the moral demands of the Old Testament and not its predictive content. These demands are incorporated by Jesus into the new era and are advanced by His moral instruction. Their permanent validity is found in Him even though their function in the kingdom may be different from the former household administration.

The two temporal clauses of 5:18 are best taken as future termination of the law's validity rather than taking the first clause as referring to the consummation and the second referring to Jesus' death and resurrection. Commandments in 5:19 refer back to the law of 5:18 and 5:17 and not to new moral teaching imposed by Jesus after the law's accomplishment through his death and resurrection.

## IMPLICATIONS FOR MORAL THEOLOGY

Exegetical conclusions concerning 5:17-20 in themselves do not complete the task of moral theology. Exegetical evidence needs to be used to affirm or deny conceptual patterns in moral theology. It is very probable that these exegetical assertions about 5:17-20 can be used to support a number of theses in moral theology. For example, David Wenham uses similar exegetical conclusions to support the thesis of a threefold breakdown of Old Testament law into ceremonial, civil, and moral.[37] No thesis can be fully established on the evidence of this pericope alone. At best the exegetical evidence from this passage can be used as converging or diverging evidence for a broad thesis that asserts the relationship of the law to Christ and His church.

John Murray's thesis (given at Fuller Theological Seminary in the Payton Lectures) that there is continuity between the creation ordinances, the ten words, the sermon on the mount, and the teaching of the epistles is certainly worthy of consideration.[38] In the Adamic administration God gave a series of ordinances for the guidance of man's conduct while in a state of created righteousness. After the Lord redeemed Israel out of bondage in Egypt, he gave her the ten words to guide her conduct as a redeemed people. The ten words are viewed by Murray as an explication of the creation ordinances. The prophets take this ancient moral content and weave it into the life of the nation in her urban setting. Jesus takes this perpetually binding moral content and reinterprets and extends it for life in the kingdom. Jesus' commands are to be integrated into the church as one of the modes of disciplining the nations (Matt 28:19, 20).

Murray's thesis goes beyond the evidence of 5:17–20. The point of the issue is to affirm that the exegesis of 5:17–20 offers strong converging evidence for this thesis. Many lines of diverging evidence could be cited, i.e., the Sabbath issue, but they cannot be settled by the exegesis of this pericope. It does appear, however, that responsible exegesis exists to support the theological idea of continuity/discontinuity in a biblical theology of morality. Continuity can be identified with the perpetually binding precepts given by Christ at creation and then developed by Him in the ten words, the sermon on the mount, and the church epistles. Many of these commands are marked with the imprimatur of the character of God. Many of the non-perpetually binding precepts were brought to completion in Christ. Although he never annulled them, he did fill them full. These constitute aspects of the discontinuity in a biblical theology of morality.

# NOTES

[1]Douglas J. Moo, "Jesus and the Authority of the Mosaic Law," *Journal for the Study of the New Testament* 20 (1984) 4–5.

[2]This position is developed by W. D. Davies, *The Setting of the Sermon on the Mount* (Cambridge: Cambridge University Press, 1977) 94–107. It is also espoused by B. W. Bacon, "Jesus and the Law: A Study of the First Book of Matthew (Mt. 3–7)," *Journal of Biblical Literature* 47 (1928) 203–31.

[3]Most of the reformers held this position as well as many recent reformed writers like Henry, Bahnsen, Ridderbos, Murray, and Stonehouse.

[4]B. H. Branscomb, *Jesus and the Law of Moses* (New York: Richard A. Smith, 1930) 260–62. Douglas Moo asserts that the majority of modern scholars hold a similar view to this one (cf. n 1).

[5]Robert Banks, *Jesus and the Law in the Synoptic Tradition* (Cambridge: Cambridge University Press, 1975). John P. Meier, *Law and History in Matthew's Gospel: A Redactional Study of Mt. 5:17–48* (Rome: Biblical Institute Press, 1976). Robert A. Guelich, *The Sermon on the Mount: A Foundation for Understanding* (Waco, Texas: Word, 1982). D. J. Moo, "Jesus and the Authority of the Mosaic Law." R. T. France, *The Gospel According to Matthew* (Grand Rapids: Eerdmans, 1985).

[6]For a threefold analysis of viewpoints see Robert A. Guelich, *The Sermon on the Mount: A Foundation for Understanding* (Waco, Texas: Word, 1982) 138–42.

[7]Frederick D. Brunner, *The Christ Book: Historical Theological Commentary* (Waco, Texas: Word, 1987) 164.

[8]Banks, "Matthew's Understanding of the Law: Authenticity and Interpretation in Matthew 5:17–20," *JBL* 93:2 (June 1974) 227.

[9]Johannes P. Louw and Eugene A. Nida, *Greek-English Lexicon of the New Testament Based on Semantic Domains* (New York: United Bible Societies, 1988), field 76.23; 1:682.

[10]R. T. France, *Matthew, Evangelist and Teacher* (Grand Rapids: Zondervan, 1989) 193–96.

[11]Robert A. Guelich, *The Sermon on the Mount*, 137.

[12]France, *Matthew, Evangelist and Teacher*, 166–205.

[13]Moo, "Jesus and the Authority of the Mosaic Law," 26.

[14]G. Delling, "πληρόω" *Theological Dictionary of the New Testament*, Vol. VI. Edited by G. Kittel and G. Friedrich. Trans. by G. Bromiley (Grand Rapids: Eerdmans, 1968) 286–311.

[15]W. D. Davies and Dale C. Allison, *A Critical and Exegetical Commentary on the Gospel of Matthew*, Vol. I (Edinburgh: T. & T. Clark, 1988) 485.

[16]Greg L. Bahnsen, *Theonomy in Christian Ethics* (Nutley, N.J.: The Craig Press, 1977) 51–72.

[17]W. F. Moulton and A. S. Geden, *A Concordance to the Greek New Testament* (Edinburgh: T. & T. Clark, 4th ed. 1963) 816.

[18]Banks, *Jesus and the Law in the Synoptic Tradition*, 210.

[19]J. P. Meier comes to the same conclusion when he says, "the Law in Mt. must be interpreted in a prophetic light, in analogy with prophecy." *Law and History in Matthew's Gospel* (Rome: Biblical Institute Press, 1976) 80. C. D. T. Moule, "Fulfillment Words in the New Testament: Use and Abuse," *New Testament Studies*, Vol. 14 (April 1968): 293–320.

[20]Ulrich Luz, *Matthew 1–7: A Commentary*, trans. by W. C. Linss (Minneapolis: Augsburg, 1989) 264–65.

[21]F. D. Brunner, *The Christ Book*, 166–67.

[22]Louw and Nida, *Greek-English Lexicon of the New Testament*, field 13:106; 1.161.

[23]See further Moule, "Fulfillment Words in the New Testament," 307–9, and France, *Matthew Evangelist and Teacher*, 171–84.

[24]Donald A. Carson, *The Sermon on the Mount* (Grand Rapids: Baker, 1978) 37.

[25]Robert Gundry, *Matthew: A Commentary on His Literary and Theological Art* (Grand Rapids: Eerdmans, 1982) 81.

[26]Banks, *Jesus and the Law in the Synoptic Tradition*, 213–20. It should be noted that Davies (487–95), Guelich (143–49), and France (115) accept this view.

[27]Luz, *Matthew 1–7*, 266.

[28]Moo, *Jesus and the Authority of the Mosaic Law*, 28.

[29]Banks, *Jesus and the Law in the Synoptic Tradition*, 220–23.

[30]France, *The Gospel According to Matthew* (Grand Rapids: Eerdmans, 1985) 116.

[31]Gundry, *Matthew: A Commentary on His Literary and Theological Art*, 82.

[32]Davies and Allison, *A Critical and Exegetical Commentary on the Gospel of Matthew*, 1.496. For further confirmation and discussion of this viewpoint see Luz, *Matthew 1–7*, 267, 268.

[33]For a discussion of the weakness of Banks' position see David Wenham, "Jesus and the Law: An Exegesis on Matthew 5:17–20," *Themelios* 4 (1979) 93, 94.

[34]Banks, *Jesus and the Law in the Synoptic Tradition*, 225.

[35]Gundry, *Matthew: A Commentary on His Literary and Theological Art*, 82.

[36]Davies and Allison, *A Critical and Exegetical Commentary on the Gospel of Matthew*, 1.501, 502.

[37]Wenham, "Jesus and the Law: An Exegesis on Matthew 5:17–20," 95. This view is shared by George A. F. Knight, *Law and Grace* (London: S.C.M. Press Ltd., 1962) 39–54.

[38]John Murray, *Principles of Christian Conduct* (Grand Rapids: Eerdmans, 1968).

# Primus Inter Pares?
# Peter in the Gospel of Matthew

## David L. Turner

Thirty years ago, in a commentary on Matthew, Homer Kent described the dilemma which the present study addresses. Concerning the words "the first, Simon, who is called Peter" in 10:2 Kent stated,

> Not the first chosen, nor merely the first one in the list, but probably a reference to Peter's prominence in the apostolic circle (cf. 26:40; Pentecost; Cornelius's house; and others). But he was first among equals. The NT knows nothing of a Petrine supremacy over other apostles.[1]

Thus Kent attempted to do justice to Peter's prominence in the gospels without going beyond the scriptural record into undue stress upon Peter. With gratitude and admiration to my former teacher I now embark upon a similar mission.

Despite the fact that Peter's prominent role in the gospels as the leader of the twelve apostles is widely acknowledged by NT scholars today, grass-roots evangelicals still seem reluctant to admit it. Pulpiteering which emphasizes Peter's impetuous remarks and regrettable deeds seems to result in Peter being the Rodney Dangerfield of apostles—he gets no respect at all! There may even be a sort of "petrophobia" as evangelicals react to the Roman Catholic view of Peter as the first of a succession of popes possessing universal authority over Christendom. So the Roman Catholic doctrine of Peter's infallibility appears to be replaced by the evangelical doctrine of Peter's invisibility! Such a view of Peter will not do. It is only the prominence accorded to Peter in the gospels which results in his weaknesses being

David L. Turner (B.A., Cedarville College; M.Div., Th.M., Th.D., Grace Theological Seminary) is Professor of New Testament and Systematic Theology at Grand Rapids Baptist Seminary, Grand Rapids, Michigan.

stressed. If the other apostles were mentioned with anything near the frequency with which Peter is mentioned, who knows what sordid details would be revealed about them?

Leaving such biased "pop theology" aside, in scholarly circles there are basically two contrasting approaches to Peter in Matthew. The first approach views Peter as the supreme rabbi whose investiture with the keys of the kingdom signifies that he is the chief guarantor and transmitter of Christian tradition. Here Peter is *primus*, first, but the other disciples are definitely not his equals. The second perspective takes Peter to be the typical disciple who exemplifies strengths and weaknesses common to Christians.[2] Here Peter is *inter pares*, among equals, but his primacy is severely truncated. It would seem that the rabbi hypothesis is more in keeping with the tenets of Roman Catholicism, while protestants will tend to be more comfortable with the theory of Peter as the typical disciple. This question will be addressed again in the conclusion of this study.

Now a word about methodology. Studies of Peter in Matthew generally assume a rather mechanical view of Markan priority with Matthew utilizing Mark and the source Q.[3] Such a view of source criticism may be falling out of favor today. France's study of the matter of literary relationships among the gospels alludes to

> a growing number of voices raised in opposition to *any* straightforward theory of literary priority and dependence, who believes it is more realistic to talk about shared traditions and a process of cross-fertilisation between the churches in which the gospels were produced than to envisage one evangelist simply "using" the work of another.[4]

Thus the present study does not assume Markan priority or indeed any simplistic theory of literary dependency.

Redaction critical studies of Matthew also generally assume the dependence of Matthew upon Mark. In such an approach Matthew's theological *tendenz* is discerned by comparing his accounts with Markan parallels and noting similarities and differences. It is common to Matthew's unique emphases to be viewed as arguably unhistorical redaction emanating from the Matthean community's own theologically creative handling of the Markan historical tradition. This approach came into its own in the United States with the appearance of the controversial commentary of R. H. Gundry.[5]

Two important matters must be mentioned concerning the approach to redaction criticism taken in the present study. First, the approach which sees Matthean *gemeindetheologie* [theological community] in virtually every verse where Matthew and Mark diverge is untenable. Matthean redaction is not necessarily to be viewed as unhistorical embroidering of Markan historical tradition. Such a perspective assumes a kind of literary dependence which is falling out of vogue today. Additionally, it assumes that the original audience of Matthew would have also needed a copy of Mark if they were to understand Matthew correctly. Neither of these assumptions are warranted. Matthew's characteristic theological emphases can be ascertained more readily and more certainly by looking at Matthew as a literary whole.[6] The second matter which must be mentioned is the matter of historicity. Granted, the gospels, along with all the narrative literature of the Bible, are theological in nature. In other words, the historical data in the gospels is not the end but the means used to accomplish the end of edifying the original audience. However, there is no reason to assume that the authors of the gospels imaginatively created pericopes made to order for the theological truths their audiences needed. Rather, the authors selectively utilized the historical data at their disposal to accomplish theological and pastoral concerns.

This approach to redaction criticism overlaps with literary criticism, which also has a legitimate place in gospel studies. Granted, some practitioners of literary criticism have a very low view of the historicity of the biblical narratives, and some are not the least interested in whether the gospels describe historical events at all. However, as Longman has argued,[7] a literary critical approach does not necessarily question the historicity of biblical narrative. On the contrary, there is reason to believe that the authors of the gospels utilized literary techniques to communicate more effectively their distinctive portrayals of the Jesus of history. Openness to the legitimate insights of literary criticism will characterize the present study.

The thesis argued here is that Matthew does portray Peter in a distinctive fashion. He is indeed *primus inter pares*, first among equals. Peter is the model disciple whose faith as well as his foibles point up the same types of characteristics in Jesus' disciples as a whole. Matthew intended his audience to see in Peter those qualities which would enable them to fulfill Jesus the Messiah's mandate to disciple all the nations. And Peter is also the rock of the church, whose christological confession supplies the church with its crucial watchword.

This thesis will be demonstrated by presenting first an overview of the Peter material in all four gospels. Then Matthew's distinctive portrayal of Peter will be traced, along with Petrine material in the other gospels which Matthew omits. Finally, a concluding theological synthesis will be presented.

## THE PORTRAYAL OF PETER IN THE GOSPELS

In the gospels Peter is most commonly referred to by the significant surname given him by Jesus. The word Πέτρος is used nearly 100 times: 24 times in Matthew, 19 times in Mark, 20 times in Luke, and 34 times in John. The gospel of John once uses Κηφᾶς, "Cephas" (1:42), the Aramaic equivalent of Πέτρος.[8] Peter is described by his given name Σίμων more than 40 times in the gospels, 5 times in Matthew, 5 times in Mark, 11 times in Luke, and 21 times in John. Generally Πέτρος is added to Σίμων when Σίμων refers to Peter in order to distinguish him from the other Simon's mentioned in the narrative. In summary, there are around 140 references to Peter in the gospels.

It is instructive to contrast the 140 or so references to Peter in the gospels with the references to the other apostles. Judas Iscariot is mentioned around 20 times.[9] John the brother of James (both the sons of Zebedee) is referred to 19 times, and his brother James 17 times.[10] Philip is mentioned 14 times, primarily in the gospel of John,[11] and next is Thomas with 10 references, also primarily in John.[12] James the son of Alphaeus, sometimes called "the less" is referred to 6 times, most frequently in Mark,[13] and Matthew occurs 4 times.[14] Bartholomew and Simon the Canaanite (or Zealot) are both mentioned only three times.[15] Judas the son of James is evidently the same person as Thaddaeus, and both of these names appear twice.[16] When all of these seemingly trivial numbers are compiled, the prominence of Peter cannot be denied. All of the other apostles combined are mentioned around 110 times, 30 less than Peter alone.

It is convenient to summarize the gospel material concerning Peter by means of a simple list[17] with the relevant passages adduced for each item:

1. In Transjordan Simon is brought to Jesus by his brother Andrew and is surnamed Cephas/Peter (John 1:40–42).

2. Simon and Andrew are called to follow Jesus and fish for men while fishing in the Sea of Galilee (Matt 4:18–20; Mark 1:16–18).

3. At Capernaum Jesus comes to Simon's home and heals Simon's mother-in-law (Matt 8:14–17; Mark 1:29–31; Luke 4:38–39).

4. Simon and others hunt for Jesus in the early morning in Galilee (Mark 1:35–37).

5. Jesus teaches the multitudes from Simon's boat and leads Simon to a very large catch (Luke 5:1–11).

6. Simon is at the first of the list of the twelve apostles whom Jesus appoints (Mark 3:13–19; Luke 6:12–16).

7. (a) On the way to heal Jairus's daughter Peter tells Jesus that multitudes are pressing upon Him (Luke 8:45).

   (b) Later Peter, James, and John observe Jesus raise Jairus's daughter (Mark 4:37; Luke 8:51).

8. Simon at the first of the list of the twelve when they are commissioned for ministry (Matt 10:2).

9. Andrew, Simon Peter's brother, says that there is not enough food to feed the 5,000 (John 6:8–9).

10. Peter walks on water (Matt 14:28–31).

11. Peter affirms that only Jesus has words of eternal life (John 6:68–69).

12. Peter requests that Jesus explain his parable about defilement (Matt 15:15).

13. (a) Peter affirms that Jesus is the Son of God (Matt 16:16; Mark 8:29; Luke 9:20).

    (b) Jesus replies to Peter with the rock and binding/loosing sayings (Matt 16:17–19).

    (c) Peter rebukes Jesus for his prediction of crucifixion and is severely rebuked by Jesus (Matt 16:22–23; Mark 8:32–33).

14. Peter, James, and John accompany Jesus to the mount of transfiguration where Peter volunteers to construct booths for Jesus, Moses, and Elijah (Matt 17:1–4; Mark 9:2–6; Luke 9:28–33).

15. Peter affirms that Jesus pays the temple tax (Matt 17:24–27).

16. Peter asks Jesus about the intent of a parable (Luke 12:41).

17. Peter asks Jesus how many times he must forgive a sinning brother (Matt 18:21).
18. Peter affirms that the disciples have left everything behind to follow Jesus (Matt 19:27; Mark 10:28; Luke 18:28).
19. Peter points out to Jesus that the cursed fig tree has withered (Mark 11:21).
20. Peter (along with James, John, and Andrew) asks Jesus about the predicted destruction of the temple (Mark 13:3-4).
21. Peter and John are sent to prepare the passover meal (Luke 22:8-13).
22. At the passover meal Peter learns about the significance of footwashing and seeks to find out who will betray Jesus (John 13:6-10, 24).
23. Jesus tells Peter that Satan desires to test him but affirms His intercession and Peter's future ministry (Luke 22:31-32).
24. Peter promises to follow Jesus to the point of death and Jesus predicts his three denials (Matt 26:33-35; Mark 14:29-31; Luke 22:33-34; John 13:36-38).
25. Peter, James, and John sleep while Jesus prays in Gethsemane, and Peter is rebuked by Jesus (Matt 26:36-40; Mark 14:32-37).
26. Peter attempts to defend Jesus with his sword and severs Malchus's ear (John 18:10-11).
27. Peter denies the Lord at Annas's court (John 18:15-17).
28. Peter denies the Lord at Caiaphas's court (Matt 26:58, 69-75; Mark 14:54, 66-72; Luke 22:54-62; John 18:25-27).
29. The angel at Jesus' tomb tells the women to tell His disciples and Peter that He is risen and will meet them in Galilee (Mark 16:7).
30. Peter and another disciple discover the empty tomb (Luke 24:12; John 20:2-7).
31. The disciples tell Cleopas and his companion that the risen Jesus has appeared to Peter (Luke 24:34).
32. After a futile night of fishing, the risen Jesus helps Peter catch fish and reaffirms his commission for ministry. Peter then inquires as to what will become of another disciple and is rebuked (John 21:1-23).

Of the above 30 or so[18] references to Peter, 22 are unique to one gospel. Matthew has six unique Petrine pericopes (## 8, 10, 12,

13b, 15, and 17). Mark has four such pericopes (## 4, 18, 20, and 29), while Luke has six (## 5, 7a, 16, 21, 23, and 31), and John has seven (## 1, 9, 11, 22, 26, 27, and 32).

Of the remaining pericopes, three are found in Matthew and Mark (## 2, 13c, and 25). Four are found in Matthew, Mark, and Luke (## 3, 13a, 14, and 18). Two are found in all four gospels (## 24, 28). Two are found in Mark and Luke (## 6, 7b). One pericope occurs in Luke and John (# 30), and one occurs in Matthew, Mark, and John (# 24).

## MATTHEW'S PORTRAYAL OF PETER

Matthew's portrayal of Peter[19] encompasses nine passages in common with other gospels as well as six passages which are unique to this gospel. There are of course several passages from the other gospels which find no mention at all in Matthew. First a list of Matthean Peter passages will be given, and then discussion of passages common to Matthew and other gospels will be undertaken. Following that will be a study of Petrine passages unique to Matthew and brief comments on Petrine materials from the other gospels which Matthew does not mention.

*Overview of Petrine Material in Matthew*

1. Simon Peter is the first disciple to be called to follow Jesus (4:18).
2. Jesus heals Peter's mother-in-law- in Capernaum (8:17).
3. Matthew's list of apostles is headed by the words "first Peter" (10:2).
4. Peter briefly walks on water but is rebuked for his "little faith" (14:28–31).
5. Peter asks Jesus to explain his saying about the cause of impurity (15:15).
6. Peter's confession leads to the crucial rock and keys sayings (16:16–19).
7. Peter rebukes Christ and in turn is rebuked by him for false thinking (16:22–23).
8. Peter accompanies Jesus to the transfiguration and again speaks out of turn (17:1–5).
9. Peter affirms that Jesus pays the temple tax and then is taught by Jesus (17:24–27).

10. Peter asks Jesus how many times a sinning brother must be forgiven (18:21–22).
11. Peter asks Jesus about the disciples' reward (19:27).
12. Peter affirms that he will never deny Jesus but Jesus predicts that he will (26:33–35).
13. Peter and others sleep while Jesus prays alone in Gethsemane (26:37–41).
14. Peter denies the Lord at Caiaphas's court (26:58, 69–75).

*Petrine Passages in Common with Other Gospels*

The calling of Peter and Andrew to follow Jesus (# 2)[20] occurs in Matthew and Mark. Mark refers to Peter simply as Simon, but Matthew anticipates the surnaming of Simon as Peter in 16:18 by referring to Simon as τὸν λεγόμενον Πέτρον. The healing of Peter's mother-in-law (# 3) is mentioned in Matthew, Mark, and Luke. Matthew's account differs from that of Mark and Luke by referring to the house as Peter's instead of Simon's, again in deference to 16:18. While both of these pericopes reveal a Matthean implication of the centrality of 16:18, their contribution to Matthew's distinctive theology is not major.

The crucial pericope where Peter confesses that Jesus is the Son of God (# 13a) occurs in Matthew, Mark, and Luke. Matthew's account differs appreciably from those of Mark and Luke. First, Matthew refers to Peter as Simon Peter (16:16), while Mark and Luke simply call him Peter. More significantly, Peter's answer to Jesus' second question ("But who do you say that I am?") is stronger in Matthew, whose σὺ εἶ ὁ χριστὸς ὁ υἱὸς τοῦ θεοῦ τοῦ ζῶντος is much more emphatic than Mark's "you are the Christ" and Luke's "the Christ of God." Of course, the really crucial section of Matthew 16 is the saying about the rock and the binding and loosing (# 13b; 16:17–19), but this unique Matthean material will be dealt with in the next section. Matthew's version of Peter's ensuing rebuke of Jesus (# 13c) also significantly varies from that of Mark. Mark simply mentions the rebuke, while Matthew mentions Peter's strong words, ἵλεώς σοι, κύριε· οὐ μὴ ἔσται σοι τοῦτο (16:22). Mark's account of Jesus' response to Peter has Jesus turn to the disciples (8:33), but Matthew mentions no disciples and has Peter bear the full brunt of Jesus' words. In Matthew, Jesus refers to Peter not only as σατανᾶ as does Mark, but significantly adds that Peter is a σκάνδαλον to him. Of course, σκάνδαλον in Matthew refers to falling away from faith or causing another person to fall away from faith (5:29; 11:6; 13:21, 41, 57; 15:12; 17:27; 18:6–9; 24:10; 26:31, 33). Thus Jesus' rebuke to Peter is of the utmost moment. Overall, then, it is clear that Matthew's presentation emphasizes both his good and bad points to a degree not seen in the other gospel accounts.

The next shared account concerning Peter is the transfiguration pericope (# 14). Here again Matthew presents Peter's weakness more starkly than the parallel accounts because Matthew narrates Peter's impetuous desire to build booths for Jesus, Moses, and Elijah without mentioning the extenuating circumstances which Mark and Luke mention as a sort of excuse for Peter's rash remarks (Matt 17:4; Mark 9:6; Luke 9:33).

Jesus' teaching about wealth forms the background for the next pericope, shared by Matthew and Mark, which concerns Peter's affirmation that the disciples have left riches behind in order to follow Jesus (# 18). In both accounts Peter states that the disciples have left their wealth behind, but Matthew alone records Peter's rather direct question, τί ἄρα ἔσται ἡμῖν? Here Peter acts as spokesman for the disciples, enunciating a question which was probably on all their minds. He asked what there would be for them as a group, not merely for himself as an individual. And Jesus gave an answer which indicated that Peter's question was not out of line.

Jesus' prediction that Peter would deny him and Peter's promise that he would not (# 24) comprise the next Petrine account, which is shared by all four gospels. Matthew's account of Peter's response to Jesus' prediction is stronger than Mark's. In Matthew Peter affirms that if everyone falls away, he will never (οὐδέποτε) fall away (26:33), while in Mark Peter simply says that if all fall away, he will not (14:29). Luke's version of the scene has Peter say that he is ready to go to jail or to death with Jesus (22:33). Thus in Matthew the scene is set more dramatically for Peter's impending denial of his Lord.

Jesus' agonizing time in Gethsemane (# 25) is a Petrine passage shared by Matthew and Mark. According to Mark, Peter, James, and John accompany Jesus (14:33). Matthew features Peter since only Peter is mentioned by name and the other two disciples are merely described as Zebedee's sons (26:37). After Jesus prays alone and returns to the disciples, Mark has him ask Peter individually about sleep and keeping watch with him (14:37; καθεύδεις . . . ἴσχυσας, 2 s.

verbs). Then Jesus urges the disciples collectively to watch and pray (14:38; γρηγορεῖτε καὶ προσεύχεσθε, 2 pl. verbs). Matthew on the other hand does not mention the question about sleep and has Jesus ask Peter about the disciples collectively keeping watch (26:40; ἰσχύσατε, 2 pl.). The exhortation to watch and pray (26:41) is collective as in Mark. Overall one could say that in Matthew the emphasis is upon Peter as a representative for his two companions.

The final Petrine pericope which Matthew has in common with other gospels is Peter's darkest hour, his denial of Jesus at Caiaphas's court (# 28). The denial occurs in all four gospels. Three features of Matthew's portrayal of this incident seem to heighten Peter's weakness and culpability. First, Matthew alone says that Peter denied the Lord ἔμπροσθεν πάντων (26:70). This intensifies Peter's shame and humiliation. Second, Matthew adds that the next denial involved an oath and supplies Peter's words: ἠρνήσατο μετὰ ὅρκου ὅτι οὐκ οἶδα τὸν ἄνθρωπον (26:72). Neither Mark or Luke mention the oath and only Luke mentions Peter's words. Third, instead of merely noting that after the third denial Peter wept (as Mark does), Matthew, as well as Luke, indicate that Peter wept bitterly (πικρῶς; 26:75).

By and large the foregoing discussion tends to validate the observation of Kingsbury that "Matthew lends greater prominence of both a positive and a negative sort to the figure of Peter."[21] To a greater or lesser extent, depending upon the individual passage, Matthew presents details which feature Peter either positively or negatively.

## Petrine Passages Unique to Matthew

Matt 10:1ff. constitutes Jesus' commissioning of the disciples for apostolic ministry (# 8). In fact, the only time the word ἀπόστολος occurs in Matthew is in 10:2. Mark 6:7 and Luke 9:1 present similar accounts of this commissioning but do not list the names of the disciple-apostles as Matthew does.[22] This unique feature of Matthew provides the setting for the mention of Peter at the first of the list.[23] The words πρῶτος Σίμων ὁ λεγόμενος Πέτρος both recall Peter's initial call as the first disciple to follow Jesus (4:18) and anticipate the "you are Peter" pericope (16:18). Thus "first Peter" does not merely mean that Peter was called first or that Peter's name heads the list. Rather it fits into Matthew's characteristic emphasis upon Peter as the leader and spokesman for the disciples.

Matthew's next unique Petrine pericope is 14:28–31, where Peter, at least for a moment, joins Jesus in a walk on the water (# 10). Here Peter's impetuosity is vividly portrayed. No sooner than he realizes that it is Jesus, not a ghost, on the water, he requests that he may come to Jesus on the water. His request granted, he walks to Jesus but soon is distracted by the crashing waves and begins to sink. His cry for help (κύριε, σῶσόν με; 14:30) recalls that of the disciples as a group (κύριε, σῶσον [ἡμᾶς; v.l.]; 8:25) in the similar incident of the stilling of the storm already recorded 8:23–27. In both cases Jesus rebukes for "little faith" (ὀλιγόπιστοι; 8:26; cf. ὀλιγόπιστε; 14:31; cf. 6:30; 16:8; 17:20). Thus the specific rebuke of Peter as the leader of the disciples reinforces the general rebuke given to all in 8:26.[24] Another noteworthy factor is the manner in which the conclusion of this pericope anticipates Peter's crucial christological confession in 16:16. Once again the interplay or even oscillation between the one, Peter, and the many, the disciples, is apparent. The disciples respond to the miraculous saving of Peter and the stopping of the storm by confessing ἀληθῶς θεοῦ υἱὸς εἶ (14:33). This confession is reaffirmed and strengthened by Peter himself in 16:16: σὺ εἶ ὁ χριστὸς ὁ υἱὸς τοῦ θεοῦ τοῦ ζῶντος. But even the confession of Peter in 16:16 is in response to a question Jesus addressed to the disciples as a group (16:13, 15). It is clear then that this pericope brings together Matthew's distinctive teaching on discipleship and his Son of God christology.[25] Peter as *primus inter pares* is at the center of both themes.

The next unique Petrine pericope in Matthew is found in the narrative about the conflict between Jesus and the Pharisees over defilement (# 12; 15:1–20). Jesus' teaching on purity stressed the heart, in contrast to the emphasis of the Pharisees on external regulations. Jesus' enigmatic saying to the crowd in 15:11, to the effect that purity or impurity came from the heart, not from externals, had evidently puzzled the disciples. In Mark's account the disciples ask Jesus to explain this saying (7:17), but in Matthew Peter asks the question (15:15). All this seems to function as a specific example of the pattern Jesus announced in Matt 13:10–17 in connection with the disciples' question concerning the parable of the sower. The crowd gets Jesus' teaching in parables because God has not granted to it the privilege enjoyed by the disciples to understand the secrets of the kingdom. In 13:10, 36 the disciples seek to understand

Jesus' parabolic strategy and imagery. After explaining both to them in his discourse, he concludes by asking them if they understand (13:51–52). Their reply prompts him to utter the final parable of the chapter, that of the householder who brings from his storeroom treasures old and new. Jesus expects that his disciples will have wisdom sufficient for them to apply his teachings to the new situations they will face in ministry for the kingdom of heaven. Their capacity to extrapolate from his teachings is crucial for the advancement of the kingdom. Thus in Matt 15:15 Peter's question about the meaning of 15:11 once again puts Peter squarely within the circle of the disciples. He may be their leader, but he, as well as they, has questions about the implications of Jesus' parables for the future. Jesus' reply to Peter's question is addressed to the disciples as a whole, not to Peter individually (15:16ff.), since Peter is speaking as a disciple for the disciples. In short, Peter is *primus inter pares.*

By common consent the central passage in Matthew on Peter and indeed on the church itself is 16:13–20. Certain features of this passage, primarily Jesus as Son of God and Peter as stumbling block, are shared with the other gospels. These have already been discussed in the previous section of this study, but now the attention is turned to the unique material in 16:17–19 (# 13b). The quest to understand these words of Jesus to Peter has produced a veritable mountain of exegetical and theological literature.[26] These verses have been appropriately described as "the passage which more than any other has figured in controversies about the role of Peter in the New Testament and the implications for the subsequent church."[27] The following brief treatment will focus on the rock saying and upon the binding and loosing. No attempt will be made to deal with the controversial matter of authenticity, which is assumed.

In approaching the passage it must be noted that Jesus had directed two questions to the entire apostolic band (16:13, 15). In 16:14 the disciples in general are represented as answering the question concerning the christology of the people. In 16:16, however, Peter answers the question directed to the disciples concerning their christology. If one has been following Matthew's portrayal of Peter, this is not surprising, for Matthew has already shown Peter to be the disciple who represents the group by word and deed. Peter's christological confession is spoken for the entire apostolic group, which occupies a unique and strategic position in redemptive history.

Through the years protestants have tended to argue that Jesus was not speaking of Peter when he said "you are Peter and upon this rock I will build my church (16:18). Instead it has been argued that Jesus was speaking of himself,[28] or at least of Peter's confession of Jesus' messiahship and deity.[29] The different gender of the words used (Πέτρος, Peter, is masculine; πέτρα, rock, is feminine), as well as subtle distinctions in meaning between Πέτρος and πέτρα have been confidently asserted to preclude any linking of Peter and this rock.[30] However, if such technicalities of grammatical precision were consistently required, it is doubtful whether metaphorical speech would ever be possible. No, it is indeed Peter who is "this rock," and it is doubtful that the above explanations would ever have arisen except as reactions to Roman Catholic developments such as the apostolic succession of the bishops of Rome as popes over the universal church and the infallibility of *ex cathedra* papal utterances. Perhaps the greatest compliment that can be paid to Cullmann's seminal work on Peter is that he argues just as strongly against the sole apostolic authority of the bishops of Rome as he does for Peter being the historical foundation upon whom the church is built.[31]

Peter acts in Matt 16:18 as he does elsewhere in Matthew as spokesman and representative of the disciples. When Jesus replies to Peter's confession, his words constitute a paronomasia or pun. The pun concerns the relation of Peter's name to his unique projected role in redemptive history, and it fits him well as the rest of the NT, primarily the book of Acts, testifies.[32] Other views of the rock do not fare so well as metaphorical speech. For example, if the foundation of the Church is Jesus, then the builder, the owner, and the foundation of the Church are the same person. This is certainly a mixed metaphor which muddles the text. While it is true that 1 Cor 3:11 does speak of Jesus as the Church's foundation, this may be accounted for by the different context and the inherent flexibility of metaphorical language (cf. Matt 7:24–27; Gal 2:9; 1 Pet 2:4–8; Rev 3:12; 21:14). Eph 2:20 combines the thought of Matt 16:18 and 1 Cor 3:11 with the statement that the apostles are the foundation and Jesus is the cornerstone. No doubt in the ultimate sense Jesus is the rock or foundation of the church. But in Matt 16:18 Jesus is speaking of Peter in particular as the representative apostle as the one on whom he will build the church.

Next the relationship of Peter as the church's rock to Peter as the one who holds the keys to the kingdom must be addressed. The keys given to Peter symbolize his authority over exclusion or entrance into the Kingdom, as is indicated by the symbolism of keys elsewhere in the Bible (Isa 22:15, 22; Rev 1:18; 3:7; 9:1–6; 20:1–3). Entrance into the Kingdom as the sphere of God's dynamic rule is featured throughout Matthew in the "gospel of the Kingdom" texts (e.g., 3:2; 4:17, 23; 10:7; 12:28; 13:19; 24:14; cf. 7:13, 21; 23:13; 25:34). It is through their response to this gospel that people enter or are excluded from the Kingdom; Peter and the twelve are to be "fishers for people," the foundational preachers of the gospel (4:19; 10:7). Their preaching of the word of the kingdom (13:19) challenges people to submit to the rule of God in Jesus, who is to be confessed as "the Messiah, the Son of God" (16:16)

This brings the discussion to the interpretation of Peter's binding and loosing (16:19b). It appears that the grammatical problem of the rare periphrastic future perfect construction is not easily solved.[33] Protestant exegesis, which generally opts for taking the construction as a true future perfect, emphasizes that the activity of binding and loosing merely carries out heaven's decisions. In this understanding whatever is bound or loosed on earth has *already* been bound or loosed in heaven. Perhaps the tendency to overreact against the sacerdotalism of Roman Catholicism reappears here. However, taking the passage as equivalent to a simple future construction is not necessarily heretical. When Peter and the church which is built on him bind or loose in the proclamation of the gospel, heaven will ratify their decisions. Heaven has set up the conditions of entrance into the Kingdom: the gospel of the Kingdom requires submission to heaven's rule in Messiah Jesus the Son of God.

One matter must be discussed further before moving on to the next Petrine passage unique to Matthew. It is the relationship of Peter to the other apostles. To what extent is Peter set apart from the eleven? Is it correct, as Brown, Donfried, and Reumann hold, that Peter in 16:16 did not merely speak as a representative of the twelve, since his confession was the result of a personal gift or revelation from God? And does Peter therefore continue to deserve ecclesiastical priority or theological prominence?[34] Though this is not an easy question, the answer seems to be a qualified "no." For Matthew, Peter's confession was no more the result of a special gift or

revelation of God than the earlier confession of all the disciples in
14:33. In Matthew, no one can know or confess the Father or the
Son apart from special divine revelation (11:25–27). Additionally, in
18:15–19 (cf. John 20:21–23), the authority to bind and loose is
delegated to the church which Jesus will build on Peter. Jesus promises to be with his gathered community in this process; nothing is
said about continuing priority for Peter. Further, in 20:25–28 and
23:8–12 Jesus instructs the disciples that they should not give special priority or prominence to any human being. They should seek to
serve, not be served. They should call no mere human "father" or
"rabbi." As the gospel concludes, the humble Jesus has become the
exalted Messiah to whom all authority has been given, and he promises to be with his disciples as they carry out the kingdom mission
which he began while still on earth (28:18–20; cf. 1:23; 18:20).
This would seem to preclude continuing ecclesiastical priority for Peter, who later described himself merely as a fellow elder with some of
his addressees and who viewed Jesus as the chief shepherd or senior
pastor (*pontifex maximus*?!) of the church (1 Pet 5:1–4). Rather,
Peter's prominence or primacy is "salvation-historical" in nature.[35]
He is *princeps apostolorum* due to his foundational historical role
recorded in the gospels and Acts, not due to a continuing ecclesiastical role promoted by a group which claims exclusive authority as his
successors.

The next to last Petrine passage unique to Matthew concerns the
matter of whether Jesus pays the two drachma temple tax (# 15;
17:24–27). In this pericope, when Jesus and the disciples arrive in
Capernaum Peter is asked by the tax collectors whether Jesus pays
the tax. Peter quickly answers in the affirmative but later Jesus
abruptly (before Peter mentions the incident) asks Peter whether the
sons of earthly kings pay taxes to their fathers. Peter observes that
the sons do not pay taxes, but Jesus, assuming the analogy with himself and his Father's temple, advises Peter to pay the tax anyway in
order to avoid offense. Peter will find sufficient funds in the mouth of
the first fish he catches for his own and Jesus' taxes. Three significant factors call for brief comment here. First, the disciples as a
group figure prominently in the context. They are mentioned in
17:24 and the tax collectors' question describing Jesus as "your
teacher" (ὁ διδάσκαλος ὑμῶν) uses the plural pronoun, referring to the
group of disciples. Second, Peter's relationship to the disciples once

again clearly appears to be that of a spokesman. It seems only natural in Matthew for the tax collectors to be drawn to Peter, given such similar incidents as 14:28; 15:15; 16:16, 22; 17:4; 18:21; 19:27; and 26:33. Third, once again Peter acts impulsively and is corrected by Jesus. This fits the pattern of 14:27–31; 16:22; 17:4–5; and 26:33–35. Here the theme of Peter's prominence features his weakness, but his weakness is not disqualifying. Jesus' kingdom authority is sufficient to overcome the weaknesses of his disciples.

The final Petrine passage unique to Matthew is 18:21–22, which concerns the intensity of obligation to reconcile with a sinning brother (cf. Luke 17:4). Jesus has just finished the solemn teaching on the church's obligation to handle offenses between members of the community (18:15ff.). Perhaps this reminded Peter of Jesus' earlier teaching on forgiveness in connection with the model prayer (6:12–15). Peter's question once again features him as the spokesman for the disciples. After the group has heard Jesus' teaching, Peter approaches him privately with a question which was likely on the minds of all the disciples. Just how radically must this principle of forgiveness be applied? Certainly one could not be expected to forgive a sinning brother more than seven times! Jesus' hyperbolic answer (cf. Gen 4:24) shows Peter that there is no limitation on forgiveness in the church, and his following parable illustrates the fact that God has forgiven believers far more than they will ever have to forgive their sinning brothers. Here Peter as spokesman for the disciples learns a lesson for all of them. His weakness in grasping Jesus' radical teaching was likely pandemic among them.

## Petrine Passages Not Mentioned in Matthew

There are four Petrine passages in Mark which have no Matthean parallel (1:35–39; 11:21; 13:3; 16:7). The first three passages do not seem to be significant theologically when compared with Matthew. In all three Peter functions prominently in the circle of the disciples, but he does so in ways which are clearly paralleled in Matthew. The fourth passage, 16:7, is not so easily dismissed, since in it Peter, along with the disciples in general, is to be told that Jesus has arisen and will meet them in Galilee. There is no such implication in Matthew, where the last time Peter is mentioned he is weeping bitterly because he has denied his Lord. The implications of this feature will be discussed in the conclusion to this study.

There are six Petrine passages in Luke which have no Matthean parallel (5:1–11; 8:45; 12:41; 22:8; 22:31–32; 24:34). Three of these passages seem to be unremarkable. Two candidly portray Peter's weaknesses (5:1–11; 22:31–32), but this emphasis is not lacking in Matthew either. As in Mark, there is a post-denial mention of Peter, this time in reference to a post-resurrection appearance of Jesus (24:34; cf. 24:12; John 20:2–6). Taken with Jesus' earlier words about a future ministry for Peter (22:31–32), this passage supplies explicit information about Peter's post-denial ministry which is lacking in Matthew.

John has more unique Petrine material than either Mark or Luke, eight passages in all (1:40–42; 6:8; 6:68; 13:6–10; 13:24; 18:10–11, 15–17; 21:2–22). Of these 6:8 is the least remarkable. The unique denial in Annas's court (18:15–17) does not seem to add much to the denial in Caiaphas's court which is reported in all four gospels. In two passages, Peter's characteristic impetuousness is underlined in a manner not unlike Matthew's (13:6–10; 18:10–11). On another familiar note, Peter appears in the role of spokesman in two passages (6:68; 13:24). The remaining two passages are considerably more significant theologically. In the first (1:40–42), Andrew is given a role which is altogether lacking in Matthew, that of introducing his brother Simon to Jesus. It may be that Matthew does not mention this because it could be understood to compromise Peter's primacy. Also, in this passage John records Jesus' surnaming Simon as Peter, and of course this differs chronologically from the context in which Matthew mentions the naming.[36] The theological implications of this chronological difference are difficult to assess.

A second significant passage is the extended treatment of Peter in John 21, which evidently serves as Christ's rehabilitation of Peter for ministry. Here Peter leads the disciples on a fruitless nocturnal fishing expedition which concludes with a miraculous catch when the risen Jesus appears and instructs the disciples on where to cast their net (cf. Luke 5:1–10). When he realizes that it is Jesus, Peter impetuously jumps into the water (cf. Matt 14:28) and swims to shore, where he and the disciples have breakfast with Jesus. The next vignette in the chapter is the well-known triple question about Peter's love for Jesus, which must have painted Peter considerably. Despite the pain this caused Peter, its purpose was rehabilitative: Peter must feed Jesus' sheep. The final emphasis of the chapter involves Christ's prediction of Peter's destiny of martyrdom, after which Peter asks an unfortunate question about the destiny of the beloved disciple. The Lord responds by repeating what he has just told Peter: "Follow me!" Even in his recommissioning for ministry Peter once again shows the tendency toward impetuous words and deeds which at times bring stinging rebukes from Jesus. But the point to be noted here is that Matthew includes no such recommissioning after the denials.

## CONCLUSION

The results of the present study confirm Kingsbury's theory of "salvation-historical primacy."[37] Kingsbury is correct that Peter should not be viewed primarily as supreme rabbi of the church. This approach exalts Peter over his fellow apostles to an unwarranted degree. The chief rabbi view may sound plausible in 16:17–19, but it fails to convince in view of 16:23; 23:8, 10; 26:74; and 28:16–20. Peter's notable mistakes, the lack of a passage in Matthew where Peter is clearly rehabilitated by Jesus, and Matthew's stress that only Jesus is worthy of the title "rabbi" all militate against the chief rabbi view. If this is true, then neither does Matthew provide support for the Roman Catholic view of Peter's successors as the sole heads of the worldwide church. However, on the narrow point of Peter as the rock in 16:18, Roman Catholic exegesis is essentially correct.

Kingsbury is also correct that Peter is more than merely a typical disciple. Matthew consistently presents Peter as *primus inter pares*, first among equals. Peter is the first of the twelve to be called by Jesus (4:18), and he is stressed as first in Matthew's list of the twelve disciples (10:2). Peter's mother-in-law is the first woman to be healed by Jesus (8:14). Peter repeatedly serves as a spokesman or representative for the twelve (15:15; 16:16; 17:1, 24; 18:21; 19:29). Though he often fails (14:30; 16:22; 17:4, 25; 26:33, 37, 48, 58, 69, 75), his failures typify the foibles of the other disciples who with Peter are blessed not due to flesh and blood but due to the Father's initiative (16:17). In this regard, Matthew includes the comment that Peter's affirmation that he would never deny the Lord was also the affirmation of all the other disciples (26:35).

To return to another question, why is it that Matthew does not mention Peter's post-denial rehabilitation as do the other three gospels (cf. Mark 16:7; Luke 22:31–32; 24:34; John 21:1–23)? Some would say that Matthew has implicitly done this by transferring some pericopes from their original post-resurrection context to a context during the life of the historical Jesus (e.g., 14:28–33; 16:15–19).[38] However, such a position involves methodological and theological assumptions which are untenable. Once again Kingsbury seems to have hit upon a plausible answer—Matthew's characteristic linking of Peter with the other disciples.[39] Though Peter is not mentioned by name after his bitter tears in connection with his denials (26:75), it is clear that Peter with the disciples has been given a mission which will not be thwarted by Jesus' death or by temporary human failure. Both Peter and the church are invested with authority to bind and loose (16:19; 18:18). Similarly, Peter is included with the apostles in both cases where they are sent out on their mission. Just because Peter is not mentioned by name at the head of a list in 28:16 as he is in 10:2 is no indication that Peter is out of the picture. The continuing presence of the risen Christ with his people, a major Matthean theme (1:23; 18:20; 28:20), precludes the need for Peter to receive the limelight of center stage attention. When the angel at the tomb tells the women to tell the disciples that Jesus is risen and will meet them in Galilee (28:7), Peter is among the disciples. And when the disciples go to Galilee to meet Jesus (28:16), Peter goes with them. And when some of them doubt (28:17), it very well may be that Peter doubted too. But Jesus as the exalted Son of Man nevertheless commissioned them for worldwide ministry and promised to be with them all the days (28:20). That Peter stopped doubting and obeyed his risen Lord as the church's rock is written large on the pages of the book of Acts.

But what of Peter's role in the church today? What impact should Matthew's characterization of Peter have upon a generation which is more aware of Sylvester Stallone's Rocky Balboa than it is of Matthew's Simon Rocky Bar Jonah? Instead of lampooning Peter's well-intentioned but misinformed impetuousness, we in these days of informed inactivity should be grateful for any modeling of enthusiasm in ministry. Peter may have often spoken too soon, but do we speak at all? Peter may have seen the waves and begun to sink, but have we even gotten out of the boat? Peter may have asked for help in understanding a difficult parable, but how many times have we feigned understanding of scripture when in reality we don't have a clue? Peter may have been wrong in suggesting that he build booths for Moses, Elijah, and Jesus, but what have we attempted to build?

Peter may have temporarily rejected the necessity of Jesus going to the cross, but have we rejected our responsibility to take up our own cross? In short we would do well in the church today to emulate Peter's enthusiasm, even if at times we make mistakes. And we would do well to emulate Jesus' patience with the mistakes of twentieth century Peters. This would be preferable to the hypercautious, defensive, fortress mentality which so often prevails. A poster on the wall of the office at the lumberyard where I worked as a seminarian said this: "Don't just stand there! Do something, even if it's wrong!" If Jesus could begin to build his church on such a foundation as Peter, "warts and all," he is able to continue its construction through us if we reaffirm Peter's christological confession and model our ministries upon Peter's enthusiasm.

# NOTES

[1]Homer A. Kent, "Matthew," in *The Wycliffe Bible Commentary,* ed. C. F. Pfeiffer and E. F. Harrison (Chicago: Moody, 1962) 945.

[2]The discussion is well summarized by J. D. Kingsbury, "The Figure of Peter in Matthew's Gospel as a Theological Problem," *JBL* 98 (1979) 67–69.

[3]E.g., R. E. Brown, K. P. Donfried, and J. Reumann, *Peter in the New Testament* (Minneapolis/New York: Augsburg/Paulist, 1973) 10–11, 13–14, 75–76. "Q" is a symbol used in the study of the sources of the synoptic gospels and refers to an assumed source for the agreements between Matthew and Luke.

[4]R. T. France, *Matthew: Evangelist and Interpreter* (Grand Rapids: Academie/Zondervan, 1989) 25. France believes that the historical complexity of the situation calls for solutions which are "more realistic than the classical hypotheses, which depend on the assumption of a literarily inactive church (and a relatively insignificant place for oral tradition) and of a method of gospel-composition by simple 'redaction' of one or at most two finished documents, in isolation from the currents of wider church life" (43).

[5]R. H. Gundry, *Matthew: A Commentary on His Literary and Theological Art* (Grand Rapids: Eerdmans, 1982). For a summary of issues surrounding Gundry's commentary, see D. L. Turner, "Evangelicals, Redaction Criticism, and the Current Inerrancy Crisis," *GTJ* 4 (1983) 262–88; 5 (1984) 37–45. See also D. A. Carson, "Gundry on Matthew: A Critical Review," *TrinJ* 3 (1982) 71–91, and the interaction between Gundry and D. Moo in *JETS* 26 (1983) 31–86.

[6]France's discussion of this topic (*Matthew: Evangelist and Teacher,* 46–49) cites works by W. G. Thompson, P. F. Ellis, and J. D. Kingsbury which accept this point. An earlier study by Kingsbury ("Peter") accepted Markan priority in principle (69) but in practice placed much greater stress on Matthew's overall theology (69, 77, 83). In this study Kingsbury called for a shift in priorities wherein "much greater attention is given

to the task of showing how the strain of 'Peter-texts' in the first gospel is properly to be integrated into the whole of Matthew's theology. At this level, exegetical decisions concerning individual passages will have to be made in the light of what one must endeavour to show is the overall structure of Matthew's thought" (83). The present study attempts to follow this agenda.

[7]T. E. Longman III, *Literary Approaches to Biblical Interpretation* (Grand Rapids: Zondervan/Academie, 1987) 54–58, 68–69.

[8]For a careful discussion of Peter's names in the NT, especially Cephas, see J. A. Fitzmyer, "Aramaic *Kepha'* and Peter's Name in the New Testament," in *Text and Interpretation*, ed. E. Best and R. McL. Wilson (Cambridge: University Press, 1979) 121–32. Recently B. D. Ehrman has argued the highly improbable theory that Simon and Cephas were two different people. See "Cephas and Peter," *JBL* 109 (1990) 463–74.

[9]Matt 10:4; 26:14, 25, 47; 27:3; Mark 3:19; 14:10, 43; Luke 6:16; 22:3, 47–48; John 6:71; 13:2, 26, 29; 18:2, 3, 5.

[10]Both are mentioned in Matt 4:21; 10:2; 17:1; Mark 1:19, 29; 3:17; 5:37; 9:2; 10:35, 41; 13:3; 14:33; Luke 5:10; 6:14; 8:51; 9:28, 54. John alone is mentioned in Luke 9:49; 22:8.

[11]Matt 10:3; Mark 3:18; Luke 6:14; John 1:43–46, 48; 6:5, 7; 12:21, 22; 14:8, 9.

[12]Matt 10:3; Mark 3:18; Luke 6:15; John 11:16; 14:5; 20:24, 26–28; 21:2.

[13]Matt 10:3; Mark 2:14; 3:18; 15:40; 16:1.

[14]Matt 9:9; 10:3; Mark 3:18; Luke 6:15.

[15]Matt 10:3; Mark 3:18; Luke 6:14.

[16]Judas son of James: Luke 6:16; John 14:22. Thaddaeus: Matt 10:3; Mark 3:18.

[17]Brown, Donfried, and Reumann (*Peter*, 58–61; 76–79) list 15 Markan passages which refer to Peter and then proceed to compare Matthew's Petrine emphases with the assumption of Markan priority. Given the methodological approach outlined above, it seems more appropriate to provide a general picture of the Petrine material in all the gospels and then to reflect on Matthew as a literary whole in comparison with the other gospels as literary wholes. The list reflects Matthew's ordering of the events.

[18]The list includes two pericopes (## 7 and 13) which have unique Petrine elements in larger stories which have Petrine elements which are common to more than one gospel.

[19]For relevant studies see J. Blank, "The Person and Office of Peter in the New Testament," in *Truth and Certainty* (Concilium 3, ed. E. Schillebeeckx and B. Van Irsel; New York: Herder, 1973) 42–55; Brown, Donfried, and Reumann, *Peter*, 75–87; P. Hoffmann, "Der Petrus-Primat im Matthäusevangelium," in *Neues Testament und Kirche*, ed. J. Gnilka (Freiburg: Herder, 1974) 94–114; Kingsbury, "Peter," 67–83; R. Pesch, "The Position and Significance of Peter in the Church of the New Testament: A Survey of Current Research," in *Papal Ministry in the Church* (Concilium 64, ed. H. Küng; New York: Herder, 1971) 21–35; B. Rigaux, "St. Peter in Contemporary Exegesis," in *Progress and Decline in the History of the Church* (Concilium 27, ed. R. Aubert; New York: Paulist, 1967) 147–79.

[20](# 2) and other numbers like it in the ensuing discussion refer to the comprehensive list of Peter passages from all the gospels, not to the list of Matthean passages.

[21]J. Kingsbury, "Peter," 69.

[22]Some prefer to view Matt 10:1ff. as a parallel to Mark 3:13–19 and Luke 6:12–16. E.g., see K. Aland, ed., *Synopsis Quattuor Evangeliorum* (10th ed.; Stuttgart: Deutsche Bibelstiftung, 1976) 138–39. However, R. T. France is correct in pointing out that "this is not an account of their [the apostles'] selection (as in Mk. 3:13–15; Lk. 6:13, to which Matthew has no parallel), but of their commissioning. They appear here for the first time as an already defined group, whose function is here seen to be that of mission. . . . " See France's *The Gospel According to Matthew* (TNTC; Leicester/Grand Rapids: InterVarsity/Eerdmans, 1985) 176.

[23]For a comparison of the NT lists of the apostles, see D. A. Carson, "Matthew" (Expositor's Bible Commentary, vol. 8, ed. F. Gaebelein; Grand Rapids: Zondervan, 1984) 237.

[24]The manner in which this pericope presents Peter as a model of the life of a disciple is recognized and well expounded by H. J. Held, "Matthew as Interpreter of the Miracle Stories," in G. Bornkamm, G. Barth, and H. J. Held, *Tradition and Interpretation in Matthew* (trans. P. Scott; Philadelphia: Westminster, 1963) 206.

[25]For Matthew's stress on Jesus as the Son of God, see 1:23; 3:17; 4:3, 6; 11:27; 14:33; 16:16; 21:37–41; 22:1, 41–46; 26:63; 27:40, 43, 54; 28:19 and also J. D. Kingsbury, *Matthew: Structure, Christology, Kingdom* (2d ed; Minneapolis: Fortress, 1989) xxi–xxiv; 40–83.

[26]See, e.g., Brown, Donfried, and Reumann, *Peter*, 83–101; J. A. Burgess, "A History of the Exegesis of Matthew 16:17–19 from 1781 to 1965" (Dissertation, Basel, 1965); O. Cullmann, *Peter: Disciple, Apostle, Martyr* (2d ed., trans. F. V. Filson; London: SCM, 1962) 161–242; P. F. Ellis, *Matthew: His Mind and His Message* (Collegeville, MN: Liturgical, 1974) 63–67; 125–34; M. D. Goulder, *Midrash and Lection in Matthew* (London: SPCK, 1974) 383–93; J. P. Meier, *The Vision of Matthew* (New York: Paulist, 1979) 106–21; and M. Wilcox, "Peter and the Rock: A Fresh Look at Matthew xvi. 17–19," *NTS* 22 (1975–76) 73–88.

[27]Brown, Donfried, and Reumann, *Peter*, 83.

[28]E.g., R. C. H. Lenski, *The Interpretation of St. Matthew's Gospel* (Minneapolis: Augsburg, 1943) 626.

[29]E.g., W. Kelly, *Lectures on Matthew* (New York: Loizeaux, 1911) 329; A. H. M'Neile, *The Gospel According to St. Matthew* (London: Macmillan, 1949) 241.

[30]E.g., Lenski, *Matthew*, 625; and S. D. Toussaint, *Behold the King: A Study of Matthew* (Portland, OR: Multnomah, 1980) 202.

[31]Note the following remarks (O. Cullmann, *Peter*, 213): "All protestant interpretations that seek in one way or another to explain away the reference to Peter seem to me unsatisfactory. . . . Upon this disciple, who in the lifetime of Jesus possessed the specific advantages and the specific weaknesses of which the gospels speak, upon him who was then their spokesman, their representative in good as well as in bad, and in this sense was the rock of the group of the disciples—upon him is to be founded the Church, which after the death of Jesus will continue his work on earth.

The Roman Catholic exegesis must be regarded as correct when it rejects those other attempts at explanation. On its part, however, it proceeds in an even more arbitrary way when it tries to find in this text a reference to 'successors.'

On exegetical grounds we must say that the passage does not contain a single word concerning the successors of Peter."

[32]The book of Acts provides a record of Peter's primary role in leading the pre-

pentecost disciples, in preaching on the day of Pentecost and later in the Jerusalem temple, in disciplining sinners, in opening the gospel to the Gentiles, and in settling disputes (Acts 1:15; 2:14; 3:1, 12; 4:8; 5:3, 29; 8:14; 10:34; 11:15–17; 15:7). This record may be coupled with other passages which speak of the apostles as the foundation of the Church (Eph 2:20; 3:5; Rev 21:14; cf. Rom 15:20; Gal 2:9).

[33]Carson's discussion of the problem (*Matthew*, 370–74) aptly and concisely handles the major issues. The construction involves the future of εἰμι coupled with a perfect participle in the predicate. In this case it is ἔσται δεδεμένον . . . ἔσται λελυμένον. The construction occurs twice as parallel apodoses to the parallel indefinite/conditional relative clause protases. The question is whether the apostolic binding/loosing of the protases is prior to the heavenly binding/loosing of the apodoses. The same construction occurs in Matt 18:18. John 20:23 is similar but uses simple perfect verbs in the apodoses.

[34]Brown, Donfried, and Reumann, *Peter*, 87, 106–7.

[35]Kingsbury, "Peter," 71, 81. See also Cullmann, *Peter*, 218–42 for a discussion of the chronological and geographical limitations of Peter's "primacy" even in the early days of the church. Kingsbury responds extensively to Brown, Donfried, and Reumann in "Peter," 74–76, esp. notes 25–26.

[36]On this matter it is sometimes stated that nothing in Matt 16:18 necessitates it being the first time that Jesus refers to Simon as Peter. Be that as it may, the discussion of this harmonistic difficulty lies outside the scope of this study.

[37]Kingsbury, "Peter," 81.

[38]Brown, Donfried, and Reumann, *Peter*, 106.

[39]Kingsbury, "Peter," 82–83.

# The Christian Hope:

# A History of the Interpretation

# of the Millennium

## Robert G. Clouse

In the introduction to a recently published handbook of theology
J. Dwight Pentecost observed that some will seek to understand Holy
Scripture by a study of

> biblical theology, in which the theologian will synthesize the teachings
> of the Bible, deriving these truths, stage by stage, within the time
> boundaries of particular biblical eras or authors' lifetimes. Others will
> develop a systematic theology, in which Bible doctrines may be consid-
> ered comprehensively and organized in a philosophical or logical for-
> mat. Others will study doctrines according to their historical
> development throughout time from the close of the canon of Scripture
> until the present day. . . . Others may concentrate on contemporary
> theology. . . . Still others may pursue the study of Scripture by com-
> paring various systems of theology which have arisen through the
> course of church history.

He concluded that there "is merit and benefit in all these approaches."[1]

As one trained in both theology and church history the writer has
found the study of the historical development of doctrine to be particularly helpful. Both Homer Kent Jr. and his father encouraged students to study the Bible in this way. As one approaches the

---

Robert G. Clouse (A.A., Grace College; B.A., Bryan College; B.D., Grace Theological
Seminary; M.A., Ph.D., University of Iowa) is Professor of History at Indiana State
University, Terre Haute, Indiana.

interpretation of Christian doctrine down through the centuries, there is no passage that benefits more from this treatment than the promise found in Rev 20:1–6 of a millennial kingdom when Christ will reign upon earth and the forces of evil will be restrained.[2]

Interpretations of this coming age have been labeled postmillennial, amillennial, and premillennial.[3] These categories continue in use despite the fact that the distinction involves much more than merely whether Christ returns before or after the millennium. The kingdom expected by the postmillennialist is quite different from that anticipated by the premillennialist, not only with respect to the time and manner with which it will be established but also with regard to the nature of the kingdom and the way Christ exercises His control over it. The postmillenarian believes that the Kingdom of God is extended through Christian preaching and teaching as a result of which the world will be Christianized and will enjoy a long period of peace and righteousness. This new age will not be essentially different from the present and it emerges gradually as an ever larger share of the world's population is converted to Christianity. Evil is not eliminated but is reduced to a minimum as the moral and spiritual influence of Christianity is heightened. During this age the church assumes a greater importance, and many social, economic, and educational problems are solved. The period closes with the second coming of Christ, the resurrection of the dead, and the final judgment.[4]

In contrast to the above view, the amillennialist believes that the Bible does not predict a period of universal peace and righteousness before the end of the world. Instead, good and evil will coexist until the second coming of Christ when the dead are raised and the last judgment held.[5]

The third major interpretation, premillennialism, affirms that the Lord's return will be followed by a period of peace and righteousness before the end of the world, during which Christ will reign as king in person or through a select group of people. This kingdom is not established by the conversion of individual souls over a long period of time, but suddenly and by overwhelming power. The new age will be characterized by the conversion of the Jews and the reign of harmony in nature to such an extent that the desert will blossom like a rose and even ferocious beasts will be tame. Evil is held in check during this period by Christ who rules with a rod of iron. Despite these idyllic conditions people are not satisfied and launch one last rebellion against God and His followers. This final exposure of evil is crushed by Christ and then the last judgment is held. Many premillennialists have believed that during this golden age believers who have died will be reunited with glorified bodies to mingle freely with the rest of the inhabitants of the earth. Usually, premillenarians have taught that the return of Christ will be preceded by certain signs such as the preaching of the Gospel to all nations, a great apostasy, wars, famine, earthquakes, the appearance of the Antichrist, and a great tribulation.[6]

It is necessary once more to caution those who approach the subject of millennialism that the usual classifications are not adequate. Although the terms postmillennial, amillennial, and premillennial have been used to present some of the variety of interpretations, one must constantly guard against a simplistic outlook because of the use of this scheme. For example, it is often stated that postmillennialism is an extremely optimistic creed that is little more than a Christian blessing on the secular teaching that humankind will progress to some utopian social goal. In reality, many of the most fervent evangelicals have taken a postmillennial view, believing that the Holy Spirit can bring a great revival to the world. This outlook has encouraged them to preach the Gospel with great fervency and led to global evangelism and missionary work. It is even possible to be a pessimistic postmillennialist, that is, one who believes the immediate future holds a time of trouble for the church, but that God will send His Spirit in a special way to overcome these problems.

Premillennialism is also a more difficult doctrine to define than it would seem at first glance. Not all premillennialists are consistent and some have decided in ages past to prepare the way for the coming of Christ, even if force was necessary. The current teaching of most premillenarians, that the Jews will be restored to their land and Jerusalem will be the center of the millennial state, has not been followed by all who hold to a premillennial advent. For example, a leading Puritan millennial scholar believed that America would be the center of Christ's kingdom.[7]

Yet another difference that confuses the usual categories of eschatological interpretation is whether the book of Revelation is interpreted in a preterist, historicist, or futurist manner. A preterist is one who believes that most of the prophecies of the Apocalypse have been fulfilled in the past. The historicist (or presentist) considers the events of Revelation now in the process of fulfillment, while the futurist believes that the bulk of the book refers to events to come. Until the nineteenth century most premillennialists used the historicist method of interpretation while today the usual premillennial emphasis is futurist. Despite these qualifications, it is still necessary to refer to premillennial, postmillennial, and amillennial interpretations concerning the second coming of Christ if for no other reason than these categories are so widely used.[8]

In each era of church history including the ancient, medieval, Reformation and modern periods one of these views has tended to predominate. During the first three centuries of the Christian era premillennialism was the prevailing interpretation. The first post-Apostolic writer to express the premillenarian faith was Papias, a bishop of Hierapolis in Phrygia. He describes the golden age of the personal rule of Christ upon earth as characterized by miracles and natural blessings. Not only would the earth yield abundant crops, but peaceful relations would be established among animals and humans. His belief was based upon a combination of Old Testament texts with Revelation 20. Irenaeus, Justin Martyr, Tertullian, Hippolytus, Methodius, Commodianus and Lactantius also kept the Apostolic witness to premillennialism alive.[9]

When Constantine legalized Christianity much of the impetus for millennial teaching passed. Premillennialism thrives when Christians are persecuted or feel themselves pressured by society, but during the fourth century official hostility was replaced by government support for the church. An alternative view of the millennium had already been developed in Alexandria by scholars such as Origen (d. 254). He believed that the Christian hope was to be in heaven not on earth and that believers should take a spiritual interpretation of the Book of Revelation. The amillennialism of the Alexandrine theologians, expanded by Tyconius, a little known Donatist writer of the late fourth century, was adopted by the medieval church because of its acceptance by the prestigious Church Father, Augustine (354–430). Early in his career he had held a millenarian view, but due to the exaggerations and crude materialism of many chiliasts he abandoned the teaching. In support of his new theory he turned to Mark 3:27, "No man can enter into a strong man's house, and spoil his goods, except he will first bind the strong man; and then he will spoil his house." The strong man was Satan, his goods Christians and he was kept away from Christians by being shut up in the abyss, the heart of the wicked.[10] The first resurrection is figurative and represents the conversion experience while the thousand years are symbolic standing for the Christian era. Thus Augustine propounded the doctrine demanded by the times and, applying an allegorical interpretation he believed that the millennium was realized in the church. This doctrine was so fully accepted that at the Council of Ephesus in 431, belief in the millennium was condemned as superstition.

For the next 1300 years Augustinian amillennialism remained the official teaching of the church. However, during the medieval period there was always an undercurrent of premillennialism among individuals such as Joachim of Fiora and the Spiritual Franciscans.[11] In the fourteenth and fifteenth centuries their teaching was revived by various pre-reformation groups including the Hussites.[12] However, the Protestant Reformers of the sixteenth century continued to hold the Augustinian view of the millennium; nevertheless they suggested changes in eschatological interpretation that led to a renewal of premillennialism in the seventeenth century. Martin Luther, for example, advocated a more literal approach to the Bible and identified the papacy with the antichrist. The attention that he called to the prophetic portions of the Bible led some Lutheran scholars to adopt a millennialist interpretation.[13] John Calvin, like Luther, was not impressed with millenarian interpretation, possibly because of the activities of certain Anabaptist groups. Despite Calvin's opposition, a German Calvinist, Johann H. Alsted (1588–1638), revived the teaching of premillennialism, putting it in a more respectable form.[14]

Alsted's work was adopted by a learned Anglican scholar, Joseph Mede, who popularized the premillennial view in the English speaking world. Mede, called by some the greatest biblical scholar that the Anglican church has ever produced, was educated at Cambridge University and afterwards became professor of Greek at that institution.[15] In his book, *Clavis Apocalypticae* (*The Key of the Revelation*) he considered that his great advance in the interpretation of prophecy was his discovery of the "synchronism" of prophecies. By that he meant that much of the prophetic teaching of the book applies to the same period and describes different beings or events during that time span. Mede held that there are three divisions of the Apocalypse and that each of these commences with a voice sounding forth as a trumpet from heaven to the Apostle John. The first of these, beginning in Rev 1:10 is the message to the seven churches; the next which begins with Rev 4:1 is the vision of the seals; and the last is that of the opened book beginning in Rev 10:8. Mede does not explain the message to the churches but he does expound the meaning of the rest of the prophecy. The occurrences of the second division dealt with the Roman Empire, while those in the third reveal the future of the Christian Church. These two systems interact in the second half of the Book of Revelation.

It is helpful to explain the historical application which Mede gave to his work since this was the usual method of early premillennialists. The first six seals picture the fate of pagan Rome, culminating in the conversion of Constantine (A.D. 311). The seven trumpets arise out of the seventh seal and are fulfilled by the barbarian invasion, the division of Rome into ten barbarian successor states, the extinction of the western empire, the war between east Rome and the Ostrogoths, the rise of Islam, the Turkish invasions, and the coming of Christ.

At the same time the sixth trumpet sounds, six vials of judgment are poured upon the anti-Christian world. The first of these vials was fulfilled when the Waldenses, Albigenses, and Hussites denounced the pope as Antichrist, and Rome as Apocalyptic Babylon. The next vial refers to the action of Luther in destroying the authority of the Roman Church over large areas of Europe. The third vial which turned the rivers into blood was fulfilled when the representatives of Rome were killed by the rulers of Europe who followed the Protestant Reformation. These three vials, Mede believed, had been poured out by his time but there were still four vials remaining to be emptied upon papal Rome. These would destroy the ruling House of Austria, the city of Rome, send the Jews to attack the papacy, and prepare the nations for the Battle of Armageddon.

The seventh trumpet begins the Battle of Armageddon during which the papacy and all the other enemies of the church are destroyed and the earth is prepared for the thousand year reign of Christ and His saints. He explains that the kingdom will be "circumscribed within two resurrections, beginning at the judgment of Antichrist, as the morning of that day, and continuing during the space of 1000 years granted to new Jerusalem (the Spouse of Christ), upon this Earth, till the universal resurrection and judgment of all the dead, when the wicked shall be cast into Hell to be tormented for ever, and the Saints translated into Heaven, to live with Christ for ever."[16]

Mede's work was extremely popular both in his own day and in the decades that followed. During the Puritan Revolution of the seventeenth century his ideas helped to fan the fire of prophetic enthusiasm. Despite the radical action of groups like the Fifth Monarchy Men who helped to discredit premillennial belief, there were always individuals of great influence such as Isaac Newton who followed Mede's ideas. Many Bible students in colonial America including Cotton Mather were impressed by the theology of the "great Mede" and followed the ideas of the English scholar.

Although premillennialism continued, it was destined to be eclipsed by postmillennialism during the eighteenth century. Postmillennialism was expressed by Daniel Whitby (1638–1725) who formulated a teaching that can be found in the works of earlier seventeenth-century Puritan writers. An Anglican latitudinarian, he published a two-volume *Paraphrase and Commentary on the New Testament* to which he appended, in place of a commentary on the Revelation, an essay entitled *A treatise of the True Millennium: Showing that it is not a Reign of Persons Raised from the Dead, but of the Church flourishing Gloriously for a Thousand Years after the Conversion of the Jews, and the Flowing in of all Nations to them thus converted to the Christian Faith.* Whitby, as his cumbersome title indicates, believed that the Jews would be converted to Christianity and that this would result in the beginning of the millennium. The golden age was to be a time of ease and plenty, universal peace, freedom from persecution, righteousness, and an era of the special presence of God on earth. He felt that this would be the result of a fresh outpouring of the Holy Spirit as at the day of Pentecost in the Book of Acts. He did not teach a literal appearance of Christ on earth or a resurrection of the dead before the millennium.

During the eighteenth century Whitby's eschatology proved to be very popular. Two writers of popular commentaries on Revelation, Charles Daubuz and Moses Lowman, both espoused the postmillennial view.[17] One of the most influential American theologians who ever lived, Jonathan Edwards, also adopted this outlook. Millennial considerations were more important to Edwards than has often been realized. In fact, he kept a notebook on the Apocalypse which spans nearly three decades of his life.[18] In this work he not only analyzed the book and kept notes on commentators on the Revelation, but he also recorded the signs of the times that he believed were leading to the millennium. Other works which he wrote dealing with this millennial enthusiasm are *A History of Redemption* (1774) and *Some Thoughts Concerning the Present Revival of Religion in New England* (1743). In these books Edwards confesses his belief that there will be a golden age for the church on earth achieved through the ordinary process of preaching the Gospel in the power of the Holy Spirit. This period was to be ushered in by the destruction of Antichrist, whom Edwards identified with the Roman papacy. As a result of papal oppression people were forced into superstition and ignorance and the Bible was taken out of the hands of laymen.

Nevertheless, in every age God had His witnesses and even in the darkest period men such as John Wycliffe and John Hus bore a testimony against Rome. The fifth vial of Revelation, Edwards believed, brought the Protestant Reformation. This movement resulted in the reestablishment of sound doctrine, the propagation of the Gospel to the heathen, and the pietist movement. Learning was revived, the power of the papacy was reduced, and persecution diminished.

The papacy was to continue in power for 1260 years (Rev 16:1) which were to expire either in 1866 or 2016 at which time a great outpouring of the Holy Spirit would result in the destruction of Antichrist. The instrument through which God would work would be the preaching of the Gospel. As a result of this revival, Satan's visible kingdom, the apostate church, would be overthrown and a great age of human happiness would follow. During this time heresy, infidelity, and superstition would be eliminated. Islam would be destroyed, the Jews converted, and the heathen of Africa, America, and India won to Christ. The millennial age was to be characterized not only by great holiness and commitment to Christ but also by a vast increase in knowledge and learning. The reign of Christ would result in international peace and understanding accompanied by the greatest prosperity and happiness the world has ever experienced. In addition to all these impressive blessings, it would be a time when Christianity and the church will be greatly respected.

At the close of the millennial age, however, much of the world was to fall away from Christ and His Church. The vast numbers who make up the armies of Gog and Magog are recruited because people abuse the prosperity of the era to serve lust and corruption. Christ will come and crush this rebellion instituting the last judgment. After the church is caught up in the clouds to meet the Lord in the air, the world will be set on fire and turned into a great furnace where all the enemies of Christ shall be tormented forever.

Just as the influence of Augustine had led the Medieval Church to adopt amillennialism so the teaching of Edwards encouraged the spread of postmillennialism in the modern era. However, there were still individuals who preached premillennialism and by the early nineteenth century their number increased because of a renewal of interest in prophecy fostered by the French Revolution. When the French overthrew their monarch, Europe was plunged into decades of turbulence that encouraged apocalyptic thinking. Many Bible scholars in Britain came to the conclusion that the end of the age was near. Most of these interpreters believed that the papacy must be destroyed before the millennium would come. The Revolution caused the destruction of papal power in France, the seizure of Church property, the founding of a religion of reason, and even for a time the banishment of the pope from Rome. Students of prophecy believed that this "deadly wound" inflicted on the papacy was prophesied in Revelation 13. Biblical chronology seemed to point to the late eighteenth and early nineteenth centuries as the decisive period for the establishment of the millennium.

The new prophetic movement centered in Britain where a vast literature on millennial themes developed in the first half of the nineteenth century. Most of these writers were from the Church of England and the Presbyterian Church of Scotland. Those who led the movement became convinced of the premillennial return of Jesus Christ. They also had a great interest in the conversion of the Jews to Christ and their restoration to the Holy Land. By 1826, Henry Drummond, an influential politician and businessman, had become interested in the conversion of the Jews and the Bible prophecies relating to the second coming of Christ. In that year he held a series of meetings at his estate attended by several important laymen and ministers. These discussions of prophecy were repeated in 1827 and 1828. Drummond himself summarized the conclusions reached at these conferences in the following six points:

1. This "dispensation" or age will not end "insensibly" but cataclysmically in judgment and destruction of the church in the same manner in which the Jewish dispensation ended.

2. The Jews will be restored to Palestine during the time of judgment.
3. The judgment to come will fall principally upon Christendom.
4. When the judgment is past, the millennium will begin.
5. The second advent of Christ will occur before the millennium.
6. The 1260 years of Daniel 7 and Revelation 13 ought to be measured from the reign of Justinian to the French Revolution. The vials of wrath (Revelation 16) are now being poured out and the second advent is imminent.[19]

Many Americans went to Britain where they were caught up in the enthusiasm about the return of Christ. One of these, Eleazar Lord (1788–1871), was a prominent businessman who with his brother David (1792–1880) began to popularize premillennialism in the United States. Eleazar's money and David's erudition and energy made a formidable combination. David wrote numerous books explaining the premillennial view but his most important activity was editing *The Theological and Literary Review.* This periodical which appeared quarterly from 1848 to 1861 featured articles by and of interest to premillennial scholars. Another reason for David Lord's prominence among premillennialists was his systematizing of their doctrine to an extent never before attempted. He set forth rules for the literal method of interpretation so that among many American premillennialists there was an agreed upon standard for prophetic analysis. The suggestions that he made include a careful distinction between "language prophecies" and "symbolical prophecies." The former should conform to the laws of language and grammar which he enumerates for his readers. "The language prophecies are easily distinguishable from those which are symbolical. The symbolical prophecies were, with few exceptions, revealed to the prophet in dreams or visions . . . [and] are all in the past tense."[20] Lord analyzed the four hundred symbols which he believed were found in the Old and New Testaments. He believed that his method, if used consistently, would stop as he stated: postmillennial interpretations. "All figurative expressions in the prophets are thus distinguishable with the utmost certainty and ease from those which are literal; the principles on which the several figures are used make their meaning clear and demonstrable; and they cut off the spiritualization of the predictions to which Anti-millenarians are addicted, as absolutely as the axioms of geometry preclude false processes in that science."[21]

Using these principles, Lord proceeded to elaborate a premillennial system based upon the historicist interpretation of the Book of Revelation. He states bluntly at the beginning of one of his books that humankind as a whole is not to be redeemed under the present dispensation. Rather it is a period of trial when men choose between good and evil and show whether they follow God or not. Mocking the idea of worldwide revival by tracing the history of spiritual awakening through the centuries, he demonstrated to his readers that every period of revival has been followed by a time of backsliding and trouble. The optimism of the postmillennialist, he felt, could be disproved from Scriptures such as John 16:32 and 33, Acts 14:22, and 1 Thess 3:3 and 4 which picture the present age as a time of trial and discipline in which evil and good are tested and made to reveal themselves. The purpose of the present age was to prepare the way for another dispensation during which the world could be redeemed and salvation extended to all nations.

Christ is to return, Lord taught, to inaugurate the millennium and to reign in person during this period. Lord consistently bolstered his views with Scripture references and appeals to the original languages of the Bible. When one reads his work he feels that here is an individual who consciously tried to follow the philological approach while the postmillennial interpreters put a greater stress upon a philosophical understanding of the Christian message.

Lord's system won many followers not only among his fellow New England Calvinists but also among other groups. These premillenarian believers would be found in such major denominations as the Lutheran (Joseph Seiss), Episcopalian (R. C. Shimeall), Methodist (John G. Wilson), Baptist (James Inglis), and Dutch Reformed (John Demarest), as well as the Congregational and Presbyterian churches. The hostility of many of these denominations forced premillennialists to create their own structures. This trend reached its fruition when millenarian conferences were held in the 1870s.

In addition to these national meetings there were local prophecy assemblies such as the Premillennial Advent Society of New York City as well as several Jewish Societies in the leading eastern communities. The formation of these new groups indicates that one had to depart from the general tenor of American life to adopt the premillennial view. The chiliast held a special set of doctrines and subscribed to a rather well defined theology including a literal approach to the Scriptures, two resurrections, and the restoration of the Jews to the Holy Land. "By 1860, millenarianism had emerged so clearly as a peculiar theology that its proponents formed virtually a sect within the larger body of American Protestantism. Like the red thread which the British admiralty used to weave into its cordage to identify it as its own, millenarianism ran through various denominations, part of the whole, but always a self-identifying thing apart."[22] Premillennialism, because it was a well-articulated theology with considerable structure and a defined leadership, was equipped to last and develop as one of the main ingredients of the Fundamentalist movement.

Despite the success of the historicist movement, a new type of premillennialism was to be prominent in the twentieth century called dispensationalism. John Nelson Darby, an early Plymouth Brethren leader, articulated the dispensationalist understanding of prophecy. Through a series of books, which include four volumes on prophecy, his ideas became popular in the English-speaking world. The line of continuity from Darby can be traced through W. E. Blackstone, G. Campbell Morgan, H. A. Ironside, A. C. Gaebelein and C. I. Scofield to more recent times. Dispensationalism has become the standard interpretation for over 200 Bible institutes and seminaries in the United States. Many famous interdenominational evangelists including D. L. Moody and Billy Graham have also adopted this understanding of eschatology. Books and periodicals such as the phenomenal best seller, *The Late Great Planet Earth*, have also popularized this approach.[23]

As the name suggests, dispensationalists believe that God deals with humanity through a series of distinct periods. Although they differ on the exact numbers of these eras, most believe that there are seven dispensations including innocence, conscience or moral responsibility, human government, promise, the law, the church, and the millennium. In each of these ages there is a unique revelation of the divine will and humankind is tested by obedience to this standard. The seventh dispensation, the millennium, is inaugurated by the return of Christ in two stages: the first, a secret rapture which removes the church before the Great Tribulation devastates the earth, and the second, Christ's coming with the Church to establish the kingdom.

The Jews have a prominent place in these events and by the time the millennium is established most of them are converted to Christ. During the millennial age the resurrected saints will rule the world with their Lord. Peace and prosperity will come to earth and worship will center in the rebuilt temple in Jerusalem. At the beginning of the millennium only believers will be alive, but some of their descendants will not accept Christ and they will join Satan in a revolt against God. This final example of human depravity will be defeated by divine intervention, the last judgment held, and the eternal state of heaven and hell established.[24] As previously suggested, this interpretation of the millennial hope is currently the most widely held premillennial view.

In summary, throughout the history of the church each interpretation of the Christian hope has had its share of adherents. During the first three centuries premillennialism seems to have predominated. Beginning in the fifth century with the teaching of the church father Augustine, amillennialism dominated the medieval church. The seventeenth century witnessed a revival of premillennialism and the emergence of postmillennialism. Due to the prestige of scholars such as Jonathan Edwards, postmillennialism prevailed and continued its popularity until the early nineteenth century. By the twentieth century a newer form of premillennialism, dispensationalism, became the major interpretation of those who emphasized the second coming of Christ.[25]

What is the proper view of the millennium? If an answer cannot be decided upon by exegetical considerations, perhaps the approach of historical theology can help to settle the question. In every age when the return of Christ has been a living reality premillennialism has been the prevailing view. Even today it is among dispensationalists that the second coming is emphasized. Those who adopt other views seldom mention the return of Christ and the fact that history will end one day with the establishment of God's kingdom. Neglecting the second coming is a failure to proclaim the whole counsel of God and deprives Christians of a powerful source of comfort. The Gospel is a message of hope and openness toward the future. Premillennialism constantly reminds the believer that no matter how discouraging the situation is today, millennial glory awaits. Perhaps one's social class is declining or his theological viewpoint is on the wane or some great personal tragedy has befallen him yet he may take heart, for one day assuredly he will rule the world with Christ.

# NOTES

[1]Paul Enns, *The Moody Handbook of Theology* (Chicago: Moody, 1989) xii.

[2]The term for a thousand is repeated five times in Rev 20:1-6. The doctrine of the thousand year reign of Christ is called millennialism or millenarianism from the Latin form of the word for a thousand or chiliasm from the Greek.

[3]Helpful information on millennialism is available in the following works: Robert G. Clouse, ed., *The Meaning of the Millennium: Four Views* (Downers Grove, Ill.: Inter-Varsity, 1977); Theodore Olson, *Millennialism, Utopianism, and Progress* (Toronto: University of Toronto, 1982); C. A. Patrides and J. Wittreich, *The Apocalypse in English Renaissance Thought and Literature* (Ithaca: Cornell University, 1984); and Ernest L. Tuveson, *Millennium and Utopia: A Study in the Background of the Idea of Progress* (Berkeley: University of California, 1949). For a general survey of literature about millennialism see Hillel Schwartz, "The End of the Beginning: Millenarian Studies, 1965-1976," *Religious Studies Review* 2 (July 1976) 1-15.

[4]For one of the more perceptive presentations of the postmillennial view see Loraine Boettner, *The Millennium* (Philadelphia: Presbyterian and Reformed, 1966).

[5]For amillennialism one should consult Anthony A. Hoekema, *The Bible and the Future* (Grand Rapids: Eerdmans, 1979).

[6]Premillennialism is explained by Clarence Bass, *Backgrounds to Dispensationalism* (Grand Rapids: Eerdmans, 1960); Charles L. Feinberg, *Millennialism: the Two Major Views* (Winona Lake, Ind.: BMH Books, 1985); Charles Ryrie, *Dispensationalism Today* (Chicago: Moody Press, 1965); and Ernest R. Sandeen, *The Roots of Fundamentalism: British and American Millenarianism* (Chicago: University of Chicago, 1970).

[7]Samuel Sewell, *Phaenomena quaedam Apocalyptica or Some Few Lines Towards a Description of the New Heavens* (Boston, 1697).

[8]Further typologies of millennialism may be found in Paul Christianson, *Reformers and Babylon: English Apocalyptic Visions from the Eve of the Reformation to the Eve of the Civil War* (Toronto: University of Toronto, 1978); James A. DeJong, *As the Waters Cover the Sea: Millennial Expectations in the Rise of Anglo-American Missions 1640-1810* (Kampen: Kok N.V., 1970); Katherine R. Firth, *The Apocalyptic Tradition in Reformation Britain 1530-1645* (Oxford: Oxford University, 1979); James F. Maclear, "New England and the Fifth Monarchy: The Quest for the Millennium in Early American Puritanism," in *Puritan New England: Essays on Religion, Society, and Culture*, ed. A. T. Vaughan and F. J. Bremer (New York: St. Martin's, 1977) 65-89; Ian Murray, *The Puritan Hope: A Study in Revival and the Interpretation of Prophecy* (London: Banner of Truth Trust, 1971); and James West Davidson's fine book, *The Logic of Millennial Thought* (New Haven: Yale University, 1977).

[9]For thoughtful material that substantiates the view taken in this article see Hans Bietenhard, "The Millennial Hope in the Early Church," *Scottish Journal of Theology* (1953) 6, 12-30, and also a longer study by the same author, *Das tausendjahrige Reiche, Eine biblisch-theologishe Studie* (Zurich: Zwingli-Verlag, 1955).

[10]Augustine, *The City of God*, trans. Gerald G. Walsh and Daniel J. Honan, *The

*Fathers of the Church* (New York: Fathers of the Church, Inc., 1954) XXIV, XX, 7, 266f.

[11]Bernard McGinn, *Visions of the End, Apocalyptic Traditions in the Middle Ages* (New York: Columbia University, 1979).

[12]Norman Cohn, *The Pursuit of the Millennium, Revolutionary and Mystical Anarchists of the Middle Ages* (New York: Oxford, 1970).

[13]Robin Bruce Barnes, *Prophecy and Gnosis, Apocalypticism in the Wake of the Lutheran Reformation* (Stanford: Stanford University, 1988).

[14]Robert G. Clouse, "Johann Heinrich Alsted and English Millennialism," *The Harvard Theological Review* (Spring, 1969) 62, 109–207.

[15]Robert G. Clouse, "The Apocalyptic Interpretation of Thomas Brightman and Joseph Mede," *Journal of the Evangelical Theological Society* 11 (1968) 181–93.

[16]Joseph Mede, *The Key of the Revelation*, trans. Richard Moore (London, 1650), compendium on chapter 20.

[17]Charles Daubuz, *A Perpetual Commentary of the Revelation of St. John* (London, 1720), and Moses Lowman, *A Paraphrase and Notes on the Revelation of St. John* (London, 1737).

[18]Stephen J. Stein, "A Notebook on the Apocalypse by Jonathan Edwards," *William and Mary Quarterly*, 3d ser., 29:4 (Oct. 1972). For a critical edition of Edwards' work on the second coming of Christ see Jonathan Edwards, *Apocalyptic Writings*, edited by S. J. Stein (New Haven: Yale, 1977).

[19]Ernest R. Sandeen, *The Roots of Fundamentalism: British and the American Millenarism, 1800–1930*, 21f.

[20]David Lord, *The Coming of Reign of Christ* (New York: 1858) 28ff.

[21]Ibid., 38.

[22]Robert K. Whalen, "Millenarianism and Millennialism in America, 1790–1880" (Unpublished Ph.D. Dissertation, State University of New York at Stony Brook, 1972) 17.

[23]Hal Lindsey, *The Late Great Planet Earth* (Grand Rapids: Zondervan, 1970).

[24]An interesting discussion of the complexities of dispensationalism may be found in *The Rapture: Pre-, Mid-, or Post-Tribulational?* (Grand Rapids: Zondervan, 1984).

[25]For a helpful study of the contrast between contemporary millennial systems see Renald E. Showers, *There Really is a Difference! A Comparison of Covenant and Dispensationalist Theology* (Bellmawr, NJ: The Friends of Israel Gospel Ministry, 1990).

# Ephesians 1:3–14:
# The Blessings of Salvation

## Robert Gromacki

David knew what God had done for him, in him, and through Him. He was thankful and full of praise. He confessed:

> Bless the Lord, O my soul: and all
>     that is within me, bless his holy name.
> Bless the Lord, O my soul, and forget
>     not all his benefits:
> Who forgiveth all thine iniquities; who
>     healeth all thy diseases;
> Who redeemeth thy life from destruction;
>     Who crowneth thee with lovingkindness and
>     tender mercies. (Ps 103:1–4)

Years later, however, the disobedient Jonah had forgotten the words of Israel's covenant king. He tried to run away from Jehovah and from his prophetic responsibilities. Subsequently, in desperation within the belly of the fish, he cried out: "Salvation is of the Lord" (Jonah 2:9). The sea monster then spit Jonah out onto the dry ground and he went on to witness the gracious salvation of Nineveh by a longsuffering God.

One characteristic of the last days in this present church age is that people will be "unthankful" (2 Tim 3:27). This ungrateful attitude should never mark the spiritual children of God (see Eph 5:21; 1 Thess 5:18). Rather, we believers should always praise God for what He has graciously done for us.

---

Robert Gromacki (Th.B., Baptist Bible College; Th.M., Dallas Theological Seminary; Th.D., Grace Theological Seminary) is Professor of Bible and Greek and chairman of the Biblical Education Department at Cedarville College, Cedarville, Ohio.

At the beginning of his epistle to the Ephesians, the apostle Paul set forth the blessings of salvation which the triune God has worked in behalf of the repentant sinner. These twelve verses (1:3–14) constitute one lengthy sentence in the Greek text, composed of 206 words.[1] The entire sentence should be read and studied many times for its sheer spiritual enjoyment. Certain emphases, however, are obvious, and these verbal themes will serve as a popular outline to our understanding of this Biblical passage.

## WORK OF GOD THE FATHER (1:3–6)

God is identified in two ways. First, He is "blessed" (εὐλογητός).[2] This verbal adjective denotes an essential attribute of the divine Being. God is blessed in and of Himself. No creature makes Him blessed. This adjective is used eight times in the New Testament, only of God and never of man (Mark 14:61; Luke 1:68; Rom 1:25; 9:5; 2 Cor 1:3; 11:31; Eph 1:3; 1 Pet 1:3). Thus, Paul praised God for who He is in His intrinsic essence. In contrast, Elizabeth identified Mary as "blessed" (Luke 1:28). This adjective (εὐλογημένη), however, meant that Mary had been blessed by God.[3] She was not blessed in herself; rather, she had received blessing from another in that God had chosen her to be the human channel for the incarnation of the Son of God.

Second, God is "the God and Father of our Lord Jesus Christ."[4] There is a twofold relationship stated here. Christ Himself once said: "I ascend unto my Father, and your Father, and to my God, and your God" (John 20:17). God is not the God and Father of Jesus Christ in the same sense in which He is the God and Father of believers. There is an eternal Father-Son relationship within the trinitarian oneness of the Divine Being, whereas He becomes the Father of believers at the time of their spiritual regeneration (John 1:12). The term "Father" probably points to the relationship with Christ's divine nature, whereas the word "God" shows a relationship to Christ's human nature. The hypostatic union of the two natures within Christ's single person thus manifests this twofold relationship.

### He Has Blessed Us (1:3)

Because God is blessed, He can bless others, and He has. What He does manifests what He is. God is immutable in His being, in His eternal essential attributes; therefore, He always acts consistently. He is the one "who hath blessed" (ὁ εὐλογήσας). This articular aorist participle points to the total redemptive purpose which centers in the accomplished work of Christ in His death, resurrection, and ascension.[5] Positionally, God has already blessed His own.

The *recipients* of the blessing are only believers. The personal pronoun "us" (ἡμᾶς) naturally included Paul and his Ephesian readers, earlier identified as "saints" and "faithful in Christ Jesus" (1:1).

The *sphere* of blessing is marked by a series of three prepositional phrases, all introduced by ἐν ("with" or "in"). The first phrase is literally translated as "in every spiritual blessing" (ἐν πάσῃ εὐλογίᾳ πνευματικῇ). The usage of the singular individualizes each specific action of God. None is excluded. The blessings are "spiritual," rather than material. They doubtless include the works of God enumerated in this passage (e.g., election, predestination, forgiveness, etc.) and countless others. In that culture, enormous wealth was centered in Ephesus and it became known as the Bank of Asia. All believers, in contrast, have been made rich in Christ (see 2 Cor 8:9).

The second phrase can be literally translated "in the heavenlies" (ἐν τοῖς ἐπουρανίοις). This prepositional phrase occurs five times in this epistle (1:3, 20; 2:6; 3:10; 6:12). Elsewhere, the adjective "heavenly" is used of God the Father (Matt 18:35), spoken truth by Christ (John 3:12), the resurrection bodies of believers (1 Cor 15:48–49), the kingdom of God (2 Tim 4:18), divine calling to salvation (Heb 3:1), the gift of salvation (Heb 6:4), the eternal country (Heb 11:16), and the new Jerusalem (Heb 12:22). The phrase does not denote a spatial, geographic location. Rather, it points to those spiritual realities which have their source in the God of heaven. These blessings correspond to the very essence of God. F. F. Bruce claimed that "they are the Christian counterpart to those temporal blessings which the Old Testament promised to those who were pressing on to an earthly inheritance."[6]

The third phrase, "in Christ" (ἐν χριστῷ), manifests a distinctive Biblical positional relationship of believers within the person of the Redeemer. To be in Christ is uniquely Christian. No advocates of other religions are said to be in Buddha, in Mohammed, or in Moses. In anticipation of the results of His redemptive work, Christ said to the apostles: "At that day ye shall know that I am in my Father, and ye in me, and I in you" (John 14:20). The predictive phrase "ye in me" is the very truth which Paul is here explaining. Through the baptism in the Holy Spirit at the time of personal regeneration, a believer is placed into Christ (1 Cor 12:13). This historical actualization within the life of the repentant sinner is the outworking of the divine elective program of God (1:4).

## He Has Chosen Us (1:4)

The conjunction "according as" (καθώς) shows manner rather than cause. God's elective decree is just one manifestation of our spiritual blessedness received from our blessed God.

The *nature* of election is divine self-interest. The verb "he hath chosen" (ἐξελέξατο) is used in soteriological passages only of God (John 13:18; 15:16, 19; 1 Cor 1:27–29; Eph 1:4; James 2:5).[7] God has chosen man; man has not chosen God. The voice of the verb is middle. Although the verb always appears in the middle, this fact does not mean that it is deponent. The stem of the verb can be traced to λέγω, a basic simple verb. It is better to conclude that when God chose, He chose in His own interest, namely for His own glorification. Salvation, including election, must be seen as theocentric rather than anthropocentric.

The *objects* of election are only the saved ("us"). Divine choice is always positive, never negative. Out of grace, God picks out from among a fallen, condemned human race those upon whom He will shower redemptive mercy (Rom 11:5–6).[8] Nowhere does the Bible state that God elects people to hell or condemnation.

The *sphere* of election is in Christ. The phrase "in Him" again denotes the Savior in both His person and redemptive work. Thus, the provision of salvation in Christ must have taken place before the election of believers within the order of the divine decree. This phrase also eliminates self-righteousness as the basis for divine choice.

The *time* of election was in eternity past, "before the foundation of the world." Before the creation of man and before the creation of this time-space universe, God purposed to elect.

The *purpose* of the election was "that we should be holy and without blame before him in love." Is the goal positional righteousness or a practical lifestyle of holiness? Foulkes stated that election is to "holiness of life."[9] Hendriksen wrote that election "does not merely bring him to conversion; it brings him to perfection."[10] The context deals with positional blessings in Christ, therefore it is more plausible to view the adjectives "holy" (ἁγίους) and "without blame" (ἀμώμους) as a reference to a positional standing. Paul later, using the same terminology, wrote in this epistle that Christ's ultimate goal was to present the church as "holy and without blemish" (5:27; cf. Col 1:22). The two adjectives show the two sides of imputed, forensic righteousness—the positive side or the impartation of righteousness in Christ (2 Cor 5:21) and the negative side or the removal of moral guilt. Today, the believer in Christ has this position; ultimately, in eternity his lifestyle will match his acceptable position.

God sees us as He sees His Son. That is the force behind the phrase "before Him." Literally, it can be "under His sight" (κατενώπιον αὐτοῦ). Because we are in Christ, God sees us through His Son.

There is a mild debate over whether the phrase "in love" should go with the elective position of believers before God (v 4) or the decree of predestination (v 5). Marks of punctuation were not in the original text; therefore, the argument cannot be resolved with total satisfaction. God is love, and everything that He does, He does in love. Both election and predestination are expressions of His love. The acceptance of believers in Christ and their eternal conformity to Christ are both the result of initiating divine love. Believers can only love God because He first loved them (1 John 4:19).

### He Has Predestinated Us (1:5–6a)

The *meaning* of predestination has often been misunderstood. It is frequently equated with impersonal fatalism; however, Paul declared it to be the action of a personal loving God. Some theologians prefer the softer term "foreordination" as a synonym for the word "predestination." The English word is based upon a compound Greek term: προορίζω—formed by the verb ὁρίζω and the preposition prefix πρό.[11] The verb literally means "to set a boundary beforehand." The verb ὁρίζω is found eight times in the New Testament (Luke 22:22; Acts 2:23; 10:42; 11:29; 17:26, 31; Rom 1:4; Heb 4:7) whereas the verb προορίζω is used six times (Acts 4:18; Rom 8:29, 30; 1 Cor 2:7; Eph 1:5, 11). Only the verb is employed by the Biblical writers, never the noun.

On the Day of Pentecost, Peter used the term to explain the significance of the crucifixion: "Him, being delivered by the *determinate* counsel and foreknowledge of God, ye have taken, and by wicked hands have crucified and slain" (Acts 2:23). The Cross is a perfect illustration of the harmony between human accountability for an evil action and the divine sovereign will. Later, Peter said that God ordained Christ "to be the Judge of the quick and dead" (Acts 10:42).

The *objects* of predestination are only believers. Note the pronoun "us." The term is never used of the unsaved. Nowhere does the Bible state that God predestinates a sinner to hell. The divine action of foreordination, thus, is positive, never negative. Only the elect are predestined.

The *purpose* of predestination is "unto the adoption of children by Jesus Christ to himself." The prepositional phrase εἰς υἱοθεσίαν literally means "unto son-placing." There is a difference between being a child of God and being a son of God. A person becomes a child of God at the moment of spiritual regeneration (John 1:12). He is then a babe in Christ, one day old, possessing the very life of God. Spiritual adoption also takes place at the time of salvation. In that event, God places the newborn child into the spiritual position of son with all of the attendant responsibilities and privileges (Gal 4:4–5). The ultimate experience of spiritual sonship will occur when a person receives his new immortal body when Christ returns (Rom 8:23).

Under Roman law, a child received the privilege of sonship through a legal process. The father selected a time (e.g., age 21 or 25) when the event would happen. The father would then remove the toga of childhood from his son and replace it with the toga of adulthood. The child was then officially put into the position as a son. In real life, there was a lapse of time between birth and official sonship. In the spiritual family of God, both occur at the same time.

Adoption is secured "by Jesus Christ." This prepositional phrase shows that the ultimate goal of predestination is total conformity to Jesus Christ. This fact can only become reality because of the entire redemptive work of Christ—crucifixion, resurrection, and return.

The *standard* of predestination is "according to the good pleasure of his will." Human merit, as the basis of divine determination, is totally eliminated by the truth of this phrase. Hendriksen noted that what God did "was a result not of sheer determination but of supreme delight."[12] There is a blending of divine joy and volition here. Why did God foreordain? He did it because He willed to do it. Yes, but also, He did it because He enjoyed doing it. The word "good pleasure" (εὐδοκίαν) emphasizes what appears to be good to God. God is good, and what He does always is good, including election and predestination.

The *ultimate goal* of predestination is "to the praise of the glory of his grace" (εἰς ἔπαινον δόξης τῆς χάριτος αὐτοῦ). Predestination exalts the grace of God. So does election (Rom 11:5–6). Neither divine action is deserved by sinful man. There is nothing which he could do to achieve the act of predestination or to keep it.

God is intrinsically gracious. That attribute of His divine essence, however, could not be manifested within the created world unless there was the divine permission for sin to occur and the presence of undeserving sinners. Men alone are accountable for their depravity— for their sinful position before God and their resultant acts of sin. They all deserve eternal condemnation. This human plight provided a perfect occasion for a gracious program of redemption, including the divine decrees of election and predestination. Later, Paul wrote that God saved sinners "that in the ages to come he might show the exceeding riches of his grace in his kindness toward us through Christ Jesus" (Eph 2:7). Throughout eternity, the children of God will praise God for pouring out His redemptive grace upon them. They will glorify God when they outwardly manifest what He is and what he has done. The angels will not be able to participate in the personal reality of this experience.

In that Roman culture, the pagan ascribed praise and glory to their respective gods in order to pacify them and to enlist their support. Biblical Christianity alone praises God for His outpouring of undeserving grace.

The ascription of praise to the glory of God occurs three times in this passage (1:6, 12, 14). Because of the descriptions of the redemptive work of the triune God, it is easy, in a popular fashion, to praise God the Father since He planned our salvation (1:3–6), to praise God the Son since He paid for our salvation (1:6–12), and to praise God the Holy Spirit since He protects our salvation (1:13–14). To Paul, the truth of redemption was not abstract nor merely objective. Rather, it was extremely personal. He was what he was by the grace of God (1 Cor 15:10), and so are we. We should be so overwhelmed by His graciousness that we constantly burst out in glorious praise to our God of loving grace.

### He Has Accepted Us (1:6b)

The *realm* of acceptance is indicated by the English connective "wherein." It is the translation of a prepositional phrase introduced by ἐν ("in") and the object stated by the relative pronoun ᾗ ("which"), followed by a relative clause. The relative pronoun refers back to the antecedent "grace" (χάριτος).[13] The realm of acceptance, thus, is the grace of God.

The *activity* of acceptance can be seen in the verb ("he hath made accepted"). Literally, the Greek verb (ἐχαρίτωσεν) means: "He has graced." The root of the verb is the word "grace." Thus, in the realm of divine grace, God has endued His grace upon undeserving sinners. This verb is used only once elsewhere in the New Testament. The angel Gabriel came to Mary and declared: "Hail, thou that art *highly favored*, the Lord is with thee: blessed art thou among women" (Luke 1:28). Mary was not intrinsically gracious; rather, she became the recipient of God's endowed grace. She did not deserve to become the mother of the promised Messiah. No woman did. In a similar vein, no human being deserves to be accepted by God. As Paul said later: "For by grace are ye saved through faith; and that not of yourselves: it is the gift of God: Not of works, lest any man should boast" (Eph 2:8–9). Salvation, from initiation to completion, is the gracious gift of the God of grace. The aorist tense of the verb locates the divine bestowment of grace at the cross through the death of Christ and its historical application in the spiritual regeneration of the believer.

The *sphere* of acceptance is "in the beloved" (ἐν τῷ ἠγαπημένῳ).[14] Jesus Christ is the beloved one. Paul elsewhere called Christ "the son of His love" (Col 1:13). Both at the baptism and the transfiguration of Christ, the Father declared of Him: "This is my beloved Son, in whom I am well pleased" (οὗτος ἐστιν ὁ υἱός μου ὁ ἀγαπητὸς ἐν ᾧ εὐδόκησα: Matt 3:17; 17:5). There is an eternal love relationship between the Father and the Son. However, the usage of the verb and its application to the concept of salvation probably show that the Father set His love upon the Son because the Son actively obeyed the will of the Father by giving Himself as the sacrifice for sin (Heb 10:7). Christ Himself said: "Therefore doth my Father love me, because I lay down my life, that I might take it again" (John 10:17). The pleasure of God the Father in the Son is focused at the cross. Isaiah wrote: "Yet it pleased the Lord to bruise him; he hath put him to grief: when thou shalt make his soul an offering for sin, he shall see his seed, he shall prolong his days, and the pleasure of the Lord shall prosper in his hand" (Isa 53:10).

Only in Christ can the believing sinner be graced. His justified standing is secure because of the Person who secured it. Someone once exclaimed:

> Nearer, nearer to God
> I cannot be
> For in the person of His Son
> I am as near as He.


## WORK OF GOD THE SON (1:7–12)

This lengthy sentence (1:3–14) ultimately has God the Father as the subject of the main verb. This section should be properly titled: Work of God the Father in and through His Son. However, the emphasis here is on the atonement and its results. Thus, the caption: Work of God the Son.

### He Has Redeemed Us (1:7a)

The prepositional phrase "in whom" (ἐν ᾧ) points back to the beloved Christ.[15] The realm of redemption is in Him, never apart from Him. It is because of who He is that what He does has eternal saving value.

The *meaning* of redemption is important. Literally, the text reads "the redemption" (τὴν ἀπολύτρωσιν). The presence of the definite article shows that Paul is concentrating on specific redemption, namely personal salvation from sin. Several words are used in the New Testament to describe the concept of divine redemption. Christ bought or purchased the provisional redemption of fallen mankind when He paid the price (ἀγοράζω: 1 Cor 6:20; 7:23; 2 Pet 2:1; Rev 5:9; 14:3–4). The cultural imagery is that we were slaves to sin and that He made the payment for our deliverance from the slave market of sin. Christ also died to remove us from the slave market of sin, never to be enslaved again (ἐξαγοράζω: Gal 3:13, 4:5). Through payment and removal, Christ has set us free forever from the penalty of sin (λυτρόω: Luke 24:21; Titus 2:14; 1 Pet 1:18). This last verb (λυτρόω) forms the basis for the term used in this verse and elsewhere (ἀπολύτρωσις: Rom 3:24; Eph 1:17; Heb 9:15). It is also the basis of the word "ransom" used to describe the concept of substitutionary atonement (λύτρον: Matt 20:28; Mark 10:45; and ἀντίλυτρον: 1 Tim 2:6).

The usage of the preposition (ἀπό: "away from") prefixed to the noun (λύτρωσις: Luke 1:68; 2:38; Heb 9:12) stresses the sense of complete freedom and total removal from the domain of sin.

The *possession* of redemption is both present and eternal. It is also very personal. The present tense of the verb ("we have": ἔχομεν) points out the constant inheritance of the entire concept of redemption by every believer.

The *means* of redemption is "through his blood" (διὰ τοῦ αἵματος αὐτοῦ). The blood is a synonym for the death of Christ, but it also specifies the type of death which was necessary to achieve redemption. It had to be a bloody death. Death through natural causes could not atone. When Christ died, He had to shed His blood for "without shedding of blood is no remission" (Heb 9:22). Moreover, Christ Himself predicted that He would have to die through crucifixion (Matt 16:21; 17:22–23; 20:17–19; John 3:14; 12:32–33). Redemption was accomplished through His blood, shed during His crucifixion. It was not achieved by His teaching or sinless life.

## He Has Forgiven Us (1:7b)

The next phrase is a further specification of the nature of redemption. Forgiveness is involved in redemption, but it is not entirely identical with it.

The *area* of forgiveness, of course, is "sins" (τῶν παραπτωμάτων). The term is used in the plural and with the definite article, thus these are particular acts of sin, not the sin principle or the sinful position of fallen man before God. The word is used 23 times in the New Testament, translated as "trespasses," "offences," "fall," "faults," and "sins" (Matt 6:14, 15; 18:35; Mark 11:25, 26; Rom 4:25; 5:15–18, 20; 11:11–12; 2 Cor 5:19; Gal 6:1; Eph 1:7; 2:1, 5; Col 2:13; James 5:16). It is a compound word, formed by the verb "to stumble or fall" (πταίω) and the preposition prefix "beside" (παρά). These sins, thus, manifest, a human failure beside the norm of divine holiness. They are deviations from the divine path of truth and righteousness.

The *standard* of forgiveness is seen in the phrase "according to the riches of his grace." The preposition, "according to" (κατά) puts forth the norm. Forgiveness is according to, not out of, divine grace. God's grace is sufficient to remove the sins of all men, and in so doing, it is never diminished. Paul concluded: "But where sin abounded, grace did much more abound" (Rom 5:20).

The noun "riches" or "wealth" (πλοῦτος) occurs five times in this epistle (1:7, 18; 2:7; 3:8, 16). The adjective "rich" (πλούσιος) appears once (2:4). God is rich in mercy and grace, and he manifests this spiritual wealth by His forgiveness of all types of human sin—both in their quality and quantity. As Micah asked: "Who is a God like unto thee, that pardoneth iniquity, and passeth by the transgression of the remnant of his heritage? he retaineth not his anger forever, because he delighteth in mercy" (Mic 7:18).

## He Has Revealed His Will To Us (1:8–10)

The English connective "wherein" is actually a relative pronoun (ἧς) which points back to its antecedent "grace" (χάριτος; 1:17).[16] God has revealed His redemptive will which manifests His grace abundantly poured out upon His own.[17]

The *sphere* of redemptive revelation is "in all wisdom and prudence" (ἐν πάσῃ σοφίᾳ καὶ φρονήσει). Robinson observed: "Wisdom is the knowledge which sees into the heart of things, which knows them as they really are. Prudence is the understanding which leads to right action."[18] How could sinful men be declared righteous before a holy God? How could God remain just and justify anyone? The issue of human salvation had a two-sided dilemma. However, divine wisdom reveals a plan of redemption which would satisfy the righteousness of God, which would balance His attributes of love, mercy, and justice, and which would glorify His total being. The application of that eternal plan in the lives of believing sinners without violating human accountability shows the marvel of the tension between divine sovereignty and human responsibility. God elects, but man receives. God provides, but man accepts. Both concepts are true.

The *object* of redemptive revelation is "the mystery of his will" (τὸ μυστήριον τοῦ θελήματος αὐτοῦ; 1:9a). The term "mystery" is used six times in this epistle (1:9; 3:3, 4, 9; 5:32; 6:19). In these passages, the concept of mystery refers to the gospel proclamation to both Jews and Gentiles and to their spiritual union as one body in Christ, forming the true church. The salvation of Gentiles in the Old Testament era was known and predicted. However, the blending of redeemed Jews and Gentiles into one body was unknown at that time. Christ predicted that He would build His church and that the foundation of the church would be His death and resurrection (Matt 16:18–21). The rejection of the promised Messiah by Israel led to the establishment of the church age. Elsewhere, Paul wrote: "For I would not, brethren, that ye should be ignorant of this mystery, lest ye should be wise in your own conceits; that blindness in part is happened to Israel, until the fulness of the Gentiles be come in" (Rom 11:25). The provision of redemption for a fallen mankind, the fulfillment of covenant promises to Israel, the establishment of the church, the spiritual body of Christ (1:22–23; 5:32), and the glorification of God all join together to manifest divine omniscience and insight in the outworking of His redemptive will. We should join Paul in his exclamation of praise: "O the depth of the riches both of the wisdom and knowledge of God! how unsearchable are his judgments, and his ways past finding out!" (Rom 11:43).

God must reveal redemptive truth in order for man to be aware of it and to understand it. No man, regardless of his intelligence or study, could ever originate or perceive the precious truths of divine salvation (cf. 1 Cor 2:9–10). They could only be known through the ministry of the Holy Spirit in inspiration and illumination (cf. 1 Cor 2:11–13). The participle "having made known" (γνωρίσας) has its primary application to Paul and other authenticated apostles who received the revealed truth and communicated it through their preaching and writing. Later Paul commented: "How that by revelation he made known unto me the mystery; (as I wrote afore in few words, whereby, when ye read, ye may understand my knowledge in the mystery of Christ) which in other ages was not made known unto the sons of men, as it is now revealed unto his holy apostles and prophets by the Spirit" (Eph 3:3–5). In a secondary sense, then, all believers can know redemptive truth as they understand the inspired Scriptures through the teaching ministry of the Holy Spirit.

The *standard* of redemptive revelation is introduced by the preposition "according to" (κατά). It is God's "good pleasure which he hath purposed in himself" (τὴν εὐδοκίαν αὐτοῦ ἥν προέθετο ἐν αὐτῷ). God's desire and decree are contingent upon nothing outside of Himself. What He wills to do, He does, and what He does is right and good, because He is right and good. The election of undeserving sinners to salvation and the passing over of others to remain in their condemned state are the total expressions of His sovereign, loving purpose. To those who would criticize such divine actions, Paul advised:

"What shall we say then? Is there unrighteousness with God? God forbid. For he saith to Moses, I will have mercy on whom I will have mercy, and I will have compassion on whom I will have compassion. So then it is not of him that willeth, nor of him that runneth, but of God that showeth mercy" (Rom 9:14–16). Even Christ said: "no man knoweth the Son, but the Father; neither knoweth any man the Father, save the Son, and he to whomsoever the Son will reveal him" (Matt 11:27).

The *goal* of redemptive revelation is the total exaltation of Jesus Christ through His supreme rule over a redeemed mankind within the new time-space universe (1:10). The English connective "that" is actually the Greek preposition "unto" (εἰς). The redemptive decree of God goes from eternity past to eternity future. The term "dispensation" (οἰκονομίαν) is a compound word, based upon "house" (οἶκος) and "law" (νόμος). It refers to governance. It can refer to a stewardship (Luke 16:2–4) or to an administration (1 Cor 9:17; Eph 3:2, 9; Col 1:25; 1 Tim 1:4). As applied to Jesus Christ, it refers to His rule as King of Kings within the millennial kingdom and ultimately to His reign as the eternal Lord of the universe. It looks forward to the time when "at the name of Jesus every knee should bow, of things in heaven, and things in earth, and things under the earth; And that every tongue should confess that Jesus Christ is Lord, to the glory of God the Father" (Phil 2:10–11). Foulkes observed: "Jesus Christ orders everything in its full time, and in infinite wisdom orders the time of all things."[19]

The phrase "the fulness of times" (τοῦ πληρώματος τῶν καιρῶν) looks at the completion of God's creative and redemptive decrees in the eternal state. The term "times" (καιρῶν) is often connected with another word (χρόνος). The latter word refers to the passing of linear time, such as days, months, and years. It is so used of the incarnation of Christ: "But when the fulness of the time [τὸ πλήρωμα τοῦ χρόνου] was come, God sent forth his Son, made of a woman, made under the law" (Gal 4:4). The word used here (καιρός) points rather to the historical events ordained of God to move history toward its ultimate goal, namely the establishment of the kingdom of God on earth and throughout eternity. God removes kings and sets up rulers (Dan 2:21). He "changeth the times and the seasons" (Dan 2:21).

The verbal concept "he might gather together in one" is an infinitive (ἀνακεφαλαιώσασθαι), compounded by the preposition "up" (ἀνα) and the word "head" (κεφαλή). Foulkes wrote: "The word was used of gathering things together and presenting them as a whole. The Greek practice was to add up a column of figures and put the sum at the top, and this name was given to the process. So the word was used in rhetoric for summing up an address at the end, and thus showing the relation of each part to the complete argument."[20] As is properly stated, history is His Story. There is a divine significance behind each human event. Ultimately, the human race will find its restoration, unity, and headship in Christ. Right now, it is not so. As one wrote: "Thou has put all things in subjection under his feet. For in that he put all in subjection under him, he left nothing that is not put under him. But now we see not yet all things put under him" (Heb 2:8). When death has finally been subjugated, then the redemptive plan of God, revealed in Scripture, will be completely realized in the sovereign rule of God through His Son (cf. 1 Cor 15:24–28).

### He Has Inherited Us (1:11-12)

The two prepositional phrases referring to Christ ("in Him" and "in whom") appear back-to-back to show the movement of thought in the passage and to stress again the position of the believer in Christ (cf. 1:7, 3, 4, 5, 6, 9, 11, 13). Every redemptive purpose of God centers in His Son.

The *nature* of the inheritance can be seen in the verb (ἐκληρώθη-μεν).[21] The AV translates it as an active voice verb ("we have obtained an inheritance"), stressing what man has gained. Actually, it is a passive voice verb and should be translated: "We were inherited" or "We were obtained as an inheritance." The emphasis is upon the fact that God has gained an inheritance, namely us believers. It is also true that believers are "heirs of God and joint-heirs with Christ" (Rom 8:17). As kings and priests, they will "reign on the earth" when Christ sits on His throne of glory (Rev 5:10).

The *standard* of inheritance again is divine purpose. Believers are "predestinated according to the purpose of him who worketh all things after the counsel of his own will" (1:11b). Several words in this verse show that the redemptive plan is God's alone. The words "counsel" (βουλήν) and "will" (θελήματος) are synonyms, but each is distinctive, especially when they are used together. The sense of "plan" is found within the concept of counsel (cf. Acts 2:23; 4:28;

13:36; 20:27). The predestinated inheritance of God in the believer manifests divine intent and goal within a plan designed by Him out of His sovereign will. Hendriksen astutely wrote: "It would seem to indicate that God never acts arbitrarily, but with deliberation."[22]

The *goal* of the inheritance is the glorification of God through human praise. The prepositional phrase (εἰς τὸ εἶναι ἡμᾶς εἰς ἔπαινον τῆς δόξης αὐτοῦ) is here translated: "That we should be to the praise of his glory."[23] Why did God create man? Why did God redeem man? What is man's purpose? What is the chief end of man? The answer is obvious. God made us and saved us to praise Him for what He has done in and through us and to glorify Him for who He is.

The identity of the group ("we") is further delineated by the English clause: "who first trusted in Christ." In the Greek, it is an articular participial phrase (τοὺς προηλπικότας ἐν τῷ χριστῷ). The verb literally means "to place one's hope beforehand." The perfect tense shows that they fixed their hope within Christ in a crisis moment of time and that they were living in hope as the result of that decision.[24] The value of hope is only as great as the one in whom it is placed. The position of hope in Christ gives the believer absolute assurance because the faithful Christ always keeps His word.

The prefix "before" (πρό) has caused many commentators to make a distinction between the "we" (1:12) group and the "ye" group (1:13). In what sense did one group believe before the other group? Some believe that the "we" group refers to Jews and the "ye" group points to Gentiles.[25] However, the "we" group could be all inclusive, including both Paul and his Ephesian readers, both Jews and Gentiles.[26] The usage of "ye" would simply isolate the readers when Paul wanted to make a special point to them. The "beforehand" concept could also distinguish those who were saved before the conversion of the Ephesians. All believers, both Jews and Gentiles, share equally the blessings of divine salvation in Christ.

## WORK OF GOD THE HOLY SPIRIT (1:13–14)

Up to this point in the passage, only the Father and the Son have been stressed in their involvement in the divine program of salvation. In these two verses, the Holy Spirit is mentioned for the first time. His ministry to believers can be seen in two areas.

## He Is The Seal (1:13)

The *objects* of the seal are believers. The personal pronoun ("ye," ὑμεῖς) indicates that Paul is specifically addressing the Ephesian saints. What is true of them is also true of all believers.

Two actions by them are mentioned. They heard and they believed. Paul briefly preached to the Jews in the synagogue at Ephesus at the conclusion of his second missionary journey (Acts 18:19–21). However, he spent three years in the city during his third trip (Acts 19:1–41; 20:17–38). During this time, "all they which dwelt in Asia heard the word of the Lord Jesus, both Jews and Greeks" (Acts 19:10). They heard "the word of truth" (τὸν λόγον τῆς ἀληθείας). The definite article appears both before "word" and "truth," thus "*the* word of *the* truth." Paul did not preach abstract, philosophical principles. Rather, he proclaimed redemptive truth—the truth that Jesus Christ alone can save the sinner from eternal condemnation (cf. John 14:6). Paul further identified the message as "the gospel of your salvation" (τὸ εὐαγγέλιον τῆς σωτηρίας ὑμῶν).

Hearing must precede believing. There is a logical order, although they may occur chronologically at the same moment. Paul explained: "For whosoever shall call upon the name of the Lord shall be saved. How then shall they call on him in whom they have not believed? and how shall they believe in him of whom they have not heard? and how shall they hear without a preacher?" (Rom 10:13–14). Both verbal actions are participles—"having heard" (ἀκούσαντες) and "having believed" (πιστεύσαντες). The actions of hearing and believing thus preceded the event of divine sealing; however, a person is sealed at the very moment he believes.[27] The phrase "after that ye believed" could also be translated "when ye believed" or "because ye believed."[28]

The nature of the seal is the "Holy Spirit of promise." The main verb ("ye were sealed"; ἐσφραγίσθητε) shows that believers do not seal themselves; rather, at the time of saving faith, they were sealed by God. Foulkes observed: "In New Testament times certain religious cults followed the practice of having their devotees tattooed with the emblem of the cult, and the initiates were then said to have been sealed."[29] Seals were signs of identification, of ownership, of authenticity, and of protection.

Again, the sphere of sealing is in Christ. Twice, the prepositional phrase "in whom" (ἐν ᾧ) is employed to show the spiritual union of believers in Christ—the sphere in which all blessings are made possible (cf. 1:3). However, the seal is the Holy Spirit. The phrase "with that holy Spirit of promise" (τῷ πνεύματι τῆς ἐπαγγελίας τῷ ἁγίῳ) technically does not begin with a Greek preposition. The dative of means, however, can be translated as "with" or "by." Every believer is sealed by God when the Holy Spirit begins to dwell permanently within his life. No believer today is devoid of the Spirit's presence. Paul wrote: "Now if any man have not the Spirit of Christ, he is none of his" (Rom 8:9).

Peter charged his listeners to repent for the remission of sins, "and ye shall receive the gift of the Holy Ghost. For the promise is unto you, and to your children, and to all that are afar off, even as many as the Lord our God shall call" (Acts 2:38–39). The promise of the indwelling Spirit was given by Christ. He said: "And I will pray the Father, and he shall give you another Comforter, that he may abide with you forever" (John 14:16). He added that both the Father and He would send the Spirit once Christ was back in the Father's presence after the Son's death and resurrection (John 14:26; 15:26–27; 16:7).

## He Is The Earnest (1:14)

The relative pronoun "which" (ὅς) introduces a clause in which the second ministry of the Holy Spirit is described.[30] He is "the earnest of our inheritance."

The *meaning* of the term "earnest" (ἀρραβών) is significant. The word is used three times in the New Testament, always of the Spirit (2 Cor 1:22; 5:5; Eph 1:14). The contexts relate the sense of earnest to the sealing of God and to the inner guarantee of an eternal, immortal body. In modern Greek, it is often used of an engagement ring. In extrabiblical documents, illustrations can be found of the word used as a security deposit, a pledge of future payment, a guarantee that more of the same would follow in the future.

The *area* of the earnest is "our inheritance" (τῆς κληρονομίας ἡμῶν). There is a switch in pronouns again, from the second person ("ye") to the first person ("us"). Both Paul and his readers, thus both Jews and Gentiles in Christ, share the same spiritual inheritance. Believers both inherit and were inherited (cf. 1:11).

The *duration* of the earnest is "until the redemption of the purchased possession" (εἰς ἀπολύτρωσιν τῆς περιποιήσεως). The verbal concept behind the concept of "purchased possession" can be seen in Paul's exhortation to the Ephesian elders: "Take heed therefore unto yourselves, and to all the flock, over the which the Holy Ghost hath made you overseers, to feed the church of God, which he hath purchased [περιεποιήσατο] with his own blood" (Acts 20:28). The noun occurs five times (Eph 1:14; 1 Thess 5:9; 2 Thess 2:14; Heb 10:39; 1 Pet 2:9). Peter identified the saved of this church age as a "chosen generation, a royal priesthood, an holy nation, a peculiar people [λαὸς εἰς περιποίησιν]" (1 Pet 2:9). Christ acquired the church when He purchased it at the Cross (Matt 16:18–21). The church, which He is building today, consists of both saved Jews and saved Gentiles. When Christ comes to take the church into heaven, all believers will receive their immortal, incorruptible bodies (1 Cor 15:51–57; 1 Thess 4:13–18).

The *goal* of the earnest is to foster the praise of God. It is "unto the praise of his glory."

## CONCLUSION

The blessings of God, worked out by the Father through the Son and the Holy Spirit, have been set forth in this lengthy sentence (1:3–14). All of us believers should praise the glory of divine grace. All of us should lift our voices and shout "Blessed be God."

# NOTES

[1]Found in the Received Text.

[2]Since it occurs first in the sentence, it is greatly emphasized.

[3]Perfect passive participle of the verb εὐλογέω.

[4]Note the application of the Granville Sharp rule of grammar: ὁ θεὸς καὶ πατὴρ (one article used with two joined nouns).

[5]Force of the constative aorist.

[6]F. F. Bruce, *The Epistle to the Ephesians* (Old Tappan, N.J.: Fleming H. Revell Co., 1961) 27.

[7]Aorist middle indicative of ἐκλέγω/ἐκλέγομαι.

[8]Note the preposition ἐκ prefixed to the verb λέγω.

[9]Francis Foulkes, *The Epistle of Paul to the Ephesians* (Grand Rapids: Wm. B. Eerdmans Publishing Co., 1963) 46.

[10]William Hendriksen, *New Testament Commentary: Exposition of Ephesians* (Grand Rapids: Baker Book House, 1967) 78.

[11]The English word *horizon* is based upon it.

[12]Hendriksen, *op. cit.*, 79.

[13]Both are feminine singular.

[14]Perfect passive participle of ἀγαπάω.

[15]Both are masculine singular.

[16]Both are feminine singular.

[17]The NIV, following the punctuation of the Critical Text, connects v 8 with v 7 and begins a new thought with v 9.

[18]J. Armitage Robinson, *Commentary on Ephesians* (Grand Rapids: Kregel Publications, 1979) 30.

[19]Foulkes, *op. cit.*, 52.

[20]*Ibid.*

[21]Aorist passive indicative.

[22]Hendriksen, *op. cit.*, 88.

[23]The definite article is omitted before δόξης in the critical text.

[24]Perfect active participle.

[25]Bruce, *op. cit.*, 34, and possibly Foulkes, *op. cit.*, 54.

[26]This is the view of Hendriksen also, *op. cit.*, 87.

[27]Both are aorist active participles.

[28]The participle can be either temporal or causal.

[29]Foulkes, *op. cit.*, 56.

[30]The Critical Text uses the neuter relative pronoun (ὅ).

# The Apostle's Watchword: Day of the Lord[1]

## Richard L. Mayhue

The biblical phrase "Day of the Lord" (DOL) stands as a key term in understanding God's revelation about the future. The NT writers' use of DOL rested upon their understanding of the OT prophets. A survey of the OT indicates that it was used by the prophets when speaking of both near historical and future eschatological events. The NT writers picked up on the eschatological use and applied DOL both to the judgment which will climax the Tribulation period and the judgment which will usher in the new earth.

## INTRODUCTION

"Day of the Lord" embodies one of the major strands woven throughout the fabric of biblical prophecy. Without a clear understanding of DOL, the pattern of God's plan for the future would remain less than clear to us.

DOL appears in four uncontested NT passages (Acts 2:20, 1 Thess 5:2, 2 Thess 2:2, and 2 Pet 3:10). However, OT prophets actually wrote more about DOL. The OT provided the basis for

Richard L. Mayhue (B.S., Ohio State University; M.Div., Th.M., Th.D., Grace Theological Seminary) is Vice President and Academic Dean at The Master's Seminary, Sun Valley, California.

whatever Peter and Paul understood about DOL. Beecher argued that

> All doctrines in regard to the millennium, the second coming of Christ, and the final judgment depend greatly on the passages in the New Testament that use the formulas, "the day of the Lord," "the day of our Lord," "that day," and the like; such passages, for example, as 2 Pet. iii:10, 1 Thess. v:2, 1 Cor. i:8, v:5, 2 Cor. i:14, 2 Thess. i:10, 2 Tim. i:12, Matt. xxv:13, etc. The meaning of these passages is, in turn, greatly dependent on the relations that exist, both in ideas and in phraseology, between them and the texts in the Old Testament that speak of "the day of the Lord," that is, "the day of Jehovah." Necessarily, the study of these places in the Old Testament will be profitable, both in itself and for the light it throws on New Testament eschatology.[2]

God's servants, the prophets, spoke of DOL as both near historical and far eschatological events. In many passages DOL moves from the near to the far. This relationship between near and far can be seen in Obadiah, Joel, Isaiah and Zephaniah. Beecher commented, "The prophets thought of the day of Yahweh as generic, not occasions which would occur once for all, but one which might be repeated as circumstances called for it."[3] Kaiser, who has been influenced by Beecher, similarly explains, "That final time would be climactic and the sum of all the rest. Though the events of their own times fitted the pattern of God's future judgment, that final day was nevertheless immeasurably larger and more permanent in its salvific and judgmental effects."[4]

DOL prophecies found fulfillment in various ways. These included (1) the Assyrian deportment of Israel ca. 722 B.C. (Amos 5:18, 20), (2) the Assyrian invasion of Judah ca. 701 B.C. (Joel 1:15; 2:1, 11), (3) the Babylonian exile of Judah ca. 605–586 B.C. (Joel 1:15; 2:1, 11; 13:6; Zeph 1:7; Ezek 13:5), (4) the Babylonian defeat of Egypt ca. 568 B.C. (Ezek 30:3), (5) the demise of Edom ca. 845 B.C. (Obadiah 1–14), and (6) the eschatological judgments of the tribulation period (Obadiah 15; Joel 2:31; 3:14; Isa 2:12; 13:9; Zech 14:1; Mal 4:5).

Specific fulfillments of DOL prophecies are detailed in Scripture. But the question arises whether there are DOL events which are not specifically named as such in Scripture. This is a difficult question because God has certainly intervened in human affairs on more occasions than the prophets specifically outlined. The Genesis flood and the destruction of Sodom and Gomorrah would seem to be cases in point. On the other hand, some seem to view every disaster in history as a DOL event. The solution to the question is to understand that the prophets were calling for present repentance in light of both a near historical judgment and an ultimate eschatological judgment. Feinberg provides a biblically balanced approach to this problem: "Some have interpreted the significant phrase [DOL] to mean any time in which God's judgments are experienced on earth. Although such an interpretation will allow for all the references to be included under it, nevertheless it empties the words of their well-known eschatological force."[5]

The prominent theme of every DOL prophecy is God's judgment of sin. God's blessings are anticipatory and attendant to the DOL but do not assume their intended expression until the DOL concludes; thus the full experience of God's blessing follows, rather than encompasses, DOL.

Imminency often characterizes DOL. In Joel 1:15; 2:1; Isa 13:6; Zeph 1:7; and Ezek 30:3, near historical fulfillments are prominent. The far event is described as "near" in Obadiah 15; Joel 3:14; and Zeph 1:14. In the prophets' minds, the event was certainly coming and would one day occur in the indeterminate future. DOL judgments are poured out on individual nations, such as Edom, Egypt and its allies, and Israel. Yet such judgments will one day be inflicted upon all of the nations according to Obadiah 15 and Zech 14:1. Tasker has written this lucid summary:

> The expression "the day of the Lord" at the time of the rise of the great prophets of Israel denoted an event to which the Israelites were looking forward as the day of Jehovah's final vindication of the *righteousness of His people* against their enemies. One of the tasks of the prophets was to insist that in fact "the day of the Lord" would be a day on which God would vindicate "His *own righteousness*" not only against the enemies of Israel, but also against Israel itself. This "day of the Lord" throughout Old Testament prophecy remains a future reality, though there were events within the history covered by the Old Testament story which were indeed days of judgment both upon Israel and upon the surrounding nations which had oppressed her.[6]

Ladd has succinctly stated the historical-eschatological tension which pressed and pulled at the prophet. His comments are worth noting:

> In all of these prophecies, history and eschatology are so blended together as to be practically indistinguishable. Sometimes, however, the eschatological Day stands in the background on the distant horizon.[7]
>
> The prophets viewed the immediate historical future against the background of the final eschatological consummation, for the same God who was acting in history would finally establish his Kingdom. Therefore, the Day of the Lord was near because God was about to act; and the historical event was in a real sense an anticipation of the final eschatological deed, for it was the working of the same God for the same redemptive purpose. The historical imminence of the Day of the Lord did not include all that the Day of the Lord meant; history and eschatology were held in a dynamic tension, for both *were the Day of the Lord*. This bond was broken in the apocalypses. Eschatology stood in the future, unrelated to present historical events. The God of eschatology was no longer the God of history.[8]

The DOL is a generic biblical phrase used by God's prophets to describe either the immediate future or the ultimate eschatological consummation.[9] It is not a technical term in the sense that it always refers only to one event in God's plan.

> It may designate a divinely-sent locust plague (Joel 1:15) or the providential fall of Babylon (Isa 13:6) or of Jerusalem (Zeph 1:14–15, 18; 2:1); and in one given context it may describe first a judgment and then a corresponding deliverance (compare with the above prophecies Joel 3:14, 18 and Zeph 3:8, 11, 16; cf. also Obadiah 15, 17; Zech 14:1, 9–11).[10]

DOL is used to describe several events and is limited only by its mention in biblical revelation. Each appearance of DOL must be interpreted in its context to determine whether the prophet expected the immediate historical act of God or Yahweh's ultimate eschatological visitation.[11] DOL is not bound to a definite time duration. It could last only for hours or it could continue for days. Only context can determine DOL longevity, and even then only general approximation can be made.

Now, with this Old Testament summary in mind, let us turn our attention to the New Testament.

## OTHER "DAYS" IN THE NEW TESTAMENT

### ἡμέρα *in the New Testament*

General Use

New Testament writers use ἡμέρα about 365 times in their literature. It can basically be outlined in four broad categories.[12]

1. The natural day (from sunrise to sunset)
2. The legal day (includes night)
3. A day appointed for special purposes
4. An indefinite period of time

Context is the key to determining a specific use of ἡμέρα.

Eschatological Use

This data is more usable when classified like this:

I. Days referring to DOL
   A. His day—Luke 17:24
   B. DOL—Acts 2:20
             1 Thessalonians 5:2
             2 Thessalonians 2:2
             2 Peter 3:10
   C. Great day of His wrath—Rev 6:17
   D. Day of wrath and revelation—Rom 2:5
   E. Great Day of God Almighty—Rev 16:14
   F. Day of visitation—1 Pet 2:12
II. Days referring to DOC[13]
   A. Day of our Lord Jesus Christ—1 Cor 1:8
   B. Day of the Lord Jesus—1 Cor 5:5
                           —2 Cor 1:14
   C. Day of Jesus Christ—Phil 1:6
   D. Day of Christ—Phil 1:10
                   —Phil 2:16
III. Days referring to eternity
   A. Day of God—2 Pet 3:12
   B. Day of eternity—2 Pet 3:18
IV. Days referring to judgment
   A. Day of final judgment

      1.  Day of judgment—Matt 10:15
                           —Matt 11:22, 24
                           —2 Pet 2:9
                           —2 Pet 3:7
      2.  The great day—Jude 6
   B.  Indeterminate day of judgment—Matt 12:36
                                 —1 John 4:17
V.  Days referring to salvation
   A.  Day of redemption—Eph 4:30
   B.  Day of salvation—2 Cor 6:2
VI.  Miscellaneous days
   A.  My day—John 8:56 (Christ's life)
   B.  Man's day—1 Cor 4:3 (human judgment)
   C.  The Lord's day—Rev 1:10 (Sunday)
VII.  Days which must each be identified contextually
   A.  The day
   B.  That day
   C.  A day
   D.  Last day(s)
   E.  Those days

### The Day of Jesus Christ

The crucial question to be answered is, Are DOL and DOC to be equated or differentiated? There is no end of speculation. As a background against which to think, a few suggestions are listed here.

A Survey of Positions

Leon Morris writes,

This thought of final judgment carries over into the New Testament understanding of the Day, and one way of referring to it is "the day of Judgment" (II Pet. 2:9). In line with this is its designation as "the day of wrath and revelation of the righteous judgment of God" (Rom. 2:5). By contrast it may be thought of as "the day of redemption" (Eph. 4:30). Again, its connection with the Deity may be stressed, for on that day God's action will be manifested as never before. Thus we find "the day of God" (II Pet. 3:12), "the day of Jesus Christ" (Phil. 1:6), "the day of the Lord Jesus" (I Cor. 1:8). It may be simply "that day" (II Thess. 1:10), or "the last day" (John 6:39f.), or "the great day" (Jude 6). It is clear that the men of the New Testament found a large place for the events of that Day, and that it was a major concept for them.[14]

George Eldon Ladd writes,

The identity of the day of the Lord and of the day of Christ is further substantiated by the conflation of these two phrases. God will confirm His people unto the end that they may be unreprovable "in the day of our Lord Jesus Christ" (I Cor. 1:8). The day of Jesus Christ and the day of the Lord are one and the same day, the day of Christian expectation. Christians are to find delight in another "in the day of our Lord Jesus" (II Cor. 1:14). Here again the object of Christian expectation is the day which is both the day of the Lord and the day of Jesus.[15]

John Walvoord, in response to Robert Gundry's *The Church and the Tribulation*, answered:

A further word needs to be said concerning the relationship of the day of the Lord to "the day of Christ." Gundry argues at length that the various forms of the six occurrences of this phrase (1 Cor. 1:8; 5:5; 2 Cor. 1:14; Phil. 1:6, 10; 2:16) do not justify any distinction from the basic term "the day of the Lord." This is an exegetical problem that does not really affect the question of pretribulationism and post-tribulationism. The contexts of these passages are taken by many to refer to the rapture as a specific event in contrast to the day of the Lord as an extended period of time. If the context of each passage, along with all the references to "the day," is taken into consideration, there is really no problem. Even if Gundry is right in holding that these passages refer to the day of the Lord, they can be understood to refer to the beginning of the extended period of time which follows. It is again begging the question to assume this teaches post-tribulationism, and Gundry does.[16]

## A Proposal

Consider these thoughts as a proposed model to understand DOC in light of its six NT appearances:

1. All DOC passages have believers as their subject.
2. The common theme of all DOC passages is a believer's present life in relationship to the time when he will be "spiritually audited," by Christ.

3. Paul appears to be referring in a very general way, without regard for chronology, to the end. Whether it is the beginning of the end, the middle of the end, or the end of the end cannot be determined by the passages.
4. There is nothing about "rapture" per se (pre- or post-) in any of the six passages.
5. All DOC passages anticipate the positive completion of a believer's redemption.

Proposal Arguments

*From Context.* Regardless of one's predisposition on the issue, there is a clear distinction between the message of the DOL and the DOC passages. God's wrath and judgment of unbelievers mark the DOL, but DOC passages communicate hope and expectation to believers.

*From Phraseology.* It is asserted that context, not phraseology, determines to what a passage refers. Because DOL and DOC passages both talk about Christ does not necessarily mean that they refer to the same event.

Within the scope of this study, two illustrations are instructive. First, these two phrases by form could be judged as synonymous:

the day of God—2 Pet 3:12;
the great day of God, the Almighty—Rev 16:14.

However, a study of these similar phrases in context yields these results:

the day of God—eternity future;
the great day of God, the Almighty—Armageddon.

Second,
the great day—Jude 6
the great and glorious day of the Lord—Acts 2:20
the great day of their wrath—Rev 6:17
the great day of God—Rev 16:14

The Jude 6 passage seemingly refers to the final judgment at the millennium's end while the other three refer to DOL at Christ's second coming. Note also on the other hand, that there is a great difference between the wording in Acts 2:20 and Rev 16:14, but both deal with DOL.

Therefore, just because of similarity in DOL and DOC phrasing, there is no necessary need to equate the two. On the other hand neither does a difference in the phraseology necessarily argue against their identity. Each passage must be handled individually.

*From Consistency.* The phrase ἡμέρα κυρίου is used consistently in the LXX to translate the Old Testament title *yôm yhwh.* In the New Testament, ἡμέρα κυρίου appears in four uncontested passages, and in each instance it is used exactly like it was in the Old Testament.

Because ἡμέρα κυρίου had taken a fixed form in the Old and because both Peter and Paul used it as such, the burden of proof rests on those who want to use DOC and DOL interchangeably to prove or show why Paul would use an entirely different phrase in an entirely different context and still refer to DOL.

Conclusions

1. The form of phraseology cannot be used alone to distinguish between the meaning of DOL and DOC.
2. Context is the interpretive key in understanding DOC phrases.
3. DOC and DOL are not identical nor interchangeable.
4. Paul was not giving a detailed exposition of eschatology when he referred to DOC. This accounts for their lack of detail.
5. Paul's main thought in all six passages is the presentation of believers before God without regard for end time chronology.
6. The judgment seat of Christ (Rom 14:10; 1 Cor 3:13; 2 Cor 5:10) is the event referred to in all six DOC passages.
7. The DOC passages make no contribution to the rapture debate. Whatever is decided about the time of the rapture from determinative passages will then have to be inferred for DOC passages.

*Rev 1:10*

John uses the expression "the Lord's day" (τῇ κυριακῇ ἡμέρᾳ) in Rev 1:10. Some have asserted that this is a reference to DOL and then concluded that the tribulational DOL includes the entire period. This passage relates to the discussion of the DOL *terminus a quo* if it can be demonstrated that John actually meant DOL.

Three positions have commonly been taken on this issue.[17]

1. The term refers to a specific Sunday celebrated annually, i.e., resurrection Sunday or Easter.[18]
2. The eschatological DOL, so prominent in the Old Testament and the subject of much of Revelation, is the time period to which John was transported in the Spirit.[19]
3. This is a reference to the first day of the week or the day which is uniquely associated with Christ because of His glorious resurrection.[20]

Against the Easter view, Stott[21] argues:

1. The usual name for the Easter season was πάσχα.
2. The common phrase for the first day of the week among the early church Fathers was κυριακῇ ἡμέρα.
3. In Ignatius' letter to the Magnesians, he exhorts them not to sabbatize but to live according to the Lord's day.[22] Certainly weekly celebrations, not annual, are in view.
4. The *Didache* speaks of the term as a weekly day of worship, not an annual commemoration.[23]

The following observations argue counter to the DOL view:

1. Regardless of whether one supports the DOL view or the Sunday view, John used this expression in Scripture for the first time.[24] If DOL was in view, it is strongly expected that John would have used the title, ἡμέρα κυρίου, which was used consistently in both the LXX and the New Testament in reference to DOL.
2. Never in the patristic literature is the term κυριακὸς used to refer to the DOL.[25]

This writer, along with the majority of interpreters, supports the Sunday position. These thoughts are offered as substantiation:

1. The term κυριακὸς does have a biblical precedent in 1 Cor 11:20 where it refers to the Lord's supper (κυριακὸν δεῖπον). It provides a model expression which helps to interpret Rev 1:10.
2. It is more reasonable to suggest that John coined a phrase which was followed by the Fathers in reference to Sunday than to believe that John alone coined a phrase which deviated

significantly from the time honored expression for DOL and which no one ever used again with that meaning.

3. The adjective κυριακὸς came from the language of contemporary constitutional law in which it meant "Imperial" or "lordian."[26]

4. In 1 Cor 11:20 and Rev 1:10, κυριακὸς would convey the respective ideas of a supper and a day which speak of Christ's death and life in His redemptive sacrifice at Calvary. Both events symbolize and proclaim the Lordship of Jesus Christ.[27]

This writer concludes with Jewett that

> . . . it is natural to suppose that the usage "Lord's Day" derived from "Lord's Supper" as a fit designation among Christians of the day on which they gathered to celebrate the meal as a culmination of their corporate worship.[28]

## DOL IN THE NEW TESTAMENT

The revelation of God through eight Old Testament prophets provided New Testament writers with a comprehensive description of the DOL concept. Peter and Paul, the only authors to use the phrase ἡμέρα κυρίου, apply and expand this central prophetic concept.

### Acts 2:20

Peter and his Christian companions were gathered in Jerusalem when the Spirit of God came upon them as Christ promised (Acts 1:8, 2:1–4). The Holy Spirit gave them the capacity to speak in other languages so that the international group that had gathered for Pentecost's celebration could each hear the wonders of God in his own language (2:5–12).

But others believed that the disciples were intoxicated and publicly mocked them (2:13). Peter's defense was twofold.

1. The time of day is too early for the disciples to be drunk.
2. The cause of this phenomenon was not alcoholic spirits but the Divine Spirit.

In order to Scripturally substantiate his reasoning, Peter quotes from Joel 2:28–32. The question becomes, "In what sense did Peter understand and use Joel 2?"

There have been four major interpretations.

1. *Fulfillment at Pentecost*—The prophecy of Joel was fulfilled fully and finally on the day of Pentecost. The fulfillment of this prophecy of grace occurred when the Holy Spirit was poured out at Pentecost (Acts 2:17).[29]

2. *Completed at Pentecost*—The fulfillment of Joel's prophecy partially occurred in Joel's day and was finalized at Pentecost.[30]

3. *The "Partial" or "Earnest" Fulfillment*—The Pentecost experience was in part a fulfillment of Joel's words. Some add the idea that the outpouring of God's Spirit at Pentecost was a guarantee that it would happen in full later:

> The gift of tongues was a *partial* fulfillment of the *general* prophecy pertaining to those times. And as the prophecy was partially fulfilled, it was a pledge that it would be entirely; . . .[31]

Another version of this basic view reasons that

> For Peter, this outpouring of the Spirit began the period known in Scripture as "last days" or the "last hour" (1 Jn. 2:18) and then the whole Christian era is included in the expression.[32]

4. *The Eschatological Only Fulfillment*—Joel's prophecy by strict interpretation deals only with DOL which occurs at the Tribulation period conclusion.

> . . . Peter used Joel's prophecy as an illustration of that which was transpiring in his day and not as a fulfillment of this prediction. In short, Peter saw in the events of his day proof that God would yet completely bring to pass all that Joel prophesied. Joel's prophecy then was pre-filled; it is yet (as the Old Testament passage on the outpouring of the Spirit shows) to be fulfilled.[33]

This writer champions the latter interpretation and offers these reasons for support:

1. The phrase that Peter uses to introduce the quote from Joel, "this is what was spoken by the prophet Joel," is not the typical phrase used by New Testament writers. The phrase "in order that it might be fulfilled" is usual fare. Even then, this explicit phrase can be used to introduce an analogous relationship (Jer 31:5 and Matt 2:18) or a preview/partial fulfillment (Isa 53:4 and Matt 8:17). While this point alone does not secure a favorable verdict, it certainly allows for it.

2. The verb εἰμί is often used, not only in the sense of equation, but also to communicate representation.[34] That is what Jesus meant when he said, "I am the door of the sheep" (John 10:7) or "This is my body" (Matt 26:26). It is reasonable to assume that it could be used that way here.

3. Peter is here most likely saying, "this is the sort of thing." He is arguing from analogy or illustration and applying it representatively to his current experience.

4. The dominant theme of DOL is judgment for sin. Because Pentecost was a day of blessing, Peter could not be saying that it fulfilled Joel's prophecy.

5. Note carefully that Peter begins with the outpouring of God's Spirit (Acts 2:17; cf. Joel 2:28) and concludes with the offer of salvation (Acts 2:21, cf. Joel 2:32). These are the only two points with Joel that Peter finds parallel to his present circumstance.

6. The very content of Joel's prophecy argues against its fulfillment at Pentecost. The Spirit was not poured out upon all mankind (Joel 2:28) but rather upon the disciples. Secondly, the cosmic signs were in no way present (Joel 2:30–31). I would agree on this point with Kaiser who calls this Acts 2 experience "a preliminary fulfillment," "mere harbingers," or "samples" of the final Holy Spirit downpour.[35]

7. It has been argued that "the last days" began with the church at Pentecost and encompasses time to the end. Both the Hebrew text and the LXX can be translated "afterward" or "after these things," noting general chronology between burden and blessing. It seems a strange methodology then to use Peter's phrase "in the last days" and make it a technical term referring to the church age. Rather, it seems best to take it at face value, meaning "the last days of the period that Joel mentions," i.e., the end of the Tribulation period and the inception of the millennium. In its most general sense, it means "days that are subsequent to the days now under consideration without regard for intervening time or event." Only context can help determine the time.[36]

This writer suggests that Peter's mention of DOL within his quote of Joel 2:28–32 was probably incidental to his purpose. It adds no interpretive value to our understanding of DOL that had not already been obtained from a study of Joel's prophecy.

## 1 Thess 5:2

Paul began his eschatological discourse in 4:13 where he answered the question, "Will our deceased loved ones be at a disadvantage when Christ comes for believers?" He answered his burdened friends emphatically, "No!" Because of Christ's resurrection (4:14), those dead in Christ will rise first at the rapture (4:16) and then those who are alive and remain will join them (4:17). Together, they will meet the Lord in the air to always be with Him (4:17).

Prophetic matters continued to occupy Paul's instruction in 5:1ff., but the introductory phrase περὶ δὲ introduces a contrast in topic within the same general subject matter, i.e., future events.[37] This becomes the first of two discussions by Paul dealing with DOL. It is interesting to note that the embryonic mention of disciplined living in 4:11 is expanded to a full chapter in 2 Thessalonians 3. What Paul dealt with briefly here became the point of major concern in 2 Thessalonians 2.

Paul began with the times (τῶν χρόνων) and the seasons (τῶν καιρῶν).[38] These terms are used in tandem at Eccl 3:1–8 and Dan 2:21 in the Old Testament. They appear also at Acts 1:7 in the New. They refer to both the general and specific aspects of time and are probably used together to form one idea which answers the question, "When?"

With regard to time, Paul asserted that the Thessalonians had no need of further instruction. He could very well be answering their question, "What is the time and indication of the DOL coming so that we can be prepared?" They knew all that God intended them to know (5:1), and they knew it precisely (5:2 ἀκριβῶς). Jesus had taught the same thing in the Olivet Discourse (Matt 24:36–44).

They were reminded that the well-known and frequently-taught DOL concept in the Old Testament would come unannounced and thus unexpectedly, just like a thief comes unexpectedly, without prior warning.[39] DOL here is to be understood as DOL was in the Old Testament—a time of judgment upon the unbelieving world. Paul's following discussion about night and darkness demands this.

There is a major grammatical indicator in 5:3. Paul switches from the second person plural pronoun referring to the Thessalonians to the third person plural pronoun referring to those who are unsaved. This indicates that the Thessalonians will not be present. Paul gives further explanation in 5:4ff.

Those who do inhabit the earth at that time will expect a time of peace and safety when in fact destruction is inevitable and inescapable. It shall come suddenly and irreversibly (like the birth pangs of a mother-to-be) upon them (5:3).

This was not a new phenomenon in the annals of history. Jeremiah cried out to God that false prophets had led the people astray by promises of lasting peace without war or famine (Jer 14:13; see also 6:14; 8:11). This was during a time which preceded the DOL manifestation in the Babylonian captivity and is analogous to the time preceding the eschatological DOL.

Ezekiel indicted the pseudo-prophets for misleading God's people when there was no peace. Significant here is that it appears in the immediate context of a primary DOL text (Ezek 13:5). The people in Amos' day also foolishly but sincerely expected blessing rather than judgment (5:18).

Paul is saying that the basic circumstances which existed and provoked the historical DOL will also bring about the eschatological DOL. It will be through the deception of Satan (Rev 12:9; 13:11–14) and the permitted delusion by God (2 Thess 2:11) that they will, like those of old, believe what is false in spite of evidence around them to the contrary.

This writer believes that 1 Thess 5:4 holds the real key to understanding the import of this to the Thessalonian church. Paul asserts that these precious believers were not in darkness. He is referring to their spiritual state. Thus, it is implied here, as well as stated explicitly (5:5), that they are sons of light and day.[40]

Because of their right spiritual relationship with God, Paul concludes that "the day," referring to DOL in 5:2, would not overtake them. That is to say, they will not be involved in the DOL.

1 Thessalonians 5 teaches several significant qualities about the eschatological DOL.

1. The Thessalonians knew all that they needed to know about the time of DOL (5:1).
2. The day like a thief will come uninvited, unannounced and unexpected (5:2).

3. The day will come as a complete shock to those expecting peace and safety (5:3).
4. The day is inevitable and irreversible (5:3), like the birth pangs of a woman entering labor.
5. The day will not come upon those of light (5:4), like the Thessalonians.

### 2 Thess 2:2[41]

As Paul concluded his prayer (1:11–12) for the Thessalonians, who were under intense persecution (1:4), he turned to a problem that severely threatened the congregation. What might have been a hint of confusion about DOL in 1 Thessalonians (5:1–11) had erupted into a major issue.

The subject of the unrest appears to have been the relationship of the Parousia to the DOL and the Thessalonian involvement in them. The source of this disturbance was a message which came to the Thessalonians to the effect that the DOL was present (2:2).

In 2 Thess 2:1, the Parousia and the gathering together refer to different aspects of the same event.[42] It pictures perfectly Christ's descent (1 Thess 4:15–16) and the believers' ascent (1 Thess 4:16–17), both parts of which comprise the rapture (1 Thess 4:17; 1 Cor 15:51–52).[43]

The Thessalonians had been shaken from their composure and alarmed by the erroneous report or teaching that they were in the midst of the DOL (2:2). The source of error was a false teacher (πνεῦμα, cf. 1 John 4:1–3), or a messenger from someone with a false message (λόγος), or the carrier of a letter allegedly written by the apostle. It is most likely that their theology was supported by and defended with the trials and tribulations that presently attended the Thessalonians' life circumstances.

Paul answers the Thessalonians' question and addresses the eschatological error by arguing that the present circumstances could in no way be the DOL.

### Background

Posttribulationists have repeatedly argued, "If Paul taught a pretribulational rapture, why did he not simply answer the Thessalonians by saying so instead of giving them the detailed answer we find in 2 Thessalonians?"[44] This is a pertinent inquiry. Many pretribulationists have replied that he did. They proceed to identify the apostasy (2:3) and the restrainer's removal (2:7) as references to the pretribulation rapture.

But it is not necessary for either of these phrases to refer to the rapture. With little support here, pretribulationists have countered with the question, "If Paul originally taught posttribulationism, why did the Thessalonians panic instead of rejoice when they thought the DOL had come?"[45]

These questions and their attempted answers have seemingly led to nothing conclusive or satisfying. Therefore another approach must be taken.

The Evidence

Four pieces of information must be correlated and harmonized to ensure that a correct re-creation of the Thessalonian dilemma has been obtained. They are:

1. Paul's original teaching on the rapture's time;
2. The false teaching that disturbed the Thessalonians;
3. The Thessalonians' response to the false teaching;
4. Paul's answer to the Thessalonians to correct the false teaching.

Three of the four pieces of data are apparently contained in 2 Thessalonians. The false teaching that disturbed the Thessalonians was to the effect that the DOL was present (2:2). The Thessalonians' response was one of alarm and disturbance (2:2). Paul's answer to correct the false teaching can easily be outlined in this way:

A. Certain future events precede or introduce the DOL, therefore you cannot be in the DOL because these events have not yet occurred (2:3–5). These events are:
   1. The mid-tribulational apostasy known as the abomination of desolation (2:3).
   2. The man of lawlessness revealed (2:3–4).
B. Certain immediate factors preclude the precursors or introduction to DOL from occurring (2:6–8).
   1. The present hindrance of lawlessness (2:6–7).
   2. The man of lawlessness is not yet revealed (2:8).

   C. Certain explainable reasons, which are not now present account for the precursors or introduction to DOL (2:9–12).
     1. Diabolical deception (2:9–10).
     2. Divine delusion (2:11–12).

The unknown of what Paul originally taught with regard to the time of the rapture must be deduced from the other three pieces of given data. The question becomes, "What original teaching about the rapture would have accounted for the Thessalonian panic over the false thought that DOL was present and also accounted for the way Paul responded in correcting the error?"

## The Possibilities

First, it is possible that the errorists taught that the Thessalonians were in the DOL knowing that Paul had taught posttribulationism. But one would expect the Thessalonians to rejoice because the rapture would be imminent. In fact, the Thessalonians panicked and thus it is concluded that this is not the correct reconstruction.

Second, it is possible that the errorists taught that the Thessalonians were in the DOL knowing that Paul had taught pretribulationism. The conclusion would be that the Thessalonians had missed the rapture. But this seems unlikely because the Thessalonians would know that the errorists themselves and certainly many others, including Paul, had missed the rapture.

A third possibility does exist. The false teachers taught the Thessalonians that they were in the DOL and additionally that Paul was wrong altogether in that there would be no rapture. Regardless of what Paul taught about the time of the rapture, they insisted that Paul was wrong about the fact of the rapture, i.e., there would be none. The following reasons make this possibility the most compelling.

   1. This third possibility explains why Paul does not appeal directly to the rapture. To do so would have opened Paul to the charge of circular reasoning, and there were no Old Testament passages to which he could point. Therefore, he possibly appealed to Daniel to show that the Thessalonians could not be in the DOL. Paul's strategy was to show that the errorists were wrong on one major point and therefore were unreliable in other major areas such as the fact of the rapture.

2. It explains why he showed them that they were not in the great tribulation of the last 3½ years of the tribulation period. He wanted to teach them how misleading it was to develop or interpret their theology based on current events.
3. It explains why the Thessalonians were shaken. They tested the errorists' theology against the times in which they lived and concluded that they were right and the apostle was wrong. If Paul was wrong on this point, he could have been wrong anywhere.
4. It explains why Paul appealed to his previous messages. His theology had not changed and it was in perfect harmony with Daniel. Paul supported revelatory authentication of theology and discredited experiential verification.
5. It explains why Paul did not assertively appeal to his apostolic authority. The Thessalonians were already under intense pressure from unbelievers in the community and from the disappointment that Paul might be wrong. Paul apparently turns them to the Scriptures.

Conclusions

If this third alternative is true, then it is impossible to determine whether Paul originally taught pre- or post-tribulationism from 2 Thessalonians 2. With a correct interpretation of the components, either position could be understood.

Therefore, 2 Thessalonians 2 is not a primary determinative passage with which to decide the rapture issue. To this writer, the Thessalonian epistles could be understood in light of either position. There are no "watershed" passages on the time of the rapture in Paul's correspondence to the Thessalonian church.

### 2 Pet 3:10

This former Galilean fisherman makes a unique contribution to the study of DOL. He applies the term of judgment to God's terminal wrath poured out on the earth. No other DOL passage uses the term in a detailed reference to the event that immediately precedes eternity future.

The figure of a thief is used, as it was at 1 Thess 5:2, to describe the uninvited, unannounced, and unexpected invasion of God into the affairs of this world. This time the results are devastating. The heavens, the elements, the earth and its works are purged by fire. Parallel passages include Isa 65:17; 66:22; and Rev 21:1. Few would dispute placing this occurrence of DOL at the millennium's end as preparatory to eternity future.[46]

Two important questions are raised.

1. Is the "day of the Lord" at 3:10 the same as the "day of God" in 3:12?
2. Does the DOL encompass the entire millennium or is it limited in 2 Peter 3 to the final judgment?

First, what relationship does DOL have with the "day of God" (3:12)? It has been previously demonstrated that DOL is a time of judgment, not of blessing. A believer according to 2 Pet 3:13 is to look for (προσδοκέω) new heavens and a new earth in which righteousness dwells. The parallel and equative statement is made in 3:12 that a believer is looking for (προσδοκέω) the day of God. Thus the day of God is the supreme blessing of eternity, not a burden. Therefore, it is different from DOL.

Note also the different prepositional phrases used to describe the two days. DOL is a time *in which* (ἐν ᾗ) the heavens and the earth depart. The "day of God," however, is the time *on account of which* (δι᾽ ἥν) the destruction comes. The "day of God" is then a time of eternal blessing which results from the final DOL judgment.[47] It is to be equated with "the day of eternity" in 3:18.

Second, is the DOL a lengthy period that includes the entire millennial period? Most dispensationalists insist that the extended period concept is right. John Walvoord is used here merely to illustrate the point.

> . . . "the day of the Lord" is an extensive time period which includes not only the tribulation and the judgments taking place at the second advent, but which includes also the entire millennial reign of Christ as a time period in which the Lord deals directly with human sin.[48]

Other than the fact that DOL is used to describe a judgment which precedes the millennium and is used to describe the post-millennial, pre-eternity judgment, there is minimal biblical evidence to warrant extending DOL into the millennium. Because DOL is chiefly a time of judgment, the millennium is *not* a part of DOL. In the New Testament, like the Old, DOL is a multiple fulfillment concept which moves toward the final and complete judgment revealed in 2 Pet 3:10.

R. H. Charles said it best:

> ... the Day of Yahweh does not in itself constitute the blessed future, but only the decisive act of judgment which inaugurates it.[49]

## CONCLUSION

### *New Testament Summary*

Peter is dependent upon Joel 2:28–32 which he quotes in his powerful proclamation on Pentecost (Acts 2:17–21). Paul mentions DOL twice in his Thessalonian correspondence. In 1 Thess 5:2 he evidences dependence on Joel 2:9 for the terminology "like a thief." Joel pictures soldiers coming on DOL and entering through windows like thieves. He also associates DOL as coming upon those who cry when disaster is imminent (5:3). This was Ezekiel's indictment of false prophets in the DOL context of Ezekiel 13. 2 Thess 2:2 makes a unique contribution to the study of DOL. Paul writes facts about the precursors to DOL that had not yet appeared anywhere else.

2 Pet 3:10 adds the most unique feature of all the DOL passages. Peter discloses that the DOL concept has an ultimate expression which even the Old Testament prophets did not envision or did not separate from that which they viewed as final. The termination of earth's history is marked by God's final judgment and cleansing of His creation. It is possible that Peter used the terminology of Zeph 1:14. However, he definitely transferred it to the end of time in preparation for the entrance of eternity future.

### *Contribution to Theological Studies*

"Theology" is a descriptive term applied to the comprehensive analysis of biblical data which leads to a theological systematization of that data. Therefore, it should be continually subject to sharpening when a restudy of Scripture warrants. DOL is one aspect of theology which needs meaningful review. A refined understanding of the OT DOL data bears fruit for NT studies.

As a result of this study of DOL in the NT, I suggest that there are two periods of DOL yet to be fulfilled on earth: (1) the judgment which climaxes the tribulation period (2 Thess 2:2; Revelation 16–19), and (2) the consummating judgment of this earth which ushers in the new earth (2 Pet 3:10–13; Rev 20:7–21:1). I would also suggest that DOL will occur only at the end of the tribulation period, not throughout its duration, and that DOL will occur only at the end of the millennium, not throughout its duration.

This study concludes where a final study should begin. That study would examine DOL theologically in light of what has been learned from the OT and NT. In this view, the traditional, dispensational definition of DOL beginning at the pretribulational rapture and extending throughout the millennium[50] or beginning with Christ's second coming and extending through the millennium[51] needs to be modified. The insight gained from both the OT and NT use of DOL provides a basis for a more precise determination of the eschatological period of DOL and a stronger defense of both premillennialism and pretribulationalism.[52]

# NOTES

[1]See Richard L. Mayhue, "The Prophet's Watchword: Day of the LORD," *Grace Theological Journal* 6:2 (Fall, 1985) 231–46, for the first essay which examined DOL as presented in the OT. It serves as essential background for this article.

[2]W. J. Beecher, "The Day of Jehovah in Joel," *The Homiletic Review* 18 (1889) 355.

[3]W. J. Beecher, *The Prophets and the Promise* (New York: Thomas Y. Crowell, 1905) 311.

[4]Walter C. Kaiser, Jr., *Toward an Old Testament Theology* (Grand Rapids: Zondervan, 1978) 191.

[5]Charles Feinberg, *The Minor Prophets* (Chicago: Moody Press, 1976) 172.

[6]R. V. G. Tasker, *The Biblical Doctrine of the Wrath of God* (London: Tyndale, 1951) 45.

[7]George E. Ladd, *The Presence of the Future* (Grand Rapids: Eerdmans, 1974) 68.

[8]Ibid., 320.

[9]Beecher, *The Prophets and the Promise*, 130, defines a generic prophecy as one which "regards an event as occurring in a series of parts, separated by intervals, and expresses itself in language that may apply indifferently to the nearest part, or to the remoter part, or to the whole—in other words, a prediction which, in applying to the whole of a complex event, also applies to some of its parts."

[10]J. Barton Payne, *The Imminent Appearing of Christ* (Grand Rapids: Eerdmans, 1962) 60.

[11]Ladd, *The Presence of the Future*, 74.

[12]W. F. Arndt and F. W. Gingrich, *A Greek-English Lexicon of the New Testament*, 4th rev. ed. (Chicago: The University of Chicago Press, 1952) 346–48.

[13]The day of Christ will be abbreviated DOC. The thrust of this discussion will be to distinguish DOC and DOL.

[14]Leon Morris, *The First and Second Epistle to the Thessalonians*, New International Commentary on the New Testament, ed. by Ned B. Stonehouse (Grand Rapids: Eerdmans, 1959) 151–52.

[15]George E. Ladd, *The Blessed Hope* (Grand Rapids: Eerdmans, 1956) 93.

[16]John F. Walvoord, *The Blessed Hope and the Tribulation* (Grand Rapids: Zondervan, 1976) 119.

[17]Paul K. Jewett, *The Lord's Day* (Grand Rapids: Eerdmans, 1971) 58–59; Robert H. Mounce, *The Book of Revelation*, New International Commentary on the New Testament, ed. by F. F. Bruce (Grand Rapids: Eerdmans, 1977) 76 n 33; and Wilfred Stott, "A Note on the Word KYPIAKH in Rev. 1:10," *New Testament Studies*, 12:1 (Oct. 1965) 70–75 offer excellent discussions.

[18]Cited by E. W. Bullinger, *The Apocalypse*, 3d ed. (London: Eyre and Spottiswoode, 1935) 9, and Stott, "A Note on the Word KYPIAKH in Rev. 1:10," 70.

[19]Bullinger, *The Apocalypse* 9–15; Joseph Seiss, *The Apocalypse*, Vol. I (New York: Charles C. Cook, 1909) 20–21, and John F. Walvoord, *The Revelation of Jesus Christ* (Chicago: Moody Press, 1966) 42.

[20]Examples include Henry Alford, *The Greek New Testament*, Vol. IV, 554; Albert Barnes, *Barnes' Notes on the New Testament* (Grand Rapids: Kregel, reprint 1976) 1547; Jewett, *The Lord's Day*, 58–60; George E. Ladd, *A Commentary on the Revelation of John* (Grand Rapids: Eerdmans, 1972) 31; Mounce, *The Book of Revelation* 76; Stott, "A Note on the Word KYPIAKH in Rev. 1:10," 70–75; and Henry B. Swete, *The Apocalypse of St. John* (London: MacMillan, 1907) 13.

[21]Stott, "A Note on the Word KYPIAKH in Rev. 1:10," 70–75.

[22]" . . . no longer observing Sabbaths, but fashioning their lives after the Lord's day. . . . " Quoted from Ignatius' letter to the Magnesians, para. 9, included in J. B. Lightfoot, *The Apostolic Fathers* (Grand Rapids: Baker, reprinted 1956) 71.

[23]"And on the Lord's own day gather yourselves together and break bread and give thanks, first confessing your transgressions, that your sacrifice may be pure." Quoted from the *Didache*, para. 14, included in Lightfoot, *The Apostolic Fathers*, 128.

[24]Jewett, *The Lord's Day*, 59, reasons, "Does not the creation of a new formula, never before used, indicate that he had something else in mind?"

[25]Stott, "A Note on the Word KYPIAKH in Rev. 1:10," 70–72, has done an excellent job in summarizing the data.

[26]Adolf Deissman, *Light From the Ancient East* (Grand Rapids: Baker, reprinted 1978) 357. He concludes that the phrase in Rev 1:10 probably refers to Sunday but acknowledges the DOL possibility.

[27]Note Paul's seven uses of κύριος in 1 Cor 11:23–32 to emphasize the point. In Rom 10:9, " . . . if you confess with your mouth Jesus as Lord and believe in your heart that God raised Him from the dead, you shall be saved"; resurrection and lordship are here inextricably joined.

[28]Jewett, *The Lord's Day*, 60.

[29]E. J. Young, *An Introduction to the Old Testament*, rev. ed. (Grand Rapids: Eerdmans, 1960) 155. Also E. Henderson, *The Book of the Twelve Minor Prophets*

(London: Hamilton, Adams, & Co., 1845) 115, and R. B. Rackham, *The Acts of the Apostles*, 2d ed. (London: Methuen and Co., 1904) 27.

[30]C. F. Keil, *Minor Prophets*, Commentary on the Old Testament, vol. X, trans. James Martin (Grand Rapids: Eerdmans, reprinted n.d.) 216, acknowledges this position but does not affirm it as correct.

[31]Albert Barnes, *Barnes' Notes on the New Testament*, 303. Also George Eldon Ladd, "The Acts of the Apostles," *Wycliffe Bible Commentary*, ed. by C. F. Pfeiffer and E. F. Harrison (Chicago: Moody Press, 1962) 1127, and Gotthard V. Lechler, "The Acts of the Apostles," *Commentary on the Holy Scriptures*, vol. 9, ed. by J. P. Lange, trans. by C. F. Shaeffer (Grand Rapids: Zondervan, reprinted 1971) 41.

[32]Hobart E. Freeman, *An Introduction to the Old Testament Prophets* (Chicago: Moody Press, 1968) 155; Keil, *Minor Prophets*, 212; and Walter K. Price, *The Prophet Joel and the Day of the Lord* (Chicago: Moody Press, 1976) 66.

[33]Feinberg, *The Minor Prophets*, 82; cf. Richard Longenecker, *Biblical Exegesis in the Apostolic Period* (Grand Rapids: Eerdmans, 1975) 100.

[34]Arndt and Gingrich, *A Greek-English Lexicon of the New Testament*, 222.

[35]Walter C. Kaiser, Jr., *The Uses of the Old Testament in the New* (Chicago: Moody Press, 1985) 99.

[36]See Hans Kosmala, "At the End of the Days," *Swedish Theological Annual*, vol. II (Leiden: E. J. Brill, 1963) 27–31, for an excellent discussion of these terms.

[37]See Arndt and Gingrich, *A Greek-English Lexicon of the New Testament*, 170. Every other use of περὶ δὲ by Paul indicates a shift in thought; cf. 1 Cor 7:1; 7:25; 8:1; 12:1; 16:1, 12; 1 Thess 4:9.

[38]James H. Moulton and George Milligan, *The Vocabulary of the Greek Testament* (Grand Rapids: Eerdmans, reprinted 1972) 315, 694, and R. C. Trench, *Synonyms of the New Testament* (Grand Rapids: Associated Publishers and Authors, n.d.) 197–99. Some assert that quantity of time characterizes χρόνος and quality of time marks καιρός.

[39]See Joel 2:9, Matt 24:42–44, Luke 12:35–40, 1 Thess 5:4, 2 Pet 3:10, Rev 3:3 and 16:15 for κλέπτης used in a prophetic motif. Note also Luke 21:34 where the illustration of a trap (παγίς) is used.

[40]See John 1:4, 5, 7–9; 3:19–20; 8:12; Rom 13:12; 2 Cor 6:14; 1 Pet 2:9; and 1 John 1:5–7 where the idea of light is used in the sense of spiritual purity.

[41]The TR reads Χριστοῦ along with D³ and K. κυρίου is overwhelmingly supported by the uncial evidence, the early versions, and both Greek and Latin fathers.

[42]H. E. Dana and R. Mantey, *A Manual Greek Grammar of the Greek New Testament* (Toronto: The Macmillan Company, reprinted n.d.) 147, describe the Granville-Sharp rule which grammatically allows this conclusion.

[43]παρουσία in 1 Thess 4:15 is paralleled by παρουσία in 2 Thess 2:1. ἁρπάζω in 1 Thess 4:17 parallels ἐπισοναγωγὴ in 2 Thess 2:1.

[44]Robert Gundry, *The Church and The Tribulation* (Grand Rapids: Zondervan, 1973) 119, and Ladd, *The Blessed Hope*, 73–75.

[45]Walvoord, *The Blessed Hope and the Tribulation*, 124.

[46]See R. Larry Overstreet, "A Study of 2 Peter 3:10–13," *Bibliotheca Sacra* 137:548 (Oct.–Dec., 1980) 354–71. George N. H. Peters, *The Theocratic Kingdom*, vol. 2 (New York: Funk and Wagnalls, 1884) 504–9, and Robert D. Culver, *Daniel and the Latter Days* (Chicago: Moody Press, 1954) 179–83, argue unconvincingly

that Peter refers to the time immediately preceding the Millennium.

[47]See also Lewis Sperry Chafer, *Systematic Theology* (Dallas: Dallas Seminary Press, 1948), vol. IV, 401, and vol. VII, 112.

[48]John F. Walvoord, *The Millennial Kingdom* (Grand Rapids: Zondervan, 1959) 273.

[49]R. H. Charles, *A Critical History of the Doctrine of a Future Life* (London: Adam and Charles Black, 1913) 83.

[50]D. E. Hiebert, *The Thessalonian Epistles* (Chicago: Moody, 1971) 211, states that "the day of the Lord is inaugurated with the rapture of the church as described in 4:13-18, covers the time of the great tribulation, and involves His return to earth and the establishment of His messianic reign." Also E. Schuyler English, ed., *The New Scofield Reference Bible*, 1372, has a note which says, "It will begin with the translation of the church and will terminate with the cleaning of the heavens and the earth preparatory to the bringing into being of the new heavens and the new earth."

[51]C. I. Scofield, ed., *The Scofield Reference Bible* (Oxford: Oxford University Press, 1909) 1349, believed that "The day of Jehovah (called, also, "that day" and "the great day") is that lengthened period of time beginning with the return of the Lord in glory, and ending with the purgation of the heavens and the earth by fire preparatory to the new heavens and the new earth (Isa 65:17-19; 66:22; 2 Pet 3:13; Rev 21:1)." See also Chafer, *Systematic Theology*, vol. IV, 398, and V. R. Edmond, "The Coming Day of the Lord," in *Hastening the Day of God*, ed. John Bradbury (Wheaton: Van Kampen, 1953) 233. For other notable examples see Peters, *The Theocratic Kingdom*, 410, and H. C. Thiessen, *Introductory Lectures in Systematic Theology* (Grand Rapids: Eerdmans, 1952) 507. Note also Paul Feinberg, "The Case for the Pretribulation Rapture Position," *The Rapture: Pre-, Mid-, or Post-Tribulational?*, ed. R. Reiter (Grand Rapids: Zondervan, 1984) 61, who suggests that DOL starts about the middle of Daniel's 70th week.

[52]A proposed third and final essay, "The Bible's Watchword: Day of the Lord," would examine DOL with the interpretation of specific OT and NT texts on DOL as the background. Subjects such as (1) precursors to DOL, (2) other dispensationalists and DOL, (3) pretribulationism and DOL, and (4) dispensational contributions would be examined.

# First Corinthians 2:1-5: Paul's Personal Paradigm for Preaching

## George J. Zemek

### INTRODUCTION

During his second missionary journey, Paul preached his way into Europe.[1] Proclaiming the Good News first in Philippi, then in Thessalonica, Berea, and Athens, he arrived at Corinth where he remained for about eighteen months.[2] Along the way, the Jews had harassed him, the gentiles often ridiculed him, and both of these major groups of God-resistant peoples regularly persecuted him. Needless to say, such circumstances presented to Paul, the preacher, many opportunities for concessions and compromises in both his message and method. However, he was always committed to doing God's business in God's way.[3]

Later, in writing to the Corinthians from Ephesus,[4] Paul reminded them of his characteristic commitment to both God's message and method while he had functioned as the Lord's mouthpiece among them. But sharing the Gospel and making disciples in that city might have been the greatest test ever of Paul's ministerial integrity. Morally, "Paul's Corinth was at once the New York, Los Angeles, and Las Vegas of the ancient world,"[5] and intellectually, "the city shared the common Greek love of philosophy and speculation."[6] From a mere scanning of 1 Corinthians it becomes obvious that these were lingering plagues within the professing Christian church at Corinth.

The opening chapters of this epistle especially target the latter of these plagues, the congregation's inordinate preoccupation with reason and rhetoric. Paul found himself being contrasted with various

---

George J. Zemek (B.A., Grace College; M.Div., Th.M., Th.D., Grace Theological Seminary) is professor of theology at The Master's Seminary, Sun Valley, California.

preachers of the Gospel, some of whom may have been giving the Corinthians more of what they wanted rather than what they needed. Not Paul! As A. T. Robertson has well noted about 1 Cor 2:1–5 in its multifaceted context, "Preaching was Paul's forte, but it was not as a pretentious philosopher or professional rhetorician that Paul appeared before the Corinthians."[7]

## THE CONTEXT OF PAUL'S PARADIGM

### Its Wider Theological Dimension

For Paul, theology always determined and regulated methodology. The *how* of his ministry in every area of Christian truth communication was governed by the *what* of his hamartiology and soteriology. Sin and self, often complicated by satanic operations,[8] have left man, in and of himself, helpless and hopeless. Paul's conclusions concerning the unregenerate man are well summarized in 1 Cor 2:14, "Now an unspiritual person never welcomes the things of the Spirit of God, for, you see, they are nonsensical to him; furthermore, he does not even have the ability to begin to know them, since they are discerned spiritually."[9] This means that "at no point does man, acting upon his adopted principle of autonomy, interpret or discern anything [in the eternal or spiritual dimension of reality] correctly."[10] Biblically, it must also be acknowledged that the regenerate man reverts periodically from a theocentric to an anthropocentric mindset, and thereby he too enters into episodes of idolatrous autonomy.[11]

In addition to understanding the utter helplessness and hopelessness of every form of human autonomy Paul acutely recognized the basic impotence of his own innate resources. Consequently, as he assumed his own personal position as a foot-soldier on the front lines of the great spiritual war he did so with only one battlecry: "But God!"[12] In a battlefield strewn with casualties and being attended by spiritual medics who are innately powerless:

> What then is Apollos? And what is Paul? Servants through whom you believed, even as the Lord gave *opportunity* to each one. I planted, Apollos watered, but God was causing the growth. So then neither the one who plants nor the one who waters is anything, but God who causes the growth (1 Cor 3:5–7, NASB).[13]

In light of this, the Commander's strategy must be carried out to the letter without any additions, subtractions, or alterations. For the spiritual soldier insubordination must become unthinkable.

Furthermore, the infantryman's armament must be of divine issue, and his military bearing should be characterized by divine dependence (cf. Eph 6:10–20). It is only then that he will be able to testify:

> For although we live our lives still experiencing creaturely limitations and weaknesses (i.e., ἐν σαρκί) yet we are not carrying on the battle according to our own command or as measured by our own resources (i.e., κατὰ σάρκα), for the weaponry of our warfare is *not* powerless (i.e., σαρκικά) *but* powerful because of its divine source (i.e., δυνατὰ τῷ θεῷ), so powerful that it is able to demolish fortresses; consequently, we, as mere infantrymen, but under God's command and outfitted with His weaponry, are bringing down human reasoning and every proud thing that raises itself up against the knowledge of God, also making every thought a POW with an objective of obedience unto Christ.[14]

In alluding to his divine armament, Paul especially had in mind his propositional weapon, the dynamic Word of God,[15] and his Personal weapon, the powerful Spirit of God.[16] Successful exploits (e.g., 1 Thess 1:5), both in Paul's time and in ours, are experienced only through the effectual synergistic operations of these divinely issued provisions.

Paul's methodological pattern, grounded upon these basic theological foundation stones, needs to be adopted by all Christian truth communicators.[17] Briefly in review, when sharing with the natural man who is sold out to sin, self, and Satan, one must plug himself into the power source of the Word of God, praying that the Spirit of God might be pleased to use His Word to accomplish His sovereign pleasure. Potentially, this is the only antidote for "pride in the pagan." One's approach should not deviate radically from this pattern when conveying the truth to professing believers. Keeping in mind their inevitable struggle with man-centeredness, the one who shares truth exercises his scriptural obligations most faithfully when he draws his dynamic data from the Word and, lovingly but firmly, presents those truths in a straightforward manner, humbly submitting himself and the results to the sovereign Spirit. This approach to the very real hazard of "pride in the pew" bears the imprimatur of God upon it.

The task of methodological assessment, however, is not complete without one final and extremely important evaluation, a self-examination of the channel of truth. This is absolutely essential since far too frequently there exists a problem with "pride in the preacher." Consequently, a paramount issue is one's own heart attitude as he shares the truth. God's mouthpiece must be consumed with his primary prerequisite for ministry, a total dependence upon God and His resources.[18] These basic theological realities will become progressively more concrete as the context and content of Paul's paradigm in 1 Cor 2:1–5 are unveiled.

### Its Narrower Polemical Dimension

#### Their Problem

Symptoms of the problem at Corinth were visible. The church was plagued with ἐν ὑμῖν σχίσματα (1:10); "divisions," "factions," "dissentions," or "cleavages," were being evidenced "among them."[19] The "watchwords"[20] of v 12 clearly document that problem.[21] Various groups within the professing "body of Christ" had been gravitating to different leading personalities and/or preachers.[22] However, that visible phenomenon constituted only the tip of the iceberg, since a larger and more basic problem lurked beneath the surface of the waters.

Stagg has done a commendable job of outlining the more basic problem that Paul faced at Corinth:

> Two wisdoms confront each other in First Corinthians: the "wisdom" of the world and the wisdom of God. . . . The "wisdom" of the world may best be defined as self-centeredness: self-love, self-trust, and self-assertion. . . . Behind all their surface problems was one problem: the "wisdom" of the world. Behind the solution to any problem at Corinth he looked to the Wisdom of God. Thus, in First Corinthians may be seen its underlying motif: God's Wisdom over against the "wisdom" of the world, judging it and offering true answer to the foolish and futile strivings of egocentric man.[23]

Consequently, one must follow Paul's argument carefully through all of its twists and turns especially since he "uses σοφία to mean rhetoric, human speculation and Christ."[24]

*Paul's probings*

After a brief salutation (1:1-3) and prayer (1:4-9), Paul enters immediately into a polemically-charged paraenesis.[25] His theological burden is captured by Scroggs's paraphrastic overview of the apostle's argument: "Let him beware who puts his trust in human wisdom."[26] In confronting the symptoms of 1:11-12, his basic message for those in dissension was: "Stop thinking of Christianity as something in which ingenuity or impressiveness counts."[27]

By employing ironical rhetorical questions (1:13) and briefly rehearsing the history of his ministry among them (1:14-16) he vindicates both his persistent attitude and previous actions with a strategic reference to his divine commission to preach (i.e., 1 Cor 1:17).[28] He had been commissioned not only to do God's business but to do it His way. Indeed, with this affirmation,[29]

> . . . Paul is fully launched on his epistle. . . . The present verse adds hints, which will be taken up in the ensuing paragraphs, about both the content of the Gospel Paul preaches, and the manner in which he preaches it. . . . Paul presents himself as a preacher, not as an orator.[30]

Not only conceptual but also semantical and literary features glue 1:18ff. to the previous verse.[31] Its most immediate connection "is as follows: 'For the preaching with which we are concerned—the preaching of the Cross—is the very antithesis to σοφία λόγου [i.e., that message and method rejected by Paul in v. 17]. . . .'"[32] In the ensuing segment, "Paul discusses wisdom and foolishness in three stages: (a) 1:18-25 fundamentally; (b) 1:26-31 as exemplified by the community; (c) 2:1-5 as exemplified by himself and his preaching."[33] Or, subdividing 1:26ff. into its usual paragraph divisions, Paul outlines: (1) "The Paradox of God's Wisdom" (i.e., 1:26-28); (2) "The Purpose of God's Wisdom" (i.e., 1:29-31); and (3) The Presentation of God's Wisdom" (i.e., 2:1-5).[34]

Paul's "simple testimony"[35] in 2:1-5 is divided literarily into two segments as indicated by emphatic occurrences of κἀγώ[36] in 2:1 and 2:3.[37] In vv 1-2, Paul affirms how he did not come to the Corinthians, while in vv 3-5 he reminds them about how he did come to them.[38] Also, by implication from his statements, he came to them, not as some of the other personalities had undoubtedly come, but contrastingly with great humility.[39]

Concerning the substance of Paul's argument in 2:6ff., "the apostle presents [God's] wisdom as inaccessible to human wisdom, thus as revelatory, known only through the agency of God's own Spirit."[40] The verses which follow 2:1–5 also carry with them much apologetical freight. In them, "he turns . . . away . . . to make a personal defense."[41] Apologetical and polemical variations, accompanied by theological flashbacks relating to the wisdom motif, continue throughout chapters 3 and 4.

## THE CONTENT OF PAUL'S PARADIGM

Within this setting, 1 Cor 2:1–5 is positioned as the methodological gem stone. This one short paragraph constitutes Paul's personal paradigm for preaching, and by extension, covers the whole gamut of conveying God's truth to needy people. Consequently, the ultimate Christian communications seminar is compressed into the affirmations of these five verses.

Organizationally, the passage could be viewed as unfolding in various ways depending upon one's controlling analytical criterion (i.e., stylistic, syntactical, and/or thematic). It has already been noted that the passage divides into two segments stylistically (i.e., vv 1–2 and 3–5).[42] It is obvious that these segments contain Paul's historical reminiscences about his arrival and stay among the Corinthians. Syntactically, his hypotactic[43] and paratactic[44] statements integrate very well into this twofold development.

In order to obtain full benefit from Paul's "seminar," however, it may be appropriate to particularize his various assertions viewing them from a thematic perspective. Therefore, in 1 Cor 2:1–5 Paul offers four personal disclosures which reflect the biblical paradigm for communicating God's truth.

### Paul's Follow-up Disclosure Concerning His Commission (v 1)

Remembering that Paul's entrance into Europe had been accompanied by "a great deal of discouragement,"[45] he nevertheless came to Corinth ministering faithfully according to his commission. When Paul arrived, he arrived preaching[46] the gospel.[47] "He came as a man who simply *announces* (καταγγέλων) a fact."[48] Among the many NT synonyms for preaching (cf., e.g., εὐαγγελίζομαι in 1:17,

and κηρύσσω in 1:23),[49] καταγγέλω places the emphasis upon "proclamation or declaration."[50] "The thought of solemn proclamation is
uppermost,"[51] especially since this word group is normally associated with the mouthpiece's mission or commission.[52]

However, his divine commission to preach, announce, or declare
God's gospel allowed no room for man's measure and method of
ministry. By the strong negation οὐ καθ' ὑπεροχὴν λόγου ἢ σοφίας,
literally "not in accordance with a superiority of word or wisdom,"
Paul bore witness that he did not do God's business man's way.[53]
He would not allow himself to be, and consequently was not, drawn
to culturally characteristic excesses[54] in the areas of articulation and
argumentation. Paul was obviously employing the pair of genitives
polemically in this context; λόγου ἢ σοφίας may respectively denote
"oratorical form" and "philosophic depth,"[55] "rhetorical skill" and
"human understanding,"[56] "eloquent and persuasive oration" and
"worldly wisdom and philosophy,"[57] "effectiveness of language"
and "skill of argumentation,"[58] "overpowering oratory" and "philosophical argument,"[59] or "rhetorical display" and "philosophical subtlety."[60] Paul rejected "elaborate diction and subtlety of argument"
as his norm for communications since those vehicles "would only
discredit his testimony."[61] For Paul, this avoidance was not merely a
matter of personal preference, but, as indicated by the parallel
words of 1:17, it was absolutely essential if he were to carry out his
commission as charged.

In order therefore to grasp the full significance of Paul's testimony
in 2:1 it is necessary to capture the thrust of his affirmations about
his divine commission in 1:17. He had not been commissioned by
Christ[62] to baptize,[63] but by contrast,[64] to proclaim the Good News.[65]
In addition, how he would fulfill the obligation of a "gospelizer"[66] was
an attendant, but extremely vital, element of his commission as indicated by the qualifying negative phrase οὐκ ἐν σοφίᾳ λόγου, "not by
means of wisdom of word."[67] The genitive λόγου is best construed as
qualitative[68] or "descriptive, and means something like 'not with a
kind of *sophia* that is characterized by rhetoric (or perhaps reason or
logic).'"[69] Consequently, the compounded phrase was intended to
exclude from Paul's mission both a "display of rhetoric" and an exhibition "of logical subtlety."[70] This is quite understandable since:

> to preach is *not a philosophy to be discussed, but a message of God
> to be believed.* . . . "To tell good *news* in *wisdom* of word" is an

implicit contradiction; "news" only needs and admits of plain, straightforward *telling*.[71]

The strategic importance of Christ's prohibition—and Paul's subsequent obedience to it (e.g., 2:1)—is indicated by the purpose clause which follows. Or, in the phraseology of Lenski, "What this mode of procedure results in, and what Christ's purpose is in forbidding it, Paul states with brevity and with force: 'in order that the cross of Christ may not be made empty.'"[72] Indeed, "to clothe the Gospel in σοφία λόγου was to impair its substance."[73] In other words, "to dress out the story of Calvary in specious rhetoric, or wrap it up in fine-spun theorems, would have been to 'empty (κενώθη) the cross of Christ,' to *eviscerate* the gospel," since "the 'power of God' lies in the facts and not in any man's presentment of them."[74]

Morris admirably shows how 1:17 launches Paul's corrective teaching and paves the way for his culturally shocking disclosure of method[75] in 2:1ff.:

> Some at least of the Corinthians were setting too high a value on human wisdom and human eloquence in line with the typical Greek admiration for rhetoric and philosophical studies. In the face of this, Paul insists that preaching *with wisdom of words* was no part of his commission. That kind of preaching would draw men to the preacher. It would nullify the cross of Christ. The faithful preaching of the cross results in men ceasing to put their trust in any human device, and relying rather on God's work in Christ. A reliance on rhetoric would cause men to trust in man, the very antithesis of what the preaching of the cross is meant to effect.[76]

Quite obviously, "the manner of Paul's preaching was determined by its *matter*."[77] This truth is documented not only by the implications of Christ's commission as summarized in 1:17,[78] but also by Paul's subsequent disclosure about his subject matter in 2:2.

### Paul's Undaunted Disclosure Concerning His Subject Matter (v 2)

With its explicit emphasis on subject matter, v 2 further explains Paul's style of ministry among the Corinthians (cf. v 1):[79] "For I did not determine (judge it fit) to know anything (*or*, know something) among you, except (*or*, only) Jesus Christ, and Him crucified."[80] This somewhat cumbersome syntactical package unfolds Paul's personal resolution[81] in two phases, the negative phase, being radically separated from the positive by the εἰ μή, "except."[82] When Paul says "for I did not decide to know anything among you,"[83] he was in effect eliminating anything that might have been perceived as man's message and/or method (cf. 2:1 and 1:17).[84] Paul "intentionally set aside the different elements of human knowledge by which he might have been tempted to prop up the preaching of salvation. He deemed that he ought not to go in quest of such means."[85] Contrastingly, after eliminating man's way, he emphatically elevated God's Way.[86] As the words "except Jesus Christ and this very one[87] crucified" indicate, Paul's exclusive subject matter was the Person and provision of the Savior (i.e., Christology and soteriology).

For Paul, giving people what they needed (cf. 1:18b, 21b, 24) rather than what they wanted (cf. 1:22) was essential, and yet, it was not easy. Indeed, when Paul wrote about faithfully heralding a crucified messiah[88] (cf. 1:23a) he possessed not only a theoretical, but also a practical awareness of mankind's resistance and rejection (cf. 1:23b): "To the Jew . . . Χριστὸς ἐσταυρωμένος was a contradiction in terms; to the Greek it would be simply meaningless"[89] "Messiah meant power, splendor, triumph; *crucifixion* meant weakness, humiliation, defeat. Little wonder that both Jew and Greek were scandalized by the Christian message."[90]

But, "instead of working miracles to satisfy the Jews, or propounding a philosophy to entertain the Greeks,"[91] Paul remained undaunted in reference to the proclamation of "Jesus Christ and Him crucified" for the sake of Christ, His commission, and the good of those God would be pleased to rescue from their own resistance. He avoided all forms of "human ostentation"[92] because he was fully aware of the fact that that very same message was God's exclusive means for unleashing the power of God which leads to salvation (1:18b; cf. Rom 1:16).[93] In Paul's decision-making process (e.g., 2:2) the pressures of man, although formidable, were not formulative because of the reality of this divine dynamic. Such knowledge would allow no room for contemplations about concessions or compromises in method, message or matter.

Paul's Transparent Disclosure Concerning His Dependence (v 3)

When Paul admitted that he was with[94] the Corinthians "in weakness and in fear and in 'great trepidation,' "[95] he was denouncing any and all forms of "self-reliance."[96] His affirmation of weakness should not be taken by itself as a reference merely to his physical stamina,[97] but needs to be taken "more broadly"[98] in concert with the other terms[99] and also in conjunction with his whole argument.

"Humanly speaking, he felt like one disarmed";[100] consequently, he ministered among them "as a frail insufficient human being."[101] Polemically directed, "the weakness, fear and much trembling (2:3)," on the one hand, "are in direct opposition to the self-confident and boastful stance of the other [i.e., most] proclaimers of the Gospel in Corinth,"[102] and on the other hand, the Corinthians, "who themselves are so haughty, are now informed that Paul performed his work without any spirit of self-sufficiency."[103]

Divinely speaking, these same words of transparent testimony implicitly convey the preacher's declaration of dependence upon God and His resources. "In the sight of God"[104] and "in the light of the task committed to him,"[105] "who is equal to such a task?" (2 Cor 2:16b, NIV). 2 Cor 2:14ff., in dealing with the glory and the awesomeness of the Christian ministry,[106] makes it crystal clear that no mere man is "sufficient," "adequate," "able," "competent," or "qualified" (2:16b).[107] Indirectly, Paul's rhetorical question about human adequacy in 2 Cor 2:16b is answered negatively throughout the development of his second canonical epistle to the Corinthians. However, it is directly answered by the stark antithesis of 2 Cor 3:5–6a wherein Paul asserts on the one hand that we are absolutely devoid of adequacy (i.e, 3:5a),[108] while on the other hand, he affirms that sufficiency for ministry[109] is resident with God and graciously imparted to those who recognize that they are indeed innately devoid of it (i.e., 3:5b–6a). As Rengstorf well summarizes it, "Confession of personal incapacity is thus accompanied by confession of God as the basis of all personal capacity."[110]

Therefore, the words of Paul's transparent disclosure in 1 Cor 2:3 constitute another specific occasion when Paul was gaining insight into the paradoxical reality that "when I am weak, it is then that I am strong" (cf. 2 Cor 12:10b). The attitude which undergirds such declarations of dependence stands as a prerequisite for real power in preaching.

Paul's Panoramic Disclosure Concerning His Ministry (vv 4–5)

What Paul generalized in 2:1–2 he now makes more specific in vv 4 and 5. Verse 4 is a reaffirmation along with a documentation of his approach as outlined in 2:1–2, which in itself was a confirmation of his faithfulness to commission as summarized in 1:17a. Verse 5 is a telic antithesis[111] which reveals Paul's understanding and subsequent motivation for ministry based upon the awesome potentiality of the revelation of 1:17b in its context. So Paul in the last two verses of this paradigmatic paragraph offers a panoramic disclosure of his ministry as viewed through power oriented (i.e., v 4) and purpose oriented contrasts (i.e., v 5).

*His power-oriented contrast (v 4)*

As Paul has done so frequently, he commences with a negative assertion, this time in reference to his λόγος, "word," and his κήρυγμα, "message" or "proclamation." Each of these terms is plagued by semantical fluidity, and furthermore, Paul's employment of them throughout this polemical context seems to make hermeneutical precision an elusive target.[112] Some argue that the respective emphases of λόγος and κήρυγμα seem to be on (1) content and (2) form.[113] Others, emphasizing the primary force of a previous occurrence of λόγος at 1:18, opt for a double emphasis upon content.[114] And still others, based both upon an appealing functional connection between the couplet λόγος and σοφία in v 1 paralleled with the couplet λόγος and κήρυγμα in v 4 and upon Paul's previous (and relatively unambivalent) use of κήρυγμα in 1:21 as "the contents of the preaching,"[115] would argue that the respective emphases of these terms are on (1) speech[116] and (2) the substance of such discourse. Consequently, λόγος in v 4 probably connotes "manner of presentation"[117] while κήρυγμα " . . . refers . . . to the subject, not to the manner of the preaching."[118]

For the sake of completeness, it should be noted that a few, apparently frustrated by the subtle nuances of the terms, dub the collocation of λόγος and κήρυγμα "a case of rhetorical duplication."[119] In the light of all these considerations, Morris's summary-conclusion regarding this significant couplet is safe and yet basically sound:

> It is not easy to see the difference between *my speech* and *my preaching*. *Speech* is literally "word." We saw it used in 1:18. . . . The word rendered *preaching* is that denoting the message proclaimed in 1:21. Probably Paul is not differentiating between the two with any exactness. He employs both terms to stress both the message he preached and the way he preached it.[120]

Irrespective of the nuances or proportions of the nuances of these two terms, the point that Paul was making via his employment of this collocation in 2:4 was very clear: "neither the one [i.e., his λόγος] nor the other [i.e., his κήρυγμα] has been corrupted in his work by the infiltration of human elements or by self-seeking."[121]

This conclusion is fully corroborated by the objectively negated prepositional phrase which follows.[122] Although the phrase is plagued by textual problems,[123] the correct reading "is probably πειθοῖς σοφίας λόγοις,"[124] i.e., "persuasive words of wisdom."[125] The key to grasping the significance of Paul's negation is bound up with a proper understanding of his skillful employment of the adjective πειθός in the sense of "enticing."[126] In reference to this adjective, Robertson says:

> It seems to be formed directly from *peitho*, to persuade, as *pheidos* (*phidos*) is from *pheidomai*, to spare. The old Greek form *pithanos* is common enough and is used by Josephus (*Ant.* VIII.9.1) of "the plausible words of the lying prophet" in I Kings 13. The kindred word *pithanologia* occurs in Col. 2:4 for the specious and plausible Gnostic philosophers.[127]

Of the related noun πειθώ in extrabiblical contexts, Bultmann has observed that it was used from the time of Aeschylus to denote "the gift or faculty of persuasion."[128]

Polemically, Paul's phraseology, "persuasive words of wisdom," therefore, appears "to have some resemblance to Graeco-Roman rhetoric."[129] The combination refers to:

> that specific, studied art of persuasive speech as was practiced by orators and rhetoricians of the Graeco-Roman world and by at least some of the Corinthian preachers.... Taken together as a phrase οὐκ ἐν πειθοῖς σοφίας λόγοις explicitly means the setting aside of the art of persuasive speech. It is a phrase which rejects the discipline of what the Greeks called ῥητορική.[130]

Consequently, Paul "used no philosophic terms, categories of thought, or reasonings that were calculated to captivate his hearers and to persuade their minds to assent."[131] Paul would not and could not have resorted to such tactics because, as the forthcoming positive member of this antithesis attests, both that prerogative and that power reside exclusively with the Spirit of God.[132]

By means of strong contrast,[133] Paul declares that if his "words carried conviction, that conviction was produced, not by any eloquence or reasoning skill of his, but by the power of the Spirit applying the message to the hearers' conscience."[134] "The Holy Spirit and the power of God (1:18, 24) manifested themselves in his preaching. And in doing so they demonstrated thereby the truth of Paul's preaching."[135] The key word, ἀπόδειξις, a "'demonstration' in the sense of 'stringent proof,'"[136] is vitally bound to and explained by πνεύματος καὶ δυνάμις, "of (the) Spirit and power."[137] Concerning the whole phrase, it

> gathers up the δύναμιν θεοῦ of i. 24 . . . ; the proof of the Gospel at Cor. was experimental and ethical, found in the new consciousness and changed lives that attended its proclamation: cf. vi. 11, ix. 1, 2 Cor. iii. 1 ff., I Thess. ii. 13 (λόγοις θεοῦ ὅς κ. ἐνεργεῖται ἐν ὑμῖν τ. πιστεύουσιν).— πνεύματος καὶ δυνάμεως are not objective gen. . . . but subjective: the Spirit, with His power, *gives the demonstration*. . . .[138]

Needless to say, such a visible evidence or proof[139] is "distinct from persuasion produced by mere cleverness."[140]

Paul's burden is concisely conveyed through this power oriented antithesis of v 4: "Mere human σοφία may dazzle and overwhelm and seem to be unanswerable, but . . . it does not penetrate to those depths of the soul which are the seat of the decisions of a lifetime."[141] Therefore, "to Paul the preaching of the Gospel is not dependent upon any human techniques of eloquence, but upon the demonstration of the Spirit and power."[142] These incontestable negative and positive realities always governed Paul's methodology: "But precisely because his preaching was so simple and unpretentious its results convincingly demonstrated the power of God."[143] Applicationally, these same truths need to control all truth communicators; since "the preacher's task . . . lies, not in wishing to act in the place and stead of the Spirit with resources of his own eloquence and genius, but in opening up the way for Him by simple testimony rendered to Christ."[144]

### His purpose-oriented contrast (v 5)

According to contextual precedent, Paul employs another antithesis[145] which now magnifies the importance[146] of his adopted methodology: "in order that your faith[147] should not be grounded on[148] (the) wisdom of men, but (contrastingly that it should be) grounded on (the) power of God."[149] With these words what has been implicit now becomes explicit. It was not only ministerially important for Paul to do God's business God's way, but more significantly from the (ad)vantage point of the Corinthians, it was eternally important. Indeed, "Paul was God's mouthpiece in declaring the Gospel; he therefore sought the very end of God Himself, *viz.*, that God alone should be glorified in the faith of his hearers."[150]

Verse 5 truly binds the major threads of his argument together. This is largely accomplished through placing the "wisdom of men" and the "power of God" in diametrical opposition.[151] Obviously, the σοφία ἀνθρώπων of 2:5a is the σοφία τοῦ κόσμου, "the wisdom of the world," of 1:20. Paul will go on to label it ἀνθρωπίνης σοφίας, "human wisdom," in 2:13.[152] On the other hand, the δυνάμει θεοῦ, the "power of God," of 2:5b is that salvific dynamic of God resident in the message of the Cross (cf. 1:18, 24), and more immediately in application (cf. 2:4b, 5b), it focuses upon "the preaching of Christ crucified, made effective in them by the Spirit."[153]

Paul, therefore, is arguing that the trust of needy people must not be grounded on a finite foundation which will surely crumble,[154] but on an infinite foundation which will never crumble.[155] "The gospel is not a wisdom, but a power; not a philosophy, but a salvation."[156] Consequently,

> right from the beginning, Paul had wished to ground his converts in the divine power, and to make them independent of human wisdom. That is why he had made no attempt to employ rhetorical arts, but had contented himself with the simplest approach. That was the reason for his concentration on that message which was so unpalatable to natural men, the message of the cross.[157]

What a communications seminar! A better methodological paradigm for preaching is unimaginable.

## CONCLUSION

Paul's example awaits our emulation. Today there is a great need, not for plausible pulpiteers, but for powerful preachers. Contemporary communicators, saturated with arrogance, given to humanistic tactics, and practiced in manipulation, abound. Yet there remains a real drought for the dynamic Word of God conveyed through humble men of God by the powerful Spirit of God. Truth communicators, publish your declaration of dependence and then, according to Paul's paradigm, "Preach the Word!"

## NOTES

[1]For a good synopsis of Acts 16:11–18:17 see Homer A. Kent, Jr., *Jerusalem to Rome: Studies in the Book of Acts* (Winona Lake, IN: BMH Books, 1972) 134–44.

[2]Cf. Everett F. Harrison, *Introduction to the New Testament* (Grand Rapids: Eerdmans, 1971) 283.

[3]A few interpreters look upon Acts 17:16ff. as an exception and therefore regard 1 Cor 2:1–5 as Paul's confession of a previously compromised message and method in the presence of the intelligentsia at Athens. For some good refutations of these misunderstandings and misrepresentations see Johannes Munck, *The Acts of the Apostles: Introduction, Translation and Notes*, rev. by W. F. Albright and C. S. Mann, Anchor Bible (Garden City, NY: Doubleday, 1967) 174; Greg L. Bahnsen, "The Encounter of Jerusalem with Athens," *Ashland Theological Bulletin* 13 (Spring 1980): 7–9; F. W. Grosheide, *Commentary on the First Epistle to the Corinthians*, New International Commentary on the New Testament (Grand Rapids: Eerdmans, 1953) 59; Gordon D. Fee, *The First Epistle to the Corinthians*, New International Commentary on the New Testament (Grand Rapids: Eerdmans, 1987) 92; and F. F. Bruce, *1 and 2 Corinthians*, New Century Bible Commentary (Grand Rapids: Eerdmans, 1971) 37.

[4]Probably in A.D. 55; cf. Bruce, *1 and 2 Corinthians*, 25; Harrison, *Introduction*, 284, 291; and William F. Orr and James A. Walther, *1 Corinthians*, Anchor Bible (Garden City, NY: Doubleday, 1976) 81–83, 118–22, 129.

[5]Fee, *First Corinthians*, 2; it is a historical fact that the city "fostered a licentious spirit that was notorious even in Greece" (Harrison, *Introduction*, 283).

[6]Harrison, *Introduction*, 282.

[7]A. T. Robertson, *The Epistles of Paul, Word Pictures in the New Testament*, vol. 4 (Nashville: Broadman, 1931) 76; cf. "Preaching was St. Paul's great work, but his aim was not that of the professional rhetorician" (A. T. Robertson and Alfred Plummer, *A Critical and Exegetical Commentary on the First Epistle of St. Paul to the Corinthians*, ICC [Edinburgh: T. & T. Clark, 1914] 15).

[8]For some Pauline confirmations of these crucial biblical facts see: Rom 1:18–3:20, the subordinate concessive (or temporal) clauses of 5:6–10, 6:17a, v 20a; 2 Cor 4:3–4, 11:3; Eph 2:1–3, 4:17–19; Col 1:21, Titus 3:3; etc.

[9]Author's interpretative rendering of 1 Cor 2:14; Boyer's illustration is appropriate: the natural man "is like a blind man in an art gallery, like a deaf man at a symphony" (James L. Boyer, *For a World like Ours: Studies in 1 Corinthians* [Winona Lake: BMH Books, 1971] 41). For exegetical documentations which confirm the theological thrust of 1 Cor 2:14, see Bruce, *1 and 2 Corinthians*, 41; Grosheide, *First Corinthians*, 73–74; F. Godet, *Commentary on the First Epistle of St. Paul to the Corinthians*, trans. by A. Cusin (Grand Rapids: Zondervan, 1957) 156–57; C. K. Barrett, *A Commentary on the First Epistle to the Corinthians* (London: Adam and Charles Black, 1971) 76–77; Leon Morris, *The First Epistle of Paul to the Corinthians: An*

*Introduction and Commentary,* The Tyndale New Testament Commentaries (Grand Rapids: Eerdmans, 1970) 60; and Fee, *First Corinthians,* 115–17.

[10]Jim S. Halsey, *For a Time Such as This* (Philadelphia: Presbyterian and Reformed, 1976) 30 (bracketed statement added for contextual clarity).

[11]Cf. Paul's development of σάρξ, "flesh," in hamartiological contexts. When the regenerated man's theocentric outlook is interrupted by his anthropocentric flashback, he temporarily functions much like the natural man, i.e., in blasphemous independence.

[12]For some Pauline confirmations of God's sovereign grace as the only antidote for man's hamartiological predicament, see: Acts 14:27 (cf. 16:14); Rom 3:21–5:11, 8:28–30, 9:16; Eph 1:3–14, 2:4–10; Phil 1:6, 2:13; Titus 3:4–7; etc.

[13]Although Paul employs a different metaphor in this context the principle remains constant.

[14]Author's interpretive rendering of 2 Cor 10:3–5.

[15]Cf., e.g., Ps 19:7–8, 119:93; Jer 5:14, 20:7–10, 23:29; Rom 1:16; 1 Thess 2:13; 2 Tim 3:15–17; Heb 4:12–13; James 1:12; 1 Pet 1:23.

[16]Cf., e.g, John 3:5–8, 16:8–11; 1 Cor 2:10b–11; Eph 6:17.

[17]I.e., whether "preachers," "teachers," "evangelists," "counsellors," etc.

[18]Cf. 2 Cor 2:16b with 3:5, and the basic thrust of 1 Pet 3:15–16 in both its narrower and larger concentric circles of context.

[19]In the opening portion of the epistle (i.e., 1 Corinthians 1–4) these schisms involved an "attachment to individual leaders," and in the latter portion of his letter Paul had to deal with the σχίσματα which had unfortunately developed over the χαρίσματα, i.e., the "grace-gifts" for the *Body* (cf. *TDNT,* s.v. "σχίζω, σχίσμα," by C. Maurer, 7:964).

[20]Barrett's appropriate designation for the slogans of v 12 (*First Corinthians,* 43; cf. 42–46 for pertinent amplifications).

[21]For an excellent survey of this initial expression of factionalism within Paul's first epistle to the church at Corinth, see "The Problem—division over Leaders in the Name of Wisdom (1:10–17)" in Fee, *First Corinthians,* 51–66.

[22]Largely due to this reason, Paul was forced to defend himself quite regularly in all of his correspondence to the Corinthians.

[23]Frank Stagg, "The Motif of First Corinthians," *SWJT* 3 (October 1960): 15–16; cf. James's development in his epistle (3:13–18).

[24]Timothy H. Lim, "'Not in persuasive words of wisdom, but in the demonstration of the spirit and power' (1 Cor. 2:4)," *Novum Testamentum* 29 (April 1987): 138, n. 6; from a strictly polemical angle, "in 1 Corinthians 1–4 . . . Paul reacts against *two* aspects of *sophia*; wisdom in speech as well as wisdom as the means of salvation" (Richard A. Horsley, "Wisdom of Words and Words of Wisdom in Corinth," *CBQ* 39 [April 1977]: 224). For some different and yet interrelated perspectives on the philosophical background, problem, paraenesis, and polemic of 1 Cor 1:10ff., see: Orr and Walther, *1 Corinthians,* 151–52; *New International Dictionary of New Testament Theology* [*NIDNTT*], s.v. "λόγος," by G. Fries, B. Klappert, and C. Brown, 3:1081–1119; *TDNT,* s.v. "σταυρός κ.τ.λ.," by J. Schneider, 7:575–76; *NIDNTT,* s.v. "Wisdom, Folly, Philosophy," by J. Goetzmann and C. Brown, 3:1023–33; and *TDNT* s.v. "σοφία, κ.τ.λ.," by U. Wilchens, 7:519–22.

[25]On the significance of παρακαλέω in Pauline paraenesis, see Hans Conzelmann,

*1* Corinthians, trans. by James W. Leitch, Hermeneia (Philadelphia: Fortress, 1975) 31–32, n. 8.

[26]Robin Scroggs, "Paul: ΣΟΦΟΣ and ΠΝΕΥΜΑΤΙΚΟΣ," *NTS* 14 (October 1967): 33.

[27]C. Clare Oke, "Paul's Method not a Demonstration but an Exhibition of the Spirit," *ExpTim* 67 (November 1955): 35.

[28]Fee correctly observes that 1:13–17 "serves as a means of shifting the focus from the problem of 'divisions over leaders' to the greater theological issue underlying its visible expression" (*First Corinthians*, 52).

[29]Later, an exegetical excursus on 1:17 will be offered in conjunction with the more in-depth analysis of 2:1–5; however, for now, note the following synopses of the great impact of 1:17 as the touchstone of Paul's overall argument: "Paul asserted that Christ sent him *not to baptize, but to preach*; further, what he was to preach is *not a philosophy to be discussed, but a message of God to be believed*" (G. G. Findlay, "St. Paul's First Epistle to the Corinthians," *The Expositor's Greek Testament*, vol. 2 [Grand Rapids: Eerdmans, 1970] 766–67); "Paul must avoid preaching which involves false synthesis in content and empty technique in form, lest the cross of Christ should lose its searching and saving content . . . " (*TDNT*, s.v. "κενός, κενόω," by A. Oepke, 3:662); and finally, "St. Paul is eager to obviate any misapprehension which might arise from his exaltation of the ordinance of preaching. . . . It is not as a mere display of rhetoric, or of logical subtlety that he exalts it" (J. B. Lightfoot, *Notes on the Epistles of St. Paul* [Winona Lake: Alpha Publications, n.d.] 156–57).

[30]Barrett, *First Corinthians*, 49; i.e., vv 1:18ff. "flow logically from the proposition of v. 17" (W. Harold Mare, "1 Corinthians," *The Expositor's Bible Commentary*, vol. 10 [Grand Rapids: Zondervan, 1976] 194).

[31]E.g., "1 C 1:18 ὁ λόγος ὁ τοῦ σταυροῦ appears to be a kind of anaphora to 17 ὁ σταυρὸς τοῦ Χριστοῦ" (F. Blass and A. Debrunner, *A Greek Grammar of The New Testament and Other Early Christian Literature*, trans. by Robert Funk [Chicago: University of Chicago, 1961] 142 [para. 271]).

[32]Lightfoot, *Notes*, 157; for an emphasis on the sovereignty of God as a thematic thread woven into the fabric of 1:18–4:20, see Scroggs, "ΣΟΦΟΣ and ΠΝΕΥΜΑΤΙΚΟΣ," 36–37; and Milton Ferguson, "The Theology of First Corinthians," *SWJTh* 3 (October 1960): 27–29.

[33]Conzelmann, *1 Corinthians*, 39; Fee analyzes this section retrospectively: "With this paragraph [i.e., 2:1–5] Paul concludes his argument that the message of the cross and the Corinthians' very existence as believers stand in contradiction to their present stance. Along with 1:26–31 it demonstrates the point of 1:18–25, this time in terms of Paul's effective ministry among them despite his weakness and failure to rely on the kind of 'powerful' speech with which they are enamored. Thus, not only the *means* (the cross) and the *people* (the church in Corinth), but also the *preacher* (Paul) declared that God is in the process of overturning the world's systems" (*First Corinthians*, 89).

[34]John F. MacArthur, Jr., *1 Corinthians*, The MacArthur New Testament Commentary (Chicago: Moody Press, 1984) 49–57.

[35]Barrett's characterization of 2:1–5 (*First Corinthians*, 28).

[36]The κἀγώ of 2:1 also functions retrospectively in a logical sense, since it ties back into the ἡμεῖς δὲ κηρύσσομεν of 1:23 (cf. Henry Alford, *Alford's Greek Testament*

[Grand Rapids: Guardian Press, 1976] 2:482). In the light of its immediately preceding context this κἀγώ stresses a precedent; cf. "It was in line with this principle . . . " (Barrett, *First Corinthians*, 62; cf. Robertson and Plummer, *First Corinthians*, 29).

[37]On this stylistic indicator, cf., e.g., Fee, *First Corinthians*, 89.

[38]Cf., e.g., Findlay, "First Corinthians," 775.

[39]Cf., e.g., Lightfoot, *Notes*, 120.

[40]Scroggs, "ΣΟΦΟΣ and ΠΝΕΥΜΑΤΙΚΟΣ," 33.

[41]Ibid., 36; Scroggs well adds that it was an apologetic encased within a polemic: "a personal defense . . . embedded in the midst of the apostle's attack" (ibid.).

[42]Respectively based upon the introductory κἀγώ with two verbals of ἔρχομαι standing at the head of vv 1–2 and κἀγώ with explicit (i.e., γίνομαι) and implicit connections with forms of the verb "to be" in vv 3–5.

[43]Cf. the explanatory γάρ of v 2 and the telic ἵνα of v 5.

[44]Cf. the conjunctive καί which introduces the antithetical (i.e., ἀλλ᾽) parallelism of v 4.

[45]Morris, *First Corinthians*, 17, cf. 52; the previous historical survey made mention of some of the discouraging events which Paul had recently encountered.

[46]I.e., κἀγὼ ἐλθὼν πρὸς ὑμᾶς, ἀδελφοί, ἦλθον . . . καταγγέλων ὑμῖν . . . , "and when *I came* to you, brethren, *I came* proclaiming . . . " [emphasis added to these two occurrences of ἔρχομαι].

[47]Note that, e.g., Metzger (Bruce M. Metzger, *A Textual Commentary on the Greek New Testament* [London: United Bible Societies, 1971] 545) and Orr and Walther (*1 Corinthians*, 156) opt for the reading μυστήριον (cf. UBS³), "mystery," herein; while, e.g., Grosheide (*First Corinthians*, 58) and Morris (*First Corinthians*, 51) prefer μαρτύριον, "witness." Orthographically, the variant seems to have arisen largely through a transposition (cf. Barrett, *First Corinthians*, 62–63), and contextually, "the reading μαρτύριον seems to be a recollection of 1.6, whereas μυστήριον here prepares for its usage in ver. 7" (Metzger, *Textual Commentary*, 545). Both words may be used as conceptual synonyms for εὐαγγέλιον, the Gospel. Therefore, after examining the textual and contextual evidence, Bruce's both-and conclusion is appealing: "The gospel was both the message to which the apostles bore witness and the divine revelation, previously concealed, which they made known" (*1 and 2 Corinthians*, 37).

[48]Godet, *First Corinthians*, 124.

[49]For helpful discussions which emphasize the interrelationship of κηρύσσω, εὐαγγελίζω, καταγγέλλω, etc., see: *NIDNTT* s.v. "σταυρός," by E. Brandenburger and C. Brown, 1:397–402; *NIDNTT*, s.v. "Proclamation, Preach, Kerygma," by U. Becker, D. Miller, L. Coenen, and C. Brown, 3:47–54; and Victor Paul Furnish, "Prophets, Apostles, and Preachers: A Study of the Biblical Concept of Preaching," *Interpretation* 17 (January 1963): 48–60. In this context the καταγγέλω of 2:1 builds upon the κηρύσσω of 1:23 (cf. Findlay, "1 Corinthians," 775). On the essence of the latter term as the activity of a herald delivering a message (in this case from God), note Morris's comments (*First Corinthians*, 46).

[50]*TDNT*, s.v. "καταγγέλλω," by J. Schniewind, 1:71.

[51]Ibid.

[52]Ibid., 1:71–72: "in their basic meaning these words always refer to the activity of the messenger who conveys a message which has been given to him either orally or in writing . . . , and who in this way represents the sender of the message himself.

... This proclamation, the authority of which is derived from its ultimate source, enters deeply into the life of the messenger and makes total demands upon him" (*NIDNTT*, 3:45, 46). In the light of this there is not only a semantical connection with κηρύσσω (cf. 1:23) and an implicit connection with εὐαγγελίζω (cf. 1:17) but also a conceptional connection with ἀποστέλλω (cf. 1:17 again).

[53]On the significance of οὐ καθ', Lenski aptly notes that it conveys "the norm which Paul repudiated when he was making his proclamation to the Corinthians" (R. C. H. Lenski, *The Interpretation of St. Paul's First and Second Epistle to the Corinthians* [Minneapolis: Augsburg, 1943] 87); these words constitute "a rejection of the bombastic rhetoric that the Corinthians liked and the rhetorical art that was so common from Thucydides to Chrysostom" (A. T. Robertson, *A Grammar of the Greek New Testament in the Light of Historical Research* [Nashville: Broadman, 1934] 85; cf. 1206).

[54]For some helpful observations pertaining to ὑπεροχή as excess, superiority, pre-eminence, etc., see: Walter Bauer, William F. Arndt, and F. Wilbur, *A Greek-English Lexicon of the New Testament and Other Christian Literature*, 2d ed., rev. and augmented by F. Wilbur Gingrich and Frederick W. Danker (Chicago: University of Chicago Press, 1979) 840–41; Joseph Henry Thayer, *Greek-English Lexicon of the New Testament* (Grand Rapids: Zondervan, 1962) 641 (cf. his rendering of "distinguished" in this context); Robertson and Plummer, *First Corinthians*, 29; Robertson, *Word Pictures*, 4:82; Lightfoot, *Notes*, 170; Morris, *First Corinthians*, 51; and Grosheide, *First Corinthians*, 58–59.

[55]Godet, *First Corinthians*, 124.

[56]Fee, *First Corinthians*, 65.

[57]Lenski, *First and Second Corinthians*, 87.

[58]Barrett, *First Corinthians*, 63; in another place he uses "rational talk" and "wordy cleverness" (ibid.).

[59]Mare, "1 Corinthians," 198.

[60]Lightfoot, *Notes*, 170.

[61]Ibid., 170–71.

[62]Note the impact of the aorist indicative from ἀποστέλλω. Also note that grammatically, the negative οὐ governs this indicative verb not the infinitive (cf. Robertson, *Word Pictures*, 4:76).

[63]"The explanation of v. 17a does not devalue baptism, but defines the personal commission to which Paul is subject" (Conzelmann, *1 Corinthians*, 36).

[64]I.e., ἀλλά.

[65]εὐαγγελίζεσθαι, i.e., to be continuously engaged in the task of preaching the Gospel.

[66]Robertson, *Word Pictures*, 4:76.

[67]Note herein that σοφία and λόγος come packaged together; cf. Lenski's hyphenated rendering "word-wisdom" (*First and Second Corinthians*, 49–50). However, the two terms λόγου ἢ σοφίας of 2:1 incontestably dovetail back into this phrase in 1:17.

[68]Cf., e.g., ibid., 87.

[69]Fee, *First Corinthians*, 64; cf. Bruce's "not with eloquent wisdom" (*First and Second Corinthians*, 17), i.e., not "in philosophical style" (Findlay, "1 Corinthians," 767). For argumentation that these words include "both the manner and the matter of the ... preaching" (Morris, *First Corinthians*, 43), see, e.g., Fee, *First Corinthians*,

64, and Scroggs, "ΣΟΦΟΣ and ΠΝΕΥΜΑΤΙΚΟΣ," 36.

[70]Lightfoot, *Notes*, 157; polemically, it abrogated any utilization of "the luxuriant rhetoric" and "the dialectic subtleties" (ibid.) which so characterized the Graeco-Roman orators and debaters. He was *not* commissioned "to proclaim the gospel with great oratorical talent" (Grosheide, *First Corinthians*, 57); therefore, in 2:1ff. Paul evaluates his method as theological and practical rather than "professional" (cf. Lim, "Not in Persuasive Words of Wisdom," 139–40; however, Lim's thesis that Paul uses this concession as a manipulative device in this epistle is totally unacceptable).

[71]Findlay, "1 Corinthians," 767.

[72]Lenski, *First and Second Corinthians*, 51–52.

[73]Robertson and Plummer, *First Corinthians*, 16; cf. Schneider: "Paul refuses to use words of wisdom because these cannot grasp or expound the saving significance of the cross of Christ. Philosophical preaching which puts human wisdom in the place of God's wisdom robs the cross of Christ of its essential content" (*TDNT*, s.v. "σταυρός," κ.τ.λ.," by J. Schneider, 7:575).

[74]Findlay, "1 Corinthians," 767; on the impact of κενωθῇ in this context, cf. Godet and Lightfoot respectively: "the term κενοῦν denotes an act which does violence to the object itself, and deprives it of its essence and virtue" (*First Corinthians*, 89); herein, it means to "dwindle to nothing, vanish under the weight of rhetorical ornament and dialectic subtlety" (*Notes*, 157).

[75]Remembering that Paul came to Corinth οὐ καθ᾽ ὑπεροχὴν λόγου ἢ σοφίας (2:1), "not with the bearing of a man distinguished for these accomplishments, and relying upon them for his success" (Findlay, "1 Corinthians," 775); his "humble mien and plain address presented a striking contrast to the pretensions usual in itinerant professors of wisdom" (ibid.).

[76]Morris, *First Corinthians*, 42.

[77]Findlay, "1 Corinthians," 775.

[78]I.e., "with such a commission he could not adopt the arts of a rhetorician nor the airs of a philosopher" (ibid.).

[79]On the syntactical force of the γάρ herein see Fee, *First Corinthians*, 92. It must be pointed out once again that 2:1–2 did not indicate a radical ministerial modification on the part of Paul immediately after his departure from Athens (cf. ibid.; Barrett, *First Corinthians*, 63–64; et al.).

[80]Findlay's expanded rendering ("1 Corinthians," 775).

[81]Cf. Robertson and Plummer, *First Corinthians*, 30; also, cf. Conzelmann: "κρίνειν here means 'resolve'" (*1 Corinthians*, 54).

[82]Cf. Orr and Walter, *1 Corinthians*, 156.

[83]Robertson, *Word Pictures* 4:82. Syntactically, the negative οὐ must be taken with ἔκρινα, "thus: 'I did not resolve to know.' In smoother English this may be tr., 'I resolved not to know' or, 'I resolved to know nothing' (NIV)" (Mare, "1 Corinthians," 199, n. 2).

[84]As a matter of fact τι εἰδέναι may have been employed by Paul deliberately in a polemical fashion: "'to be a know-something' (*aliquid scire*)—to play the philosopher—according to the well-known attic idiom of Plato's *Apol.*, paragraph 6, and *passim*, where οἴεται τὶ εἰδέναι = δοκεῖ σοφὸς εἶναι . . . " (Findlay, "1 Corinthians," 775). The unfortunate perpetuation of such a humanistic obsession is not only documented quite directly in the Corinthian correspondence but also implicitly by Luke's parentheti-

cal comment in its context of Acts 17:21.

[85]Godet, *First Corinthians*, 125–26.

[86]Cf. respectively, Alford and Robertson and Plummer: "The only thing that I made it definitely my business to know, was" (*Alford's Greek Testament*, 2:483); "not only did I not speak of, but I had not thought for, anything else" (*First Corinthians*, 30).

[87]Rendering the demonstrative emphatically (cf. Blass, Debrunner, Funk, *Greek Grammar*, paragraph 442, 229).

[88]"Paul's *theologia crusis*" (Lim, "'Not in persuasive words of wisdom,'" 138; cf. 145, n. 24); cf. *TDNT*, s.v. "σταυρός," by J. Schneider, 7:575–77.

[89]Lightfoot, *Notes*, 162; cf. respectively, *TDNT*, s.v. "σκάνδαλον, κ.τ.λ.," by G. Stahlin, 7:354, and *TDNT*, s.v. "μωρός, κ.τ.λ.," by G. Bertram, 4:845–47; *NIDNTT*, s.v. "Wisdom, Folly Philosophy," by J. Goetzmann and C. Brown, 3:1023–33, esp. 1025–26. By referring to both "Jews" and "Gentiles" in 1:23, "Paul includes all mankind in the rejection of the crucified Messiah" (Morris, *First Corinthians*, 46).

[90]Fee, *First Corinthians*, 75.

[91]Findlay, "1 Corinthians," 770.

[92]Mare, "1 Corinthians," 194.

[93]Morris appropriately comments: "Nor is it a message about God's power. It *is* God's power" (*First Corinthians*, 43).

[94]Taking ἐγενόμην πρὸς ὑμᾶς as Paul's ongoing condition while at Corinth (cf. Fee, *First Corinthians*, 92–93) rather than merely his condition upon arrival (cf. Robertson, *Word Pictures*, 4:82). Cf. Acts 18:9–11.

[95]Barrett's conceptual rendering of τρόμῳ πολλῷ (*First Corinthians*, 64).

[96]Cf. Fee, *First Corinthians*, 96; he well adds that this "is hard to teach in a course in homiletics, but it still stands as the true need in genuinely Christian preaching" (ibid., 97).

[97]Cf., e.g., ibid., 93.

[98]Findlay, "1 Corinthians," 776; cf. Lightfoot, *Notes*, 171–72.

[99]Note Conzelmann's "threefold characterization" of the preacher (*1 Corinthians*, 54); for argumentation, cf. Godet, *First Corinthians*, 127–28, and Grosheide, *First Corinthians*, 60.

[100]Godet, *First Corinthians*, 127.

[101]Mare, "1 Corinthians," 198. Cf. 2 Cor 10:3–6.

[102]Lim, "'Not in persuasive words of wisdom,'" 147.

[103]Grosheide, *First Corinthians*, 60.

[104]Lightfoot, *Notes*, 172.

[105]Morris, *First Corinthians*, 52; cf. Bruce, *1 and 2 Corinthians*, 37, who argues that in 2:3 Paul conveys "a sense of complete personal inadequacy in view of the task of evangelizing such a city as Corinth."

[106]A. T. Robertson's practical but yet profound treatment of this passage is a classic: *The Glory of the Ministry: Paul's Exultation in Preaching* (Grand Rapids: Baker, 1967).

[107]Cf. *NIDNTT*, s.v. "ἱκανός," by W. Von Meding, 3:728–30; and *TDNT*, s.v. "ἱκανός, ἱκανότης, ἱκανόω," by K. Rengstorf, 3:293–97. Consequently, "cool complacency is not the mood of the finest preaching" (Robertson, *Word Pictures*, 4:83).

[108]Note the objective negation with ἐσμεν and the force of the complementary prepositional phrases with the reflexive pronoun, i.e., ἀφ᾽ ἑαυτῶν and ἐξ ἑαυτῶν.

[109]Cf. esp. 2 Cor 2:15–16a.

[110]*TDNT*, 3:295.

[111]Cf. ἵνα . . . ἀλλ᾽. . . .

[112]By way of example, the following comments illustrate the complexity of these phenomena: λόγος "has no uniform English equivalent, but suggests 'speech in rational form,' with the emphasis lying now on 'speech,' now on 'rational,' and now on 'form'" (Barrett, *First Corinthians*, 65); "there is a *logos* (speech) that belongs to wisdom and there is a *logos* (message) whose content is the cross; but they are mutually exclusive. . . . But unlike the Corinthians, who attached wisdom to *logos*, Paul attaches *kerygma* ('preaching' or 'proclamation')" (Fee, *First Corinthians*, 68, 94); and in reference to the more immediate context, λόγος is juxtaposed with σοφία in 2:1 and with κήρυγμα herein at 2:4. For a survey of other pertinent data, see Horsley, "Wisdom of Word and Words of Wisdom in Corinth," 229–31.

[113]Cf., e.g., Fee, *First Corinthians*, 94; Godet, *First Corinthians*, 128; Grosheide, *First Corinthians*, 61; and Lenski, *First and Second Corinthians*, 91–92. Lenski does however make his preference tentative by acknowledging that both terms "include the substance and the form of its presentation" (ibid., 92).

[114]Cf., e.g., Findlay, "1 Corinthians," 776.

[115]Grosheide's accurate expanded rendering of κήρυγμα (*First Corinthians*, 57); cf. Boyer, *For a World like Ours*, 35.

[116]Cf. λόγος as "speech in progress" (James H. Moulton and George Milligan, *The Vocabulary of the Greek Testament* [Grand Rapids: Eerdmans, 1971] 379), or as "continuous *speaking, discourse*, such as in the N.T. is characteristic of teachers" (Thayer, *Greek-English Lexicon*, 380–81).

[117]Oke, "Paul's Method not a Demonstration but an Exhibition of the Spirit," 35.

[118]Lightfoot's summary (*Notes*, 161) of the τοῦ κηρύγματος of 1:21; although at times he seems reluctant to characterize λόγος and κήρυγμα in 2:4 respectively as "the form and matter of his preaching," he does admit that this distinction "is not far from the right distinction" (ibid., 172); cf. Alford, *Alford's Greek Testament*, 2:484.

[119]Conzelmann, *1 Corinthians*, 54.

[120]Morris, *First Corinthians*, 52.

[121]Godet, *First Corinthians*, 128; i.e., "he did not use any illicit means with respect to either contents or form" (Grosheide, *First Corinthians*, 61).

[122]οὐκ ἐν . . . , i.e., "not 'enforced by' . . . " (Barrett's appealing rendering of ἐν herein [*First Corinthians*, 65]).

[123]For data surveys and/or interactions, see: UBS³ apparatus; Metzger, *Textual Commentary*, 546; Conzelmann, *1 Corinthians*, 55; Bruce, *1 and 2 Corinthians*, 37; Robertson, *Grammar of the Greek New Testament*, 157; Lim, "'Not in persuasive words of wisdom,'" 146, n. 25, who tabulates 11 variants; and Orr and Walther, *1 Corinthians*, 156, who count 16.

[124]Lim, "'Not in persuasive words of wisdom,'" 146, n. 25.

[125]The genitive σοφίας is best construed as subjective, contextually being a reference to man's, i.e., worldly, "wisdom" (cf., e.g., Barrett, *First Corinthians*, 65). It must be remembered that in the context of 1:17–2:16 "'words of human wisdom' is a Corinthian value" (Fee, *First Corinthians*, 64).

[126]Morris, *First Corinthians*, 52; he further comments that with this adjective following οὐκ ἐν "Paul roundly eschews the methods of human wisdom" (ibid.).

[127]Robertson, *Word Pictures*, 4:83; cf. Robertson and Plummer, *First Corinthians*, 32, who subsequently conclude that "the cleverness of the rhetorician, which the apostle is disclaiming and combating throughout this passage, was specifically directed to the art of persuasion" (ibid., 32–33).

[128]*TDNT*, s.v. "πειθός, πειθώ," by R. Bultmann, 6:9; therefore, based upon the utilization of the adjective in 2:4, he well concludes that "Paul is stating that his preaching does not derive its power to convince from the rhetorical art of human wisdom" (ibid.).

[129]Lim, "'Not in persuasive words of wisdom,'" 137.

[130]Ibid., 146–47.

[131]Lenski, *First and Second Corinthians*, 92; i.e., Paul totally rejected any approach which was intended "to entice or force human minds by attractive or overwhelming rhetoric" (Oke, "Paul's Method not a Demonstration but an Exhibition of the Spirit," 36. "But his preaching did not thereby lack 'persuasion' [cf. v. 4b]. What it lacked was the kind of persuasion found among the sophists and rhetoricians, where the power lay in the person and his delivery" (Fee, *First Corinthians*, 94). "Paul's preaching" therefore, "carried conviction because of the power of the Spirit" (Morris, *First Corinthians*, 52); cf. v 4b.

[132]Some of the other preachers and the Corinthians desperately needed Paul's insight; i.e., "as it is all from God, why make a party-hero of the human instrument" (Robertson and Plummer, *First Corinthians*, 33).

[133]The antithetical parallelism which pivots on the ἀλλά has several facets; e.g., "ἀπόδειξις 'demonstration' is opposed to πειθώ (in πειθοῖς) 'plausibility'; and πνεῦμα καὶ δύναμις to λόγοι σοφίας . . . " (Lightfoot, *Notes*, 173).

[134]Bruce, *1 and 2 Corinthians*, 37.

[135]Grosheide, *First Corinthians*, 61; cf. Godet, *First Corinthians*, 129, and Furnish, "Prophets, Apostles, and Preachers," 54–55.

[136]Robertson and Plummer, *First Corinthians*, 33; they continue, "in ἀπόδειξις the premises are known to be true, and therefore the conclusion is not only logical, but certainly true" (ibid.). On the occurrences of this word in the LXX (cf. 3 Macc 4:20 and 4 Macc 3:19) and concerning its use as a technical rhetorical term in extrabiblical literature, see Lim, "'Not in persuasive words of wisdom,'" 147.

[137]Although the terms are often closely associated (for examples and discussion, see Findlay, "1 Corinthians," 776, and Orr and Walther, *1 Corinthians*, 156), it is not necessary to view this collocation as a hendiadys, e.g., "powerful spirit" (Orr and Walther, 1 Corinthians, 156; cf. Fee, *First Corinthians*, 95).

[138]Findlay, "1 Corinthians," 776; for some appropriate comments regarding the *testimonium Spiritus sancti*, cf. ibid., and Lenski, *First and Second Corinthians*, 92.

[139]Cf. Fee, *First Corinthians*, 95, on the force of ἀπόδειξις herein.

[140]Robertson and Plummer, *First Corinthians*, 33.

[141]Ibid.; cf. Lim, "'Not in persuasive words of wisdom,'" 147.

[142]Lim, "'Not in persuasive words of wisdom,'" 148; cf. Barrett, *First Corinthians*, 65.

[143]Morris, *First Corinthians*, 51.

[144]Godet, *First Corinthians*, 130.

[145]I.e., ἵνα . . . μή ἦ ἐν . . . ἀλλ' ἐν. . . . Not only does this compounded purpose clause grammatically complete v 4 but it also serves as a telic summation for the first four verses of chapter two (cf., e.g., Lenski, *First and Second Corinthians*, 92) and

conceptionally relates back to 1:17b in particular (cf., e.g., Barrett, *First Corinthians*, 49; and Findlay, "1 Corinthians," 777) and to 1:18ff. in general (cf., e.g., Fee, *First Corinthians*, 96; and Godet, *First Corinthians*, 130). Prospectively, it dovetails into the argument which follows, esp. 2:6–16 and 3:18–21.

[146]Cf. *TDNT*, s.v. "δύναμαι, δύναμαις," by W. Grundmann, 2:313.

[147]I.e., "'their Christian faith'" (Mare, "1 Corinthians," 199); cf. Grosheide, *First Corinthians*, 62.

[148]"The preposition marks the medium or sphere in which faith has its root" (Robertson and Plummer, *First Corinthians*, 33), i.e., "'to rest upon'" (Grosheide, *First Corinthians*, 66), "be grounded on,—owe its origin and stability to" (Alford, *Alford's Greek Testament*, 2:484).

[149]Author's expanded rendering.

[150]Findlay, "1 Corinthians," 777.

[151]Cf. Conzelmann, *1 Corinthians*, 55; and Godet, *First Corinthians*, 131.

[152]Cf. his σοφίᾳ σαρκικῇ, "fleshly wisdom," i.e., sinfully autonomous wisdom, in 2 Cor 1:12; for commentary on these syntheses, see Findlay, "1 Corinthians," 777.

[153]Bruce, *1 and 2 Corinthians*, 37.

[154]As Barrett appropriately contends, "Preaching that depended for its effectiveness on the logical and rhetorical power of the preacher could engender only a faith that rested upon the same supports, and such a faith would be at the mercy of any superior show of logic and oratory, and thus completely insecure" (*First Corinthians*, 66).

[155]Because "the real power does not lie in the person or presentation of the preacher but in the work of the Spirit as experienced by their own existence" (Fee, *First Corinthians*, 94).

[156]Godet, *First Corinthians*, 130.

[157]Morris, *First Corinthians*, 53.

# Bibliography of Articles, Books, and Reviews by Homer A. Kent, Jr.

*1954*

"The Life of Christ." *The Brethren Teacher* 4:1 (January–March 1954).

"The Life of Christ—Part II." *The Brethren Teacher* 4:2 (April–June 1954).

"The Origin of the Agape." *Brethren Missionary Herald*, 22 May 1954, 343–44.

*1955*

"Was Jesus Born in December?" *Brethren Missionary Herald*, 24 December 1955, 815.

*1958*

*The Pastoral Epistles.* Chicago: Moody Press, 1958. Rev. ed. 1982.

1959

"The Day of Crucifixion." *Brethren Missionary Herald*, 28 March 1959, 199–200.

*1960*

"Paradise." *Baker's Dictionary of Theology.* Grand Rapids: Baker Book House, 1960.

*1962*

"Commentary on Matthew," *Wycliffe Bible Commentary.* Chicago: Moody Press, 1962.

"The Qumran Community and New Testament Backgrounds." *Grace Journal* 3:2 (Spring 1962): 35–44.

## 1963

"Nourished in the Words." A series of 30 Greek word studies appearing in the *Brethren Missionary Herald* from 28 November 1959, to 19 October 1963.

"Romans-Ephesians-Philippians-Colossians." *Brethren Quarterly* 24:4 (July–September 1963).

## 1964

"Matthew's Use of the Old Testament." *Bibliotheca Sacra* 121:481 (January–March 1964): 34–43.

## 1966

"How We Got Our New Testament." *Moody Monthly* 66:6 (February 1966): 24–26, 40. Reprinted in *Grace Journal* 8:2 (Spring 1967): 22–26.

## 1968

*Adult Teacher's Guide* and *Comprehensive Bible Study*. David C. Cook Publishers, variously beginning 1968.

"Can We Trust the New Testament?" *The Sunday School Times and Gospel Herald* 66:22 (November 15, 1968).

## 1969

"Gospel of Mark." *The Brethren Teacher* 19:2 (January–March 1969).

"Paul Departed From Athens and Came to Corinth." *Brethren Missionary Herald*, 27 December 1969, 18–19.

"The Gospel of John." *The Brethren Teacher* 16:2 (January–March 1969).

## 1971

*Ephesians: The Glory of the Church* (*Everyman's Bible Commentary* series). Chicago: Moody Press, 1971.

"The Centrality of the Scripture as Reflected in Paul's First Epistle to Timothy." *Journal of the Evangelical Theological Society* 14:3 (Summer 1971): 157–64.

## 1972

"Books: A View From the Other Side of the Typewriter." *Brethren Missionary Herald*, 14 October 1972, 24.

"Is the King James Version Inspired?" *Brethren Missionary Herald*, 15 April 1972, 16–18. Reprinted in *Sword of the Lord*, 3 November 1972.

## 1974

*Jerusalem to Rome: Studies in the Book of Acts.* Grand Rapids: Baker Book House and Winona Lake: BMH Books, 1974.

*Light in the Darkness: Studies in the Gospel of John.* Grand Rapids: Baker Book House and Winona Lake: BMH Books, 1974.

*The Epistle to the Hebrews: An Expository Commentary.* Grand Rapids: Baker Book House and Winona Lake: BMH Books, 1974.

## 1975

"Feetwashing." *Wycliffe Bible Encyclopedia.* Chicago: Moody Press, 1975.

"The Pastoral Epistles." *Wycliffe Bible Encyclopedia.* Chicago: Moody Press, 1975.

## 1976

Excerpts from "Inaugural Address." *Grace Seminary Spire* 4.1 (Fall 1976): 2–3.

"God's Choice of a Family." *Winona Today* (Winter 1976).

*The Freedom of God's Sons: Studies in Galatians.* Grand Rapids: Baker Book House and Winona Lake: BMH Books, 1976.

## 1977

"The First 300 Days." *Brethren Missionary Herald*, 15 August 1977, 20, 22.

Untitled article on personal devotions. *Grace Seminary Spire* 4.3 (Summer 1977): 4–5.

"Writing! Why Bother?" *Grace Seminary Spire* 4.4 (Fall 1977): 3–4.

## 1978

"Commentary on Philippians," *Expositors Bible Commentary*, vol. 11. Grand Rapids: Zondervan, 1978.

"Have You Considered a Week at Winona?" *Winona Today* (Summer 1978).

"The Languages and Personal Bible Study." *Grace Seminary Spire* (Fall 1978).

*Treasures of Wisdom: Studies in Colossians and Philemon*. Grand Rapids: Baker Book House and Winona Lake: BMH Books, 1978.

## 1979

"How Many Years Between the Covenant and the Law?" *Grace Seminary Spire* 6.3 (Summer 1979): 14–15.

"The King James Only?" Grace Theological Seminary brochure, 1979.

"The Land of Christ's Birth." *Winona Today* (Winter 1979).

"The Value of Counsel." *The Seminary Spire* 6.4 (Fall 1979): 3.

## 1980

"A Time to Teach." *Grace Theological Journal* 1:1 (Spring 1980): 7–17.

"Highlights of an Exciting Year." *Brethren Missionary Herald*, January 1980, 35–36.

## 1981

"College Education in a World of Change." *Brethren Missionary Herald*, February 1981, 32–33.

Review of *The Epistle of Saint James*, by Joseph B. Mayor. Reprint. Minneapolis: Klock & Klock, 1977. *Grace Theological Journal* 2:1 (Spring 1981): 145–46.

"The Glory of the Christian Ministry: An Analysis of 2 Corinthians 2:14–4:18." *Grace Theological Journal* 2:2 (Fall 1981): 171–89.

"The Greatest Tribulation." *Winona Today* (Summer 1981).

### 1982

*A Heart Opened Wide: Studies in 2 Corinthians.* Grand Rapids: Baker Book House and Winona Lake: BMH Books, 1982.

"An Interview with Dr. Kent." *Brethren Missionary Herald*, January 1982, 32–33.

### 1983

"Becoming Involved in Christian Higher Education." *Brethren Missionary Herald*, November 1983, 26–27.

Review of *Commentary on James*, NIGTC, by Peter Davids. Grand Rapids: Eerdmans, 1982. *Grace Theological Journal* 4:2 (Fall 1983): 310–11.

"Grace Schools." *The Brethren Encyclopedia.* 3 vols. Philadelphia: The Brethren Encyclopedia Inc., 1983.

"Winona Lake Christian Assembly," *The Brethren Encyclopedia*, 3 vols. Philadelphia: The Brethren Encyclopedia Inc., 1983.

### 1984

Review of *Commentary on Galatians*, NIGTC, by F. F. Bruce. Grand Rapids: Eerdmans, 1982. *Grace Theological Journal* 5:2 (Fall 1984): 298–99.

"Footwashing." *Evangelical Dictionary of Theology* (formerly, *Baker's Dictionary of Theology*). Grand Rapids: Baker Book House, 1984.

### 1985

"The New Covenant and the Church." *Grace Theological Journal* 6:2 (Fall 1985): 289–98.

### 1986

*Faith That Works: Studies in James.* Grand Rapids: Baker Book House and Winona Lake: BMH Books, 1986.

"In Christ, But Not Secure?" *The Seminary Spire* 14.2 (Winter 1986): 3–4.

### 1987

Review of *The Epistles to the Colossians, to Philemon, and to the Ephesians*, NIGTC, by F. F. Bruce. Grand Rapids: Eerdmans, 1984. *Grace Theological Journal* 7:1 (Spring 1986): 131–33.

### 1989

"Fellowship—A Call to Commitment." *Brethren Missionary Herald*, 15 July 1989, 14–15.

Review article of *The Gospel According to Jesus* by John F. Mac-Arthur, Jr., *Grace Theological Journal* 10:1 (Spring 1989): 67–77.

### 1991

"Four Fulfilled Prophecies in the Olivet Discourse." *Salvation* 45:1 (January–February 1991): 3–4.

Dr. Homer A. Kent, Jr., completed forty years of faithful service to Grace Theological Seminary and Grace College at the end of the 1990-1991 academic year. He has served as Professor of Greek and New Testament and Academic Dean in the Seminary as well as presiding as President of both the College and the Seminary during the years 1976-1986. Dr. Kent has had an active role in the Fellowship of Grace Brethren Churches and is known by the larger evangelical community for his helpful publications on several books in the New Testament. His volumes on the book of Acts, the Pastoral Epistles, and Hebrews, have been widely circulated.

The present volume is called a "festschrift". This means that it is a book of essays intended to honor the recipient for his life of service and contributions to the cause of Christ. These essays are written by individuals who have studied and taught with Dr. Kent over the years. Each author has expressed their appreciation for Homer Kent's life of ministry by the articles which appear in this volume.

Some of the biblical subjects treated in this book are:
"Form and Function in the Letters of the New Testament"
"Inspiration, Preservation, and New Testament Textual Criticism"
"The Background to the Good Shepherd Discourse in John 10"
"Peter in the Gospel of Matthew"
"The Christian Hope: A History of the Interpretation of the Millennium"
"Ephesians 1:3-14: The Blessings of Salvation"
These articles along with seven others provide a wide range of helpful information for students of the Bible.

**Gary T. Meadors**, editor, is Professor of Greek and New Testament and Chairman of the Division of Biblical Languages and Literature at Grace Theological Seminary, Winona Lake, Indiana.

**BMH BOOKS**

P.O. Box 544
Winona Lake, Indiana 46590

ISBN: 0-88469-23